Th. 31st Sept. Ride (accompd by J. McD.) to Don=
=manan, N.B. Phil. Fol[illegible] & Organ building & cleanhouses
— dine & sleep at Kilbrane — meet there Mrs Day
my poor Bro's Widow for the first time since our mis=
=fortune — much affected —

F. 2d We visit Rockfield — where Thompson is
building a cleaner House & Almon has built one —
dine & sleep by invitation at Jack Duggan's —

Sat. 3d after breakfast visit Clonmelanan fix
upon a situation for J. McDonogh's intended house
— N.B. necessary to charge him about taking strict
care of the plantations repairing the walls &c. —
return to dine & sleep at Poulonough —

Sund. 4. drive to Tralee — breakfast wth Jas
Day — go to prayers — the excellent condition of
the Church does great honour to James who
from a Ruin has by stimulating & working
at Vestry upon the Parishrs converted it into
one of the nicest Country Churches I know —
dine with him —

M. 5 - dine wth Robert Hickson
Tu. 6th dine wth Dat Connell
W. 7th dine wth Steph. H. Rice
Th. 8th dine wth Will Rowan!
Fr. 9th dine wth John Rowan
Sat. [illegible]

S. 11th Dine wth Ld Mac.
M. 12th Dine again wth J. Day
Tu. 13 - Dine wth Wilson

Robert Day

(1746-1841)

The
Diaries
and the
Addresses
to Grand Juries
1793-1829

Gerald O'Carroll

Robert Day, published in 1807 by Edward Orme, Bond Street, London, included in the collected charges.

Robert Day (1746-1841)

The Diaries
and the Addresses to Grand Juries
1793-1829

Polymath Press

First published in 2004 by Polymath Press,
Courthouse Lane,
Tralee, County Kerry, Ireland.
Printed in Ireland by Alphaset, Tait Business Centre,
Dominic Street, Limerick.

ISBN 0-9547902-0-0

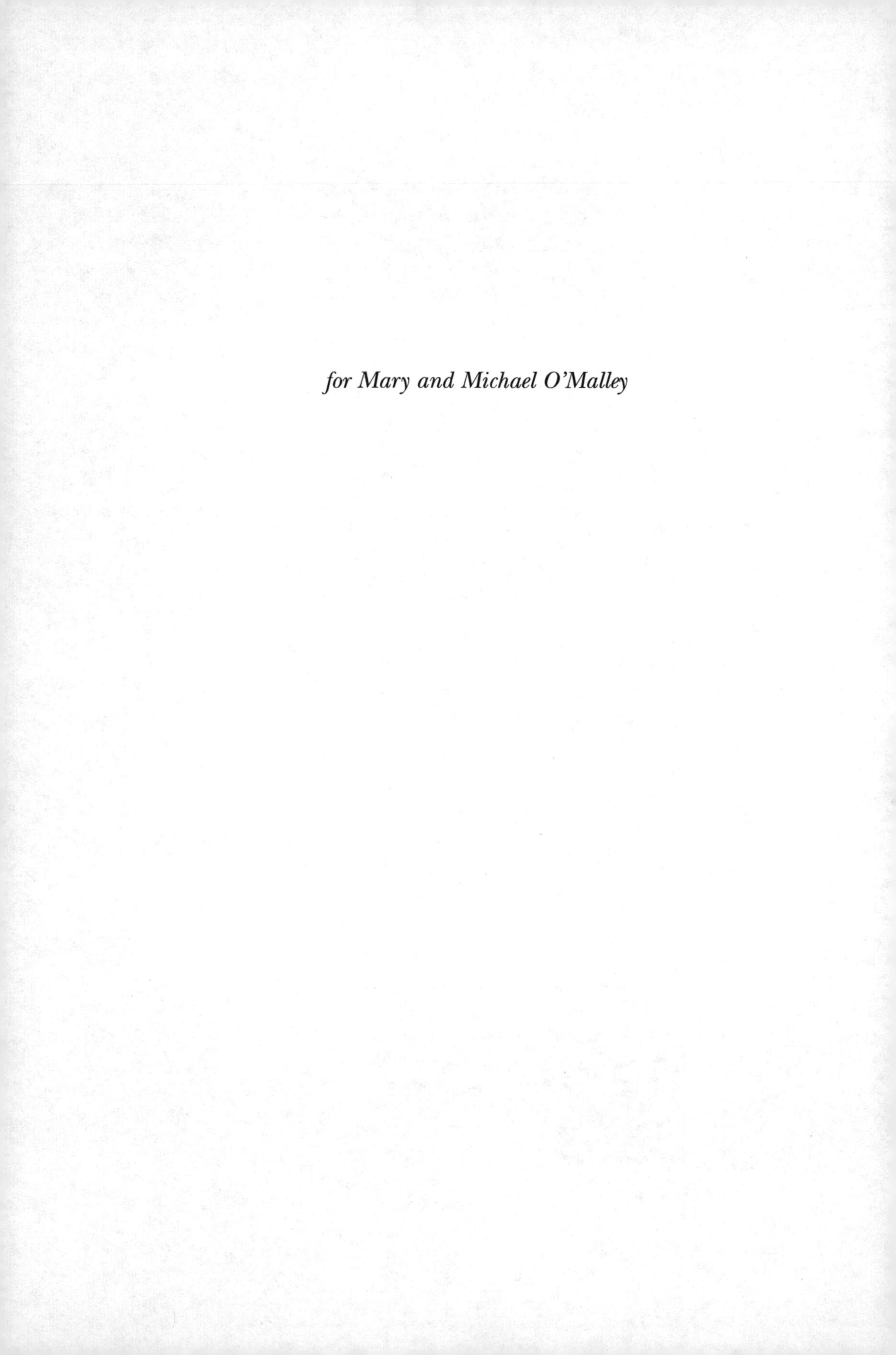

for Mary and Michael O'Malley

Preface and Acknowledgments

Mr Justice Robert Day makes an important contribution to the study of moderate political thought in the era of the French Revolution and the Napoleonic Wars, despite his obvious indebtedness to the restricted and elite political system of the eighteenth century, including the Tory control of politics in Britain and Ireland right up to the Emancipation act of 1829 and the great Reform act of 1832. A number of factors are worth bearing in mind in the case of Day in order to dissociate him from the forces of reaction and to establish his moderate credentials. One is that his links with the south-west of Ireland, a region which in his own words had a very 'scattered' settlement of the governing elite, caused him to depend perhaps more than others on the informal, almost feudal, system of bonds and obligations characteristic of eighteenth-century life and which cut across the social strata. Second, it was the French Revolution that converted Day, as it converted so many others, into a conservative. His political formation was in the gallery of the houses of Parliament in London when Pitt the Elder, Earl of Chatham, was still there. Chatham attacked the political monopoly of the Whig grandees which dominated the reigns of the first two Georges and which withheld the liberties won at the Williamite Revolution of 1688 from the wider population; under Chatham, Britain's empire became the vehicle for the extension of not only of commerce, but of political institutions and religious liberties as established during the Protestant Reformation. Day came under the influence – how early and with what degree friendship we cannot be sure - of Lord Shelburne, Chatham's successor and holder of vast estates in the south of Kerry. Shelburne assembled a coterie of radical thinkers at Bowood, and Day met him officially on behalf of Henry Grattan and the Irish patriots in 1782. Finally, Day's political career coincides with that of William Pitt the Younger, whose reform administrations perpetuated the legacy of his father, before Pitt passed the torch to Canning and others who completed the Day pantheon. With justification therefore, one of Day's obituaries wrote that 'he was a Whig of the old, but not of the modern school', a reference to the turbulent first years on the throne of George III as the domestic political instability echoed that in the American colonies. The term he liked most to apply to others was that of 'enlightened', because in his own work to reform the penal system and dismantle the penal laws against Catholics he was operating quite consciously under the aegis of both the Reformation and the European Enlightenment of the eighteenth century.

The original inspiration for this research was a lecture on the subject of the Dennys given to the Kerry Archaeological and Historical Society in October 1990 by the Rev. Canon A.E. Stokes of Ashford, Co. Wicklow, who assisted me subsequently with his great knowledge of the Kerry families and of Irish and British history, particularly the reigns of William and Anne. Day is the Dennys' ancestor from the fourth baronet, but his importance became clear to me in subsequent encounters in the correspondence and biographies of Ireland's 'Liberator', Daniel O'Connell. I am indebted also to a considerable number of local historians who contributed what they knew of the Irish regions, and to numerous academics for their expertise in the 'long' eighteenth century: Russell McMorran, who knows Tralee better than any of us, the Knight of Glin and the Knight of Kerry for genealogies and assistance with portraits, Tony Browne, for families and houses of the Shannon region, Robert Fitzsimons M.D. for Tralee doctors, infirmaries and certain ailments, Bertie O'Connor, for the land war in North Kerry, Paddy Lysaght, who contributed the book containing letters of Day and John Fitzmaurice of the 95th Rifles; Matthew Potter shared his experience of liberal unionists from his work on the Monsells of Tervoe, John Cussen donated a print of Lord Courtenay. I am also indebted to John Gerard Knightly and Valerie Bary for information on Miltown and the Godfreys, Liam O Duibhir for Tipperary gentry, Joseph M. Carroll who drew my attention to the work of Michael Quane on Banna School and the Erasmus Smith foundation on Valentia Island. Philip Samways assisted with astronomy records and Kenneth Ferguson, who has written the Robert Day entry in the forthcoming Irish Dictionary of National Biography, assisted with legal issues and the identification of some legal personages. Tom Seaver made some Latin translations, and Michael Potter used his digital camera to good effect to produce a number of images of buildings such as churches. Donald Cameron of Beaufort House was generous with information about his Crosbie and Talbot-Crosbie forebears and also with a number of portrait images from his ancestral collection. I have tried to follow all of Cian O'Carroll's advice on aspects of presentation, for which I am very grateful and without which the book would have been the poorer. Enid O'Toole, a descendant of Rev. James Day, has researched the pedigrees of Kerry families and checked those included in this book. I am indebted to both the Royal Irish Academy and the Beinecke Library for permission to publish. Research facilities were generously afforded me by the Hon. Society of the Middle Temple, London, Hon. Society of King's Inns, Dublin, the Royal Irish Academy, the National Library of Ireland, the Registry of Deeds, the British Library, the Library of the Representative Church Body, Limerick City and County Libraries, Mary Immaculate College and University of Limerick, Kerry County Library, Cork City Library, the Boole Library in University College Cork, the Public Record Office of Northern Ireland, and the Royal Irish Fusiliers Regimental Museum, Armagh.

The bequest of Day papers made to the Royal Irish Academy by Ella B. Day was the collection of her husband, Col. John George Day, a grandson of Judge Day by his second wife Mary FitzGerald.[1] Previous to the bequest Ella Day wrote to the County Kerry Society (January 1935) to state that 'a number of manuscript letters and copious diaries of Mr Justice Robert Day have come into my hands at the death of his grandson, Colonel John George Day (late R.E.)', an event which 'has tempted me to collect them into a volume with illustrations'. That the manuscript volumes of the judge's charges – addresses - to the grand juries of Ireland formed part of this bequest is clear from the fact that one of the volumes contains the inscription 'Property of Col. J.G. Day'.[2] Ella Day abandoned her plan for a publication of what one assumes were the diaries and the charges; what materialised instead was the memoir which appeared in 1938.[3]

Individual Day charges first appeared in the newspapers, then as pamphlets, finally in volumes of the judge's selection. The present book contains all of those which appeared in volumes, and I have added charges in Cork, 1803, and Kerry, 1811, because they are relevant to issues raised by the diaries, and because they bring the reader away from Dublin and into the provinces. A number of sentencing charges are also included – are indeed essential - to understand the controversies into which Day appeared to stray from about 1811 to 1815. His earliest collections may date from about the time of his appointment to the court of King's Bench in 1798: an entry in his diary of September 1801 while in London has him thanking the Speaker, Onslow, 'for the very flattering and handsome language he was pleas'd to hold of my Charges to the Grand Juries of the county of Dublin'. King George III had read them 'and his Majesty was graciously pleased to express his warmest approbation of them'.[4] Though circulated abroad, the print run may have been quite small; surviving volumes carry dedications, something which suggests that they were produced as much for distribution to friends as to gratify the grand juries who begged him to publish them. A copy of the 1808[5] is inscribed 'To the Honourable Sir William Cusac Smith, with the most affectionate regards from Rob Day'. Another, of 1810, containing a charge of January of that year,[6] is dedicated to 'Serj. Thomas Goold'. Ella Day's book reproduces an inscription dedicating a volume to Henry Grattan, while some descendants of Judge Day have recently purchased one, via the internet, containing a dedication to his patron and cousin Lord Glandore. The Library of King's Inns, Dublin, has a collection published in 1830 which includes a charge given after the Emmet Rebellion of 1803. All of his selected charges appear in the present volume.

Turning to the surviving diaries, all but one, that of 1807-13, are held by the RIA. The exception is in the Beinecke Rare Books Library in the University of Yale, N.H.[7] Did Ella Day know of the Beinecke diary? She knew of others, because her book reproduces fragments of them, which appear not to have survived. The gaps are significant, most obviously those of 1801 to 7 and 1813 to 27.

To facilitate reading, modern punctuation has been superimposed in order to replace a document filled with dashes. For the most part abbreviations and spelling inconsistencies have been removed, and spellings of proper names, like Macromp for Macroom, Massey for Massy, Atea for Athea, Rathkeal for Rathkeale, Main for the river Maine, have been retained unaltered. Where Day has used different spellings for the same word, the version most commonly used today has been adopted, though confusion continues with such as Kilcolman / Kilcoleman, Kilgobbin / Kilgobban, etc. Capital letters appear with much greater frequency in the original diaries and I have reduced some of these to lower case; in the charges to grand juries I have retained capitals for legal and constitutional terms. His italicisation of certain words in the pamphlets of his charges has been retained, and his underlining of words for emphasis in the diaries. Numbers, as in miles travelled, have been reproduced in order to retain the character of the diaries. Dating has been reproduced almost exactly in an attempt to convey the haste in which many of the entries were made.

1. Genealogical information from John W Day, 5 Jubilee Road, Parkstone, Poole, Dorset, BH12 2NT.
2. RIA Day Papers, Ms. 12w12.
3. Ella B. Day, 26 Jan. 1935, Fisher's Hotel, Farnham, Surrey, to the County Kerry Society in The County Kerry Society, Annual Reports 1922-40; same to the same 14 Dec. 1935; Ella B. Day, *Mr Justice Day of Kerry, A Discursive Memoir* (Exeter 1938).
4. 11 Sept. 1801, RIA ms. 12w15.
5. *Seven Charges Delivered to the Grand Juries of the County of Dublin by the Hon. Mr. Justice Day while Chairman of the said County, to which is added a Charge Delivered by him to the Grand Jury of the County of Tipperary on 7 March 1808,* printed by Graisberry and Campbell, 10 Back Lane, Dublin 1808: NLI, call no. Ir 3404 di
6. NLI, Joly 3404.
7. The James Marshall and Marie-Louise Osborn Collection, Beinecke Rare Book and Manuscript Library, Yale University. Yale, NH.

Contents

Appendices

Maps

List of Illustrations

Biographical Chronology

1746	Born July 1 at Lohercannon near Tralee.
1754	Attends the school of a Catholic, John Casey, at Banna; later attends Midleton School.
1761	Matriculates at Trinity College Dublin. 1766 Graduates B.A.
1764	Admitted to Middle Temple, London.
1769	Enters Middle Temple, renews friendship with Henry Grattan.
1774	Marries (August) Mary Pott of the parish of Marylebone. Called to the bar at King's Inn, Dublin. Takes a house in North Frederick St.
1775	Birth of his daughter Elizabeth.
1777	Trustee in the marriage settlement of John Crosbie, later 2nd Earl of Glandore.
1779	Joins the 'Order of St.Patrick' aka 'Monks of the Screw'; the society includes Lord Charlemont, Grattan, Barry Yelverton, John P. Curran.
1780	Doctor of Laws.
1781	On the death of Robert FitzGerald (17th Knight of Kerry) he assumes the guardianship of the 18th Knight, Maurice FitzGerald (b. 1772).
1782	Representative of Grattan and the patriots to Lord Shelburne in talks to finalise the arrangements for 'legislative independence'. Moves house to Merrion Square.
1783	Elected to Parliament for Tuam. Attends the Rotunda Volunteer Convention. Commissioner for Revenue Appeals (£300 p.a.). Commences to undermine the democratic (Reform) party in Kerry.
1785	Appointed Advocate of the Admiralty Court.
1789	Chairman of the Dublin Quarter Sessions, Kilmainham. Bencher at King's Inns.
1790	Takes Silk. Returned to parliament for Ardfert, in the general election.
1793	Chairman of the parliamentary committee on the Great Catholic Relief bill and supports the bill in parliament. His judicial 'charges' begin to appear in the Dublin (later in the provincial) press.
1794	Appointed by the Committee of Secrecy to travel in Cork.
1795	Daughter Elizabeth marries Sir Edward, 3rd Bart., in May.
1797	Appointed by the Committee of Secrecy to travel in five counties of Leinster and Ulster. Becomes Provost of Tralee. Re-elected for Ardfert in general election.
1798	(Feb.) Appointed justice of the King's Bench, Ireland in the vacancy created by Justice Robert Boyd. Leases Loughlinstown House, 12 miles south of Dublin, as his country residence, but retains his house in Merrion Sq. Assists the Special Commission which tries the leaders of the 1798 Rebellion. Re-elected Provost of Tralee. Prepares to promote the Union of Britain and Ireland.
1801	Travels to Scotland and England.

1802 Returns George Canning to Parliament for Tralee.
1805-13 Denounces the new Catholic campaign. Favours gradual concessions and government 'veto'
1808 Sentences the leaders of the Shanavests and Caravats in Tipperary.
1809 Receives the Viceroy, the Duke of Richmond, at Tralee Castle.
1811-12 Participates in high-profile trials of the Dublin Catholic delegates. Visits Parliament, witnesses the defeat of Canning's pro-Catholic proposals.
1813-14 Presides at the trials of newspaper editor John Magee.
1815 Fails to prevent O'Connell's duel with d'Esterre (d'Esterre killed).
1819 Retires from the Court of King's Bench.
1820 Presides at the meeting in Dublin to elect Henry Grattan's (Jnr.)
1822 Assists famine relief in Kerry
1823 Death of his wife
1824 Testifies on 2 June to the Parliamentary Commission on Disturbances in Ireland, Chairman Lord Palmerston. Marries Mary FitzGerald of Bandon, a nurse assistant to his wife, a Catholic, and the mother of his two sons.
1823-31 Promotes construction of the new Protestant church of Monkstown, and a Chapel of Ease at Killiney (legislation 1828, consecrated 1835).
1828 Death of his daughter Lady Denny. Travels in England and France for six months; appears in Parliament in time to witness the passage of the Catholic Emancipation bill.
1841 Feb. Death. Burial at Carrickbrennan cemetery beside his first wife. Later joined there by Mary FitzGerald (d. 1849), his second.

Introduction

For somebody with such a strong Jacobite ancestry Robert Day's embrace of the British state was remarkable, particularly remarkable when we consider the still strongly Gaelicised and Jacobite character of the South West of Ireland where he was raised.

Robert's father, the Rev. John Day of Lohercannon, near Tralee, was a comfortable Protestant clergyman whose family is said to have settled in Ireland in the seventeenth century. But the name could also derive from O'Dea and therefore suggest a native Irish and convert background.[1] More is known of his mother. Lucy FitzGerald was descended from the leading native and Norman lords of the West Munster region. Of these, representatives of the FitzGeralds (Knights of Kerry) and the O'Briens (Viscounts Clare) were on the defeated side of King James at the Boyne in 1690. The FitzGerald who fought at the Boyne married a Crosbie to turn Protestant and retain his estates, while O'Brien lost his estates and became the founder of the regiment of Clare in the service of the King of France. In the year before Robert Day was born, Charles O'Brien, sixth Viscount Clare, led the Irish brigade in the army of Marshal Saxe in the defeat of the English at Fontenoy, supposedly to the cry of *Remember Limerick and the treachery of the English.*

Any nostalgia for the Stuarts on the part of Robert Day was certainly less than that of his uncle Robert FitzGerald who corresponded with his Jacobite relatives in Europe. The Days, unlike the FitzGeralds, were great Irish Protestants. The family would supply numerous clergymen to the Irish church in the generations to come. Many of them served in the parishes in and about Tralee, the county town of Kerry. The Dennys settled this region as 'Undertakers' during the Munster Plantation, which followed the defeat and death of the 'Rebel' Earl of Desmond in 1583; they occupied the Desmond Castle in Tralee and were soon presenting the clergymen to St. John's and the neighbouring parishes. Robert was undertaking legal and financial responsibilities for the Dennys long before his daughter's marriage to the third Baronet gave him a commanding role in the estate from 1795. He may also have used the Dennys to advance his parliamentary career. Prime Minister Lord Shelburne was a cousin of Robert's cousin and patron Lord Glandore, but there was a second connection in the person of Arabella Fitzmaurice, Shelburne's aunt, who had married Arthur Denny; when Robert stepped on to the political stage by entering the Irish parliament in late 1783 he wrote a flattering letter to Shelburne with an offer of his political allegiance.

Day's allegiance to the status quo explains his support for a negotiated approach to the admission of the Irish Catholic majority to the Constitution, to the extent that it was only when Britain was about to capitulate finally to unqualified Emancipation during the 1820s that he appeared to make his peace with the radical Catholic campaign. However, he was uncomfortable in the environment of Protestant reaction. He told Parliament at the time of the great Catholic Relief Act of 1793,

> 'No man was more strongly attached to this ascendancy than he – it was connected with the state, and inseparable from it; but he could distinguish between the ascendancy and a struggle for power and monopoly which enshrined itself in the altar of the church.' [2]

Concessions to the higher tiers of Catholics, such as the franchise and membership of the grand juries, (those he tried to include in the 1793 Act), would be a continuation of the work of the first generation of pro-Catholic activists (including his uncle Robert FitzGerald, MP Dingle) which culminated in the Gardiner relief acts of 1778 and 1782, which granted the right to purchase property, the open practice of the Catholic faith, the right of Catholics to teach school, and the admission of Catholics to the bar. A definition of citizenship on the basis of property qualification rather than religion would give political recognition to the powerful Catholic presence in commerce, which in turn agreed with the priority which Day gave to the equalisation of trading relations within the Empire. With a greater investment in the Empire, Catholics would see their interests as interconnected with the Empire's security, and all of this agreed with another of Day's priorities: his consistent support for the inclusion of Catholics in the officer ranks of the regular army. Relief legislation would include 'wings', or securities: the right of the government to 'veto' appointments by Rome to the Catholic hierarchy, and the payment of a salary to the Catholic priesthood, which it was hoped would detach the priests from the laity. We find him in an entry in his diary of 1801 defining Emancipation as 'to level all distinctions as far as is consistent with the Protestant Establishment.' But he was about to be drawn for a number of years into a phase of inflexible opposition. One reason was his belief that the political environment was no longer propitious to further relief legislation, and that forcing the issue had caused the war effort to lose the services of his great hero William Pitt: the failure of Pitt's efforts to deliver Emancipation with the Union was connected with the King's belief that his coronation oath prohibited him from doing anything that would jeopardise the position of the Established church, but it had the effect of causing Pitt's resignation. The Emmet Rebellion played a part, because, though small in scale, it shocked Day and appeared to vindicate the reactionaries. A third reason was Britain's lonely isolation in the struggle with Napoleon: Britain was – to use his words – in no mood to attempt fixing the roof while a storm was blowing. A final reason, connected with the last, was that her isolation appeared to cast Britain in the role of a chosen people – not only in a secular struggle but in what it believed to be an attack on its leading role in the Protestant Reformation: High Anglican and leading Tories opinion became entrenched in the view that the limits of Catholic relief had been reached, and this opinion became powerfully represented in Dublin Castle in the years ahead, and among the Irish lord chancellors and the law officers. As well as having to work in this environment, Day was strongly connected in London and was very sensitive to British public opinion; all of which explains the very discernible venom in his private correspondence on the Catholic question in the first decade after the Union as the new Catholic campaign under Daniel O'Connell gathered pace, and later, as he clung to the compromise

Veto solution in the parliamentary strategy of Grattan and Canning, his alienation from both the Catholic movement and the liberal press after 1810. In matters of religious belief Day was doctrinally broad, a position which is reasonably clear from his diaries during his visits to the Presbyterian Lowlands of Scotland. The monarchy was the defender of the broad, tolerant tradition of the Reformation, on the one hand against political extremism represented by the radical wing the seventeenth-century Puritanism, on the other against continental Catholicism which, as a good Irish Protestant, he associated with absolutism, superstition and the temporal and spiritual power of the papacy. The excesses of Presbyterianism had been curtailed by the payment of the Regium Donum: what worked with them could have the same beneficial effect if applied to the Catholic priests. To some considerable degree therefore Day was out of sympathy with the influence on secular politics exerted by High Anglicanism and Tory conservatism in the decade after the Union, ; which is why we find him criticising those who opposed Canning's Catholic relief bill of 1812. It was a difficult time: he was sentencing the Catholic delegates in the court of King's Bench in Dublin, meantime he was a spectator in the visitor's gallery at Westminster while people he otherwise admired for supporting a vigorous prosecution of the war, Tory *Ultras* such as Lord Eldon, continued to oppose a formula of Catholic relief which included the securities agreed by moderate Protestants like himself.

The Day brothers and their cousins were sent to the school of the Catholic John Casey at Banna a few miles from Lohercannon. The school was illegal under the Penal bar against Catholics schools and Catholic school masters, making it a remarkable symbol of post-Penal era collusion in the world of Day's upbringing. He won a scholarship[3] to Trinity College, Dublin, where he achieved grades of distinction, though he was overlooked in the awarding of a fellowship; the circumstances annoyed his uncle Robert FitzGerald who was sitting in the audience at his viva voce and felt that his nephew was the victim of an injustice. From 1769 he kept his terms at the Middle Temple, being called to the bar in Dublin in 1774. Before returning to Ireland that summer he married Mary Pott, daughter of Percival Pott, an eminent surgeon at St. Bartholomew's Hospital. They lived in Frederick St. from which base Robert began to build a career on the Munster circuit and in property transfer.

In London he and his Trinity contemporary, Henry Grattan, had witnessed the beginnings of Britain's dispute with her American colonies. The old biographies of Grattan, including Grattan's *Life,* by his son, draw on Day's recollections of this period. Grattan was a regular visitor to the visitor's gallery of the House of Commons to hear William Pitt the Elder (Earl of Chatham) argue the case for conciliating the Americans. Day, more committed to his legal training, appears to have haunted the courts, something which appears in the remark in the diaries about 'those law lords of with which my youth was familiar'. Both sympathised with the claims of the Americans on trade discrimination and taxation without representation. We find Day later viewing a portrait of the author of the Stamp Duties, George Grenville, and recording the comment that it was Grenville 'who severed America from us'. The outbreak of hostilities with the colonists – the Boston Tea Party in December 1773, Lexington and Concorde to follow – coincided with Day's first years back in Dublin, and their impact was felt in the two Irish general elections of 1776 and 1783 which returned many candidates who were for the first time controlled by the demands of reform-minded electorates. Before Day sought a seat in parliament for himself – something not to be considered seriously perhaps while uncle Robert FitzGerald represented Dingle – he entered the spirit of democratic-reform agitation in Dublin. This took the form of attendance at a patriotic dining club known as the *Order of St. Patrick*, or the *Monks of the Screw*, which included such patriotic and anti-government figures as Lord Charlemont, John Philpot Curran, Grattan, and a number of future judges whose careers would be as conservative as Robert's. Lord Charlemont headed the new Volunteer movement which protected the coasts against attack from America's ally, France, now that the regular army was withdrawn from the country to fight the Americans. The Volunteers also gave an armed support to a range of political demands made by the parliamentary patriots. Henry Grattan took over the mantle of patriotic leader from Henry Flood, and Day represented him and the patriots in May 1782 in the final negotiations with Secretary of State Lord Shelburne to arrange legislative independence. He believed that legislative independence corrected the Irish privy council's 'usurpation' of control over the enactment of legislation in Ireland's parliament, in effect restored Ireland's parity with England under the crown; the other concessions of that period included 'Free Trade' (what he referred to in a Tralee speech in 1789 as 'a share in the West India trade') and the security of Irish judges against arbitrary dismissal. Years later when they were trying to elect Grattan's son in Dublin he stated:

> 'Mr Grattan found his country a slighted and dependent province, governed by a legislature in which she had no voice, and by laws to the enactment of which she gave no consent.' [4]

But this is where Day's democratic phase ends. The fact that Britain was forced to make Irish concessions as her forces were suffering their final defeats in America always troubled Day. He now opposed extra-parliamentary pressure for reforms of parliament and the extension of the franchise the consequences of which must be to take Ireland down the American road to separation and republican government.

Robert FitzGerald died in 1781 and Day entered parliament in 1783 for the borough of Tuam, Co. Galway. He had already parted from the Volunteer movement, and his attendance at the great Volunteer convention in the Rotunda just after the new parliament convened found him apathetic, even hostile, to its proceedings. For one thing, he complained that the final compromise definition of reform ignored the three million Irish Catholics. His personal interests were also at play. He hoped to advance as a crown lawyer, and he had strong personal vested interests in the private boroughs of his native Kerry where his patron and cousin Lord Glandore was the principal political figure. These were some of the reasons why he embarked on a career in the government support. From almost immediately he entered Parliament he worked to undermine the democrats in his native Kerry, while at the same time he continued to identify himself with the cause of Catholic relief. He worked with government to bring reforms to the administration of justice, which was the area in which he was held in high regard both as a legal figure and as somebody who understood the rural agitation against rents and tithe.

Promotion to the chairmanship of the Dublin county court at Kilmainham came in late 1789, some weeks after the fall of the Bastille prison in Paris. The first phase of the French Revolution does not appear to have perturbed him unduly. He was a great francophile, but he hated Bourbon expansionism, and that of Louis XIV in particular. In common with many others he watched with interest what at first appeared moderate constitutional reforms. Could it be that France was about to inaugurate a replica of the English revolution of a hundred years before? His first charges from the bench at Kilmainham are silent on the subject, probably a sign that he was adopting the approach of 'wait and see'.

If these were his first impressions he was about to be disillusioned. The defeat of the French émigrés and the forces of the Duke of Brunswick at Valmy in September 1792, following hard on the capture of Louis by the Paris mob and the massacres of prisoners in the Paris prisons, undermined the possibility of moderate reform: the Revolution became republicanised and atheistical, and it proclaimed to the world its intention to export its principles. By the time Day addresses the Kilmainham court in January 1793 (the first of the collected charges) he has abandoned any ambivalence about events in France. (The address will become memorable for its forecast of the execution of Louis XVI a few days later.) In the following month Britain goes to war to liberate the Netherlands and to defend the monarchical order in these islands and in Europe.

Revolutionary France's threat to these islands would have meant little without the growth of revolutionary clubs and correspondence societies in Britain and Ireland. Irish Protestants democrats, whose reform campaign Day had helped undermine after he entered parliament, now revived volunteering and made common cause with a new and radical Catholic leadership, which from 1791 became infiltrated by membership from the United Irishmen. Day had only known the venerable and mainly aristocratic Catholic leadership of men like Lords Fingal, Gormanston and the Killarney peer, Lord Kenmare. The new movement summoned a national convention; it arranged to present a petition in London and by-pass the Irish parliament including long-time supporters like Day. Day kept his nerve and chaired the parliamentary committee which brought in the great relief bill of 1793, which, among other concessions, granted Catholics the franchise and the right to membership of the grand juries.

The bill became law but failed to deflect revolution. The feeling was widespread that it was enacted only under pressure of events outside the House and deteriorating circumstances abroad. Day said as much himself when he contributed to the debate on the Convention bill some months later: he stated that it was the advance of French armies under Dumouriez in the Netherlands which helped the bill's passage into law. It was one of those occasions when Day blended into the reactionary background when it suited him. His nerve was deserting him, and it finally broke after the failure of William Ponsonby's parliamentary reform bill of 1794, when the United Irishmen sent emissaries to the French to seek assistance for revolution. One of them, the Rev. William Jackson, was apprehended. Following Jackson's trial Wolfe Tone fled to America and the United Irishmen were banned. Day's charges from 1795 justify the repressive measures of the regime of Lord Lieutenant Camden, particularly the

Insurrection and Indemnity acts and the suspension of the Habeas Corpus, though he made oblique – and compassionate – reference in a charge of April 1797 to the displacement of the Ulster Catholics after the Battle of the Diamond: 'those atrocities in the North at which humanity sickens, and to whose active and sweeping progress our mild and merciful code of criminal jurisprudence is in vain opposed.' The work of containing revolution in the country meant that he was more and more absent from parliament. He appears to have handed responsibility to his cousin Maurice FitzGerald. Robert's son had a more youthful and conciliatory approach to the Catholic issue after he made his parliamentary debut in 1795 with a speech in support of Grattan's emancipation bill. The bill was defeated by the reactionaries, and there is considerable reason to think that Day's sympathies were at least temporarily with them, and that it may have suited him not to be present in the house for the occasion. At least one of his future judicial colleagues was present and voted for: Judge Fletcher would later become the hero of the O'Connell movement for presenting, at this time and during the second decade after the Union, a more amenable and liberal face of the Irish bench than Day. It would be many years before Day succeeded in extricating himself from association with the Tory *Ultras.* As a member of the Irish judiciary he would have to face the combined attacks of the independent press and the radical Catholics in the second decade after the Union, and he only emerged to take his place alongside the Catholics again when in retirement during the 1820s, by which time the case for emancipation had won very wide acceptance. But conservatism held sway until the appointment of Canning as prime minister in 1827.

In his native Kerry Day's profile was raised considerably from 1795 when his daughter Elizabeth married Sir Edward Denny, who succeeded his brother in the baronetcy after Sir Barry was killed in a duel in October of the previous year. In Sir Edward's marriage settlement to Betsy Day her father became the principal trustee of the estate. Encumbered with debts and settlements, the trusteeship imposed a number of time-consuming duties. It was from this time that he became widely known in Westminster circles as the single individual responsible for the nomination of Tralee's parliamentary representative, the sale of which now became a lucrative source of income for the estate. At the same time he brought a 'hands on' and efficient direction to the running of the estate, redistributing farms out of lease, developing the Spa for tourism, and arranging mortgages in order to balance the books and meet the cost of settlements: 'I am now entering upon the very troublesome but indispensable duty of surveying with Denny those great farms which have lately dropt out of lease and which well managed will give him some chance of independence and comfort.' [5] There were difficulties with Denny from the start. Sir Edward's decision to reconstruct Tralee Castle about 1804 caused Day to remark that his son-in-law, had 'exhausted and involved himself with his gloomy Chateau as to leave himself without the means at present of giving a suitable education to his eldest son':

> 'He is unfortunately one of those who cannot be argued from wrong to right and whom nothing but suffering and bitter experience can beat out of any wayward propensity of his. How often and earnestly have I pressed upon him your early

advice to abandon that grave of his family's reputation and consequence and to reserve some one of his fine western farms for a family seat – to proceed with the work deliberately and prudently, first forming with the assistance of skilful artists the plan for a house and demesne, and then executing both at his leisure according as his circumstances and inclination prompted. But never was hog more attached to mire than he to the town of Tralee, though now he repents of his works and expenses there when he has advanced too far to retreat…' [6]

Sir Edward and family may have moved to live in Worcester before the decade was over. Day may have suggested the better education their young children would obtain there. Now Day had a free hand, but quarrelling continued at long range and up to Sir Edward's death in 1831: Sir Edward objected to the judge's second marriage in 1824 for the effect the prospect was having on Lady Denny, while Day blamed Denny's improvident ways for plunging Lady Denny into poor health leading to her death in 1828.

The delayed progress of democratic opposition to the Tralee oligarchy owed more than a little to Day's personal popularity and to a certain populism in the government of the town and region. For example there was the inclusive character which appears to have marked public occasions. Typical was the king's Jubilee celebrations in October 1809, when toasts were given to Wellington's Peninsular successes and by inference to the many county families represented in the ranks of his army.[7] Wellington's progress was to be seen as a struggle to liberate not just England, but Catholic Europe and places further afield like Spain's colonies in South America which were in danger of falling under the power of the French. Another of Day's strategies was to try to return pro-Catholic representatives from Tralee to Westminster. Such a figure was George Canning (1802-6). Canning was the political heir to Pitt and Shelburne, and when he was returned for Tralee in 1802 he and Pitt were very identified with the cause of Catholic relief. (Pitt had resigned after failing to carry Catholic emancipation after the Union, while Canning objected to Pitt's support for his successor Addington, and therefore he sought a 'free seat' and obtained Tralee.) Wellington's return for Tralee (though he sat instead for Newport on the Isle of Wight) hardly seems a popular nomination, but his government delivered Catholic emancipation in 1829. James Stephen (1808-12) belonged to the evangelical wing of the Tories, whose programme and achievements greatly impressed the practical, non-doctrinal evangelism of Day: prison and penal reform, the struggle against slavery, the spread of education, the spread of Christianity under the flag of empire, alleviating of suffering among primitive communities now ruled by Britain, and so on. These were also popular issues with the Whigs, including the Whig opposition in Kerry, and issues which promised to demote the Catholic issue against a background of wider imperial and humanitarian concerns.

The slip in Day's personal influence with Dublin Castle was something which he foresaw at this time, and it was something of which his opponents began to take advantage as he tried to juggle Denny and judicial duties. Loss of influence with Dublin and his desire to maintain a kind of political consensus in Kerry helps explains why the government found Day an elusive figure, somebody whose intentions were not always easy to read and who, if the price was right, was prepared to return a member of the Whig opposition.[8] We find him taking heed of the wishes of the townspeople in the construction of the barracks in 1809: he stressed that the iniative came from 'the Corporation of Tralee and its inhabitants', who considered it essential for 'the morality of the people and the discipline of the army.' [9]

It was the twin forces of political revolution and rural insurrection, rather than disaffection with the oligarchical government of Tralee, which helped rock Kerry in the first decade of the Union. The Emmet rebellion of 1803 affected Kerry more than the far greater and more widespread rebellion of 1798, which left the county largely unscathed. Emmet had cousins in Kerry, notable St. John Mason who had tried to run a counter-Union campaign. The rural campaign against rents and tithes now revived also, while the advance of the Whigs in 1806 meant a political support for republicanism and the United Irishmen: 'the sworn friends of Arthur O'Connor and the panygerists of the French Revolution. Alas poor Kerry, what an abyss of degradation hast thou fallen into! If such a miscreant as John Segerson be among their idols, what abject beasts must the votaries be?' [10] From Kerry also emerged the leader of a new and militant phase of the Catholic campaign, Daniel O'Connell.

O'Connell, the future 'Liberator', was one of the group of young county lawyers which included Day's nephews Ralph Marshal, Bob Day and the Frankses. The O'Connells and the Days had known each other in the previous generation, even cooperated in schemes of 'friendly discoveries' to give legal protection to Catholic farmers against forced subdivision under the Penal laws. Count O'Connell and Day were contemporaries; the Count left Ireland for the continental regiment about the time Day entered the Middle Temple. They remained friends through life. Amity yielded to tension from the time when Daniel helped arrange the renewed Catholic petition to parliament in 1805, stepping out of the shadows finally in 1808 to become the director of the new campaign. In late 1810 he attacked the Union in an important speech in Dublin. On the issues of emancipation and the Union O'Connell considered Day to have betrayed his political roots. He also considered that Day's control of the government patronage under the Duke of Richmond (1807-13) exaggerated Day's real political weight in the county. For his part, Day saw the Grenvillite and anti-war opposition pulling the strings of the revived Catholic campaign in Ireland. Having failed to defer all discussion of Catholic relief while Britain was at war, Day now attacked the concept of emancipation itself: unqualified emancipation would favour a narrow group of lawyers and was irrelevant to the needs of the mass of the people labouring under rent, tithe and grand jury cess. Relief should come as a series of concessions following negotiation, the reward for good behaviour, and when British opinion and the conditions in Europe permitted.

Day drew some inspiration from the Pope's concordat with Napoleon, writing to one correspondent that this compromise, like the Canada Act of 1791, provided a blueprint for Ireland.[11] The constitution for Upper Canada established Anglicanism as a counterpoise to the Puritan bias of the neighbouring United States, and at the same time recognised Catholicism. It was this evolving view of the constitution which he tried to defend against die-hard opposition in British public opinion on the one side and Irish Catholic intransigence on the other. From the trials of the Dublin Catholic delegates, which began in the court of King's Bench in late 1811, Day appeared to take the fight to the new Catholic movement and the campaign against the Union, both of which were identified with O'Connell. A central allegation, one he repeated a number of times, was that the Catholic movement was involved in the rural disturbances and intent on bringing in the French. Unfortunate for Day, he was also attacking the press. The popularisation of politics from the period 1811-13 is nowhere more in evidence than in the court of King's Bench in Dublin and in the reporting of its cases. The culminating trial of newspaper editor John Magee was only one of a series of very high profile trials which received wide coverage in Britain and in the Dublin and provincial press, partly because these were trials of the press itself, and partly because it was in the courts that popular politics of the time were confronted. Day was on the bench for all of these trials, and it was to him that the other judges handed the task of sentencing. It was at Magee's trial that Day and O'Connell appeared to first conflict openly, Day rebutting O'Connell's attack on the Huguenot attorney general with one of his own on O'Connell:

> 'The sluices of slander were opened wide, and the mountain torrent roared and rushed along, sweeping viceroys, law officers, judges, juries, the Church, the State, everything revered and sacred in society, down its muddy and turbulent tide, without discrimination or decorum.'

The Irish courts were in the vanguard of conservatism at this time, and the defeat of Napoleon in 1815 helped pospone democratic politics in Britain and Ireland until the achievement of emancipation in 1829 and the the great Reform law of 1832. But Day made a number of errors in the years immediately after the Magee trial which handed the advantage to his legal opponents and which may have hastened his decision to retire from the bench. He made the error of travelling the Munster circuit for the Spring assizes of 1816 and presiding in Tralee at the trial of the duellist Rowan Cashel. There were numerous conflicting testimonies about how Cashel killed Henry Arthur O'Connor in a duel at Ballyseedy the previous year, but the complaints of the O'Connor family subsequent to the trial about Day's charge to the jury are said to have played a part in the judge's retirement from the bench in early 1819. It is difficult to know. The names of those testifying give some cause to believe that the rumpus may have been created by Day's opponents, though Day's hesitation to condemn Cashel appears not consistent with private doubts about duels which he confided to his diary after the trial of Alcock in Wexford in 1808. Whatever the underlying causes, the unpopular Cashel walked free after the jury heard a charge from Day which all but instructed the jury to find him not guilty. A petition was brought to the house of commons and Sir Robert Peel lent his weight to persuade parliament to reject it.

Day served as foreman of the Dublin Grand Jury after his retirement (according to his testimony to a parliamentary commission on disturbances in Ireland in 1824). He was in Kerry to assist efforts to alleviate the famine of 1822 by appeals to England for aid. He continued to spend considerable time in Kerry during the autumn. 'I generally visit it for two or three months in the year', he told the parliamentary commission. The poet and song writer Thomas Moore heard that Day was one of the two best landlords in Kerry. The other name given to Moore was the Marquess of

Lansdowne. It was a curious inclusion and probably owed something to Lansdowne patronage of Moore and his high profile in the Whig opposition. Lansdowne was one of the 'lords paramount' complained of by Day for their absenteeism. In the troubled northern half of Kerry he nominated Lord Ennismore for the same distinction, telling Dublin Castle in his communication from Listowel in September 1808 that 'the vast peasant population of the northern barony of this county have either been dispossessed of their ancient holdings and turned adrift, or reduced by rack-rents to a state of abject beggary'.

In physical appearance Day was a big and imposing man. The accent appears to have retained little trace of his Kerry origins, or so the Duke of Clarence said in the summer of 1801.[12] He practised the grand manner of speech. In handing down a sentence he could wring a confession from the offender or a sympathetic response from the gallery. In Cork he sentenced to death a father and two sons, 'in a manner so solemn and affecting as to draw tears from a number of the spectators.'[13] Then there were the puns on his name. The Day papers contain the following newspaper cutting: 'An Hibernian having been found guilty of a burglary before Mr Justice Day, in Ireland, shrewdly observed that he had lost by day what he had got by night.'[14] The political message tended also to vary in order to suit the audience; in Dublin or the North he would emphasise the centrality of King William of Orange, while in the South or West he would dwell on the share of Ireland in the common law since the Norman settlement, and the legacy of George III in terms of inaugurating an era of prosperity and rolling out the institutions of state to benefit all its citizens.

1. The historian Mary Agnes Hickson believes that the great-grandfather of Judge Day came from Bristol, that he was 'a Quaker agent for the Pretender, who was arrested and confined in Tralee gaol, which, however, he "broke" ... and escaped to Cork' (*Kerry Evening Post*, 10 Sept. 1872). Robert's friend and cousin Sir John Day, who appears in the following pages, is given in the British Library card index as the descendant of a family which settled in Ireland in the seventeenth century.

2. *Parliamentary Register*, speech of Robert Day, 21 February 1793.

3. From Casey's school he appears to have gone to the school of the Rev. George Chinnery at Midleton Co. Cork (Michael Quane, 'Midleton School, Co. Cork', *JRSAI*, vol. 82, 1952, PP1-27., 17, 20)

4. *Freeman's Journal*, 14 June 1820., extract from a speech of Judge Day to a Dublin meeting at the Royal Exchange to plan Grattan Jnr's election campaign for Dublin city).
5. National Library of Ireland, photocopies of the FitzGerald Papers: Day, Tralee, 4 October 1802 to Maurice FitzGerald. Elsewhere Day had to arrange a settlement for the very young widow of the deceased baronet. She was Anne Morgel, who appears as Lady Floyd in the pages of his diaries. Her settlement necessitated an act of parliament in 1804.

6. NLI, Talbot-Crosbie Papers, Day, Loughlinstown House, to Lord Glandore, Ardfert, Wed. 4 June 1806.

7. See the *Limerick Gazette and General Advertiser*, 3 Nov. 1809.

8. NLI, photocopies of the FitzGerald Papers: Day, at Lifford, to Maurice FitzGerald,1 April, 1807. 'I am very sorry we are losing Mr Elliot (William Elliot, Chief Secretary, Ed.) who I take to be an

amiable virtuous man. But I have some reason to complain that he has never done me the honour so much as to this hour to answer an application which I made two or three months ago for what I conceived to be a very reasonable favour... that his Grace would permit the Archdeacon to resign a small benefice in favour of his son'.

9. Robert Day, Listowel, to Sir Edward Littlehales, Dublin Castle, 14 Sept. 1808, NLI, HO 100, vol. 148, p. 410.

10. NLI, photocopies of the FitzGerald Papers, Day, Loughlinstown House, Wed. 16 April 1806, to Glandore. See also, for example, J. Godfrey, Tralee, 19 June, 1809, to Robert Dundas (the Chief Secretary) 'for the information of his grace the Lord Lieutenant' (the Duke of Richmond), reporting a search by parties of yeomen from Listowel and Tralee at Tullig, and enclosing a copy of a United Irishman's Oath and a paper containing the names of 95 persons, 'all of whom I suppose belong to the Society' (NLI, Melville Papers, 55 a).

11. British Library, Chichester (Thomas Pelham) Papers, Add. Ms 33112, Day to Pelham, Friday, 11 December 1807.

12. RIA, Day Papers, Ms. 12w15, p 66

13. *Limerick Chronicle*, 29 August 1804.

14. RIA, Day Papers, Ms. 12w11, newspaper cutting.

William Pitt addressing the House of Commons, by K. A. Hinkel; picture also includes John Jeffreys Pratt (Earl Camden), George Canning, Thomas Erskine (Baron Erskine) and Charles James Fox. (National Portrait Gallery)

1

'That tremendous convulsion': January 1793

A Charge
delivered to the Grand Jury of the County of Dublin
at the Quarter Sessions of the Peace
held at Kilmainham
on the 15th of January 1793
by Robert Day, Esq., M.P. Chairman.

Published at the request of the Hon. Sheriff and Grand Jury

Printed by Henry Watts of Dublin and in 1796 by Richard Edward Mercier and Co, 31 Anglesea St.

Gentlemen of the Grand Jury,

You are brought together at this periodical return of our General Sessions of the Peace, to discharge a duty of great and vital importance to the county of Dublin and the community at large: to call forth into life and action the criminal law; to deliberate and weigh in the scales of equal and dispassionate justice, such charges as shall be submitted to you against divers of your fellow subjects; to put such of them in a course of trial as shall be made out to your satisfaction, either upon the evidence of your own senses, or upon the *viva voce*, or written, evidence of accusers; and thus to vindicate and promote the general police and good order of our county. I am sensible that the duration of each session, and the frequent return of this duty to the County of Dublin, are attended with no inconsiderable inconvenience to country gentlemen; but you will reflect how small a price you pay in this occasional trouble for the essential advantages derived upon yourselves and the public from a conscientious and diligent discharge of your duty. In order to impress you with a just sense of the importance of this trust, it may not be amiss, particularly at this critical juncture, to trace briefly the criminal law of your country from its elementary principles.

When civil society was established, it was found necessary that the constituent members would resign a certain portion of their natural liberty (or to use the current expression of the day, a certain portion of the 'Rights of Man') in order to secure the remainder. The unlimited enjoyment of every individual in a state of nature were found incompatible with human happiness, or the existence of civil society for which man was obviously formed; for the weak it is evident, must in that state be victims to the strong – the simple and the honest must be the unprotected dupes of every designing or daring knave. To obviate these evils it was that civil government was established, wherein rules of conduct and the moral obligations of justice from man to man were prescribed, the impulses of appetite were controuled by commensurate penalties, strength and power ceased to be the arbiters of property, and universal equal protection was substituted for the wild excesses and dominations of the passions. How far that *professed object* of all civil government has been attained in other states, it is not our business now to inquire; it is enough for us to know, that every peaceful subject who reposes under the shade of the British Constitution – 'the proudest Monument of human wisdom and integrity'[1] - enjoys the most perfect security for his life, liberty, property and reputation. The means whereby that important end is obtained, are the civil code and the criminal code, the latter of which is your peculiar and appropriate office; a code instituted for, and competent to, the punishment and controul of public offences, and which, with the impartiality of death, knows no distinction between the Prince's palace and the poor Man's cottage.

But while the British Constitution provides adequate punishment for guilt, it has encompassed innocence with impenetrable lines of defence and security. The life and liberty of an Irishman are sacred: the law doth tender them so dearly, that no man can be convicted but on the oaths of 24 at least of his equals; 12 at least of the Grand Jury (whose condition is likely to raise them above undue influence) must concur to find the bill of indictment, and 12 Petit Jurors (secured by the privilege of challenge against all prejucice to the prisoner) must concur to convict upon that bill. I ask you, Gentlemen, is there a man among you who is not conscious, and feels not that under the British Constitution to be innocent is to be secure? To be innocent, is to be independent of, and beyond the reach of power? We know of but one law for the proudest Peer of the realm, and the poorest Peasant who crawls upon the earth; a mild and equal code, which, like the Deity, is no respecter of persons, but pervades, controuls, and cherishes alike the whole system. The poor man's friend – his shield and security against the strong arm of power! The popular order of the state, in fact, is the most essentially interested in maintaining inviolate the law, under whose happy influence and protection, industry, ingenuity and personal exertion (the only patrimony of that class of mankind) are stimulated, fostered, and invigorated.

The British Constitution is so familiarized to us by uninterrupted enjoyment, that no wonder if weak or thoughtless minds surveyed its beauties without much emotion or sensibility. The charming scene always lying in our view, one is too apt at last to behold with apathy and indifference. But, Gentlemen, who that has a heart to feel, or an understanding to reflect upon the calamities of France but must be roused to an animated sense of the unrivalled excellence of our Constitution and of the rational liberty which is our indefeasible birth-right? Mark the effect of these distractions upon our fellow subjects of Great Britain, that nation of philosophers, that sober, dignified, and manly people; they know the value of their Constitution, and they venerate it with the enthusiasm of idolater – happy combination of the highest degree of practical liberty with the energy and vigour of the monarchical form – a well-poised system of Government, perfect and unaltered by the wisdom of age, admired and celebrated by the most enlightened sages of ancient as well as modern times - 1700 years ago by the Roman Historian[2] in its cradle, and in the present century by the French Philosopher[3] in its maturity. If sedition assail the venerable fabric they embrace its columns, resolved to stand by it or perish in the ruin – they rally round the Throne of their good, their beloved King, and drown the storm with acclamations[4] of loyalty from end to end of the Island. They laugh at the malignant folly of those human devils who offer them wild theory for substantial enjoyment, and under pretence of mending their condition would substitute for genuine liberty the vilest and most savage of all dominations, the tyranny of an unbridled multitude. If our system, say they, has in the lapse of years contracted specles, there is a recuperative quality in the Constitution which enables it to purge and slough off without danger or innovation or violence its own impurities. Judge, then, the tree by its fruit – prosperity unexampled in the world, a gigantic growth in commerce, manufactures, wealth, arts and learning; and a corresponding and still more rapid growth in the wealth and prosperity of this kingdom since the year 1782, when we were restored to the enjoyment of that constitution.

Gentlemen, the same restless and evil spirit has been busy here too. In fact, the richest soils will often throw up the most noxious weeds. So in the best constructed systems of government there will be found men of misguided and vicious propensities, who discover too late that honest industry is the straightest road to wealth, and a just applications of talents the road to honest fame. Bankrupt in fortune and character, they sicken amidst the universal prosperity of their country, they survey with envy and disgust that general happiness which they do not share, and they confederate without remorse against the most revered establishments of the country in a diabolical hope by such summary and compendious process of lifting themselves upon its ruins. Such men, as long as they escape in public elections, have an interest in agitating the country; they have nothing to lose, and in a scramble they may gain something. Who can behold without affliction the desperate labours of Parricides to disturb the peace and interrupt the growth of this flourishing Kingdom? Fictitious grievances and chimerical expectations of I know not what new-fangled *Equality* are held forth to delude the credulous and uninformed classes of people. The most pernicious doctrines are circulated in newspapers, cheap pamphlets, and handbills. Bodies of people have actually been invited, with the most unparalleled audacity,[5] to arms. Indefatigable pains are taken to disaffect the public against the legislature; to bring the executive authority of the land into contempt; to hold forth as a model to our imitation a bankrupt and distracted nation, stained with the blood of her best citizens; and exulting perhaps at this moment, in the murder of a mild and innocent Sovereign;[6] a nation lately the seat of arts, elegance, refinement and science – now undone in the pursuit of an impractical liberty, whose religion is atheism, and whose politics are universal conquest, and the dissolution of all legitimate government.

Gentlemen, the alarm became so serious and general as to call loudly for the interposition of government, and it must be owned that the Government has stepped forth with the most laudable vigour and the happiest effect. A seasonable Proclamation has been issued by the Lord Lieutenant and Council, warning those disturbers of the peace of the dangerous precipice on which they stood – Fortunately the hint was taken; for let me tell you, Gentlemen, that the raising and keeping together numbers of armed men, against the express commands of the executive authority, particularly if for the reform of imaginary or even real public grievances, has been adjudged to be a constructive levying of war against the King, and of course High Treason. The Constitution avows no course of proceeding for a redress of grievance, but by petition to any one or all of the three branches of the legislature, conducted in a peaceable, orderly, and respectful manner; a right disputed by the arbitrary and infatuated House of Stuart, but unequivocally asserted a the Glorious Revolution in the famous Bill of Rights. But, Gentlemen, an attempt by intimidation and violence to coerce a redress of grievances, to force the enacting of a new or the repeal of a subsisting Act of Parliament, is a proceeding of a very different complexion indeed; it is a construction of law nothing less than to wage war against the King – it is High Treason. The Government has also taken vigorous measures to crush every symptom of insurrection and tumult in the country, and to apprehend and bring to justice all sowers of sedition, and let me remind my brethren the Magistrates in the solemnest manner in the presence of the county, that a more than ordinary vigilance and exertion is expected from them in this crisis, when the friends of anarchy and confusion are unusually active and industrious. They are called upon to disperse all meetings of a seditious tendency, to seize and commit all persons distributing seditious writings, or holding seditious and treasonable conversations. For, Gentlemen, though their words cannot amount to an overt act of treason, unless uttered in contemplation of some traiterous purpose, yet when spoken in contempt of the King or his government, whereby his Majesty may be lessened in the esteem of his subjects, and his Government weakened, I say such words are highly criminal and punishable by fine and imprisonment and even pillory. Much more criminal must seditious writing be, as writing imports a deliberate act, and if published may under certain circumstances amount to an overt act of High Treason. The Magistrates are also periodically called upon to caution all publicans and victuallers within their jurisdiction, against suffering their houses to be converted into dens of sedition and confederacy, on pain not only of being stript of their licences but of being held responsible for the crimes of the wanton they harbour.

The most dangerous and destructive Being in the Universe would be Man but for the restraints imposed upon him by divine and human institutions. Religion and Law are the chains which are thrown round Man in the Social state, and which fetter and bind him down to his good behaviour But in vain does the Legislature speak, if the Magistrate will not act; in vain do we boast of the best system of Criminal Jurisprudence in the world, if it be allowed to sleep in the Statute book, instead of being executed with vigour and inflexibility. It can not be denied that a general relaxation and imbecillity in the administration of Criminal Justice has long been the reproach and misfortune of Ireland. It is the observation of a humane Philosopher[7], 'that the greatest check to crimes is not the cruelty but the infallibility, not the severity but the certainty of punishment'. Let the Executive authority be liberal and mild, but let it be vigilant, firm and inflexible, and we shall seldom have occasion to resort to the severities of the Law. We know that the most likely means of human happiness are obedience to the Laws and the maintenance of established Order and well-regulated power. In England it is well and truly said that a Constable's Staff executes the Law.

The solid and rational liberty of that happy Nation - her splendour in arts and arms, in commerce and literature, in every thing that elevated and refined the nature of Man, is not more the result of just and equal Laws, than the reward of a vigorous execution of those Laws, and of a willing and implicit obedience to them.

But vain will be the exertions of Magistracy, vain the interposition even of Government, if gentlemen of influence and authority amongst us do not step out and second those exertions. We must not content ourselves with wishing well to our country; the time is come when men must Act; when every friend of Social Order will form round our unrivall'd constitution, and by a spirited and determined conduct in his neighbourhood sustain the magistrate in preserving the public peace. Whatever speculative differences may exist in the country, depend upon it every man loves order in proportion as he loves liberty – in short, the very existence of that sacred liberty, without which we should be but tenants at will of all we hold dear in this life, depends upon a vigorous execution of the laws and a prompt co-operation with the magistrate.

One word more before I dismiss you. At a former Session I had occasion to deplore the fatal spirit of Combination which raged in that part of the capital to which our juristiction extends. That baneful spirit happily hath been suppressed through the vigour of some of our Magistrates, and some seasonable examples made by this court, and the artisans have once more returned to their loom and to the peaceful exercise of their several occupations. Nay, more, it is well known that much pains have been taken to enflame and excite some of the neediest and most desperate among the journeymen, and to affiliate them into subordinate Jacobin Clubs for the blackest and most atrocious purposes; but that they have in general had the virtue and good sense to resist the infamous proposals. Thus deporting themselves, they have an irresistible claim upon our best offices and exertions, while they are employed in honest industry, and in advancing the manufactures of their country, it behoves us to see that forestallers and ingrossers do not enhance the necessaries of life and add further burdens to our tradesmen already struggling under too many difficulties. Gentlemen, this abominable practice demands your most serious enquiry; you ought not to wait for the return of informations upon the subject, but are bound by your oath (if any of you knew of the practice) to discover the offenders that he may be indicted or presented. And let us address one word to you out of your capacity of Grand Jurors, as Gentlemen of feeling and sensibility: Let me recommend to you an Association - nay, start not at the word – an Association for the relief of distressed Artisans. If we must have associations among us, for God's sake let us set the example of one for a virtuous purpose – not for preserving game, nor for preserving covers and propagating vermin, nor for circulating libels and sedition – in short, not to administer to the luxuries, the follow or malignity of mankind: Let us associate for the relief of the poor manufacturers of the Liberty, whose suffering at this dear and pinching season, challenge our sympathy, and whose patience and good conduct under these sufferings demand our warmest approbation and applause.

Gentlemen, I have detained you too long from the discharge of your duty and of the imporant public business which awaits your consideration.

1 The observation of a great statesman (Mr. Fox) most egregiously misapplied to the French Revolution, that tremendous convulsion which has crumbled into dust the Throne, the Church, the State, all the sacred and venerable Institutions of a towering and powerful Monarchy – that Revolution (if a much-honoured term must be so prostituted) which has degraded, exiled, exterminated the old Nobility and original Gentry, the clergy and the landed proprietors of a great and ancient Nation, and delivered it over a prey to a few desperate and detestable Adventurers, governing by a furious and sanguinary Rabble! Even the Founders of this "proud monument" have been successively swept off amidst the general havoc in one Equality of ruin – Canum fera facta suorum; the prey of their own Hell-hounds, victims to their own diabolical doctrines, and the only consolation left is the awful warning held out to mankind by this horrid history against the rage of Innovation.

2 RIA, Ms. 12w10, gives the following footnote: Tacitus – vide Agricolae Vita, p. 721 & seq. Elziv. Edit. & passim, & de moribus German, 693.

3 RIA, Ms. 12w10: Montesquieu, L.2, c. 8.

4 Alluding to the Addresses from all quarters of the United Kingdom to his Majesty, expressing the most rooted abhorrence of the new Philosophy of France, and an ardent and unshaken devotion to the British Constitution.

5 Among many criminal effusions of the press at this time, the most conspicuous perhaps is a libel published 16 Dec. 1792, of a most inflammatory and seditious tendency, intitled "An Address from the Society of United Irishmen to the Volunteers of Ireland"– Wm Drennan, Chairman, Arch. Hamilton Rowan, Secretary, summoning the Volunteers in express terms to arms. The obvious design of this paper is to excite the people to overawe the Legislature with an armed force, and finally to subvert the Constitution and Government of the country.

6 The savage and deliberate murder here foreseen, which shocked and revolted mankind, was perpetrated the 21st inst., upon charges unsubstantiated by a shadow of evidence and even in violation of the express articles of their own short-lived constitution.

7 Beccaria (Cesare Beccaria, Italian prison reform advocate, Ed.).

To ROBERT DAY, Esq.

Chairman of the County of Dublin,

The Address of the SHERIFF, GRAND-JURY *and* MAGISTRATES.

SIR,

WE cannot suffer this busy and fatiguing Session of the Peace to close without acknowledging, in terms of the warmest approbation, our Sense of your Conduct since your appointment to the Chair of the County of Dublin. We know not whether to commend most, your indefatigable assiduity in the discharge of a difficult duty, your patience, temper and humanity in the administration of Justice, or your professional abilities in the interpretation of the Law; and we doubt not as your exertions have already contributed much to the good order of our County, so a steady perseverance in the like conduct will be crowned with the most salutary consequences.

Accept also our thanks for your many judicious and instructive Charges, but particularly for your late most seasonable and constitutional one, the publication of which we unanimously desire; and be assured of our sincere esteem and respect.

Signed by order of the Meeting,

JOSEPH ATKINSON, Sheriff.
THOMAS LIGHTON, Foreman.

To the High Sheriff, Grand-Jury and Magistrates of the County of Dublin.

GENTLEMEN,

Your Address was as unexpected as it is flattering. I did not know that my humble endeavours in the discharge of my duty had entitled me to observation so distinguished and so honourable. Had I wanted incentive to the execution of a Charge whose importance I feel, and to which I am devoted, your over-rating partiality has furnished the most powerful—the praise of men, themselves the most praise-worthy and respectable.

ROBERT DAY.

Urging loyalty in 1795: the United Irishmen league with France

A Charge delivered to the Grand Jury of the County of Dublin at the Quarter Sessions of the Peace held at Kilmainham by Robert Day, onc of his Majesty's Counsel learned in the Law and Chairman of the said County.

Published at the request of the Hon. Sheriff and Grand Jury. 1795

The Reign of Terror in France was brought to an end with the execution of Robespierre in July 1794. In that year Day's best work was done in Cork where he arrived in March to act as prosecutor for the Crown, - in his own words, 'to inquire into the state of that country, to discover the real and true cause of the present disaffected state of the west of that county, and to maintain a constant correspondence with the Lord Lieutenant's secretary and the Attorney General'(RIA, Day Papers, ms. 12w14).

No month is given for this address, and it is not included among the collected Charges in the Day mss. (Ed.).

Gentlemen of the Grand Jury,

The duty which we are this day in our combined capacities called together to discharge, however familiarized by its frequent return, is the most serious and awful incidental to the human condition. In this solemnity we see nothing less than Man exercising one of the great prerogatives of his Creator, and sitting in judgment upon Man.

It cannot be denied that civil society, for which we are formed, could not hold together without the right to ordain, and the authority to inflict, capital punishment. Man is the slave to turbulent and domineering passions, which can hardly be controuled, or public order preserved, even by the formidable sanction of death. But if heavy and exemplary punishments, and even death itself, *must* be inflicted for the benefit and maintenance of society, it becomes a sacred duty to ourselves, while we discharge this momentous trust, to examine whether our system of Criminal Jurisprudence be so contrived, that the sword of the law shall fall only upon the guilty neck; and whether the precautions thereby provided for the protection of life and liberty be such as innocence may well confide in, and power, wealth and malice assault in vain. Nor will the inquiry into that vital part of our laws and government be thought unseasonable at a time when men are found amongst us who would depreciate, and with rash and parricidal hands pull down, the whole of that ancient and venerable fabric. At such a time you will not think a few moments ill-employed in contemplating the happy effects of our criminal system, appreciating its eminent advantages, and renewing thus occasionally our homage of gratitude to that best of Constitutions under which we may all enjoy in fearless security every civil blessing of life.

The Criminal Jurisprudence of these realms consists of three great component members – the Grand Jury, the Court, and the Petit Jury; to each of which are assigned their distinct and appropriate functions.

In this distribution of functions, to the *Grand Jury* is allotted the grateful task of protecting innocence against false and malignant accusation. Such is the caution and tenderness of our criminal law, that it allows no subject to answer any charge which has not previously been submitted to the scrutiny, and receive the sanction, of a Grand Jury. Where the right of accusation is uncontrouled, the security of innocence must be precarious indeed. Poverty, simplicity, virtue, are but feeble and unequal competitors with power, cunning and malice. The institution, therefore, of an intermediate body between accusation and trial is a proud and beautiful feature of the British Constitution; worthy of its benignity and wisdom; founded in a just jealousy of power and human malignity, and in a tender solicitude for the Civil Rights of the subject. The Grand Inquest, composed of twenty-three of our peers, selected for their independence and character from the body of the County, acting under the solemn obligation of an Oath, are appointed to exercise a severe and inquisitorial judgment upon every charge, and to stamp it with their verdict, before the party accused shall be at the trouble of accounting for the particular act imputed to him.

The province of the *Court* is to see that the crime be alleged in the indictment so clearly and precisely, that the defendant may know what the charge is which he is called upon to answer; that all evidence in its nature ambiguous, irrelevant and incompetent, be rejected at the trial; that the law arising out of the evidence be faithfully and correctly interpreted to the jury; that the Judge do watch over the legal rights of the defendant, and, as far as they are concerned, even be his counsel; and that justice be executed in mercy, according to the true spirit of our constitution, solemnly inculcated in the coronation oath. "Judges," says the humane and eloquent Foster, "should have written on their hearts the solemn engagement of their King, to cause law and justice to be executed in mercy in all his judgments."

The Charge, and of course, the Fate of the prisoner, finally depend upon the uncontroulable voice of the *Petit Jury*, that simple, excellent and effectual bulwark against injustice and oppression. What greater security for life and liberty can be easily imagined, or can innocence desire, than the certainty that we cannot be divested of either but by the unanimous decision of twelve of our honest and impartial equals? The invention of this species of trial has been attributed to the superior genius of Alfred; but however improved it might have been by him, its institution seems coeval with the first civil government of England. Our sturdy ancestors considered the Trial by Jury the Palladium of their Liberties; they enforced its confirmation by *Magna Charta*, and preserved it unimpaired through every conquest and change of government.

And what have been the effects of this happy system of jurisprudence? Has it not assured our property, stimulated our husbandman and manufacturer, and generated and fostered that industry and ingenuity which have glutted the markets of the world with the commodities of the British Empire? Here the universal confidence in the vigour and indiscriminating equality of our law, which hath converted these little islands into an asylum for Misfortune, and a depot of the specie and wealth of Europe. But the most flattering testimony to this excellent system, as well as to the general principles of our constitution, is that of France itself. That unhappy nation, after wading through seas of blood and horrors unutterable in pursuit of her favourite phantom, seems at last awakening from her fatal delusion; and we hear her now acknowledge the pre-eminence of the trial by jury, and that true rational liberty is to be found only under a government composed of three balancing Estates[1]. Those important truths, however, she might have learned at less expense; truths so clearly exemplified amongst her neighbours of Great Britain, who are the first people in the world that have taught the true theory and science of government. There she might have seen a people possessing as large a portion of real liberty as is consistent with a state of society; - the liberty of doing every thing right, and restrained only from doing wrong; - every man's just rights, the fruits of his industry and talents, his person, the free exercise of his religion – all secured to the extent of his most sanguine wishes.

Gentlemen, we have the same common law, and nearly the same statute law, with England. We boast of the same happy temperate constitution, placed midway between the extremes of chilling despotism and intemperate democracy. Why not then yield the same fruit here as in England? Whence proceeds that savage spirit of insurgency which never dies amongst us, but bursts forth at different periods in the different provinces with all the fury and desolation of a volcano? Whence, but because just and equal laws are not sufficient to practical liberty without a certain and vigorous execution of them. Because it is as much the fashion there for all ranks to assist the Civil Power in executing the law, as it is here to resist it. Because, in one word, her magistrates are active, her country-gentlemen public-spirited, and her peasantry sober, amenable and industrious. Such was the system of the great Athenian law-giver[2], who boasted that he attained his object "by the co-operation of strength with justice;" thereby implying that the legislative power could produce but little advantage, unless seconded by a vigorous executive authority.

At the same time it is but just to allow that, however the laws may be administered in other parts of the kingdom, there is no indolence or inactivity amongst the Magistracy of the county of Dublin. It cannot be forgotten that much pains were taken to purge and reform our Magistracy, and to give to the county an efficient and respectable Commission of the Peace[3]. Hence we see of late but scanty Calendars; hence we find this county, considering its overflowing population, enjoys a singular share of tranquillity and good order; while some others, even on our borders, continue to be disturbed and ravaged by the most savage and cruel Banditti. The vicinity, however, of the mischief is alarming; and I trust it is unnecessary, under the awful circumstances of these times, to animate the Magistracy, and all the property and power of the county, to a more than ordinary degree of vigilance and attention. By the Calendar it appears that one man stands committed for tendering an unlawful oath, which may be punished by Transportation. The offence, it should at first seem, would not lead to consequences of such serious or general mischief as to warrant a punishment so extreme. But we know by long experience that this is one of the earliest symptoms in every county of approaching Insurrection. The first step of the agents of sedition is, to engage in their cause the simple and half-inclined peasantry, by the obligation of a prophane oath, "more to be honoured in the breach than the observance." The next is, to disarm all the property and virtue of the country. The progress from thence to insurrection, and to the perpetration of those barbarous crimes which stain our country at this period, is natural and obvious. The evil acquires strength as it advances; the civil power is set at defiance; the military must be resorted to; and the musket and the halter close the last sad scene of the tragedy! The nature, therefore, of this case well deserves your most serious consideration. Call the Informant before you, and examine and sift him diligently. If the charge appear to be well-founded, you will of course put it in the way of trial. But you will not stop there: You will be able, probably, by this personal examination, to learn whether this be an unconnected substantive offence; or whether it be not a branch of one general system of devastation, intended to embrace the whole island; a system promoted by Traitors, conspiring with the enemies of their king and country. If it be (as it is likely to turn out) a spark of that flame which rages in our neighbourhood, you, Gentlemen, as having a deep interest in tranquillity and the security of persons and property in your county, will not delay an hour to take the most vigorous precautions against the progress of the mischief. Sensible as you must be of the benefits we enjoy under a mild and happy government, you have heard with regret and horror of the savage outrages committed in several of our counties. Possessing the just influence attached to well-applied property, you cannot exercise it so much to your own advantage or honour as in promoting a due submission to the laws, and such dispositions among the humbler and uninformed ranks of life, as may best secure to us the blessings of good order and civil liberty; - to win them by persuasion, protection and mild controul, from turbulent and uncivilized habits to the discipline of law; and by a sympathetic benevolence, and an ear ever open to the complaints of the peasantry, to reconcile them to that inequality of condition under which some wild or wicked men would teach them to repine, but which is the inseparable lot of human nature. But if conciliating measures shall fail, you will then stand justified in the sight of God and man, in resorting to that force which the wisdom and foresight of government have happily provided for us, fully competent to our protection, and proportioned to the critical and peculiar circumstances of these times.

There is another species of offence, as wicked in its principle as pernicious in its effects, to which the present scarcity of provisions loudly calls your attention – that of forestalling and ingrossing. It is well known that many of the necessary articles of life pass through the hands of several successive purchasers, each of whom must have a profit before those articles reach our markets, whereby the ultimate price is advanced unconscionably, and an artificial scarcity is created. The law has provided very heavy and exemplary punishment for this offence so mischievous to trade and oppressive to the poor. The Legislature I say has done its part; do you yours. Institute an active and strenuous inquiry after those bad members of society, who, instead of resorting to honest industry, stand between the farmer and consumer, lift the necessaries of life beyond the lips of our manufacturers and tradesmen, and traffic in the sufferings of poverty and hunger.

Gentlemen, I shall not pay so bad a compliment to your experience and understandings, or to my own humble labours in the chair for so many years, as to suppose it necessary at this day to detain you by a dissertation upon the duty of a Grand Juror. The sum and substance of it is compressed into your oath, and may be conveyed in three words – *Diligence, Secrecy, Impartiality.*

As to *Diligence,* I confess I do not see how gentlemen can reconcile that express injunction of the oath with the lazy habit which has grown up among Grand Jurors, of going to business at a late hour, and even then of not assembling their whole number. The obvious consequence is, that the public business is sometimes very injuriously retarded, and the burden of duty thrown upon the diligent and conscientious, to the indulgence of the less scrupulous. I have no fear of such default in the course of this session; but should it so happen, I must rely on you, Mr. Foreman, to signify the same to me forthwith, in order that the Grand Jury may be called over upon a fine.

With respect to *Secrecy,* nothing can be more express than the oath upon that head of your duty: "Not to disclose his Majesty's counsels, you fellow-jurors, or your own." And yet, strange to tell! we have sometimes known some of the most important proceedings of Grand Juries transpire even to the minutest circumstances attending them! Gentlemen, the evidence for the Crown is a sacred deposit which you are not at liberty to betray. Anciently the Grand Juror who did so was held an accessory to the offence, whether it was treason or felony; and though the law be now otherwise, still he is guilty of a *high misprision,* and liable to fine and imprisonment. Such disclosure serves but to give the party accused an opportunity of practising upon the witnesses, to discourage criminal prosecutions, and expose every Grand Juror to the most indecent solicitations.

On the subject of *Impartiality,* I shall not offend men of your condition and sentiment by dwelling on its necessity. You stand, Gentlemen, in a post not only of honourable confidence, but of serious and grave responsibility. On one side you see the King himself, as the public accuser, suing for justice at your hands; on the other, your fellow-subject, with every thing that is dear to him, his life, liberty, honour – all committed to your protection. You will, I doubt not, hold an honest and even balance between the public and the individual; remembering while you bestow due attention upon the good order and police of our county, that you are not at liberty to doom any man to the hardships of a public trial but upon the most satisfactory evidence. On this part of your duty give me leave to enlarge a little, it being, as I conceive, not sufficiently understood or felt in this kingdom.

There are three species of evidence which our Grand Juries are considered as competent to entertain: 1. *The evidence of their own senses,* which obviously is the best and most conclusive. Upon that it is that a *Presentment* is founded; that is, the notice which a Grand Jury is *bound* to take of an offence committed within their knowledge, without waiting for a bill of indictment from the Clerk of the Peace. If you, or any of you, know any thing presentable, you are sworn not to leave it unpresented. 2. The *viva voce* evidence of such witnesses as are sent by the Court to the Grand Jury to be examined for the Crown. In England the uniform practice is, for the clerk of the crown or peace to swear the witnesses for the Crown in open court, and to indorse their names on the indictment; and upon their testimony alone the bill is found or ignored. 3. The sort of evidence most in use in Ireland, and which, allowing it to be legal, is certainly to a conscientious and discerning mind the least satisfactory, is the written depositions of witnesses for the Crown, called *Informations,* sworn before a magistrate, and sent up to the Grand Jury with the bill of indictment. Were this question a *res integra,* and now fit to be discussed, I should have no difficulty to declare this secondary evidence of depositions to be illegal and inadmissible, and that nothing less than the *parol* testimony of a witness ought to be received by a Grand Jury to ground an indictment upon. Such inferior proof would in general[4] be inadmissible before a Petit Jury; and how much more to be rejected by a Grand Jury, who are precluded from receiving any evidence on behalf of the party accused. It is a manifest violation of an established rule of evidence, "that none but the best evidence which the nature of the case will admit of ought to be received." The practice, however, has obtained, I know not how, in this kingdom, time out of mind; the Judges of the land acquiesce in it invariably, and it is our duty to submit to it. Nevertheless, without presuming to shake the established usage, I may be allowed to recommend earnestly to you, in all cases of the slightest doubt, to resort to the English course of personal examination. Consider whether you can sufficiently satisfy the oath you take, "*well and diligently to enquire,*" by merely reading the information of an angry and prejudiced witness in his own cause, "with the blow still glowing on his cheek," and often taken in a very slovenly and reprehensible manner. Consider whether a Grand Jury can act in general with impartial justice to the accused party for whom no witness can be examined, but by cross-examining and diligently sifting the witness *against* him, and by an actual enquiry from the witness's lips into all the circumstances of the case. The Irish practice of finding bills upon the slighter evidence than in England, multiplies them in this kingdom inordinately; and it often happens, very little to the credit of the Grand Jury, that a culprit shall be acquitted even upon the testimony of the prosecutor. Thus the county is burdened, the public time is wasted, and an innocent fellow-subject involved in the manifold inconveniences of a public trial, without any means in general of compensation or redress.

I am aware that delay may be objected to personal examination; but if such an objection could be seriously urged, where the dearest interests of a fellow-creature are at stake; if an argument could be gravely offered to a Christian tribunal which a pagan poet[5] would blush to listen to, it is only at assizes the objection can have any weight, where the Judges are limited in time, and not at sessions, where we are under no such difficulty. I have, therefore, always exhorted Grand Juries, for the better investigation of truth, to adopt as closely as possible the just and humane practice of England; and it is with great satisfaction I perceive it has grown very much into use with the Grand Juries of this county.

In a word, Gentlemen, let me remind you, in the language of Lord Coke, "that indictments should be formed upon plain and direct *proofs* and not on probabilities and inferences." [6] The moment Grand Juries yield to mere probability, or think themselves at liberty to ground their verdict on less than positive evidence, they betray the trust reposed in them – they cease to be the guardian of innocence and shield of civil liberty – and there is an end of that happy freedom, that calm tranquillity of life, which is the great object and forms the prime blessing of the social compact.

Gentlemen, I shall detain you no longer.

1 In the Revolutionary calendar the Ninth of Thermidore (July 1794) ended the Reign of Terror, overthrew the Committee of Public Safety and executed Robespierre (Ed.).

2 Solon, the Athenian law giver, came to power in 594 B.C. Placing himself on the side of the poor he was responsible for making economic and political reforms and challenging the abuse of power on the part of the aristocracy (Ed.).

3 The reference here is to the Magistry Act of 1787, Irish Statutes, 27 Geo. 3, c. 40, in the enactment and implementation of which Day took an active part.

4 Unless it appeared upon oath, to the satisfaction of the Judge, that the informer was dead, or so sick as to be unable to travel, or spirited away by the prisoner.

5 Nulla unquam de morte hominis cunctatio longa. Juvenal.

6 2 Inst. C. 12, p. 384 (Day). Sir Edward Coke (1552-1634), Chief Justice of England. Coke was a great exponent of the common, against statute, law, and a leading parliamentary opponent of Charles I. His magisterial Reports and Institutes were a survey of English law (Ed.).

'The French are in the Bay': charges of 1796

A Charge
delivered to the Grand Jury of the County of Dublin
at the Quarter Sessions of the Peace
held at Kilmainham on the 12th day of January 1796
by Robert Day, Esq., M.P.

Published at the request of the Hon. Sheriff and Grand Jury

Rev. William Jackson, agent of the United Irishmen to France, was captured in 1794 and tried in April 1795. What he revealed to the Irish authorities had a bearing on Day's remarks in the following two addresses, which contain the theme of Catholic ingratitude. The United Irishmen were suppressed immediately the trial ended and Wolfe Tone fled to America. In the north the defeat of the Defenders at the Battle of the Diamond in September was followed by the formation of the Orange Order and the flight of large numbers of Catholics from south Ulster to settle in Connaught. Near the year's end Carhampton dragooned Connaught.
French dominance in Europe caused the First Coalition to unravel. Belgium (Austrian Netherlands) was already under French control, and the final defeat of Holland (now the Batavian Republic) was sealed with a punitive treaty in May 1795. Later Prussia abandoned the Coalition and signed a peace with France, and Hoche defeated the rebels in Brittany and their British military support.

Gentlemen of the Grand Jury!

It is impossible for any Irishman not dead to all public virtue, to contemplate without exultation and national pride the stability of their kingdom amidst the convulsions and disastrous events which in the lapse of a few years have desolated the greater part of Europe. While we prostrate ourselves in grateful adoration before the throne of God for his stupendous goodness, it may not be unprofitable to enquire into the more immediate causes of our redemption from those awful calamities which it has pleased Providence to visit upon so large a proportion of our fellow creatures. Such calculations, while they teach us to form a just sense of the importance and value of our establishments, must naturally lead every man of prudence and reflexion to sustain and cherish them as the sure means of our preservation amidst this wreck of nations.

The frame and structure of our Government is the great and primary cause, to which under God, we stand indebted for our security – that government in which Monarchy, Aristocracy, and Democracy combine their forces and best properties, and controul the vices and excesses of each other, that government in which these three rival powers are tempered into an apt consistence; and so many advantages seemingly irreconcilable, like the jarring elements of nature, conspire to produce this harmonious, well-poised order of things. – From this form of Government, in which the interests of all are alike considered, result our system of just and equal laws, and the principles which regulate the administration of justice amongst us. From the same source is derived the happy state of our society in these kingdoms; where protection is extended equally to all, where there is one law civil, where merit finds free access to the emoluments and honours of the state thrown open without distinction to all. In a word, it is by the energy and free principles of our Constitution that the British Empire has risen to its unrivalled greatness, and the people to the highest gradation in the scale of political and civil happiness.

Among the various means which secure the civil rights and happiness of our people (which in truth are public security and strength) none is more distinguished than that which the present solemnity draws into action. You perceive, Gentlemen, that I allude to the administration of criminal justice amongst us. Our whole judicial constitution is indeed a blessing, but particularly the Trial by Jury. In the construction of our criminal tribunals, which are separated into distinct parts, the more effectually to guard against corruption, caprice, and error, the leading principle, which has been steadily kept in view, is Equality. The Grand and Petit Juries are composed of persons who themselves are liable to be tried and judged by others of their fellow-subjects acting in the same capacities. That measure of justice which the juror deals to his fellow-subject today, may be measured out to himself to-morrow; it behoves him therefore that it be a just one. So also they are indiscriminately called to those services, from time to time as each occasion requires, from the great mass of the Freeholders of the county; no distinction observed, save that of character and a very moderate qualification of property. It must strike you therefore that, being transitory and occasional bodies, they are not exposed, as a permanent Jury would be, to the exercise of any corrupt or undue influence, which the rich and powerful can always best command.

Nothing can more clearly illustrate this equality amongst all conditions in these realms, than the dire effects of a permanent standing Jury in France. That unhappy country got a glimpse of our establishments, and adopted from us the institution of juries. But they were juries in name only, and not in principle or construction. Instead of impannelling them for each occasion, their sanguinary legislators established standing Juries; not to exercise any judgement upon the cases submitted to them, but to sanction the most unparalelled enormities. The consequences were what might be expected. These permanent juries soon became the convenient organ of each succeeding Monster in power, and at the nod of every ferocious leader, with scarcely the forms of law, consigned whole hecatombs of innocent victims to judicial sacrifice. Gentlemen, your indignation rises at this horrid prophanation of the sacred institution of juries; an institution which you habitually contemplate as the sure refuge and sanctuary of innocence, the poor man's best friend, his tutelary God; the strong curb of insolent power and licentious authority; the terror of guilt alone.

But in the remaining branch of our criminal tribunals, such fluctuation is not necessary to an equal dispensation of justice. On the contrary, the judge, being independent of the Crown, may safely be permanent; and indeed of necessity he must be so, as long as we prefer a system of known and fixed laws to novel and chimerical opinions; as long as industry, experience, education and science, are essential ingredients in the judicial character.

In a word, we may with truth assert, that there is no nation under the sun where justice is so equally and impartially administered as in these realms; and of the law it may with no less truth be said, that as it provides a remedy for every injury, so it affords that remedy equally to the proudest and the poorest.

One should suppose that under so favoured and providential a dispensation of things, no man in his senses could wish to change his political condition. No one, it might be hoped, who was not actually distempered in mind, or bankrupt in fortune or fame, could be seduced from an habitual sense of the singular advantages derived from a system of laws 'as broad and general as the casing air'. But alas! It can no longer be concealed that the industry of sedition and treason has been too successful in both countries. The wicked conspiracy has been traced through many of its ramifications in Great Britain and Ireland. What the proceedings[1] of the British Parliament and courts of justice have been these two last years to probe the evil and check its progress, it would be going out of our way to detail. But we know that Treason of late has thrown off the mask of our sister kingdom, and disdains all concealment. The late direct and immediate attempt upon the person and life of the Sovereign[2] no longer leaves the object of the conspirators questionable, or the Treason matter of construction or inference. It was reserved[3] for the peculiar and daring atrocity of modern principles to assail the father of his people, surrounded by his devoted and exulting subjects; in the exercise of that august function, which dispenses happiness to millions, which gives life and motion to the most sublime system of legislation that history has recorded. Phrensy alone it was thought could have armed itself against the life of a Monarch, as distinguished for his inviolable fidelity to the constitution, as for his exemplary piety and domestic virtues; whose life, in addition to our allegiance, challenges the tribute of our love; and whose death would be the bitterest calamity that could be inflicted upon his subjects.

In this country the plot has been carried on with more colouring and disguise, but perhaps with a still deeper degree of malignity. The object of the conspirators in Great Britain was to subvert the Monarchy, and in its place to substitute a Republic; that is, to let in all the confusion and anarchy of France. This was to be accomplished by means of a National Convention, to be openly and avowedly held, to which they had the folly to hope that the people might be persuaded to transfer their allegiance and confidence from their King and Parliament. But the object here was no less than to procure an invasion from France; from a people whose progress has been invariably marked by desolation, famine and blood. *Gallorum gentem infestissumam nomini Romano intra moenia arcessunt.* This was to be seconded by a general rising of the great mass of our people, who were represented as *semi-barbarous,* [4] ready for any change, and harbouring a rooted and confirmed aversion to the British name and connexion. Gentlemen, you know that to promote this diabolical purpose Jackson visited this City, an accredited Ambassador from the Daemons of France to certain traitors and parricides of Ireland. You know that through the vigilance and address of Government in both kingdoms, that unfortunate man was brought to justice, and his cabinet of conspirators, taking the alarm, prudently fled, and escaped the punishment due to their crimes. But the seeds of Treason unhappily had been previously scattered through the island, and it must be owned that they have produced an abundant crop. It now comes out on the clearest evidence, that those deluded men stiled *Defenders*, apparently but a lawless rabble, confining their views, as it at first seemed, to meer acts of plunder and felony, have in truth been regularly embodied and organised under leaders and committee-men. It appears that the plot had rooted itself so extensively, that the insurgents through no less than nine counties, have been leagued together by the most sacred (or rather the most accursed) obligations, to rise upon notice; that all were bound by the same oath to the National Convention, used the same mysterious signs, acted in unison, and were moved as it were by one spring. With the same traiterous purpose they have been disarming every man in those counties, upon whose co-operation they could not count, and who wanted courage and public spirit to resist them. With the same view they learned the use of arms, levied contributions, purchased ammunition, recruited avowedly for the National Convention, employed emissaries in the experiment, and vain as wicked, of debauching our brave and ready soldiers; and in short, took every step to strengthen themselves and give effect to the long expected descent. - Mean time the conspirators were not idle in the Capital. In a City[5] so populous and so profligate, the most desperate enterprise will not long want an army of advocates. All men goaded by bankrupt, evil society, or conscious guilt, have an interest in confusion, and were pleased to find a rallying-point: neglected apprentices, needy journeymen, seditious masters, hoping to 'ride the whirlwind', here formed themselves into Societies, Committees and Clubs, and familiarly discoursed of Rebellion as the sacred birthright of the people. The Philanthropic Society enlarged with great sensibility on the virtue of assassination and the use of the poignard. The dregs of the dissolved *United Irishmen* thought a civil war the best expedient for promoting a general uniformity and harmony of sentiment. And there is reason to believe, that a massacre upon a comprehensive scale was in agitation, as the surest means of promoting political morality and the Christian religion!

Such, Gentlemen, is the dark and formidable conspiracy, which, through the signal mercy of Providence, has been brought to light when at the very point of explosion. Much praise is fairly due to government for the perseverance and energy with which the infernal plot has been followed up and defeated. We have awakened on the brink of a precipice. We have been walking in dull obscurity over a mine, which by good fortune has not sprung under our feet. But though the electric cloud be passed, the sky still lowers. "We have scotch'd the snake, not killed it!" The diligence of bad men never sleeps, and has the additional danger of being mingled with cautious observance of times and seasons. They can withdraw when the aspect of things is unfavourable; but if the alarm which they have raised shall subside, if your vigilance shall be lulled into security, then like summer flies after a storm, they will again come forth with fresh zeal and renewed activity. Can it be doubted that Republican Agents and disaffected men of no mean condition foment this traitorous spirit, and administer to the support of those deluded wretches, who can have no resources of their own to rest upon through this barbarous warfare, so long and obstinately waged by them upon all order and civil Government in the country?

Gentlemen, it is needless to trouble you with any legal observations of my own upon the subject. The law has been[6] lately laid down definitely by higher authority, the concurring authority of three learned Judges; and I cannot express it more clearly than in the words of the learned Baron, your late worthy Municipal Judge[7]: "It is now evident (said he) that the Defenders are not merely Felons, but *Traiters*." The oaths and tests under which they are enlisted, declare expressly that they are concerned with the National Convention of France for the purpose of subverting our government. And it is now fit that it should be made known, that it is High Treason to incite or encourage a man to become a Defender; that it is Treason to harbour, comfort or abet the Defenders – all persons in any wise concerned are Traitors. And further, all men who know, and do not disclose to government or the magistrates their knowledge of the Defenders, and of their criminal actions or purposes, are guilty of *Misprision of Treason* – the judgment for which, Gentlemen, is no less than that the convict be imprisoned for life, forfeit the profits of his lands for life, and forfeit absolutely all his personal property.

These observations,[8] Gentlemen, I address not only to you, but to this assembled Multitude; in the anxious and fond hope, that every man who hears me will with his utmost industry circulate them, and impress the law upon the minds of the deluded peasantry in his neighbourhood. Say to them, that at the moment when Parliament had been most busy in ameliorating their condition: - when the only price[9] which they paid to the state for protection had been remitted and the burden transferred to their landlords – when they had been relieved, in a great degree, of Tythe, at the expense of the Protestant Clergy – when a liberal provision had been appropriated to the education of the Roman Catholic clergy – and above all, when a Protestant Legislature, by a bold and enlightened policy, struck off those religious and political fetters, which for a century had galled the great body of our fellow-subjects: tell them, that, false to the acknowledged loyalty of their own Communion, the first use they have made of long-lost freedom, the first record of their gratitude for this accumulation of bounty, was a foul conspiracy, with the Eternal Enemy of the British Empire, to dethrone that virtuous and beneficent Monarch who had himself become a mediator for the Catholic Body with his Parliament of Ireland! to bend the neck of free-born Irishmen to the vile yoke of French Usurpers drenched in blood; of the fiercest domination that ever blotted the page of history, or scourged any portion of the human race! Tell them, that their guilt is the highest in the scale of crimes – that the punishment which awaits them is the severest known to the law – that the public indignation is at its height, and calls aloud for vengeance on them – and that no resource remains but that they return forthwith to their allegiance, and to those long deserted paths of industry in which alone they can find competence, and comfort for their unhappy families, balm for their wounded consciences, and favour from their offended GOD. Tell them, finally, that the best evidence they can give of contrition, and the surest title they can have to Mercy, will be a voluntary disclosure (before any information shall be given against themselves) of their whole Plot, and of the nefarious incendiaries who have thus led them to destruction.

The detail in which I have so long detained you will not, I trust, be deemed altogether foreign to the duties of this day. We are assembled here to let loose the terrible judgments of the law, even death itself, upon the comparatively small offences against property; knowing at the same time that principles are instilled, and plots conceived, which would confound all property and its owners in one undistinguishable ruin. Can we with a safe conscience execute those avenging laws upon paltry plunderers, unless we also in our several capacities exert our authority to check the levelling principles which have generated so many and such enormous crimes? Unless we use our best endeavours to trace to their sources and dry up those waters of bitterness which overspread and pollute our land? Such persons and such societies, if any be known to you within our jurisdiction, I recommend to your serious attention and severest reprehension. So also, all places where those seditious and treasonable associations assemble, of which you have any knowledge or shall receive information, should be presented as common nuisances. The publicans who knowingly suffer their houses to be converted to such criminal purposes (and it is incredible that they can be strangers thereto) are deeply implicated in the guilt of the conspirators; and the only question would be, whether they were not principal in the Treason, for receiving and comforting Traitors, or guilty only of an atrocious and most penal misdemeanour in concealing the Treason. An here let me solemnly, in the face of our country, conjure my brethren the magistrates to be particularly chaste and cautious at this juncture, in granting licenses; and to have a vigilant eye on all public houses in their several vicinities; to proceed summarily and severely against all unlicensed publicans; and to withdraw their licenses from all publicans whose conduct and character justify suspicion; but those above all who keep their houses open at unseasonable hours. It would indeed be a regulation of great public advantage to shut up all places of mean and obscure resort at an earlier hour than would perhaps be necessary in times less critical. There can be no hardship in requiring men to retire early to rest, who must rise early to earn their daily bread. It is in the dead of night, when all nature seeks repose, all but animals of prey, the conspirators assemble, and hatch dark and bloody treasons and other atrocious crimes. And it is in those hot-beds of corruption and debauchery, that the first deeds of vice and criminality are sown, which afterwards ripen into full-blown guilt, and find so much exercise for this and every other criminal tribunal.

Upon the face of the Calendar it appears, that two men stand committed for plundering a dwelling-house of arms, and two more for administering unlawful oaths. Charges of so serious a nature, at all times demand your best attention, but more especially at this juncture, when such are known to be among the crimes of Defenders. Gentlemen, let me recommend to you in these cases, (as indeed I most seriously do on every occasion of importance or doubt) to call the prosecutors before you, and to sift and search them with all your diligence; such personal examinations will not only enable you to form a competent and sound judgment upon these particular charges, but may also lead you to further discoveries touching the general plot which I make no doubt it is your wish, as it is your duty and interest, to pursue into all its mazes and concealments.

Gentlemen, I shall not trespass further upon your time than just to remind you, that you are the constitutional guardians of the lives and liberties of your fellow-subjects; you are the sacred shields of innocence against power, wealth and malice; and that, whenever a Grand Jury finds a bill of indictment upon insufficient evidence, they betray the solemn trust reposed in them by the law, they do an irreparable injury to the party accused; and, as far as in them lies, they shake one of the main pillars of our unrivalled constitution.

1 Reports to both Houses of the British Parliament in early 1794, and in October the State Trials at the Old Bayly, revealed 'that a traiterous conspiracy had been formed and acted upon, by certain societies and individuals in different parts of England and Scotland, corresponding and intimately connected, for subverting the established laws and constitution, pulling down the Monarchy, and for introducing in its stead that anarchy and those extravagant notions of false liberty, which have transformed the fairest and once the most civilized region of Europe into a wilderness of tygers.' (Pamphlet footnote.)

2 King George was attacked en route to open parliament (Ed.).

3 The sentence beginning 'It was reserved for ...' and the next, down to 'as distinguished for his inviolable fidelity to the constitution... ,' replace an original of less oratorical flight: *Faulkner's Dublin Journal,* 26-28 January, 1796, has: 'It is hardly credible, were not the fact so notorious, that a savage attack could have been made upon a Monarch, as distinguished for ....'

4 See Jackson's Trial, p. 81 and passim. (Rev. William Jackson died in the dock on 30 April 1795 from a dose of arsenic before sentence could be pronounced on him, Ed.)

5 In tanta tamque corrupta Civitate, Catalina, &c. See Sallust in bello Catal.

6 By Chamberlaine, J., Finucane, J., and Baron George in The King against Weldon for High Treason at the Commission held 14 December, 1795 (pamphlet footnote).

7 Denis George, Recorder of Dublin 1785, Baron of the Exchequer 1794.

8 This paragraph is not included in the press report of the charge.

9 Pamphlet footnote: The Hearthmoney Act, which transferred that Tax from all Houses having but one Hearth to such as have more; the Barren Land Act, which exempted all heath and waste unimproved ground from Tythe for seven years after improvement; the great Catholic Act, which gave to the Catholic, in common with the Protestant peasantry, every political privilege of which that order of the community is susceptible – these liberal measures, calculated generally for the relief of the poor at the expense of the rich, were among the many excellent laws of the Westmorland Government.

William Ashford, Opening of the Grand Canal Dock at Ringsend, near the mouth of the Liffey, Dublin, St. George's Day, 23 April 1796
(National Gallery of Ireland)

The Substance of a Charge delivered to the Grand Jury of the County of Dublin on the 4th of October 1796 by Robert Day, Esq., M.P., one of His Majesty's counsel learned in the law and Chairman of said county.

Published at the request of the Magistrates and Grand Jury

The United Irishmen, still seeking French assistance to establish a republic, joined with, or took over, the Defenders, a movement more linked to agitation against landlords and the Established church. 1796 saw the passing of repressive legislation, also an act to embody a Yeoman force from the Protestant population. Day justified all of these measures. In the provinces however, Day was regarded as too humane, too eager to clear the prisons of improperly detained suspects. Lord Longueville, writing from Cork, complained that 'General Coote has come to great disgrace. All the people he committed were acquitted, or turned out of jail by that General Jail Deliverer Mr. Day, whose office at Cork, or conduct there, we are all at a loss how to account for by law' (National Archives of Ireland, State Papers 1016, 11-18, Lord Longueville to (not recorded) 2 October 1797).

Gentlemen of the Grand Jury,

I have no doubt that the Oath which you have now taken has made a deep and due impression upon your minds – that your conduct in the important office which you have undertaken will be conformable to the spirit of that Oath – and that you will discharge the duties which it imposes, diligently and conscientiously, not less to your own credit than to the advantage of the public.

What those duties are, it is hardly necessary to detail to Gentlemen of your experience and condition. No words indeed can more clearly express them, than those of that solemn obligation by which you have just bound yourselves. "You are well and diligently to inquire, and true presentment make. – You are not to disclose his Majesty's counsels, your fellow-jurors' or your own. – You shall present no person or thing through malice, nor leave any one unpresented through fear, favour, or affection."

As long as the world is inhabited by imperfect Beings, it will happen that "Offences come." To controul and punish offences, and to protect Innocence and Virtue, it is that certain known rules of action, or Laws, are made; and to execute those Laws, by which Society is held together in this Kingdom, and to administer Justice to your county, you, Gentlemen, are now called together.

The first object of the laws is to preserve the Government and Constitution of the state. For this purpose have been enacted the Statutes relative to High Treason, and for this purpose have been instituted the late prosecutions for treason, conspiracies and sedition; offences till of late strangers to this loyal and humane country. God grant that the numerous and severe examples which have been made in the Capital and on the Circuits may have extended their beneficial influence to this, and to every other county of the Kingdom! God grant that the ignominious fate of those obstinate victims to public justice may have taught the deluded abettors of insurrection and treason the fatal folly of grappling with the Law! That Justice, like the merciful Author of our being, though slow to mark what is done amiss, is sure to overtake with multiplied vengeance the persevering and incorrigible offender! - That such prosecutions should have been necessary, to every good man must be matter of no less surprise than regret; because the most prominent feature of our Constitution is, that all classes of men amongst us are equally intitled to the benefit of the Laws – that the highest are not above the law – and that the lowest are within its protection. The next object of the laws is to protect our lives, our persons, and our property. Fortunately there appears no charge in the calendar of an offence against any of these, but such as your experience has rendered you perfectly conversant with. It is unnecessary therefore to trouble you with any comment upon the nature of them.

For the execution of the Laws and the punishment of offences, the most usual and effectual course of proceeding is by Indictment; which is your proper and peculiar province. But in deliberating upon such bills as shall be sent up to you by our officer, you will ever bear in recollection the sacred maxim of our law – "that every man is to be presumed Innocent 'til he be proved Guilty." It is true that the Grand Jury can receive evidence, only in support of the charge; for an Indictment when found is an accusation only, and not a trial. But before you entertain that accusation and adopt it with the solemn sanction of your verdict – before you declare upon your oath that there are just grounds for dooming a fellow-subject to a trial, eventually affecting his property, liberty, character, perhaps his life – you are bound to satisfy yourself thoroughly, as far as the evidence goes, that the charge is true. The Grand Jury Room is not an office in which every Bill of Indictment, which the crown shall think proper to prefer, is to be implicitly registered. You have still prouder and more imperious duty incumbent on you – the protection of innocence against malice and power. The Grand Jury is stationed as an out-post upon the very frontier of Civil Liberty, to repel the first inroads of injustice; and the moment you find a Bill of Indictment without due consideration and satisfactory proof, you betray that critical post confided to you by a jealous and provident Constitution. – And here allow me to repeat an admonition which I am fond of inculcating upon Grand Juries – not to trust too confidently to Informations, which at best are but secondary evidence; and which are often taken as negligently by the Magistrate, as they are sworn vindictively by the Prosecutor. It is for want of a due and patient investigation of the charge by the Magistrate, that our Grand Jury table is so often loaded with angry and frivolous Informations. In all cases of reasonable doubt, suspicion, or obscurity, you ought to reject the bill; or certainly not to find it, 'till you have called the witnesses for the Crown before you, and satisfied yourselves of the truth of the charge by a strict *viva voce* examination.

But, Gentlemen, your duties are not confined to the walls of your Grand Jury Room. As the Grand Inquest of the County, your are bound to inquire after and make *Presentment* of all offenders, and of all offences and nuisances coming directly within your own knowledge and jurisdiction, and which from your local advantages you have the best opportunities of discovering. Under this head of Inquisitorial Duties, falls that which requires you to present all places of unlawful resort within your county, especially such as are kept open at unseasonable hours, or upon a day sacred to other purposes, the Sabbath; not for innocent recreation, but for dissipation and wanton debauchery. So also all meetings, associations, and clubs held for Combination among tradesmen; or for any disorderly, seditious, or other unlawful purpose: - But above all, any Assemblies for promoting that modern complication of all crimes of robbery, burglary, assassination and treason – called *Defenderism*: - Such are proper objects for the most vigorous prosecution, and demand of course your most active and serious inquiry. – And it may not be amiss thus publicly to apprise the County, that the Legislature last session made the County of Dublin responsible for all robberies, burnings and other such outrages therein committed, by giving to the sufferers compensation for their losses by Presentment; in other words, by extending the operation of the 15th and 16th of the King, called the Whiteboy Act, to this county. – It is easy to discover the principle of this wise provision, in the simple but happy regulations which the great Alfred adopted to reduce his licentious subjects under the salutary restraints of Government and Law. He authorized the People to raise the *Hue and Cry*, and to make *fresh Suit* from place to place 'till the offender was apprehended. And in order to interest the disturbed District in such immediate pursuit, he made the several divisions and subdivisions, into which he distributed his Kingdom, answerable in damages for all robberies therein committed.

Gentlemen, in your Inquisitorial capacity devolves upon you another duty, painful perhaps in the execution, but dear to humanity, and such as on reflexion will well reward your trouble – that of visiting your Jails and seeing that they are regulated according to Law. Since the last Quarter Sessions our prisoners have been turned over to the New Jail – that splendid monument of humanity and munificence of our county, and of the taste and talents of the ingenious Architect[1] whom they employed. Let us follow up and second the benevolence of the County of Dublin, and take care that this noble Establishment, so happily contrived for the reformation of the criminal, be not converted into a Seminary of wickedness and vice. Let us take care that the crimes and inveterate abuses of the Old Prison be not transferred with the Prisoners to the New. Let us see that the scanty rights of the unhappy be not abridged. – Gentlemen, let me recommend to you, when the Crown business (which always claims your first attention) shall be dispatched, to appoint a Committee to visit the Jail before the Court shall finally adjourn; and let them on the spot inquire into the conduct of the Jailer and his inferior officers towards the prisoners. A Jailer should be taught that he is the Keeper, not the Tyrant, or Lord of his Prisoners – that the powers intrusted to him over his prisoners are for their safe custody, and not for extortion, persecution, or oppression – and that as long as a prisoner conducts himself in a decent and orderly manner, he is intitled to humane treatment, and to every indulgence consistent with security and his sentence. In a word, it is the duty of a jailer to command with temper, and to inforce his just authority with firmness, but without violence, insolence, or brutality. – Your Committee will perceive also the necessity of extending their inquiry to the conduct of the Inspector-General, the Local Inspector, the Distributor of Bread, the Chaplain, the Physician; in short, of every officer whom the county hath attached at very liberal salaries to the Jail. Let them see whether the Regulations prescribed by the Jail Acts, particularly the specific rules ordained by the 15th of the King, be strictly observed; - but above all, whether spirituous liquors, cards, dice, or any other game for money be permitted in the prison. – And of all these matters you, Gentlemen, will be pleased at your leisure to make a Report[2] in writing to this Court; to the end that we may adopt the most effectual Regulations within our competence for correcting any existing abuses, and for the better government of our prison in future. – Such was the daily occupation of the benevolent Howard, who laid down his life in mitigating human misery; whose Divine Spirit purged the pestilential vapour, lightened the fetters, and softened the horrors of every dungeon in Europe!

From many years' acquaintance in my judicial capacity with the Grand Juries of the County of Dublin, I am aware how unnecessary it is to detain you longer upon the subject of your duties. Of both Grand and Petit Juries I will say, that I have ever found them governed by a conscientious regard to their Oaths; and let me add, that of late, under very trying circumstances, they have uniformly and to their immortal honour evinced an unshaken zeal for our good King and unrivalled Constitution; displaying to their fellow-subjects of both kingdoms a bright example of loyalty and true love of their country. But before you withdraw, permit me to address a word to you upon the present critical state of the country. If ever there was a period which loudly and imperiously called for the active and vigorous exertions of every good subject in his various capacities and relations, it surely is the present. It is not merely our political existence as an important limb of the freest and happiest Empire in the world that is at stake, but the physical existence of every individual amongst us. We know that the favourite and avowed object of the French Government is to devote their whole concentred force to the extermination of the British Empire. We alone have stood in their way to universal dominion; which doubtless would lead to the utter extinction of all religion, property and social order. We know that an invasion of these happy and flourishing islands (flourishing even amidst the desolation of Europe) is the Golden Expedition with which they amuse their wretched impoverished country; and that if they can detach the few Allies who faithfully stand by us, they will, no matter at what hazard, attempt the desperate experiment. At a period so alarming and awful, fortunately all prudent and well-affected men see the indispensable necessity of stepping forward and straining every nerve to repel the common danger. Upon that vital subject, involving national independence and personal security, no difference of opinion can subsist amongst us. The external urgent danger must bind and compress us internally; common interest will excite us to general action; and while the danger prevails, all projects of ambition, all religious and political controversies will surely be suspended, and give place to a cordial co-operation of all parties against the common enemy. The juncture admits but of one distinction – the Friends of our Constitution, and its Foes. I see the old military enthusiasm of Ireland – which in the late war presented an invincible front to the combined powers of Europe. I see your characteristic gallantry once more in motion. I see all the energies of the Island – her whole property and power pressing forward to embody and array[3] under the sanction of Government *pro aris et focis*[4] - in defence of our Country, our Liberties, our Families, of every thing dear to the heart of man. In such a season Neutrality would be folly, or something worse. In such a season it was that the great Athenian Statesman[5] pronounced Neutrality to be a treason: - at the best it would argue that infatuated Apathy, which in a time of danger is the forerunner of ruin. – Mean time it is necessary to watch narrowly our domestic enemies, the more dangerous because disguised. It cannot be doubted that Treason[6] rankles in our bosom; that men are to be found amongst us leagued with France, deep in her interest and councils; who invite invasion, who labour to introduce into the heart of their country a destructive and implacable Foe. At a time when conspiracies have been discovered against the very being of the state; when men, once of consideration and popular influence amongst us, stand fugitives and outlawed traitors; when so many atrocious criminals have forfeited their lives for enormities 'till of late unknown amongst us – for assassination, conspiracies, treason; - at such a juncture no honest man will deny that a comprehensive Plot exists in the state, or damp the ardour of manly and spirited precautions. Among other too-successful means of mischief they have got possession of some of our public Prints; turning the very Palladium of our Liberty, a Free Press, into an instrument of our own destruction – that press which should be guarded as our most precious inheritance; guarded alike against licentiousness and encroachment. In their language too as well as in their writings you perceive them acting as the zealous emissaries of France; extolling the power of our enemies, yet lulling their Country into a fatal security – rejoicing in their victories – extenuating their atrocities – deriding our conquests – misrepresenting the measures of a vigilant and virtuous Government – and scattering with unceasing industry the seeds of discontent and rebellion through the land. – To Gentlemen of your education and character it would scarcely be respectful to vindicate, against the calumnies of bad men, a Constitution from which we all derive unparalleled protection. It is engraved upon your hearts in characters of indelible veneration, the object of your grateful and most rational affection. Were evidence required of its pre-eminence, seek it not beyond these walls – look for it in the high trust committed to yourselves. Here, to be suspected is not to be guilty – well-earned Property, Moderation, Religion are not crimes – accusation is not conviction – nor is conviction instant and inevitable death. Here, no trembling victim is dragged by the reeking hands of assassins before a Bench of blood-stained Monsters, and consigned to immediate butchery, "cut off even in the blossoms of his sin." Here, you behold the reign only of the Laws; the confidence of Innocence, and the reasonable hope even of Guilt truly penitent of its crimes. Here Innocence may scorn all the puny efforts of Malice and Wealth and Power, as long as the great Centinel of Civil Liberty, the Grand Jury, sleeps not on his post. – Compare then the British Jurisprudence, as thus conducted amongst us, with that Tribunal of Blood which will be erected here if ever the malignant labours of our Parricides prevail; with the horrid outrages committed under the semblance of Jurisprudence in that distracted country: - Compare their Fraternity, which is but another name for confiscation, massacre and ruin, and which will be our lot if ever the peaceful shores of Ireland be disturbed, and a rapacious Enemy shall find his way into our country; compare that frightful state of things with the present security of your manifold comforts and solid enjoyments, with the prosperity and rapid growth of your people: and say – are you prepared for such a transition? Are you prepared to be severed from the British Empire, and to purchase by requisitions, contributions and forced loans an incorporation with France? Are you prepared to resign this venerable fabric, constructed by the combined virtue and wisdom of ages; the sanctuary of Freedom; - to exchange the British Constitution – this fostering Parent of every thing that can adorn or ennoble human nature – for a Revolutionary Government, where Property, liberty, Life are but the sport of unrelenting Caprice?

The most fervent prayer of my heart is, that the British Empire may prove an example, and France a warning, to the World!

1 Sir John Trail, the architect of the new Kilmainham prison; the prison was begun in 1785 and completed in 1796 (Ed).

2 It would be unjust to the respectable Gentlemen composing the present Grand Jury to conceal, that this advice from the Bench has been followed with the most laudable and humane punctuality. A Committee was selected, who proceeded to the New Prison; and presented a very well-digested and comprehensive Report. It was satisfactory to observe the favourable testimony in general borne by them to the conduct of the present Jailer and of the several other Officers; but particularly to that of the Rev. Mr. Stubbs, the Chaplain and Local Inspector, whose assiduity and benevolence in both capacities are vouched in the most flattering terms by the Committee.

3 The Yeomanry Act of 1796 (Ed.).

4 literally, 'for the altars and the hearth'.

5 Demosthenes, the Orator, in his Phillipics opposed the rise of Macedonia under King Philip II (Ed.).

6 "The offence of inciting Foreigners to invade the Kingdom is a Treason of signal enormity. In the lowest estimation of things and in all possible events, it is an attempt on the part of the Offender to render his country the seat of blood and desolation." Foster, 196 (Day). Michael Foster (1689-1763), judge and author of *Crown Cases and Discourses upon a few branches of the Crown Law,* 1762 (Ed.).

Loyalty and Disaffection in the Hierarchy: two charges of 1797

An Address delivered to the Grand Jury of the County of Dublin on Tuesday, the 10 January 1797 by Robert Day, Esq., MP, one of His Majesty's Counsel learned in the Law and Chairman of said County.

First published in Dublin at the request of
the Magistrates and Grand Jury

A storm at Christmastime forced the French fleet at Bantry Bay to weigh anchor and return to France. Day interpreted the event as proof that divine providence was on the side of Britain. The gentlemen of West Yorkshire commended this address for its 'piety and patriotism', and having obtained his permission to publish the address they 'directed many hundred copies thereof to be distributed in this Riding'. The apparent loyalty of the Munster population when the French fleet anchored at Bantry Bay provided Day with the opportunity to conciliate Catholic opinion. The charge is most often quoted for the praise it gives Doctor Francis Moylan, Bishop of Cork, whose Pastoral had condemned the French attempt to land in Ireland. Worthy of note is the reference to Moylan as 'the pious Catholic Bishop of Cork' rather than the more condescending 'Titular' Bishop of Cork', Day's customary usage (Ed.).

Gentlemen of the Grand Jury,

The present tranquil and orderly state of our country and Capital, and the scanty Calendar in my hand, call scarcely for any other expression from me than that of the most lively and cordial congratulation. The times, it is true, have been turbulent; the Laws have lost their energy and just authority; and Humanity must for ever deplore the streams of blood which the insulted justice of the country has exacted. But it is a consolation of much moment that so many unhappy victims have not died in vain. Our misguided fellow-subjects, warned by numerous and severe examples, have discarded their evil counsellors and abandoned the criminal courses into which they had been deluded. They have opened their eyes at last to the blessings of that Constitution which protects them; and have returned to the paths of honest and sober industry, and a due submission to the laws of the land.

Gentlemen, I feel that it would be an insensible and disgusting waste of the public time to detain you at this joyful moment by a cold phlegmatic dissertation upon your duty, the threadbare theme upon which I have so often solicited public attention. I feel that at this proud juncture such a discourse would be deemed as it ought, a pedantic mockery of your best and finest feelings, engrossed as no doubt they now are by one of the most exhilarating and sublime subjects that ever presented itself to the enraptured mind of man. Yes, Gentlemen! Virtue has triumphed over Crime, Order over Anarchy, Liberty over Slavery, Religion over Atheism.- The right arm of our gracious God hath been stretched out to crush an impious Foe, and to save and protect his favourite Island. The long patient vengeance, the slumbering wrath of a just and terrible Divinity hath at last been awakened, and hath vindicated his power and justice upon the heads of an hardened and apostate race, who have proscribed him from his temples, and denied even the existence of the living God.

In contemplating this signal mercy, there are certain facts too prominent and emphatical to escape the notice of the most superficial observer; facts which might impress conviction upon infidelity itself, were infidelity capable of conviction. The discomfiture and utter confusion of the Enemy steeped in blood, steeled 'against every compunctious visiting of nature,' have been the sole and exclusive work of the Almighty; Providence it would seem had reserved to himself the punishment of those declared enemies of all order, virtue and religion. *Affavit Deus et dissipavit eos.* It was the breath of the Almighty which dispersed them. He uttered his will, and straitway the enemy who had eluded the British fleet, and had already in imagination rioted in the golden spoils of this plundered and devoted land, were scattered. This proud armament, the last effort of their expiring Navy, invited hither by traitors, advanced with all the confidence of another Armada to a certain and easy conquest, and has closed its career with the same disastrous tragical catastrophe. – Nor can it be forgotten by any well-regulated mind, that this awful visitation had been appointed for the great festival of Christianity; as if to recall by a tremendous warning at that sacred season a lost and infatuated people to a due reverence for our holy Religion, which had been the object of their derision, and which they had with great formality abjured.

But this is not all: if the pompous enterprise, from which your destruction was promised, has been miserably frustrated, your preservation has been accomplished by means not only the most effectual, but the most judicious and best selected. It is true a fair opportunity has been lost of emblazoning another day in the crowded calendar of British glory; but humanity and true policy, frugal of the blood of patriots and heroes, shrink alike from the blood-stained triumphs which feed the unfeeling pride of nations and conquerors! Your deliverance has been effected by wiser and more providential means; it has not cost you a single life or a single ship: that storm, which burst upon the hostile fleet, locked up ours secure in port – and what at first was felt by us all as a misfortune, proves ultimately but another instance of Divine favour.

For my own part, as a steady and confirmed Christian, I cannot but descry, in the strong marked events of this auspicious hour, the Divine finger – the immediate interposition of an avenging, a protecting, a just Ruler of the Universe: I can discover in these providential occurrences a superintending Dispenser of good and evil, 'scattering a people that delight in war;' scourging the perfidy[1] of a Government who project the destruction of your country even while they present to you the olive-branch of peace, mortifying their contumelious insolence, their pride, their gigantic arrogance, inspiring the Five-headed Despot of France by practical lessons of bitter adversity, with sentiments of becoming moderation, and holding forth to exhausted humanity some reasonable prospect, some fair omens, of returning repose.

But, Gentlemen, it would be unjust to pass over the effects of this much-vaunted expedition amongst ourselves, happy beyond the most sanguine hope. When I had the honour to address the last Grand Jury of the County, I took the liberty to draw their attention to the critical state of public affairs, and to suggest the necessity of arming ourselves under the sanction of Government, in conformity to the Yeomanry Act of this Session; but well as I had reason to recollect the martial alacrity and genius of our countrymen, my mind, I own, had not been prepared to expect or to conceive the possibility of what has since happened; high as I knew their pulse to beat at the call of danger, of honour and of their country, I hardly could expect that all party animosities, religious and political, could instantly have subsided – that all professions, trades and occupations, would be abandoned for arms – that in the space of three short months, you would have become a nation of soldiers, and another volunteer army would have arisen more sudden, more systematic, and better regulated even than the former. This mad and desperate Enterprise has developed the true character of Ireland to admiring Europe; it has displayed your gallantry, your patriotism, and your public spirit: These, however, are virtues which were never denied to the Irish character; but it has proved also, what perhaps was not before so well understood, the sound and loyal principles of the Southern peasantry, their just and inveterate conception of French *Fraternity*, and their ardent devotion to their good King, and to the British Constitution and Government. It has produced the Pastoral Letter[2] of the pious Catholic Bishop of Cork,[3] breathing a spirit of peace, loyalty and philanthropy, worthy of an Apostle: it has, in a word, vindicated the great Roman Catholic mass against the misconceptions of men prejudiced because uninformed, and (what was more difficult) against the disaffection and criminal tardiness of certain discontented individuals of their own body. – The Elements *have* saved us; a British Fleet *may* save us; - but whilst we are thus united at home, thus animated by a just sense of the incalculable blessings we enjoy – the perfect security of our Liberty, our property and our persons – confident in our own resources, we may bid defiance to any future experiments which our implacable enemy shall be rash enough to repeat.

One very serious and alarming fact is now confirmed beyond a doubt, that a traiterous correspondence has been maintained by miscreants in this kingdom with the government of France. It now appears that the invasion, thus happily averted, has been promoted by domestic traitors, scandalously misrepresenting the general spirit of the Irish peasantry; that invasion, which was to lay waste your fields, to sack and pillage your cities and habitations, and consign your honest acquisitions, the well-earned fruits of long and laborious thrift, your virtuous matrons and beloved children, to the spoil, the brutality and butchery of a famishing licentious and inveterate soldiery, culled (for their pre-eminence in crime) from the gaols and gallies of France, and recently schooled in the ensanguined, desolated and smoaking ruins of La Vendée. Whether the French rulers have reason to thank their parricide correspondents for belying the purity of our country, for their confident assurance that Ireland was impatient for French *Liberty* – that is, to league with ruin and embrace death, let the present triumph and universal glow of patriotism and loyalty decide. But allow me to express an earnest and anxious hope, that the Magistracy and all good subjects may not be deluded by the present flattering calm, but that they continue to watch with jealous vigilance, all suspected individuals and associations. In the best constituted communities there will always be found men of splenetic and malignant minds, or surfeited by too much happiness, or intoxicated by sudden prosperity, or having no property or character to lose, who eagerly pant for change, are ready to overturn the venerable fabric of Government, and labour to spread their own contagion amongst a happy and contented people. The old and flimsy veil under which these innovating spirits cloak their pernicious purpose is Parliamentary Reform. – When the House is no fire, they refuse to join in extinguishing the flames, until a certain chamber, which in their wise and profound judgment is ill constructed, shall be altered according to their taste. But whatever they profess, there seems no violence in suspecting that the object of such projectors is the destruction of the whole building, and not its improvement – those cold-blood Reformers, who in the hour of danger would capitulate and parley with their country, and must make their bargain even when the enemy is in your harbours. If there be men amongst us surrounded with all the means of human happiness safe in their persons, secure in their property, in the full fruition of every species of rational and social liberty, who yet are discontented and complain – if there be men, who warmed by the animating beams of the sun, make no other use of his cheering light but to discover the spots upon his glorious disk, I can only pity lamentation so unfounded, and occupation so unprofitable and unavailing. Be it our study to cherish with a jealous care, a Constitution our protection and pride, the parent of every civil blessing, and which it would be our greatest misfortune to survive.

But in vain has all this profusion of bounty been showered upon us, unless we turn with grateful hearts to Him from whom it flows – unless impressed with a deep and lasting sense thereof, we allow it to mingle with our lives, and colour all our conduct; but above all, unless we resolve to cling fast by that sacred Revelation of the Divine Will, which is the best consolation under misfortune in this world, and the strong anchor of our hope in the next. It is an imperious duty upon men of your condition and influence to promote by example and admonition, among the inferior classes of the people the practice of industry and temperance, a willing obedience to the laws, and all the moral and religious virtues. The prevention of crimes is far more lovely and acceptable in the sight of God than the punishment. Virtue and happiness go hand in hand even in this life; and depend upon it, the greater the stock of individual virtue in any state, the happier will be the general condition of that state.

Gentlemen, the surest pledge which I know for public order, personal security, and universal happiness, is to be found in that divine compendium of ethics – '*Fear God, and honour the King*'.

Doctory Francis Moylan,
To His Beloved Flock,[4]
The Roman Catholics of the Diocese of Cork

At a moment of such general alarm and consternation, it is a duty I owe to you, my beloved flock, to recall to your minds the sacred principles of loyalty, allegiance and good order that must direct your conduct on such an awful occasion. Charged as I am, by that Blessed Saviour, whose birth with grateful hearts we on this day solemnize, with the care of your souls, interested beyond expression in your temporal and eternal welfare, it is incumbent on me to exhort you to that peaceable demeanor, which must ever mark his true and faithful disciples.

Loyalty to the Sovereign and respect for the constituted authorities, have been always the prominent features in the Christian character; and by patriotism and obedience to the established form of government, have our ancestors been distinguished at times, and under circumstances very different from these in which we have the happiness to live. For, blessed be God, we are no longer strangers in our native land, no longer excluded from the benefits of the happy constitution under which we live, no longer separated by odious distinctions from our fellow-subjects. To our Gracious Sovereign we are bound by the concurring principles of gratitude and duty, and to all our fellow citizens by mutual interest and Christian charity.

Under these circumstances it is obvious what line of conduct you are to adopt, if the invaders, who are said to be on our coasts, should make good their landing and attempt to penetrate into our country. To allure you to a cooperation with their views, they will not fail to make specious professions, that their only object is to Emancipate your from the pretended Tyranny under which you groan; and to restore you those Rights of which they will say you are deprived.

You, my good people, whom I particularly address, who are strangers to passing occurrences, had you known in what manner they fulfilled similar promises in the unfortunate countries into which, on the faith of them, they gained admittance, you would learn caution from their credulity, and distrust men who have trampled on all laws human and divine; Germany, Flanders, Italy, Holland, to say nothing of their own, once the happiest, now the most miserable country in the world, can attest the irreparable ruin, desolation and destruction occasioned by French fraternity.

Be not deceived by the lure of equalizing property, which they will hold out to you, as they did to the above-mentioned people; for the poor, instead of getting any part of the spoil of the rich, were robbed of their own little pittance.

Be not then imposed on by their professions – they come only to rob, plunder and destroy. Listen not to their agitating abettors in this country, who endeavour by every means to corrupt your principles, but join heart and hand with all the virtuous and honest members of the community, who are come forward with distinguished patriotism, as well to resist the invading foe, as to counteract the insidious machinations of the domestic enemies and unnatural children who are seeking to bring to their native country the train of untold evils that flow from anarchy and confusion. – Obey the laws that protect you in your persons and properties – Reverence the magistrate entrusted with their execution, and display your readiness to give every assistance in your power.

Act thus, my beloved Brethren, from a principle of conscience, and you will thereby ensure the favor of your God, and the approbation of all good men; whereas a contrary conduct will draw down inevitable ruin on you here, and eternal misery hereafter.

I shall conclude with this simple reflection, if the sway of our impious invaders were here established, you would not, my beloved people, enjoy the comfort of celebrating this auspicious day with gladness and thanksgiving, nor of uniting with all Christians on earth, and with the celestial spirits in Heaven, in singing glory to God on high, and on earth peace to men of Good will!

F. Moylan, R.C.B.C., Dec. 25, 1796.

1 The Negotiations for Peace continued till the Expedition was ready, and then were abruptly and contumeliously broken off. The Fleet sailed from Brest on Thursday evening the 15th Dec., and on the 19th Lord Malmesbury received the French Minister's note commanding him to quit Paris in 48 hours.

2 This excellent Divine did not hang back or temporize till the danger was past. With a courage not less striking than his loyalty and benevolence, he delivered this impressive and spirited exhortation upon the first appearance of the hostile armament on our coast. Ardent in the cause of his God, his King and his Country, and regardless of evey personal consideration, he did not balance between duty and danger. At the very crisis of our fate, when the force and peril (swelled by panic and credulity) could not be known or calculated, he lost not a moment in giving battle to an Atheistical Enemy, and exposing himself in case of any untoward event to their most rancorous vengeance. The Cork Committee, composed of 31 Citizens of the first rank and character, without any regard to religious distinction, caused 3000 copies of this salutary and seasonable admonition to be immediately printed and circulated through the city and county.

3 Dr Francis Moylan, Bishop of Kerry 1775-1787, Cork 1787-1815.

4 The pastoral appears as a footnote in the pamphlet edition of this charge.

A Charge
delivered to the Grand Jury of the County of Dublin at the Quarter Sessions of the Peace held at Kilmainham on Tuesday the 25th April, 1797 by Robert Day, Esq., M.P., one of His Majesty's counsellors learned in the law and Chairman of the said court.

Published at the request of the High Sheriff, Magistrates and Grand Jury.

Printed in Dublin by Richard Edward Mercier and Company, 31 Anglesea St., Booksellers to the Honourable Society of King's Inns[1]

(It was printed some weeks later in London by John Stockdale of Piccadilly.)

In 1797 Doctor Thomas Hussey, Bishop of Waterford, issued a famous Pastoral. He attacked the practice of compelling Catholic militia men to attend Protestant church services, and he urged Catholic parents to withhold their children from non-Catholic schools. Day's anger at Dr Hussey owed much to feelings of betrayal, as Dr Hussey had been favoured with appointment as the first president of Maynooth College, set up by the Camden administration in 1795 for the training of Catholic priests in Ireland. The London pamphlet of this charge omitted Day's attack on Doctor Hussey (Ed.).

Gentlemen of the Grand Jury,

You are called together this day to bear your part in dispensing Criminal Justice to our county. You are called together to cooperate with the other component members of this tribunal, in administering the best system of Criminal Jurisdiction which the wit of man has ever been able to devise; that mild and benign system, which, from the earliest ages of antiquity hath distinguished and exalted the British Constitution and Empire above all others, where the wisest precautions are adopted to protect innocence, and to disappoint malice, corruption, prejudice, and every other evil affection of the mind; where twenty four honest, respectable neighbours, above all exception, must be fully satisfied in their consciences that the accused is guilty, and must unanimously, and upon their oaths, pronounce him so; where the small man is heard as patiently as the great, the poor man as favourably as the rich; where no man is respected for his rank, or feared for his power. The nature of the office which you have just undertaken, and the true character of a juror, may be summed up in a few words: To be a juror, is to be the guardian of innocence, the avenger of guilt, a friend to justice, and the most perfect organ of truth; - to be a juror is to be the best benefactor of the people, the best preserver of their public and personal rights; it is to defend the Constitution alike against anarchy and arbitrary power; against the silent and undermining encroachments of the monarch on the one hand, and on the other against the boisterous and overbearing encroachments of the many. In a word, next to the legislative trust, there surely is no other which concerns more essentially the well-being of the state, than that of juries. It is therefore much to be wondered at, that so many gentlemen of education and property in our county should make so much difficulty in serving upon the Session and Commission Grand Juries. Can their time and trouble be better bestowed than in administering justice to their fellow subjects? In truth, this reluctance is a serious public misfortune, because every man, in proportion to his stake in the community and the cultivated state of his mind, is most likely to feel the weight of that trust; most likely on the one hand to resist with firmness the undue interference of Power; on the other hand to promote a reverence for the laws, by a strict and scrupulous execution of them, without which the fruits of honest industry and every other blessing of social life must ever be precarious. Surely those men are but ill intitled to the proud privileges of a British subject, who decline to take their share in the public duties which are but the price we pay for those privileges; and which, however burdensome, are the surest means of maintaining us in the undisturbed enjoyment of our most precious rights.

You will hear with concern that the crimes on the face of the Calendar are not few, and that their quality in general is of considerable enormity. This too is the more observable as our magistrates are active, our criminal tribunals assiduous, and the war, into which we have been forced by anarchy and atheism, has weeded our county as usual of many malefactors and idlers. But the times are distinguished by some striking and peculiar features. You have never before known Sedition[1] to stalk so publicly and confidently thro' the land, or so daringly and powerfully patronised. You have never before known Irish men and Irish prints, (disclaiming that old-fashioned virtue which once embraced every other, the love of their country), openly to exult in our domestic embarrassments, in the miscarriages of a magnanimous ally, and the successes of a merciless and exterminating enemy. You know the pains which are taken to disparage the whole frame of our Legislature, and to render it disgusting and odious in the eyes of the people; that Legislature to whose wisdom and patriotism we owe the unexampled growth and rapid prosperity of Ireland. The laws under which we have thus happily flourished are represented as unjust, unequal and arbitrary, and the administration of them corrupt, partial and sanguinary. Magistrates are calumniated and vilified, from the most exalted and venerable down to those of the most ordinary functions. The iron reign of Bigotry with its horrid train of intolerance disunion and religious rancour is preached up and fervently inculcated;[2] the enlightened and happy progress of National Union is arrested in its most efficient source, in the fond and susceptible season of youth, in the social and endearing habits of education[3] and early fellowship; the most sacred[4] of our establishments is insulted and libelled; even the fidelity of our brave and loyal soldiery is practised upon – that implicit submission to authority which is the main-spring of the military machine, the soldier's first and paramount duty, without which an army becomes a rabble, formidable only to those who pay it – by a Minister of peace; bending under the favour of that government whose main pillars he thus, with a boldness beyond all parallel, attempts to shake. The most abominable doctrines touching revealed Religion and Civil Government, levelling all distinction, order and property, and alienating the lower classes from their rulers, are daily presented in the most seducing forms to the great body of the people, who are too ignorant to foresee the practical mischiefs resulting from such principles, and from their credulity and numbers are the most likely to prove the dupes as well as the instruments of them.

No wonder then if such malignant industry has produced an abundant crop of crimes; no wonder if it constantly recruit our prisons, and overload our gibbets. If the great props and buttresses[5] of the State be thus assailed with impunity; if the venerable institutions of our country, habitually revered from long experience of their excellence, be traduced and trampled without restraint or disguise; if the people be instructed to despise and deny the authority even of their legislature, no wonder that the laws are become a dead letter, and that the civil power hath lost all efficiency and controul. Hence proceed those atrocities in the North at which humanity sickens, and to whose active and sweeping progress our mild and merciful code of criminal jurisprudence is in vain opposed; that alarming ferment, which so loudly called upon Parliament for strong and extraordinary measures in proportion to the extreme emergency and danger of the times. Among others is the Insurrection Act which continues in force to the end of next session of Parliament; and as it is possible that in the conflict with treason, our magistracy may be driven to the painful necessity of resorting to that statute, it may not be amiss to state thus publicly to you and to them, the principal provisions of it.

By the Insurrection Act administration of any oath importing to bind the persons taking it to be of any seditious association, or to obey the rules of any unlawful committee or to commands of any unlawful leader, or not to give evidence against any confederate,[6] is now made Felony[7] of Death; and the taking such oath is subjected to transportation for life. And surely no good subject who knows that the scope and tendency of these Oaths is nothing less than the subversion of the state, that they form the bond of that deep laid Conspiracy now notoriously existing for a general Insurrection, will think that any punishment known to our law can be too rigorous for them. This provision is general, and extends to the whole Kingdom.[8] Then come certain local clauses, applicable only to proclaimed districts. Upon the representation of seven magistrates in special sessions assembled, a power is given the Lord Lieutenant and Council to declare by proclamation any county or district to be in a state of disturbance; and therefore a summary jurisdiction over all *idle and disorderly persons* in that district vests in the magistracy - analogous to, but very short of, the permanent powers given over such offenders to a single justice in England. From the earliest dawn of a police in the sister kingdom, a single magistrate has been authorised to commit to hard labour, to inflict corporal punishment, or to send into his Majesty's service, all idle and disorderly persons, rogues, and vagabonds, according to the degree of their delinquency. But the Insurrection Act commits no power of impressments or of corporal discipline to our magistracy; no less than two have any jurisdiction, from whom an appeal lies to the quarter session and in case of conviction, the magistrates can only transmit the offender to the navy. And the Act describes distinctly who shall be deemed idle and disorderly persons – all who take unlawful and seditious oaths, and who are already transportable for life, all who have no visible means of subsistence, and who also are already transportable, all who in the disturbed districts assemble tumultuously in the day, or are found assembled in public houses at unreasonable hours in the night, all who have or disperse seditious papers and such like. Such alone, who, in fact are offenders of a much higher order, are the idle and disorderly persons upon which this act attaches, and who, upon conviction, are liable to be impressed. Thus by a happy process good is extracted from evil – the crimes of individuals are converted to the benefit of the state; and those malefactors who conspire the subversion of government are compelled to serve in its defence.

Thus then you perceive that the English authority and statute book not only full warrant, but go considerably beyond this measure. If the crown can force the gallant and generous sailor from his fire-side and family in war time, without the formality of a trial or pretence of delinquency, into the service of his country – if state necessity and public policy can justify the exercise of an authority so harsh and summary over the most valuable class of our fellow-subjects, what claim to milder treatment have men, convicted before two magistrates, with an appeal to the quarter-sessions, of a conduct bordering upon treason? Surely if ever a just occasion arose for suspending the trial by jury, it is in the case of miscreants who systematically assassinate witnesses, jurors and magistrates, for their zeal in public service, and thus would render that immemorial and sacred depository of our liberties incompetent to the administration of justice. It is the proud boast of these conspirators that they can murder faster than juries can hang. The laws of civil society are framed to restrain such offences only, as the ordinary state of civil society is exposed to; and not in the vain and silly hope of stemming anarchy and insurrection, and all the enormities incidental to a state of smothered rebellion. In England, where the principles of true and rational Freedom are well understood and felt,[9] the present awful times have given birth to stronger measures than the Insurrection Act – to the suspension of the Habeas Corpus Act, which we have since adopted, a multiplication of treasons, a considerable enlargement of the summary jurisdiction of the magistrates, and a very strict regulation of the invaluable right of petitioning. Upon the whole, no man can lament more sincerely than myself[10] any departure from the line of the constitution, however inevitable its necessity, or short its duration, and it is the anxious hope, that this promulgation of the act may save the pain of resorting to it in our country, that I have in this discussion of it so long trespassed upon your time.

Gentlemen, the present awful crisis calls for the best exertions of us all in our several stations. The *High Sheriff*, as principal conservator of the peace in his bailiwick, is bound to watch every spark as it rises, and to extinguish it before it kindles into a flame. The Constitution hath committed to him the custody of the county for his year; and with it ample means for suppressing tumult and preserving the public peace. He is authorised upon any emergency to call out the power of his county, that is, every male from sixteen to sixty; and they are bound to attend him on summons, well armed under pain of being fined or imprisoned. So also, the *Magistrates* are armed with adequate powers for the like purpose, and the county expect at this juncture the vigilant and active exercise of those powers. Let it be their special care, as it is their bounden duty, to disperse all the unlawful assemblies, whether under colour of funerals or any other pretence, calculated by display of numbers to inspire the disaffected with confidence, and the well-disposed with just alarm and dismay. Let it also be their care to take up every suspicious stranger, skulking through their jurisdiction, to examine him strictly, and upon oath, as to the object and motive of his visit, into this county; and if he cannot give full satisfaction, to commit him till he shall find security for his good behaviour. Let them remember the munificent provision which the legislature, recording the obligations and sensibility of a grateful nation, hath bestowed upon the families of those virtuous magistrates who have perished in asserting the laws of their country; those intrepid martyrs to civil liberty, who have been butchered by the bloody hands of remorseless traitors. – for myself, Gentlemen, I feel it to be my first duty, one to which I devote myself, before which every other vanishes to my view, to co-operate by every other means in my power to the tranquillity and good order of our county. Under that impression, I give this public notice of my determination to hold this court by short adjournments throughout the present quarter-session, because, in my mind, no measures can be more effectual to controul crimes and criminal excesses, than speedy justice. – With respect to you, Gentlemen, I have no doubt that as Grand Jurors you will do your duty as becomes good subjects and honest men – faithful to your king, your country, and yourselves. It has been said by a splendid and enlightened Statesman,[11] alluding to the State Trials of 1794 in another kingdom, "That public prosecutions were become little better than schools for treason; of no use but to instruct criminals in the dexterity of evasion; or to shew with what complete impunity men may conspire against the commonwealth." Surely if ever the stain shall sink so deep as to reach and tinge our juries, the triumph of treason will then be complete; this indeed would be the consummation of all moral as well as civil depravity and desperation. If the laws, which are made for our security, become inoperative through the corruption of those who are entrusted with their execution, all our rights and liberties, all the safeguards of persons and property must give way to the disorganising system of the day; and our boasted institution, the trial by jury, would, instead of being (what it is) our first blessing, become a curse. In the soundest political, as well as in natural bodies, there will be found occasionally some sour and noxious humours, which fester and rankle, and in spite of the wisest regimen, will sometimes break out into serious heats and disorders: but the evil, even when most alarming, can never be deemed incurable; the commonwealth must never be despaired of, as long as juries, impressed with a religious reverence for their oaths, and a deep sense of the transcendant trust reposed in them, pursue untainted the even tenor of their duty; as long as juries, uncorrupted by wealth or power, unseduced by faction, undismayed by sedition, menace, or danger, acquit themselves in the face of God and of their country with courage, integrity, and an inviolable regard to truth.

But it is not in your official capacity that I am now most anxious to address you: as gentlemen of consideration and property in your county, embarked with your families and all your dearest concerns in the same vessel with your country, let me conjure you to look beyond the walls of your Grand Jury Room, and to survey the awful dangers which surround us. Never surely before this magazine of moral plague was opened upon the world, never till this ruinous and accursed trade of politics had superseded every other trade, did any country advance with such swift career in the race of cultivation and prosperity as Ireland. Looking into the Grand Jury Box, I cannot forget that the Constitution happily had been communicated to every sect and persuasion in our country; that religious distinctions no longer divided our people; and that, as experience shall justify the liberality of Parliament, a perfect political equality will bless without distinction the whole community. Commerce, agriculture, and manufactures had 'burst their cearments,' and revived amongst us; the face of the whole island, but of that part most of all which now heaves with discontent, smiled with plenty, encreasing population, and every useful and elegant improvement; even that war, which impoverished and exhausted Europe, wafted treasure to our shores and promoted enterprise amongst our countrymen; and we feel, through all the classes of our people, the rapid progress of comfort, independence, and civilization. Such hath been the growth of this country within the memory of the youngest of you – let the incendiary misrepresent as he may, such could be the offspring only of wise laws and of enlightened legislature. "Now look upon this picture, and on *this*." Turn your eyes to the desolation which now reins in Ulster, which approaches our own frontier with hasty strides, and may wrap our county in horrors unutterable, if not speedily encountered by the most spirited precautions. Mark the accumulated evils, the pillage, burglaries, burnings, and assassinations, which disfigure the whole face of that fair and once contented province, tarnishing the national character, hitherto so famed for every humane, generous, and manly sentiment. Whence this frightful change, this incredible revolution in the temper of that distracted province? Is all this laid in the character and natural propensities of Ireland? Ask the simple, unadulterated peasant of the south and west that question – ask their instantaneous, generous emotion upon the late invasion, that instinctive impulse which is the voice of nature, and never errs – and you will be answered with the indignant warmth of injured honour, that treason is not the characteristic of an Irishman – that treason is not a plant congenial to the mild and happy temperature of Ireland, but a baneful exotic, transplanted from the burning region of anarchy and regicide. Yes, Gentlemen, these are the ravages of no mean incendiary leagued with France: these are the bitter fruits of those pestilential doctrines, which are propagated amongst us with an assiduity and zeal beyond all example, in daily publications of every size; in pamphlets, newspapers, and hand-bills. The fever is kept up to delirium, and the infection diffused by committees and corresponding associations, acting by these cheap inflammatory publications, and by secret missionaries and open professors and preachers of their infernal gospel, affiliated after the Jacobin model, now too flagitious and anarchical even for the meridian of France.

Let not these criminal labours depreciate in our minds the solid blessings we possess. Let not the fatal love of innovation, let not the vile suggestions of political fanatics, or of bankrupt revolution-hunters, persuade us to hazard substantial comfort in pursuit of visionary perfection above the lot of man. Let us, on the contrary, unite in defence of those precious possessions. Let the virtuous and wise, the friends of order and rational freedom, of settled property and government by law, form a compact and determined counter-union to put down their foes, whose object is a scramble for your property, and who have blasted the rising hopes and happy promise of their country. Let us rally round that constitution, whose excellence we trace from the practical blessings it bestows, resolving to deliver it and our dishonoured country from the sacrilegious hands of paricides, or perish in the ruins.

1 The earlier Dublin version adds 'that fruitful parent of the most disastrous crimes!'

2 The London pamphlet adds 'the most sacred of our establishments is insulted and libelled; even the fidelity of our brave and steady soldiers is practised upon by a minister of peace, with a boldness altogether without parallel.'

3 "Remonstrate with any parent who will be so criminal as to expose his offspring to those places of education where his religious faith or morals are likely to be perverted. If he will not attend to your remonstrances, refuse him the participation of Christ's Body: if he still continue obstinate, denounce him to the Church, that according to Christ's commandment he be considered as a Heathen and a Publican."
Such is the liberal language of one who thro' a whole page affects to inculcate liberality – of one whom the government recalled to his country, and selected to preside over the education of the Roman Catholic youth, now destined by this anathema to be immured in exclusive seminaries, and trained up in uncharitable and unchristian sentiments of their Protestant brethren; - in return for their frank and unreserved communication of political rights and power.
Viscount Dillon, an ardent friend to Catholic equalization, and who in common with every other friend to the measure must lament the indiscretion of that mischievous publication, observed in the Lords: "that the Titular Bishop of Waterford Doctor Hussey had published the most inflammatory libel he had ever read, abounding in falsehoods and calumnies the most gross and mischievous – and this too from a gentleman highly indebted to the Government, and placed at the head of a seminary instituted under its auspices."

4 From 'the most sacred' down to 'to shake' appears only in the Dublin version.

5 Later London pamphlet replaces 'props and buttresses of' with 'pillars of'.

6 The press gives 'against any confederation, which before was a clergyable felony'.

7 By the 27 G. 3. 15, called the Riot Act, any person who shall administer or tender an Unlawful Oath may be transported for life; and the person taking it, for 7 years.

8 The sentence beginning 'And surely no good subject ...' was added for the London pamphlet.

9 A celebrated writer, whose bias certainly is not to arbitrary power, observes, "that very strict notions of Liberty may be unfavourable to a great degree of personal security. It is no doubt a capital advantage that our lives, liberties and properties are not at the mercy of Men, and that they can not be deprived of them but by express Law rigorously construed. Hence the proof of a crime is so difficult that many criminals escape for one who suffers. Thus the chance of impunity is so great, that there is too much encouragement for crimes." Priestley's Lect. on Hist. L. 47.

10 The sentence containing this reflection was inserted for the London pamphlet.

11 Burke. This sentence, containing the reference to Burke, was omitted in the London pamphlet.

Robert Day and wife Mary Pott, collection of A.E. Stokes

January 1798: reporting William Orr's execution

A Charge
Delivered to the Grand Jury of the County of Dublin at the Quarter Sessions of the Peace held at Kilmainham on Tuesday, Jan. 9, 1798 by Robert Day, Esq., M.P., one of His Majesty's Counsel learned in the law and Chairman of the said Courts.

Published at the request of the High Sheriff, Magistrates and Grand Jury of the County Dublin.

Printed by Mercier and Co. Booksellers to the Hon. Society of King's Inns & to be sold at their shops in the N
ew Courts & No. 31 Anglesea St.

This charge includes his response to the controversy generated by the trial and execution of William Orr. In September 1797 Orr was tried on a charge of having administered the United Irish oath to two soldiers of the Fifeshire Fencibles. Found guilty, he was executed on 14 October. The Judge, Barry Yelverton, Lord Avonmore, and the Attorney-General, Arthur Wolfe, were friends and colleagues of Day. Orr's counsel was John Philpot Curran. The emotion of the occasion affected Yelverton, who wept as he rejected Curran's plea for a stay of execution.

Gentlemen of the Grand Jury,

The frequent return[1] of the General Sessions of the Peace and of the Commission of Oyer and Terminer, which the wisdom of our Legislature has provided for the preservation of tranquillity and good order in our populous county, hath so trained you all in the important trust of a Grand Juror, that it might seem altogether unnecessary to take up your time by any explanation of it. But this is not a moment for any public man to relax in the discharge of duty. At a period so portentous and awful, I should fear that my veneration had abated for the great boast of British jurisprudence, the Trial by Jury, or that I had become indifferent and cold to the affecting scenes now passing in this country, could I dismiss you from the box without a few words of respectful address.

The knowledge of the criminal Law and of the administration of criminal justice, is indisputably one of the most important subjects which can employ the human understanding; for upon the wise formation and structure, the enlightened interpretation, and the upright execution of that class of laws, depend the liberty of the nation as well as the safety and happiness of each individual. In the investigation of this subject we naturally lament our departure from the simplicity of the ancient criminal code, the multiplicity of our statutes, the immense catalogue of offences known to our law; and the various and intricate legal questions which arise upon the application of the law to particular facts and cases. But this multiplicity and complexity are the indispensable price which a free people pay for the security of persons and property. In an arbitrary government the rights of the subject are precarious, and the positive laws simple and few, because the will of the tyrant regulates all. – But a nation of freemen, commercial, populous and refined, can be governed in their transactions, protected in their acquirements, and controuled in their excesses only by established, promulgated and permanent rules; and these rules, and the controversies arising upon their construction, will multiply in proportion to the increasing depravity of the times, and to the increase of civil and commercial intercourse among the inhabitants. But let us for a moment see whether, for these inconveniences, the unavoidable result of our improved condition, we shall not discover abundant consolation in the pure, the equal and benign dispensation of Criminal Justice under the British constitution.

In every controversy that comes before a court of law, two questions present themselves for investigation – *quaestio juris,* and *quaestio facti* : the *facts* and circumstances which form the case, and the law which is applicable to those facts. In other countries the offices of deciding the law and exploring the facts are united in the same magistrate; but it is one of the many happy peculiarities of the British law that these two duties, so distinct in their natures and requiring qualifications so very different, are committed to distinct and very different descriptions of men: the decision of the law, to the judge, who is sworn 'to decide according to the laws of the land', the decision of the facts, to the jury, who are sworn 'to give a true verdict according to the evidence'.

The arduous and important trust of expounding and interpreting the law is wisely reposed by our constitution in men elected for their abilities, education and learning; whose lives have been spent in study, and in the exercise of all those moral virtues which conciliate public confidence and favour; who outshine with unsullied integrity and unshaken firmness the patient temper and placid manners which exalt the judicial character even higher than more shining qualities; who though appointed by the Crown, are no longer the ministers of arbitrary power, but the independent depositaries of the laws and customs of the realm, declaring them openly and intrepidly without regard to person or party; who converse and consult together, and by mutual communication preserve an uniformity of judgments and a consistent administration of justice; and whose dignified station and lofty character afford the best pledge for the assiduous, able and upright discharge of their sacred function.

The office of investigating the *facts* and truth of the case (to which plain common sense united with integrity are fully competent) is executed in a manner not less entitled to general confidence, by the County - not by officers appointed by the Crown, but by a jury of fellow-subjects; a mode of trial sanctioned by immemorial antiquity,[2] and calculated above all others to guard against error, partiality and perjury. When twelve sensible impartial men, returned by an officer of deep responsibility from the vicinage of the transaction and of the witnesses, aided by the authority and experience of a judge, present when the witnesses are openly and in the face of the world searched and sifted by the counsel, the jury and the judge, shall upon their oaths declare the truth upon controverted facts; no wonder that such a trial should be pronounced, "confessedly to be the best criterion for investigating the truth of facts that ever was established in any country." No wonder if such a trial has begot a settled confidence in the public mind, a fond attachment to the country where justice is thus administered, and a grateful reverence for a constitution which bestows and secures so inestimable a privilege.

But to secure the advantages of this institution, the distinction of *Law* and *Fact* is essential, and must be inviolably preserved. "For Juries, saith the Oracle of our law, are to try the *Fact*, and the Judges ought to judge according to *Law*." If the Judge should dictate to the Jury in matters of *Fact*, he usurps an office which the Jury have sworn to discharge "according to the evidence," he presumes to decide what each Juror individually is as competent to form a sound opinion upon as the Judge, and what the twelve collectively are much more competent to decide. On the other hand, any encroachment of the Jury upon the province of the Judge would be still more dangerous. The education of unprofessional men, even the most cultivated, does not qualify them to determine points of law; their decisions consequently would fluctuate, and accord with no steady or permanent principles; and the Law for want of certainty would cease to be, what it is well defined, "a Rule of Conduct." Thus a gradual loss of liberty would inevitably follow; for the essence of liberty consists in the certainty of law. – In a word, it is the duty of the Jury to exercise their own judgments in matters of Fact, to receive the Law as it is declared to them by the Judge, and to mould out of both a General Verdict. The constitution has appointed the Jury to be the organ for pronouncing the combined result of both investigations; expecting that they shall therein faithfully incorporate the law, as declared from the Bench, with the facts as found by themselves.

Gentlemen, I dwell the longer upon this great boundary between the provinces of the Judge and of the Jury, because among the many novelties of the day it is not the least curious and daring, that men even of professional authority, who should never forget that they are "the ministers of Truth and Justice," [3] have laboured to draw the cognisance of the law from the Bench, and to invest the Jury with the decision thereof as well as of the fact. We find at various times an uncommon display of ingenuity and eloquence most criminally perverted to mislead Juries upon that important subject: as if by inspiration they could acquire a competent knowledge of that intricate and complicated science; or were at liberty to exercise their own clashing opinions upon the law, instead of being bound to receive it from its proper organ, the presiding Judge.

These provisions for the pure and perfect administration of justice amongst us obtain alike in civil and in criminal cases. But in criminal proceedings the jealous spirit of our constitution hath not left the subject to these safeguards alone. The law, in its mild caution and tender regard to human life and civil liberty, hath not committed the subject to a single jury, but exacts a double test for the investigation of the truth; requiring the accusations of a Grand Jury, previous to a trial by a Petit Jury. In civil proceedings the object of which is to discuss the differences, and adjust the right of individuals, the Defendant is immediately and without previous inquiry, required to answer the charge, however groundless of his adversary. But in criminal cases, where the defendant is exposed to corporal punishment, the law interposes between the complaint and the trial a solemn inquiry into the nature, motives and evidence of the charge. It would be hardship, which the free genius of the British constitution would not endure, that a subject should be exposed to the discredit and danger of a public Trial, whenever any prosecutor thought proper to prefer an accusation; and therefore the Grand Jury is most mercifully stationed as a barrier against the prosecutions of thoughtless levity, vindictive justice, or overbearing power; a centinel to challenge and arrest unjust accusation in the very commencement and first steps of its march. But if this twofold security be thought unnecessary in all ordinary criminal cases, where the King in truth is but nominally the prosecutor, how much more important is the institution of a Grand Jury, now happily calculated to guard the liberties of the people in all prosecutions of a public nature, where the Crown or its government may be supposed to have a personal interest, and to take an active and personal part! The administration of criminal justice originates in fact with the people by means of Grand Juries; the Crown cannot exhibit a capital charge against any subject without the consent of the people, that is, without the sanction of a Grand Jury returned from the body of the people. And therefore in times of political heat and difficulty, such unfortunately as we now live in, this institution is admirably contrived to protect the subject against the abuses of the executive power in the prosecution of crimes. While therefore, this twofold barrier of the constitution shall subsist in proper vigour, and criminal judicature remain with the great body of the nation, no avenue will be open to civil oppression. The interests of the state may be ignorantly or corruptly managed; but the people will continue free.

Such, Gentlemen, is the nature of the high trust to which you are this day called by your country, and which you have sworn with your best ability to discharge. The Grand Jury composed of gentlemen of respect and property in the county, superior to corruption, to menace, and to every other undue influence, are pledged to a double duty: to put guilt, however elevated in a course of trial; and to screen innocence, however humble, from unfounded, light or malicious accusation. You have sworn, "well and diligently to enquire and true presentment make" - that is, to examine with patient attention (the only evidence which you are at to receive) the evidence of the Crown, the nature of the charge, the credit and consistency of the witnesses, the character of the party accused; and to satisfy yourselves of his guilt, as far as *ex-parte* evidence can satisfy, before you involve a fellow-subject in all the inconvenience of a public trial - . It is in truth a serious and awful situation to be brought to that bar, polluted by the presence of many a hardened criminal. Reflect upon the abased and degraded condition of a culprit stigmatised by the solemn verdict of a Grand Jury, already half condemned by the giddy and flippant malice of the world, holding up his hand with trembling anxiety in defence of his liberty, his life, his honour. What reparation, what atonement can the deep wounded sensibility of injured innocence receive for such an outrage? Alas, what an inadequate and scanty consolation even from acquittal! – Perhaps too in the present gloomy hour, when every feeling heart is rent with the mingled emotions of indignation, shame and grief, when the proud character of Ireland, once so eminent among the nations for every generous virtue, is levelled with the dust by the poniards of vile conspirators and midnight murderers; when your jails are overflowing, and in the general sweep the innocent will sometimes inevitably be confounded with the criminal; at such a time it behoves you most perhaps to be upon your guard, to discuss each case with more than ordinary circumspection and calmness, to suspect even your own impartiality, and to see above all things that you become not the dupes of your public virtue, or of your just and natural alarm. And, in justice to the accused, and as the best and surest means of acquiring a clear understanding of each charge, let me earnestly recommend to you, at least in all cases of importance or doubt, to adopt the English practice of personal examination. This course, which I have invariable advised in preference of the imperfect evidence furnished by informants, I now press with the greater confidence, as it appears to have been strongly inculcated at the late commission by the high judicial authority (Judge Downes) who there presided. We know that the magistrate can sometimes take an information with as much indifference and flippancy as an ordinary affidavit, though it is his duty to sift the accuser strictly as to the matter of his information, to receive it from his own lips, and to satisfy himself thoroughly as to the justice and importance of the charge, before he transmit it to the Crown office to ground so serious a proceeding as an indictment.

But while I state thus anxiously what you owe to the party accused, let me not be understood as wishing to create any improper bias in your minds, even on the side of mercy. It is your duty to hold an even and steady balance between the public and the individual; always recollecting that where the charge is fairly substantiated by credible *prima facie* evidence, you have no discretion, but are concluded by your oath to find the bill. 'It is the interest of the state that malefactors should not remain unpunished'. And surely, Gentlemen, if ever the strict and rigid execution of that sound maxim was necessary, it is at this portentous period of the country. That a foul and flagitious conspiracy has for some time existed in the bowels of this Kingdom, in concert with the irreconcilable Enemy of the Empire, to subvert our free Government, the source of all your comforts and glory, and in its place to substitute a Democracy, the source of all those miseries which now grind the race of Europe; that this conspiracy has attained a degree of shape and body of the most alarming and formidable maturity, are truths too broad and palpable to be seriously disputed: we trace it bloody progress from its head-quarters in the Capital through the kingdom in all the records of the late circuits; we discover that a denomination of traitors, impudently assuming the popular and imposing appellation of *United Irishmen*, have, with a perseverance that would do honour to a good cause, under the flimsy pretence of seeking political improvement, propagated a spirit of insurrection and rebellion from one end of the island to the other. Such are those perturbed spirits who confront and brave the public scorn, who languish and pant in the sunshine of a settled and well-regulated government, who hold it 'better to reign in hell than serve in heaven', whose pastime is confusion, commotion and blood. Until the existence of this execrable confederacy, Ireland was a stranger to midnight violence, to pillage, to wanton cowardly, cruelty. The public-spirited magistrate, after discharging his duty to his country, might return to his family, his fire-side and domestic comforts, in perfect confidence and security. The virtuous juror and the honest witness might acquit themselves to God and to their consciences, without the risk of being way-laid, or the fear of murder. Committees of assassination did not exist, and meet in the noon-day, in the most public streets of the capital, applauded and stimulated by their blood-thirsty journalists. Individuals were not till then designated for the dagger, by name and in print, for no other crime than their virtuous exertions in the service of their country. Wherever this conspiracy advances, plunder, desolation and death are in its train. The most laborious enormities, perpetrated by their emissaries and agents, from their frequency and familiarity have so stupefied and benumbed our moral sense, as to have lost all power of exciting horror amongst us. All the crimes of civil society in its ordinary state, those offences which heretofore employed our criminal judicatures, however numerous or flagitious, dwindle to nothing and actually disappear, in comparison with the vast and awful system of atrocity concerted and acted upon by the ferocious association of conspirators. And to consummate and crown this disastrous catalogue of criminality, their bloody rites are gravely and formally opened with a solemn oath of fidelity to this infernal cause – the God of purity and mercy is blasphemously invoked to attest; and thus to become an accomplice in their foul deeds! to be present in aiding and abetting this gang of assassins in wading through the blood of their fellow subjects to the subversion of the state. We read in history of another celebrated conspiracy, not more sanguinary in its means or detestable in its ends, commencing with the same[4] monstrous and incongruous combination of religion and impiety. We recollect also, what, though vouched by the grave Historian and the brilliant Orator[5] who immortalise that subject, would seem incredible were it not confirmed by the transactions of our own time, that in Cataline's Plot there were some of the *Patrician*[6] order implicated, but masked in cautious or cowardly concealment; not from any bankruptcy of condition, but goaded by mortified ambition and diabolical lust of power; hoping upon the ruins of the old government to erect another of which they looked to be the leaders and managers. –In such a relaxed and disjointed state of things, when the doctrines of the day have multiplied the sources of destruction, when the very existence of society is at stake, and your throats and purses are the avowed aim of the plot, it becomes necessary to cloathe injustice in all its terrors. Public policy not less than conscience and justice, forbid you in this unhappy state of the country to compromise with delinquency. When examples are necessary to intimidate and controul the wicked, lenity (were it in your discretion) would be unseasonable, perhaps fatal; it would be cruelty to your country.

But of all the calamities inflicted by this French faction upon their country, perhaps the most deplorable and deadly is the abuse and prostitution of the Press. The liberty of the press consists in this, that every man may write and publish what he pleases; but he is answerable for the matter of his publication, and it is at his peril if he offend. A free press is essential to a free government: and the extinction of the one would infallibly be followed by the ruin of the other. Let us never grow so fastidious with the vital nutriment and *pabulum* of liberty, as to reject it, however nauseously and disgustingly it may sometimes be presented to us; let us never argue from the abuse of the thing, to the use of it. Whatever corruptions have occasionally obtained in the press (as what is there in human affairs so excellent that is not liable to corruption?) we must not forget that to its labours we chiefly owe the deliverance of these countries from religious and civil tyranny. As long as it is open to fair, manly and bold discussion, no people can be enslaved without their own consent; no people oppressed, who do not conspire against themselves. The never-sleeping Watchman of the constitution fails not to sound the alarm, to hang out the signal of an enemy's approach; so that arbitrary power cannot steal upon the nation, cannot come unperceived or unawares. But the press, like the elements of life, like fire, air and water, if not restrained from excess and confined to proper limits, instead of vivifying serves but to continue and to destroy. That the press, hitherto the bulwark of our liberties, is in these our times degraded into a vehicle of defamation, infidelity and treason, into a filthy receptacle and sewer of every thing vile, abominable and loathsome in society, is a melancholy truth which no rational being will deny. We can not wonder that monsters, who in cold blood conspire or abet the assassination of their innocent fellow-creature, should exult in the cowardly murder of virtuous reputation. Against bold and open violence I can provide – I may repel, avert, or deprecate it; but against the poison of the lurking coward, the poniard of the assassin, or the keener poniard of the libeller's pen, what precaution can protect, what courage or strength can defend? When we reflect upon the extravagant licentiousness of the press in this country, sparing neither sex, condition, or character; vilifying the executive authority, conspicuous for its moderation and humanity, merely for the discharge of its primary and most indispensable duty – for employing in the protection of the people the great military force which they pay, when the civil power proved utterly incompetent; for standing forward at the loud call of the community, in defence of the lives and futures of his Majesty's peaceable, loyal and industrious subjects, against a traiterous banditti, leagued with the foreign enemy, and by a system of rapine and terror preparing the way for its reception – when we see the administration of justice degraded in the eyes of the people, and that the judgment seat (till now held sacred amongst us) can no longer protect our mild virtuous and constitutional dispensers of the law[7] - we are at a loss to account why in a country, where the greatest subject cannot with impunity invade the civil rights of the meanest and most worthless, the latter shall without interruption asperse the honour and reputation of the former. When, under the hollow and lying mask of *Union* men labour to *divide* and embroil the different orders, conditions and sects of the nation; to excite the citizens against the soldier, who alone protects him in his virtuous industry; the emancipated and grateful Catholic against the generous Protestant, who has broke his chains; the people against the Legislative and executive authorities, under whose fostering care we have grown to this towering height of prosperity; and finally, Ireland against the British connexion: when we are stunned with so much profligate nonsense about arbitrary power, which in this country exists only in the gloomy and crazed imagination of the restless Republican, at a time when there is but one substantial ground of terror in the world – one against which we should converge every faculty, and 'bend up each corporal agent,' the Demon of Democracy, threatening the earth with its infernal train of incalculable ills; in a word, when nothing human is so intrenched in character, nothing Divine so sacred and exalted, as to escape the immeasurable rancour of libellers; the conclusion is inevitable – that our press is become the indented property of the enemy, that France has erected and pays for the Press in this country, which she has put down in her own; and our honest indignation is lost in grief at this deplorable debasement of the brightest privilege of liberty, a Free Press.

If long experience of the genuine liberty and unparalleled blessings which we enjoy cannot cure our political Bedlamites, one might have hoped that the hideous despotism exercised in France upon persons and property, the utter extinction of the press even to the name, the destruction of all the talents and virtue of the country even without the formality of a trial, might have opened the eyes of the blindest and most prejudiced. It might be hoped that the storm, which has shaken Europe to its centre and shattered it into fragments, might teach them the wisdom of clinging fast to the British constitution, which, like their oak, forms the strength, while it secures the happiness, of the people; that constitution and connexion under which these little specs in the Northern Ocean, scarcely discernible in the map of the earth have grown to be the envy and wonder of the world.

But Gentlemen, the country is not without resource. The legislature with equal wisdom and public virtue hath by the Libel Act committed to juries the final decision of all questions of libel or no libel; and the event has fully justified this honourable confidence in the impregnable bulwark of our freedom. The event has proved that juries, uninfluenced by popular clamour or the most impassioned inflammation from the Bar, will investigate the subject with a conscientious regard to the oath, and the duty they owe to their King, their country, and themselves. The juries have performed their part boldly and firmly; at no one period of this country has justice been administered with more purity, with more perfect indifference to persons or party. While Grand and Petit Juries shall thus act with a steady and dispassionate respect for truth, the Law and constitution may yet triumph. Ireland, resting upon the sacred volume of her liberty may bid defiance to her insolent ferocious foe, and with the immortal assertors of Magna Charta exclaim – "We will not suffer the law of England to be disturbed!"

Gentlemen, I feel that I have trespassed too long upon your indulgence; much longer in truth than I intended; but at such a juncture, when so much awful matter obtrudes itself for observation, the difficulty is to select and to compress. I shall now relieve you, after expressing the ardent prayer of my heart, (in which I am sure of your concurrence), that the British constitution moulded by the wisdom and virtue of ages, cemented by the best blood of our ancestors, and finally settled at the Glorious Revolution, may, through the energy of our rulers and courage and good sense of our country, rise superior to the wicked machinations of conspirators and traitors, and be transmitted unimpaired as a sacred inheritance to our latest posterity.

1 The Commission of Oyer and Terminer is held by adjournment four times every year for the County of Dublin; and by the 26 Geo. 3, c. 24 it is enacted "That the Session of the Peace for the City of Dublin and the County of Dublin shall not be adjourned for any greater length of time than from six weeks to six weeks".

2 He footnotes here that the jury system, originating in the countries of northern Europe during feudal times, and consisting originally of the 'panel of one hundred', was supplanted by the old Roman Law 'as transmitted by Justinian'. 'But in England, where the Civil Law was reluctantly and sparingly admitted, our sacred Palladium was not only religiously preserved, but gradually improved into its present admirable form.'

3 Lord Holt's character of a Lawyer.

4 *Catalinam oratione habita, cum ad jusjurandum Populares sceleris sui adigiret, humani corporis sanguinem vino permixtum in pateris circumtulisse: indepost exsecrationem aperuise consilium suum; atque eo dictitare secisse quo inter se magis sidi sorent.* Salust, Catal. C. 22 (ref. to Gaius Sallustius Crispus, War Against Cataline, the story of the conspiracy of an impoverished aristocrat, Lucius Catilina, in 63 B.C.-Ed.).

5 Cicero, who also wrote the history of the Cataline conspiracy (Ed.).

6 *Eo convenere Senatorii ordinis P. Lentulus, &c. – Erant praeterea paulo occultius consilii hujusce participes Nobiles, quos magis Dominationis spes hortabatur, quam inopia aut alia necessitudo.* Ibid. c. 17. See also Cicero in Catal, passim.

7 It is impossible to forget the late indecent practices resorted to by the advocates and confederates of Orr to discredit the verdict in that case, and to raise a clamour against the enlightened and virtuous Judge (Barry Yelverton, Lord Avonmore – Ed.) who refused to recommend him for a pardon, and against the Chief Governor (Lord Camden – Ed.) who suffered (as was his duty) the law to take its course. To solicit a Juror to disparage or reflect upon or explain away the verdict, after the Jury have gone at large and mingled again with the world; to apply to Jurors after being discharged, to enter upon a private and ex parte examination of witnesses after a public trial, and thereupon to make affidavits expressing regret for their verdict, is a practice of the most criminal nature and leading to consequences the most mischievous.

2

The Preliminaries of a Peace with Napoleon are in course of preparation. Day is anxious for peace and also for a healing of religious divisions in the North of Ireland. During the circuit to the North-East of Ireland he regrets that the Orange Order refuses to admit Catholics, though orangeism in the beginning 'was productive of much good'.

1801[1] In the Orange North: *Ireland's North-Eastern Circuit*

Wednesday, July 21st Set out from Dublin on the N. W. Circuit, accompanied by my wife and Judge Finucane, my associate. Sleep at Kinnegad.

Longford, Th. 22nd Arrive at this paltry town and Finucane J.[2] opens the Commission. Crown and Civil business very light; 5 Records only tried.

On Friday we all dine with our amiable friends, Maj.and Mrs. Nedham, and after supper are much gratified by some agreeable singing from the Miss O' Farrells. Next evening too I find Mrs. Day[3] at the Major's where she dined and where we remain to a late hour. N.B. Not to forget the kind attention of the Nedhams. The Kerry Light Company are quartered here and are commanded by Captn. Gun,[4] who I learn with great pleasure (from Maj. Nedham, Commander of the garrison) is a very well conducted young man and likely to redeem his family's fortunes from the ravages of his worthless father.

Sunday 25th We breakfast at Granard (a small but neat and thriving town) with Mr. Ker, agent to the Greville estate, where we are very hospitably received. After breakfast I climb the Mote which commands a fine extensive view and which was rendered famous by the gallant stand made by a handful of Yeomen commanded by Commsr Cottingham against a desperate body of Rebels in the summer of 1798, who after some struggle were at last routed. Mrs Ker on that critical occasion displayed great heroism: in the absence of her husband a party attacked his house in the rear, expecting to meet with little or no resistance. But after stationing her children in a place of safety she proceeded to the window commanding the Insurgents and fired several shots among them; two were left dead in the garden and the rest beat a precipitate retreat. Dine at Lord Farnham's[5] – a noble seat- 1500 acres in the demesne. Find here a Kerry colony: Lady Anne FitzGerald, Mrs. Letitia Blennerhassett, Miss Herbert, &c &c. After dinner examine his Lordship's Devonshire cows, wild and almost as active as deer, recommended much for the plough and other country work as lighter and more efficient than the sluggish bullocks generally employed. Pass a pleasant day, and at a late hour reach Cavan.

Cavan, Mon. 26th July. I open the Commission & dispatch all the Crown business this day.

The Maguires' Castle, Enniskillen.

Tues. I assist Bror. Finucane, whose Record Calendar is heavy, and whose good natured and accommodating spirit intitles him to every attention on my part.

Enniskillen, W. 28th Judge Finucane opens the Commission in the evening. On our way hither Lough Erne presents a distant but interesting view, and near town I drive (by permission) through the demesne of Lord Belmore and take a passing view of his Lordship's magnificent Chateau,[6] supposed to have already cost from 80 to £100,000. The Demesne seems unworthy of such a princely house, which by some perverse mismanagement commands not the lake from any of its windows.

Thurs. Dine at Dr. Burrowes' School house – fine command of the lake and town, but an exposed situation. Receive a very polite invitation from the venerable Lord Ross to pass Saturday at his beautiful seat, Belisle, and my friend Sir Richard Hardinge, his son-in-law, promises to show me the lake in great stile.

Castle Coole, Co. Fermanagh, built for Lord Belmore

Saturday 1st August. – the perverse wetness of the morning forces us, much to our mortification, to send an apology to Lord Ross,[7] and to decline the tempting occasion of enjoying that enchanting scene. (N.B. Belisle is 7 miles from Enniskillen.) About 12 the day holds up and I ride a few miles along the charming lake westward towards Col. Archdall's. On our return we witness a great Orange Procession marching in 51 Lodges, each wearing a Banner emblematical of loyalty and attachment to the Glorious Revolution, headed to the number of 4500 by Lord Cole,[8] "the Prince of Orange" in the County Fermanagh – the object was to commemorate the accession of the illustrious House of Hanover; and it is but justice to that vast assemblage of young and high-spirited men, to state that no excess or irregularity was said to have happened in the course of the whole day, and that they returned to their homes at an early hour and none intoxicated.

Upon the subject of the Orange Institution I would say a word, and whatever my present sentiments upon it may be, I am free to confess that in the commencement of our late troubles the Institution was productive in Ulster of much good; for it served as a rallying-point for the well-affected, and enlisted all powerful Fashion in the service and cause of loyalty. But it were to be wish'd that the Societies had been founded upon a principle of loyalty only, and not of Religion; and that every subject of whatever denomination or religious persuasion were admissible who could give satisfactory proof and testimony of his loyalty. No man will say that a severer test of loyalty or a stricter qualification are necessary for the Orange Clubs than for the glorious guardians of our lives, liberties and properties, the Navy and Army; and yet, who ever asked a recruit for either what his religion was? Or will any man pretend that the Catholic seaman and soldiers who form so large a proportion of our gallant defenders are not as ardent and unshaken loyalists as any of these fellow subjects? If a Bishop Hussey has sounded the trumpet of treason from the altar and employ'd his influence in the cause of rebellion, a Bishop Moylan[9] on the other hand has been found by his preaching and practice to inculcate most officiously peace and loyalty and brotherly love through his populous diocese. Hence we do not find that loyalty is the exclusive property of one religious sect more than another. Popery in truth, however erroneous in its religious doctrines, inspires a love of Monarchy and a submission to government, even to non-resistance; it is the struggle between the persuasions, wherever that unfortunately happens, for political power which produces collision, heat and fire, and therefore in those counties where either sect predominates decidedly there is no conflict or bad blood – none in the Northern counties where the Catholics are too insignificant in point of numbers and property for competition, none in the county of Kerry where the Protestant bears no proportion to the Catholic. It is only in the counties where political adventurers place themselves at the head of these sects respectively and make religion a stalking horse for electioneering purposes that these sanguinary and atrocious crimes have been committed, for the love of God! I should therefore, for one, most anxiously wish to see all religious badges names and distinctions abolished and forbidden amongst us. The Orange Institution, like the old Irish Volunteers, was of infinite use for a season; but like them it has degenerated into an invidious faction and ought to be discontinued. The Orange Ribbons, prescriptive (in its spirit) of Popery, is considered as a declaration of war on the part of the Protestants against the Catholics; it acts as a challenge or call upon the Catholics to unite and make common cause against the Protestants – he mounts accordingly a green or a white cockade, both symbols of disaffection; and meaning at first no more than measures of self-defence he insensibly glides into disaffection and rebellion. In the Tipperary Regiment of Militia, quartered at Cavan, this religious spirit was excited by these distinctive badges, and were it not for the laudable activity and uncommon courage of Major White, would have certainly blazed out into a fatal flame. The like was near happening in the Light-Infantry Brigade quarter'd at Longford; and if such distinctions be suffered among our Military, the most sour and dangerous spirit will taint the whole infallibly. How much wiser and better to second and promote the principles on which the Government and Legislature of Ireland have long acted – viz. to bury in oblivion all mutual injuries, to level all distinctions as far as is consistent with the Protestant Establishment, and to unite in bonds of harmony and affection all British subjects in defence of that admired constitution whose blessings are now communicated nearly alike to all denominations .

Enniskillen is the only tolerable town I have yet seen on this circuit, and even this is good only by comparison. It consists of little more than one long wide irregular street of thatched houses built on an island of Lough Erne and entered at both ends by bridges of some length. The Market-House and still more the Church are respectable – the Barracks are spacious and handsome. Its insular situation gave great security and confidence to the inhabitants in the late Rebellion; but the town is surrounded by Hills and could not stand an hour against artillery. The surrounding country is very beautiful rich and populous.

Omagh, Sund. 2nd Aug. Built on the side of a hill; very ordinary indeed for a county town, and thatched for the most part like the rest.

Mon. I open the Commission. Here I have the pain for the first time this circuit to pass a capital sentence. The inordinate extravagance and rapacity of Grand Juries call for - and from the United Legislature will probably receive - a speedy and radical reform. One simple measure would correct all – let the Collector's receipt for the county cess be a discharge of so much of the rent due of the landholder to his landlord; as the Irish-rent and Crown-rent receipts now are. The landlords compose our Grand Juries and impose the tax upon the subject; but what is it that regulates the tax? Not the rentall or income of the party who is tax'd, but the quantity of land which he happens to hold or farm. It is the land holders and not as in England the landlord, who pays the tax. But were the farmer or tenant intitled to credit out of his rent for the county charges paid by him, it would among many advantages have two obvious ones: 1 the Grand Juror would be frugal and discreet in the imposition of a tax which must ultimately come out of his won pocket. 2 The absentee landlord, who now pays not a single shilling towards that tax which so essentially benefits his estate and advances his income, would in that case contribute alike with the resident a just proportion of the tax. I could write a volume upon this very beneficial but much abused trust; sed non est hic locus. It is obvious were some such controul upon the prodigality of Grand Juries created, that the juristiction might be very safely transfer'd from the assizes to the Quarter Sessions; and perhaps very wisely; for the latter not being limited in duration the magistrates would have ample leisure to discuss each presentment applied for – and the public would in the magistrates possess a permanent instead of fleeting responsibility which Grand Juries afford.

Tuesday 4th August. Visit twice this day Rash, the beautiful seat of my poor murdered friend Lord Mountjoy.[10] Delighted as I was with the scenery, the extensive plantations, the happy course and reaches of the river, yet sentiments of deep melancholy would ever and anon steal across my mind in reflecting on the tragical fate of the enlightend, benevolent and amiable Nobleman who projected and formed that fine young seat - remarkable that he and Lord O'Neill[11] who were perhaps the most strenuous amongst us that asserted Catholic Emancipation, should be the victims of a Rebellion tinctured and exasperated by religious bigotry; two amongst the brightest ornaments of the Peerage.

Lifford, Wednesday 5 August. Arrive at the county town of Donegal after passing through Strabane. The first comfortable town I have seen since I left Dublin. Why is not Letterkenny, situated more centrally, the Assize town of Co. Donegal? The Marquess of Abercorn[12] possesses £30,000 a year from Strabane inclusive along the East side of the Foyle. His Lordship has formed a handsome basin at Strabane and made a canal of a few miles length as to open a navigable communication between that town and Derry. I am not aware that he has made any other return to the county for the immense income which he draws out of it.

Sunday 9th Mrs Day and I go to prayer at Raphoe, 5 miles from Lifford – visit the Venerable Prelate Hawkins[13] after prayers – walk with the Bishop's son-in-law, Ball, to my worthy friend Dean Allot, where Mrs. Day and I dine and pass the night – charmed in the evening with sacred music, his amiable daughter playing and singing accompanied by her father and mother

Londonderry. Monday 10 August. Arrive here early in the morning from the Dean of Raphoe's. Remarkable that – this Virgin Town as it is call'd (that is, which never yielded to the filthy embraces of James 2d or of any other spoiler), which pours forth every year hogsheads of Libations to the Glorious Memory, does not possess a single picture, statue or bust of William. I strongly urge the Grand Jury to build court houses which are much wanted here; and in the presentment provision might be contrived to be made for a handsome pedestrian statue of their immortal Deliverer to be placed in some conspicuous situation in the Crown Court.

Thursday 13 August. Circuit ends – the lightest which I have experienced since I became Judge (in March 1798) but indeed the only circuit which I have not found laborious beyond expression. In truth the country was never known to have enjoyed more confirmed tranquillity; not a single symptom thro' the whole circuit of treason or sedition; and only one solitary capital sentence pronounced, and that for a man for whom the Grand Jury in a body interceded; every individual engaged at his loom, his harvest or the fisheries, and universal peace, loyalty and respect for the laws prevails among all orders.

Downhill, from John Preston Neale, Views of the Seats of Noblemen and Gentlemen in England, Wales, Scotland and Ireland, publ. 1819-23

Arrive at the hospitable and plenteous seat of Mr. Dominick McCausland of Daisyhill, near Newtownards, 15 miles from Derry, at dinner – a most elegant and comfortable habitation, planted with great taste and luxuriance by himself and now fully grown – and next morning

Fr. 14th We proceed by the Strand round the bluff head of Magilligan to breakfast at Downhill, and are there astonished and delighted by the splendid collection of pictures and statues and by the costly architecture of the eccentric Mitred Earl,[14] the Lord of that wild scene. But it is impossible not to regret the misapplication of so much treasure upon a spot where no suitable Demesne can be created, where trees will not grow, and where the northern blast and the trade-wind of the west almost forbid all vegetation; where the salt spray begins already to corrode the sumptuous Pile of Grecian architecture, and the imagination, anticipating no distant period, weeps over the splendid Ruin, a sad monument of human folly! The Chateau fronts the South and commands an extensive view of a fine but naked country – in the rear is the ocean over which upon an elevated, abrupt and prominent Cliff the Bishop has built a handsome Grecian Temple full of valuable but mouldering books, some on shelves and some piled in disorder upon the floor. Round the architrave of the

Temple is engraved the following distich, I believe from Lucan –

Dulce mari magno tollentibus aequora ventis

Terra alterius magnum spectare laborem[15] –

A distich conveying, I fear, a just but not favourable sentiment of the human heart.

Dine at the Jackson

arms, Colerain, about 5 miles from Downhill, an opulent well built town seated upon the beautiful Bann. This town too, as well as Derry, had its walls, and we trace some considerable remains of them.

Sat. 15th Aug. We visit the stupendous wonders of the Giant's Causeway.

Monday. Breakfast at Belfast and dine and sleep at Donaghadee. It is observable on this circuit that though the country gentlemen and peasantry seem in general very comfortably appointed, the towns for the most part afford but indifferent accommodation. The four first indeed of the country towns are no more than each a long street of thatch'd houses. Slate seems not in such general use in the counties of Longford, Cavan, Fermanagh and Tyrone, as in every other county of Ireland that I have visited, and it is not uncommon for houses otherwise respectable to be thatch'd. Lord Mountjoy's fine seat of Rash is a striking instance.

1 RIA, Day Papers, Ms. 12w15,.

2 Matthias Finucane (1737-1814) of Lifford, near Ennis, Co. Clare. Justice of the Ct. of Common Pleas 1794. An old acquaintance of Day since they were both *Monks* in the drinking-dining club of *St Patrick*, or *the Screw*. Finucane served on the special commission after the Emmet rebellion in 1803, and resigned 1806.

3 Mary (Polly) Pott was daughter of Percival Pott, surgeon at St Bartholemew's Hospital, London. She and Robert Day were married in 1774. Day uses Pott and Potts interchangeably.

4 Townshend Gun was commissioned Captain in the Kerry Militia on 6 Sept. 1797 *(A List of the Officers of the Several Regiments and Battalions of Militia and of the Several Regiments of Fencible Cavalry and Infantry, Dublin 1799)*. His father, William Townshend Gun of Rattoo, near Ballyduff, Co. Kerry, was connected with the Blennerhassetts and Lord Ventry, political rivals of Day.

5 John Maxwell Barry, 5th Lord Farnham, a Lord of the Irish treasury.

6 James Wyatt built Castle Coole in Co. Fermanagh in 1788-98 for Armar Lowry Corry, 1st Earl Belmore.

7 Sir Ralph Gore (1725-1802). A distinguished military man. Wounded at Fontenoy, Commander-in-Chief in Ireland 1788. MP Donegal 1747. Viscount Bellisle 1768, Earl of Ross 1772.

8 William Willoughby Cole, 1st Earl of Enniskillen (1768-1803), Lord Lieutenant and Custos Rotulorum Co. Fermanagh. Seat Florencecourt.

9 Doctor Francis Moylan, Bishop of Ardfert (Kerry) 1775-1787, Cork 1787-1815, who issued a famous Pastoral after the French appearance at Bantry Bay which impressed Day.

10 Luke Gardiner, Lord Mountjoy, was associated with important Catholic relief legislation in 1778 and 1782. Was killed on the bridge of New Ross during the Rebellion of 1798.

11 John O'Neill, MP supported Catholic relief policies. He was killed in Antrim town during the Rebellion of 1798.

12 John James Hamilton (1756-1818) was 9th Earl of Abercorn. Seat Baronscourt, Co. Tyrone.

13 Rev. James Hawkins, Bishop of Raphoe 1780-1807.

14 Frederick Augustus Hervey, Earl of Bristol and (1768-1803) Bishop of Derry. Day's correspondence contains an account of this individual's eccentric appearance at the Rotunda Volunteer Convention in 1783.

15 'It is pleasant, when the winds blow up on the mighty ocean, to view a great event from another's land' (Ed.).

View of the High Street of Edinburgh, from Edina Delineata, 1798, by Aeneas Macpherson (Edinburgh City Libraries)

Through Scotland to Edinburgh

W. 19. Dispatch my chaise and servants Dumfries to Longtown (about 90 miles), there to wait for us while we resolve upon a trip north-east to Edinburgh.

Sat. Edinbro'. Reach the Caledonian Capital thro' a very highly-cultivated country, and on entering at the west end of the town are struck with the Castle, seated upon a rock of towering elevation, abrupt and altogether inaccessible on all its sides save one which connects it by means of a draw-bridge with the main street of the Old Town. It accommodates 1000 Infantry, a park of Artillery and about 400 French prisoners whom we found in great spirits selling toys and chatting very cheerfully over the pallisades with the visitors. Make our way to Heriot's School, which is a noble foundation established and endowed in the year – by – Heriot for the education of Freemen's sons. The building is very respectable and the accommodation said to be excellent. Almost facing it is another, more modern foundation for the same purpose, called Watson's Academy. Ramble thro' the town and are delighted with the cleanliness of this City. Remarkable that there is no river in Edinbro'; but a strong and deep current rushes constantly down the Main street supplied from pipes.

Sun. 23 Aug. Go to St. Andrew's beautiful church in a most beautiful street, George's St., and are very highly edified by the prayers and sermon of the Minister, Dr. Richie, successor to the learned and illustrious Dr. Blair.[1] In the evening repair to the great High Church in the Old Town (stiled St. Giles's in the days of Episcopacy, and the Cathedral of the Diocese) and there hear another very good sermon. Both prayers in the two churches were very impressive and deliver'd with great devotion; still the manner of delivering upon the whole is so monotonous and phlegmatic that I found it difficult to command my attention thro' the whole Service tho' considerably shorter than our own. But leaving to others to decide the question whether this (aparently) extemporary course or a set form of prayers be preferable, I cannot but condemn and reprobate the arrogance of the erect posture in which the Presbyterian addresses his creator in prayer, instead of the humility of kneeling or at least of an inclined attitude. Not even at the Lord's Prayer do they condescend to incline their stiff necks. Nor can I reconcile myself to the omission of the Creed and Commandments in their service, for these as well as the Lord's Prayer can not be too frequently inculcated and ought to be impress'd by regular and periodical repetition. There is reason to believe that Family Prayer and even private Individual Prayer are not in use among Presbyterians. Quaere, whether their whole system be not too relaxd and philosophical and leads not unavoidably to Deism?

Heriot's Hospital, founded by George Heriot, goldsmith to James VI, for 'poor and fatherless boys' and 'freemen's sons' (Edinburgh City Libraries)

Old Edinbro' stands upon the Ridge of a narrow hill commencing on the West with the Castle and running along in a regular well-proportioned street of a mile long call'd High Street till it terminates with the Palace of Holyrood-House on the East. This Ridge falls down most abruptly on both sides; on the South to the Street call'd Cowgate, and on the North to the valley call'd the North Lock, both of wch are cross'd by bridges connecting the Ridge wth the opposite sides of the valleys. Cowgate seems to be the St. Giles's of Edinbro', consisting only of mean habitations and crowded wth the dregs of the people – passing along - Street you look thro' the rails of the Bridge down upon Cowgate and the perpetual stream of passengers flowing as it were under the Bridge wch you stand upon; the one, in short, (to continue the allusion) is an Aquaduct conveying a clear and copious stream across the turbid and foul torrent wch passes under it. The North Lock was formerly a Marsh and occasionally so filled wth water as to present the appearance of a Lock (i.e. Lough); but it has been effectually drain'd by sewers and is now perfectly dry, and forms a handsome verdant valley bounded on the South by the rear of High St. and on the North by the beautiful terrass and row of houses call'd Prince's Street. High St. is the Strand or Dame St. of Edinbro; and for an old street is wide, regular and handsome; but the houses are raised to the inconvenient height of 6 or 7 stories to the front, and to the rear (on account of the abrupt declivity) to that of 10 and often of 12 stories. These buildings however, generally speaking, are not each a distinct dwelling-house, but rather a Stair-case (here call'd a Land) like those in Colleges and Inns of Court, where one common entrance and passage leads to as many distinct habitations as there are floors, and where the several families reside unconnected and often unacquainted with each other. They possess not a foot of background; and hence in past times, when a relax'd and inefficient Police existed here, it was the practice to discharge even from the windows into the open street at early hours the sordes of each habitation and to heap their dirt often in the recesses of the Stair-case. But a perfect reform has of late years taken place here in that great essential – each Individual is forced to bring down upon the ringing of the Dustman's Bell the collected dirt of each day at a very early hour, wch is immediately carted off; and we had curiosity to ascend a few of the Lands wch we found invariably to be as nice and clean as the Staircase of any private house could be.

Considering our short stay here we have contrived to do much. We have seen the Register Office, a noble modern building terminating the North Bridge, and forming a splendid and wise establishment highly creditable to this Country. Here in a spacious circular Room are arrang'd on shelves abstracts (or rather counterparts) of all Scotch Deeds; for here as in Ireland there is an universal Registry, and titles and changes take effect from the date of registering each Deed and not from the date of its execution. There is no timber used in the construction of any of the apartments; the floor, walls, shelves are stone, the doors iron, &c – no lighted candle admitted – the whole is kept well-air'd by conceal'd stoves – in short every precaution is adopted wch ingenuity could suggest to guard against both fire and damp. I had scarcely seen this noble institution when I reflected with shame and regret upon the criminal neglect of our ci-devant Legislature and of our Government in this particular. What can be more disgraceful and more alarming for the landed property of Ireland than the mean and miserable apartments in which all the memorials of our Deeds are huddled, unprotected alike against damp and fire? The Scotch office has instantly suggested to me also another important idea and which I shall not fail to mention to Mr. Abbot,[2] that the very best use which could be made of our fine House of Commons, now vacant and disengaged, would be to convert it into a Register Office. This most momentous application of that great ornament of Dublin might well console even those who regret (if any sincerely regret) the incorporation of our Legislature with the British.

On Mon. I deliver my letters. Mr. Montgomery, the Chief Baron's son is out of town. We dine and spend a very pleasant day with Mr. Allan the Banker in Queen St. which commands a charming view of the Forth and Fifeshire beyond, and on Tuesday we dine with Mr. Kerr, secretary to the Post Office, at his Box near town.

W. 26 Aug. I had determined to visit Hoptown House, about 12 miles from Edinbro, and which according to Lord Glandore[3] (who is an excellent authority in the picturesque) is one of the most magnificent seats in Great Britain. But my English engagements force me away, and I leave this City early this morning for England, having first received a visit from Mr. Kerr to announce to me the Gazette account of the capitulation of the French Army in Cairo.

Th. 27 Aug – breakfast at Lockerby – post to Gretna Green, the last stage in Scotland, seated on the Sark, wch separates it from England on the West side as the Tweed does on the East. The Matrimonial Operator[4] is neither a Blacksmith nor a Minister but an abandon'd old rogue who puts the hands of the Runaway couple into each other, witnesses their vows of everlasting constancy, sees them together under cover of a quilt, and then tells them that forsooth they're married. But none who are not willing to be deceived will believe that this impudent ceremony can be ought but a mockery marriage.

To London and 'the days of my youth'

Drive on from Gretna-Green across the Sark into England to Longtown.

Fr 28 Breakfast at Hesket (a poor but clean place) – after breakfast cross a dreary Moor till we reach Penrith, a well-built good Town. Here we resolve upon a short detour to the Lakes, and no sooner said than done – away we post (leaving our own Cavalry &c at the Crown Penrith) to Keswick.

Sun. 30th Aug't. Take leave of this enchanting scenery at 6 this morning and post for Ulswater – 17 miles from Keswick. Having enjoyed as much of the charms of the Ulswater as the rain and our limited time would allow, we returned to Penrith. We proceeded with our own horses to Appleby, the county town of Westmorland, where we sleep at an excellent house, the King's Head on the banks of the Eden.

M. 31st Before breakfast I visited the Jail and Court-Houses. See also the Castle, one of Lord Thanet's seats – he holds this Estate under condition of entertaining the Judges, who accordingly with their whole suite are very handsomely lodg'd and boarded during the Assizes. N.B. The Earl[5] was convicted of a Riot in endeavouring to rescue (assisted by certain notorious Republicans) the illustrious Arthur O'Connor[6] after the unaccountable acquittal of that Traitor at Maidstone in 1798.

Th. 10th Sept. Leave Cantab. after dinner for Royston where we meet our Cavalry & sleep at the Red Lion – Cambridge a mean town without the colleges.

F. 11th breakfast at Polleridge – dine at the Rose & Crown, Enfield highway; leave our cavalry there for the night & take post for London, where we stop & sleep at the Oxford Hotel, Arlington St. Piccadilly – cursedly dear house.

Sat. 12 Sept. Our Horses come up from Enfield and take us after breakfast to Richmond, where we find our dear friends bursting with impatience and mad wth joy to see us. The Horses arrive in very good spirits and health tho' a good deal reduced in plight after a British journey of abour 440 miles. Henceforth I do not mean to load my paper with a diurnal detail. Residing with the good sisterhood of Kew-Lane there was of course for some successive days so little of occurrence or variety amongst us that the account of one day might serve for a Journal of many. I shall therefore content myself with a general sketch of our life while Richmond continued our head quarters.

Upon my arrival I found a note from my affectionate friend Sir John Day,[7] desiring to receive the earliest intimation of the moment I should arrive. However, I anticipated his kind invitations by paying him an early visit next morning. Nothing could exceed the cordiality of his reception. After prayers he took me to Lord Onslow[8] and presented me to his Ldp – and I availed myself of that opportunity of returning my grateful thanks to the good old Peer for the very flattering and handsome language he was pleas'd to hold of my Charges to the Grand Juries of the county of Dublin. So highly indeed and so far beyond any merit which they possess did he deem them, that he took occasion when in waiting as Lord of the Bedchamber, to present a copy of the Charges to the King; and he reported to Sir John that his Majesty was graciously pleased to express his warmest approbation of them.

At a handsome dinner from my friend Mr. Dundas, the King's surgeon, we met the celebrated Monsieur Lally Tollendal,[9] son of the famous Genl. Count Lally, whose attainder he procured, by his talents as an Avocat and his indefatigable perseverance, to be reversed. He had been very active in the first years of the French Revolution against the Court; but seeing the profligate views of the Leaders, he separated from them and emigrated to England. Here, as descended from an Irishman, (for his grandfather followed the fortunes of James from Ireland and forfeited), His Majesty, at the instance, I understand, of Lord Loughboro',[11] has confer'd upon Tollendal a pension of £300 a year upon the Irish establishment. He was introduced to me as a compatriote – an acute, lively, eloquent man, professing much attachment to Britain and gratitude to her beneficent Monarch; but I suspect introrsum a Jacobin, tho' speciosa pelle decora.

Lieut. Gen. Count Lally, guillotined 1766, taken from O'Callaghan, Irish Brigades

But it was at Sir John Day's that we experienced cordial hospitality accompanied wth. a taste approaching to elegance. Before my arrival Edward and Betsy[12] dined there more than once – afterwards we repeatedly dined wth them. At one of his Entertainments consisting of 2 courses & an elegant Dessert (served up indeed in very handsome stile) our party I remember were Lord Onslow, Sir George and Sir Robert Baker and their Ladies &c. – gold plate and exquisite Seve china at the Dessert, and in the evening at coffee with friends meeting, nothing can compare. I think Lady Day,[13] beside being a very kind good natured being, is a very clever, intelligent mistress of a family.

My usual occupation was to saunter after breakfast to Wall's Library to read the news; after that "an ambulation of conference" with my friend Sir John; or a walk perhaps to the Hill to enjoy the luscious Landscape wch feasts the sight from thence even to cloying; or with the Ladies to some of the many curious places wch abound in this unrivall'd neighbourhood, eg one day by the ferry Sion Gardens; another day very agreeably spent in viewing the King's small but select collection of pictures at

Looking down Richmond Hill, Richond-on-Thames

Kew and promenading thro' Richmond Gardens under the auspices of old Mr. Tunstall and his daughter the Housekeeper – sometimes I took a ride to London; or thro' the country; one day accompanied by my nephew Bob Day (who formed a very important and agreeable member of our family party while at Richmond) I rode through Richmond Park and Kensington to Hampton Court. Here the exiled Stadholder[14] and family live in all the magnificence of a Monarch at the King's expense; here his Serene Highness slumbers away his days as well as nights in luxurious lethargy undisturbed by any reflexions upon the fallen greatness of his House.

Meantime some of our remoter friends lost no time in paying their compliments of congratulation upon our arrival in England after an absence of 7 years. Our sweet-tempered, plain and unaffected friend, John Watts, and his warm-hearted, affectionate but eager and crabbed little wife, breakfast with us from Hampstead – in return for which we pass's Sunday 20th Sept. very agreeably with them at dinner, and upon a subsequent day we were entertain'd very hansomely indeed by his nephew Bob Watts of Hampstead, who is a very well-conducted, well-manner'd young Gentln, thriving rapidly as a Broker.

But it is time I should come to Alderman Skinner[15] and the substantial friendship of that excellent man. After visiting us at Richmond accompanied by his amiable daughter and Wright and Harvey, his sons-in-law, he invited Edward and me by authority from the Sheriffs Elect to dine with them in the London Tavern.

Sat. 26th Went to London early – breakfasted at St. James's Coffee-House. Returning up St. James's St. who should stop me but my amiable friend Lord Pelham?[16] Walk'd together for an hour in the Park. Delighted to find him so entirely recover'd from the pulmonary complaint which threaten'd in Ireland to carry him off as it had done his brother and sister. It seems that he and all the Ministry are highly pleas'd with Genl. Hutchinson in Egypt; if he brings the campaign to the happy issue – which there is reason to hope from his prudent and judicious conduct – it will lay the foundation of his fame, fortune and elevation.

N.B. Let it not be forgotten that I owe to him (Pelham) and Lord Camden my elevation to the Bench in February 1798, a year memorable for the breaking out of the Irish Rebellion (23 May) of sanguinary and ferocious memory.

Mon. 28. Call upon Lord Glenbervie[17] – out of town – pass an hour with Lord Carleton[18] in Jermyn St. By appointment with the worthy Alderman I proceed from his house to the London Tavern and dine with one of the new Sheriffs in the great Ball Room – a very sumptuous entertainment – at 3 long tables disposed in the form of a Gallows, the Lord Mayor, Aldermen, Sheriffs and their Guests dining at the transverse table at the upper end of that noble Room, and the Commons at the other two. Excellent Band in the Orchestra, and 'Rule Britannica' sung in fine stile by Townsend.

Tu. 29th Sept. – after breakfast[19] Edward and I proceed by instructions from Skinner to ...[20] Church in King Street, Guildhall, where we find the whole Corporation dress'd in their proper robes, and hear a most excellent sermon from Mr. Gregory, the Lord Mayor's Chaplain.

Th.1st October. We return to our good friends at Richmond.

1. Hugh Blair (1718 - 1800), divine, appointed to High Church, Edinburgh in 1758, where he served to his death. Professor of Rhetoric and Belles Lettres at the University of Edinburgh.

2. Charles Abbot (1757-1829), Chief Secretary of Ireland February 1801 to January 1802, later Speaker of the English House of Commons.

3. John Crosbie (1753 - 1815), 2nd Earl of Glandore, Ardfert Abbey, Co. Kerry, the writer's cousin and political patron. He was a strong advocate of Catholic relief legislation.

4. Joseph Pasley, or Paisley, (1730-1814) was the son of a dissenting clergyman. He was a fisherman and smuggler, and a hard drinker.

5. Sackville Tufton, 9th Earl of Thanet (1767-1825), was present with leading Whigs at the trial of O'Connor in May 1798. O'Connor was acquitted but not released as another warrant was expected. Thanet was later convicted and served a year in the Tower of London for attempting to rescue O'Connor in the court.

6. Arthur O'Connor (1763-1852), MP Philipstown in the Irish parliament, where the writer would have known him. Leading United Irishman and editor of *The Press.* Tried for high treason in Maidstone 1798. Brother of Roger, also in this diary, both nephews of Lord Longueville.

7. Sir John Day (1738-1808), former Advocate-General of Bengal and a cousin of the writer. He had attended Trinity College a few years before Robert. He died on June 14 1808 (RIA Day Papers, Burtchaell and Sadleir, *Alumni Dublinensis,* 1935, British Library card index).

8. George Onslow (1731-1814), son of the former Speaker of the House of Commons, Arthur Onslow. Became Lord of the Bedchamber 1780, created Viscount Cranley and Earl of Onslow in June 1801

9. Trophime Gerard, Marquis de Lally Tollendal, son of Lieut.-Gen. Count Thomas Arthur Lally. Born 1751, died 1830, by which time his titles included Marquis de Lally Tollendal (title taken from a place

near Tuam in Co. Galway where the family originated), Peer of France, Minister of State, Grand Officer of the Legion of Honour, Chevalier Commander and Grand Treasurer of the Order of St Esprit, Member of the Royal Academy of France. He was married and left one daughter, 'through whom the family peerage was conveyed to her husband, the count d'Aux' (John Cornelius O'Callaghan, *History of the Irish Brigades in the Service of France*, London 1870, p. 579). In 1778 the Marquis succeeded in having his father's attainder overturned.

10. Lieut.-Gen. Count Thomas Arthur Lally, b. Dauphine where he was baptised January 1702. Son of Sir Gerard Lally, Col.-Commandant of the Irish Regiment, and nephew of Arthur Dillon. In 1744 he was commissioned Colonel of a new regiment which came to bear his name. It served with Lord Clare in the Irish Brigade that assisted Marechal de Saxe to defeat the English at Fontenoy the following year. This result was reversed in the Seven Year War: he commanded his regiment in India, where he lost Pondicherry to Eyre Coote, for which, on his return to France, he was imprisoned in the Bastille and guillotined in 1766. (O'Callaghan, *Irish Brigades*, passim; pp. 562-577.)

11. Alexander Wedderburn, first Baron Loughborough (1733-1805). Lord Chancellor 1793 in succession to Thurlow; held office to 1801 when succeeded by Lord Eldon.

12. Elizabeth (Betsy) Day, Robert Day's daughter, married Sir Edward Denny of Tralee Castle in May 1795.

13. Benedicta, wife of Sir John Day.

14. William V (1748-1806), Prince of Orange and Stadholder of the Dutch Republic. He ruled until the French invasion of 1795 which ended the Republic and forced William and his wife to flee to England where they lived until their deaths. He was a first cousin of George III.

15. Alderman Thomas Skinner was Lord Mayor of London in 1794: 'our much to be honoured friend', infra.

16. Thomas Pelham (1756-1826), 2nd Earl of Chichester, Chief Secretary of Ireland to Viceroys Lords Northington in 1783 and Camden from 1795 to 98; Home Secretary 1801.

17. Sylvester Douglas, Baron Glenbervie (1743-1823). Lincoln's Inn, called to the bar in 1776. Day probably knew him since his time as Chief Secretary to Lord Westmorland, Viceroy of Ireland, from 1794 to January 1795. MP 1796 for Fowey, Cornwall.

18. Hugh Carleton (1739-1826), Chief Justice of the Common Pleas (Ireland) 1787-1800. Was head of the special commission after the Rebellion of 1798; supported the Act of Union after which he became a representative peer at Westminster. Day also participated in the special commission and was one of Carleton's successors as representative for Tuam in the Irish parliament.

19. He has lodged in London at Bury Street.

20. left blank

"Peace and Plenty"
– the Preliminaries of a Peace with Napoleon

Day has a circle of friends in Richmond-on-Thames, some difficult to identify but first among whom is his cousin, Sir John Day, retired Advocate-General of Bengal. His and Robert's connection goes back to Trinity College and the Middle Temple. There is a letter from the 1770s among the Day papers in which Robert congratulates Sir John on his first appointment in India. Indian colour is to be found throughout these diaries with the return home of numerous Stokes, Collis and Day relatives serving in the military or the civilian service of the H.E.I.C. Sir John Day may have been the first of the relatives to go to India.

Friday 2 Oct. "Pray, Ma'am, what means the merry ringing of all the bells at this early hour? Has immortal Nelson destroy'd the gunboats at Bouloyne; or has Alexandria surrender'd? Or does it announce only the return of the King from Weymouth to Kew?"

"Why, Lord bless you (answers Miss Sayer, whom I stop in Kew Lane at 8 in the morning with joy sparkling in her eyes) have not you heard the news?"

"What news?" "Why, Peace, Peace, let me go."

"Depend upon it, Madam, I have not the most distant idea of breaking the peace with you or any one; I presume thus to hold you only to ask the news."

"Why, good G -, how can you be so dull; I tell you we have made Peace wth France! the Preliminaries were signed last night by Lord Hawkesbury and M. Otto –"

My first impulse in the exstacy and delirium of the moment was to fling my arms about Miss S.'s neck and to "have hugg'd the painted rogue, she pleas'd me so" – but she vanishes and relieves me from ballancing upon the thought –

Ter conatus ibi finstra dacde brachia

Ter frustra comprensa manus effugit Imago.[1]

Did I dream all this, did I hear her distinctly; or do not my astonish'd senses deceive me? Have not the stocks fallen in confidence of another Campaign? While wrapt up thus in astonishment & doubt, not daring yet to swallow a delicious draught wch I thought it certain I must disgorge, whom shd I meet a little farther on but Dundas going his morning circuit among his patients. Old Dundas launches into an extravagant eulogium upon Bonaparte, the Augustus of his day, who now gives universal peace to a subjugated world & closes the Temple of Janus. The latter sally I could have dispensed with; nevertheless, such is my transport that I overlook this Jacobinical effusion. Persuaded that we have been taken care of, my first joy is that Human Blood is no longer to flow; that Jacobinism must now perish in both islands even to the root, that the Union will now operate and rapidly fructify to the advancement and growth of both the contracting parties; and that two great neighbours may have discovered that the world is wide enough for both, may abandon the diabolical maxim that they are by fate and nature to be enemies, and instead of cutting each others throats may commence a glorious race in arts and sciences – in commerce and agriculture – in the important science of good government, which establishes the Throne in the happiness of the people – in short, may have no competition but in a generous and magnanimous friendship and a beneficence bounded only by the limits of the world. Away I stride to Cheek-House & rejoyce the hearts of the Fum, of my Lady Cocklifty, the Fox & the Bear; & returning home to breakfast I find the Sisters three dancing the Hays & actually mad with exstacy at this unlook'd-for termination of human misery. Dispatching breakfast I make but 3 strides to Jack Day. "Here (said I on my way) am I sure to find an exultation coresponding & flowing from the same pure sources with my own; founded in benevolence & an ardent love of his Country." But what is my astonishment when instead of a cheerful countenance with wch my cordial friend was wont to receive me, I see nothing but gravity, sometimes like confusion & an evident depression of spirits.

"Cheer up (said I) my dear Jack, let this unlook'd for blessing cause you to banish for the present all sense even of pain."

"Bob (answered he with a sigh), I have no pain but that of the mind – we have indeed got Peace, but such a peace as establishes Bonaparte upon the throne of the Bourbons, consolidates at our door a greater Empire than Louis 14th in his dreams of universal domination ever aspired to, and flings proud England after all her waste of blood and treasure, after all her brilliant victories and numerous conquests, at the feet of a Tyrant as perfidious as he is sanguinary."

Saying this he handed me the Porcupine of the morning containing an outline of the Preliminaries wth some very harsh strictures on them. After reading a passage a while I professed myself contented with the terms. If France is now enlarged beyond the limits of Ancient Gaul, has not England acquired a greater and more powerful Empire in the East, an Empire more productive of wealth, commerce and power, which Bonaparte recognises and in effect confirms to us by this peace? And if we restore to France her colonies let it be remembered that we have retained two most important Islands from her allies, Ceylon which furnishes the most valuable spices and the finest Harbour in Asia, and the centinel, as it were of Indostan; and Trinidad, which gives us the command of the Spanish Main and an uninterruptable intercourse with the South American provinces of Spain – and as to more Islands, we do not want them for we have enough, and we have not population or forces to retain them. The Cape is to be a Free Port, so that we are to have all the benefit without the heavy burden of it. Had Malta been preserved to us my joy would be unalloy'd; that Island besides giving us the command of the Levant and Turkey Trade would always keep Toulon in check and blast in the bud all future speculation of France under Egypt, and through Egypt upon India, the basis of British Greatness. Still however, Malta would require a great army to garrison it, perhaps 7000 men; to be maintained (considering the distance from home) at enormous expence and probably it might give umbrage to our ally Alexander and to other Europe "powers". And as to the terms were they more brilliant they might no doubt flatter our national pride; but if our honour be maintained and our most precious possessions, the sources of all our wealth and power and glory, be secured and strengthen'd, then in my mind the

London, Fleet South.

moderation of these terms is the best argument in their favour, as it is the surest pledge for the permanency of Peace.

Sun. 4th Rise early – Mrs Day & I & Mary FitzGerald[2] go to the Chapel Royal in the Castle at 8 a. m. The King comes accompanied by Princess Elizabeth. After prayers we plant ourselves wth the Crowd in the gang-way to take a nearer view of our good King, & are delighted to see him in such excellent plight, health and spirits – his dress was a green coat, wth brass buttons, blue pantaloon and half-boots, round hat and brown bob wig –

Thursday, 8 October. We all proceed post haste to Alderman Skinner near Tooting and are received by him and his sweet daughter with their usual cordiality – nothing can exceed the comfort of our accommodation.

F. 9th The worthy Aldn. takes me to London before breakfast – dine wth Lord Carleton in Jermyn St. after seeing an excellent 3-room'd house fitting up for him in George's St. Hanover Square – our company Ldy Carleton[3] & her mother Mrs. Mathew. In the evening parade a great part of the Town to see the splendid Illuminations, the signature of Bonaparte to the Preliminaries having arrived in the forenoon. St. James's all in shade – the Quakers don't illuminate and their windows are smash'd everywhere – so also Mr. Peter Porcupine,[4] edited by Cobett (who in America had done the British interests much good); his House in Pall-Mall and his office in (I believe) Southampton St. are sadly abused for his impudent obstinacy in refusing to Illuminate – a Paper till now strongly in favour of administration breaks loose into the most virulent immesurable abuse of the Peace; supposed to be a retainer of Mr. Wyndham and the Grenvilles, who it seems quit their ci devant friends and give the Peace no quarter. The Illuminations, after being eclipsd by the most vivid lighting I ever saw for some hours, are soon put out & the Mob are dispersed by 10 0' clock by the heavy rain.

Sat. 10th the Illuminations are resumed this night with encreasd spirit & brilliancy.

Sun 11 return to Tooting and rejoin my friends under the hospitable roof of the good Alderman - his daughter Lady Saunderson spends the day wth us -

Monday 12th The mighty Fum, Ursa Major and myself drive to Richmond and pass a very pleasant day with Sir John Day - the Town splendidly illuminated at night, this being the 3d P & P (i.e. Peace & Plenty) were a general device - but after those letters over the door of Peg Jefferies (a masculine old maid of this town) some wag added inconspicuous characters, "& may they never fail us".

Tu. 13th We meet our friends of Tooting at Lady Saunderson's pretty house on Clapham Common at dinner & very handsomely entertained - Cards in the Evening but she never plays - Lady S. is widow of Sir Jas. Saunderson Bt. and Alderman of London - he married her when old enough to be her father & died leaving a very fine & promising daughter & an income of abt. £1,500 a year durant viduitate; or if she marries, £10,000. She became the year after Sir James's death a Quaker & assumed all at once the dress, language formality & tenets of that solemn sect in the most rigid degree - However in the course of another year upon the expostulation of her Father & other friends she resumed her former dress & habits & is become once more a good Church of England woman, retaining nevertheless a good deal of the sober formal &self-denying rules of conduct which Quakers practice - but her leading & prominent feature is an extensive & most liberal charity applying a great proportion of her income in acts of benevolence. At night we all return from lady S's to Tooting, abt 3 miles

W. 14th - The Richmond families take leave after breakfast of this worthy Toothing family & return by Lord Spencer's noble seat at Wimbledon Common to dinner.

Thursd. 15th Oct. 1801 One day last week Sir J Day took me to see the Duke of Clarence's Gardens at Bushy-park of wch. H.R.H. is Ranger, upon the invitation of poor FitzGerald the Gardener of Tralee whose father & mother had always lived under the protection of my father. Upon our arrival the Maitre d'hotel received us at the steps & said that H.R.H. who was out riding had directed that the House shod be shewd to me, as well as the Gardens; & we were accordingly conducted thro' it even to the very cellars, & without any pretensions to elegance it certainly is a very complete family house. From thence we proceeded under the auspices of Kerrykee FitzGerald thro' the Gardens, wch to say the truth "are no great things". In the gardens I found another acquaintance, the gardener's wife of the name of Trant. Their account was that nothing cod exceed their comfort & happiness - that they had lived under their Royal Master above 4 years & found him a courteous, beneficent Master and did not doubt of dying in his service-their Garden House was very neat & comfortable, & they presented to me 6 fine children.

Upon retiring from the Gardens to our coach whom shod we meet but H.R.H.[5] returned from his ride & on his way to the Gardens in search of us. Sir John, who had long the honour of the Duke's acquaintance & friendship, presented me immediately to H.R.H. who rec. me with very gracious & unaffected courtesy & was pleasd among other civil things to say that he had long known Mr Justice Day by character & had wish'd much for the favour of his acquaintance. We then returnd to the Gardens & took a hasty second view of them wth the Duke, who then conducted us thro his Farm-Yard & Haggard. - H.R.H. then orderd his Sociable for Sir John & me; & after shewing his Stable, Horses, Carriages &c, all in excellent stile, about half a mile distant from the House he attended us thro' the whole of his farm, computed to be abt. 300 acres, H.R.H. riding at my side & conversing wth us the whole way wth great good humour, excellent information & good sense & the most amiable, unaffected condescension. In the course of our ride he spoke wth great severity of Mr Pitt & said that his Father was so disgusted wth him that he was sure H. M. wod never again consent to take him back –that if the Prince of Wales were King (wch. perhaps on the verge of 40 he might think it high time to be) he certainly cod not be expected to adopt Pitt after his arrogant treatment of the Prince on the Regency - so that there seemd but little probability of Mr Pitt's ever returning into power. H.M.'s disgust was for P.'s deserting him at the most critical period of that War into wch he had plungd H. M.; & still more for attempting to force the Popery relaxation upon him contrary to his Coronation Oath. He was very inquisitive about Ireland, express'd a high opinion of the 28 Irish Peers, particularly the Chancr whom he described to be an acute eloquent man - surprised to find they had so little of their native accent; the Chancr had but little; Ld Carleton more, Archb. Cashel[6] a good deal. He was pleasd to say he wod not have suspected me to be Irish from my accent.

After spending a very pleasant day we return'd to the House abt 5; & on our alighting H.R.H. desired I wod name my own day for giving him the pleasure of our company at dinner - &we did accordingly fix upon this day (15th Oct).

Upon alighting at the door I was agreeably surprised to meet an old College acquaintance of mine whom I had never seen since the days of my youth, the Revd. Mr. Loyd, His R.H.'s Chaplain; grown so bloated & gross from having been a light & slender person that I did not know him till he mentioned his name - he shewd me a room to dress in; after which operation we assembled a while in the Hall, a spacious room well aired with a large fire, to hear a Savoyard playing on a non-descript instrument wch produced much such music as a Dulcimer -from thence we proceded to the Drawing-room where we found the agreeable Mrs. Jourdan[7] wth her eldest son, a fine boy abt 8 years old. Knowing me to be from Kerry she inquired wth much anxiety about her relations the Blands & other acquaintances of hers of that county - grown very fat, but continues very pleasing still without however any pretension of beauty - indeed a few nights before in the character of Hayden on the Richmond stage she acted with as much spirit & vivacity as in her best day. Sir J. Day arrives & dinner is announced; Mrs J. sits on H.R.H.'s right hand, who sits at the head & his Chaplain at the foot of the table - an excellent dinner - 2 soupes, Turbot & Venison &c &c - 2 courses & desert - Champagne, Cape, Claret &c

After dinner all the children are introduced; the eldest boy & girl handsome & like the Bland family, 4 more fine children very like the Royal Family, particly the youngest child, a white-headed, good humd pug daughter the very picure of the Queen - all educated as carefully & treated wth as much respect by the Domestics & tenderness by the Duke as if legitimate - her behaviour modest, easy & unaffected throughout - the surname of the children it is said will be Fitz-Clarence, but this I have only upon report.

After a chearful glass we follow Mrs J. & get Coffee - & then Sir John & I make our bow & retire about 9.

Such was the polite & flattering reception wch I met wth from the King's 3d son in whose way to the Throne there stands by the course of nature but the young Princess Charlotte.

F. 16th Oct. Both families visit London - dine that day wth Fredk. Smith, our Quaker cousin, at his country House on the New Road - are entertained by him & his excellent wife & most amiable daughters & family with the most generous open-hearted hospitality & the most unaffected chearfulness & good humour. The Quaker does not pray. He meditates much, reviews his own life in silence, and prescribes a strict reformation to himself. But the great pride & glory of this sect consists in extensive charity & secret acts of goodness & benevolence. Fredk. (who is a chymist in the Haymarket of great repute & employment) bestows his cousin Mrs. Day a beautiful medicine chest stored wth a multitude of the best medicines accompanied wth a most affectionate & sensible letter.

Tu. 19th Visit my excellent friend Lord Glenbervie at the Pay Office & sit for a couple of hours wth him. Dine this day wth th Revd. Mr. Ward in Portland St. where we meet Dr. Gillies,[8] successor to the illustrious Dr. Robertson[9] as Historiographer in Scotland to the King & author of a Grecian history - an acute interesting conversable Scotchman - suspected to have been democratic, but in office conducts himself speciously. We accompany Mrs. Ward to Covent Garden to hear the divine Billington in Mandane.

W. 20th. Bob Day[10] & I spend our morning getting Cash & jobbing in the City - dine at Dolly's - in the evening join the Sisterhood at friend Smith's, sup & pass away a few very agreeable hours - Bob a great favourite with all; even the young ones weep at his departure.

Th 21st Oct. Ld Alvanly calls upon m abt 10. His Lordship & I walk to Lord Camden in Arlington St. who receives me wth great cordiality - call on Lord Pelham, Shafton St. Picadily, but don't find him at home - he sleeps at Fulham Mr Abbot's

Fr. 22 d Bob & I take a coach to Watt's in Hampstead - spend a couple of hours there & dress for his neighbour Lord Alvanley's- go there at 5 to dinner & find Thompson B.[11] & Le Blanc J. before us- treated wth great attention & brotherly respect by the three Judges.

M. 25th Oct. Wth heavy hearts & sorrowful countenances we take our leave at length of our afflicted & dear friends the Sisterhood - & surely at this painful moment of separation it is but a small tribute of gratitude to acknowledge the indelible obligation wch we owe for their affectionate & generous hospitality to Sir Edwd., Betsy & Bob Day for 3 months, & to Mrs. Day & myself for 6 weeks of this long vacation. Meet the Oxford Post coach (wch I secured last week) at Kew-bridge, dine at Henley & sleep at Oxford.

Tu. 26 Oct. Our time is so limited that we reluctantly leave Oxford this morng & travel to Birminghim.

W. 27th proceed for Wolverhampton – never was there a more execrable conveyance, never in Ireland in its worst days -from thence take post chaises to Shrewsbury 3 stages

Th. 28th. Rise early & are persuaded to take a coach & four as a more expeditious as well as more sociable conveyance than in 2 chaises & pair - within 4 miles of Oswestry one of the hind wheels loses a felly[12] - Sir Edwd & I walk to the town, while the coach is drag'd with the rest of our party the 4 miles in 2 hours - after breakfast a lawsuit takes place between the drivers & Mr Justice Day touching the fare (17 halfcrowns), as if they had fairly performed their contract & that no Judge but an Irish one wod lay down the law differently.

Dine at Llangollen, after visiting the pretty Hermitage of Lady Eliz Butler & Miss Ponsonby - The Fum while in the act of sketching off one of the Bar gates is most politely rebuked by those sour lumps of stale virginity; as if he had been taking off the gate itself, and not a mere drawing of it.

Modern ceramic of the Two Ladies of Llangollen, Ponsonby and Butler

Sat. 30 Breakfast at Jackson's excellent House at the Ferry - hear wth great pleasure that the Road is going on wth great spirit along the foot of the great Snowdon from Bangor & coming out I fancy about Keniog, abridging the road, as it is said, about 20 miles; and another piece of intelligence, that an Act will pass this session for an Iron Bridge at Bangor Ferry to the southward considerably of the Ferry, at a place where there are two large rocks in the channel whereby a Bridge of three arches may well be thrown across.

Sund 1st Nov. Spend this day insipidly in Holyhead - calld on board abt 9 in the evening; a calm dark night.

Tu 3d –land at the Pigeon IIse abt 9 o'clock this evening, after having been 48 hours at sea, suffering an uninterrupted sickness of the severest kind, & escaping by the divine goodness a most tremendous storm.

The Sunday following (Nov. 8) the servants, horses & equipage arrived safe & unhurt from Parkgate, having taken refuge from the storms of the preceding week in Beaumaris Bay – after a few days rest the horses appeard as fresh as they were on the 21st last July after travelling above 1000 miles in less than 3 months.

1. 'Thrice I endeavour'd to embrace her charms, Thrice her bright Image vanish'd from my arms.' (He supplies the translation.)

2. Mary FitzGerald, of Bandon, Co. Cork, was the lady companion and nurse of Day's wife. In 1824, the year following the decease of his wife, Day and Mary were married: the ceremony legitimised two sons.

3. Judge Carleton m. as his second wife Mary, daughter of Abednego Mathew, Dorsetshire, in 1795.

4. Peter Porcupine was a psuedonym for William Cobbett, the widely read pamphleteer and journalist. When in America he became a fierce critic of American democracy.

5. The Duke of Clarence (1765-1837) was the 3rd son of George III. He became King William IV in 1830 and died in 1837, when he was succeeded by Queen Victoria.

6. Charles Agar, Archbishop of Cashel 1779-1801.

7. Dorothea Jordan (1762-1816), Irish actress and mistress of the Duke of Clarence, with whom she had ten children. She was the wife of one of the Blands of Derryquin, near Kenmare. Day may have seen her on the Dublin stage when she acted in Crow St. Theatre during the 1770s. She fled to England from an abusive relationship with her manager, Daly, and in England assumed the name Jordan. She became the Duke's mistress about 1790 and remained so until 1811.

8. John Gillies LLD (1747-1836), historian and classical scholar.

9. William Robertson (1721-1793), historian, author of History of Scotland.

10. Robert Day, Judge Day's nephew, second son of Archdeacon Day, m. Christina Marshall of Dublin. Entered Trinity 1792 aged 14; called to the bar in 1802 (*Alumni Dublinensis*). High Sheriff of Kerry in 1808. He lived at Lohercannon.

11. Chief Baron Sir Alexander Thomson (1744-1817), Baron of the Exchequer fom 1787.

12. felly (felloe), or exterior rim of a wheel

3

'That Fortress built by Nature for herself': the Irish courts in time of war

When Day addressed the Grand Jury of Co. Cork in August war had resumed in May and Robert Emmet was under arrest following his insurrection of July. The Chief Justice, Day's friend and colleague Arthur Wolfe, Lord Kilwarden, became the principal victim of the Emmet insurrection when he was dragged from his carriage in Dublin and piked to death in the presence of his daughter. Day avoided remarks which might prejudice Emmet's trial. Instead he concentrated his remarks on Britain's isolation in the struggle with Napoleon and on the heroic end of Lord Kilwarden, propagating the martyrdom of his friend by repeating Kilwarden's dying instruction that Emmet should receive a fair trial. Emmet was tried, convicted and executed in September. Day was then at liberty to comment more. The report of the Cork charge is taken from the Cork Mercantile Chronicle, 29 August 1803.

Judge Day's Charge to the County Grand Jury of Cork of the 14th August 1803

After expressing much concern at the crowded state of the Jail and the enormous crimes imputed to so many of the prisoners, his Lordship proceeded to observe, that these lamentable excesses (by whomsoever committed) were the natural consequences of that utter contempt and relaxation of all laws, human and divine, which had characterised our unfortunate country for some years past. The treason of our days possessed a new and peculiar malignity; it soared in turpitude and audacity beyond flights of treason in any other civilised period of our history. Our former civil wars were but a struggle for the sceptre between rival families and their respective adherents; each party professing a religious reverence for the venerable establishments of the country. But what is the object of modern treason? To erect a new government (if a compound of despotism and atheism can be called a government) upon the ruins of morality and religion; to subvert all those happy institutions under which the British Empire hath attained its matchless pitch of prosperity and power; to glut individual vengeance and lust, and all the fierce passions of the human breast, but an unlimited perpetration of cruelty and pillage, rape and murder; to confiscate property, to annihilate all the orders of the state; and finally to overturn the Altar and the Throne.

But whatever currency their detestable doctrines might have had, whatever might have been the illusion of French principles, that spell, thank God, is long dissolved; France herself, had she had a Press to speak for her, would own, so too would all her nick-named new fangled provinces, Batavia, Belgium, Liguria, but above all Helvetia, the peculiar object of the protection and favour of the Great Nation, that there never before existed so revolting a tissue of tyranny, infidelity, rapacity and blood as the Revolution of France, and of all those ill-fated countries who have fraternised with her.

It was hoped that the bitter sufferings of our infatuated peasantry in the 1798

Rebellion would have taught them the danger and folly of renewing their traiterous confederacy with that pestilential people. But the late explosion in our capital has awakened us to the lively sense of our error, and to a distinct view of our danger. The bloody tragedies of that disgraceful night have disclosed a system of treason, organised and matured to an alarming degree. The cold-blooded butchery of the excellent Man, of whose wisdom, justice and moderation it had been his Lordship's happiness and pride to have long been the daily witness, whose expiring breath, in the true spirit of that benign Code which he so admirably administered, commanded "that his murderers should not suffer without a fair trial", displays the genuine character of the crisis which is preparing for us; it demonstrates that no assemblage of virtues can subdue, no elevation of character assuage, the sanguinary thirst of a ferocious populace. The depots of arms, the magazines of ammunition, the eloquent Proclamations, the artful and well-contrived concealment of the preparation and materials of destruction; while all these exhibit the advanced state and murderous purpose of the plot, they prove that the great impulse comes from wealth, education and talent.

Under these critical circumstances of the country, it has pleased the wisdom of his Majesty and of the Parliament to demand a great and extraordinary force from his people. This will necessarily induce no light burdens, and binds of course the Grand Juries of Ireland to the severest and most rigid frugality; it loudly calls upon them to confine their presentments to mere works of absolute and indispensable necessity. His Lordship felt that he should wrong the characteristic loyalty and ardent public spirit of a County of Cork Grand Jury, were he to doubt for a moment their promptitude and zeal to give every possible facility to the Acts of Parliament for the defence of the country. They would recollect what a burden the Militia Family Bill imposed upon the country, what a further burden is induced by the Army of Reserve; they would reflect upon the faulty principle of Grand Jury taxation sustained by the land holder and not by the land owner, charging for the most part the industry and not the income of the country; and they would feel as long as the legislature judged it expedient to raise those large supplies through the instrumentality of Grand Juries instead of direct parliamentary taxations, that nothing could guarantee the tranquillity and contented state of the county but the strictest economy and moderation on the part of the Grand Jury.

The question now at issue is no less than the very existence of the British Empire. The present vast and awful question is, whether the British Empire, the nursery of Heroes, Sages and Patriots, the generous asylum of fallen greatness and persecuted religion, the last refuge in Europe of expiring liberty, morality and law, shall exist in its distinct and independent state, or whether we shall bend our free born necks to the …ing yoke of France, submit to the vilest and most degrading Slavery, and sink into a tributary province to an implacable Enemy, whose overwhelming ambition we alone have hitherto controuled. The struggle which it is our destiny to sustain, I would presume to call a spectacle worthy of the Divinity to contemplate: these little Islands advanced to paramount eminence by the vigour of an unrivalled Constitution, standing forward the intrepid champions of freedom, of Christianity, of a benumbed and stupefied world, against the most ferocious power that ever shook the earth.

What the final issue of this awful contest will be it would be blasphemy for a moment to doubt. If there be a God in Heaven (and all nature proclaims aloud that there is) he will make our cause his own, and in due time dash the presumption of this intoxicated and sanguinary Usurper against our Wooden Walls and well-defended Coast.

This deviation from the direct course of his duty his Lordship trusted would not, under the gloom which covered us, be deemed unworthy of the high commission which he had the honour to bear. His object was not to awaken fear, but to rouse to vigilance; not to excite despondency, but to animate to activity. England had much to do, but Ireland much more. England is an unanimous, loyal and enlightened people, and will rise as one man to exterminate the invader; we unhappily are a divided people, we cannot rise in mass, nor venture to arm indiscriminately our people. The sister island prepares her enthusiastic millions for invasion; we must prepare for invasion and be feared for rebellion too. The moral peculiarities and difficulties of the state of society amongst us demand an increased exertion and activity from every man of education, influence, and authority. If the poverty and ignorance of our peasantry expose them to the wiles and seductions of treason, they form an affecting appeal to the higher orders for protection, sympathy and instruction. The best specific for the ills of our situation would be to enlighten the understandings of the humbler orders; to open the eyes of our credulous and corruptible people to the criminal views of their flagitious leaders; and thus, by a due mixture of vigour and moderation, by a persuasive and parental discipline, to win them back to a true sense of their real interests, and a just respect for the laws which protect them.

A Charge
delivered to the Grand Juries of the City and County of Dublin
on the 6th November, 1803
by the Right Hon. Mr. Justice Day

Published at the request of both Grand Juries. Dublin.[1]

Printed by P.D. Hardy, Cecilia-St., 1830

The brilliant Emmet was a palpable loss to the community to which he and Day belonged, and to the work of reform which unionists were undertaking at this time. Day would have known his father, who was the state physician; also Temple Emmet, Robert's eldest brother, from the time when both were Monks of the Screw, and his other brother, Thomas Addis, from his and Day's time in the Irish parliament. The tentacles of Emmet's insurrection extended into Day's political heartland in the South West: Emmet's cousin and associate St. John Mason promoted an anti-Union campaign in Kerry, and we even learn that the Emmets were 'the intimate associates' of Tralee provost William Rowan who dines with Day many times in these diaries.[2] Regarding St. John Mason, Day wrote the following to the Chancellor, Lord Redesdale, shortly before he delivered the above charge:
'That young barrister, Mr St. John Mason, who was lately arrested on his route hither from Dublin, and who is cousin german to the Emmets, was busy at the pious work of treason in the county of Kerry, of which he is a native, in Spring 1799; and I remember to have then denounced to the Grand Jury a most inflammatory printed paper sign'd with his name circulated with great industry and calculated to excite that county. I have a copy of it now in my possession.'[3]

Gentlemen of both Grand Juries,

By the much lamented death of Lord Kilwarden, and the consequent promotion of my Lord Chief Justice Downes (a promotion by which His majesty's Government has administered the best possible consolation to the country for its late incalculable misfortune), the task of charging you this day devolves on me. If I execute it imperfectly, it is fortunate for the public, and affords much comfort to myself to reflect, that I address Gentlemen of well-known experience in the office of a Grand Juror, and whose condition and character offer the best guarantee for the intelligent and conscientious discharge of that important duty.

The loss of that excellent man, whose inhuman fate you all deplore – whose departing spirit, whilst yet it trembled on his lips, bore testimony to his virtues, both as a settled Christian and a benign despenser of the British code[1] which he so admirably administered, is felt by all as a great public calamity. But with what peculiar weight does that calamity press upon this Court, where he presided with so much lustre, and from whom the aid and lights of his deep learning, sound judgment, and solid talents have been so abruptly snatched! For us, the surviving associates of his judicial toil, who had so long the happiness and pride of being the daily witnesses of his wisdom, his justice, his moderation, and mercy – his firm and inflexible integrity, his very failings (and who has not his failings?) bottomed in purity and goodness – what greater glory can we propose to ourselves, than an humble but steady pursuit of his conduct, and an animated imitation of his virtues!

Gentlemen, you are assembled to assist this the supreme Court of the land, where the King himself in contemplation of law is present, in the administration of the criminal justice of your respective bailiwicks – so it is in theory. But, in point of fact, your criminal jurisdiction is become little else than a name, that duty having, by reason of the great influx of civil business into this Court, been for many years past executed by the Commission Court. Should, however, any bills be sent up, you are not to be informed, that of all the objects within your cognizance they are entitled to a priority of your attention, that it is your duty to dispatch them by a sober and dispassionate investigation of the evidence for the Crown alone, and to adopt or reject each accusation as you shall or shall not, upon such evidence, be thoroughly persuaded of its truth. It will, moreover, be your duty, as the Grand Inquests of the City and County of Dublin, to present to the Court every offence and every nuisance of a public nature which shall fall within your knowledge through the course of the term, together with the offender. You, Gentlemen of the City, where no doubt nuisances abound, and some indeed of a notorious and frightful kind, are sure of receiving considerable aid and relief in this important branch of your duty from our excellent Lord Mayor, who has already, in the lapse of a few weeks, achieved some essential reforms in our capital, and whose firm, virtuous, and loyal conduct entitles him to the thanks and support of every lover of religion, morality, and good order.

Light, therefore, would be your labours, were they limited to your criminal jurisdiction. But you are aware that certain statutes of Ireland have superinduced upon the original common law jurisdiction of Grand Juries another duty of great weight and importance. I allude to those laws which have invested our Grand Juries with a discretionary power of taxing their fellow-subjects, for the repair and construction of the highways and other public works of the several counties, and thus in effect committed to them the prime and paramount branch of legislative function. (His Lordship then traced the progress of this jurisdiction, from the common law through its various changes; and after showing that it was first entrusted here as in England to the Magistrates in sessions, and from thence gradually transferred to the Grand Juries at Assizes upon its present extended scale, he thus proceeded.) This you must perceive to be a high and transcendant trust, committed no doubt to the Irish Grand Juries, with a view to accelerate by such extraordinary powers, the settlement and civilization of the country. And it must be owned, that however abused it has been, and continues to be in some of our counties, no course could be more successfully adopted for improving the habits of our people and the face of the island. It is obvious that every road which traverses the country, which pierces our morasses and unlocks the fastnesses and retreats of its inhabitants, in the same degree facilitates an execution of the law, whilst it opens an intercourse amongst the people, drains and improves the soil, and by providing considerable employment for our labouring poor, supersedes, in some degree, the necessity of poor laws. In a word, this tax is expended for the benefit of the country in which it is raised, and like the genial and refreshind dew of Heaven, it descends upon, and meliorates the soil from whence it was exhaled. But, Gentlemen, in the execution of this trust, so precious in the discreet use of it, and so pernicious in its abuse, it is your duty to look most especially to two or three obvious principles: - First, that your grants be not oppressive. Second, that they be appropriated to necessary, or to well-selected works. And third, that they be committed only to Supervisors of known integrity and established character in their neighbourhood. If the agriculture and industry of your counties are to be burthened (as it is fit they should for their own improvement) it is your duty to see that the tax be not absorbed by private avenues, lanes, and byways, for individual accommodation, whilst the great approaches to your capital (upon which, too, I regret you will not suffer turnpikes to be erected) are in too many instances neglected and left to shift for themselves.

But, Gentlemen, that discreet and judicious economy, which should ever be the ruling principle of your grants, was never more incumbent upon you than at this present period. If the unprecedented circumstances of the country require an unprecedented supply for its defence, they call with a commanding voice upon the Grand Juries of Ireland to limit their presentments to works of absolute and indispensable necessity; and by a severe frugality to preserve unimpaired the resources of the people for the weighty demands of military preparation. That preparation in the City of Dublin, it is impossible for any man not dead to the fate and honour of his country, to view without exultation, pride and confidence.

It was impossible for any honest man to witness, on the late anniversary of our Glorious Deliverer,[2] your brilliant display of numbers, zeal, and loyalty, and of those free and constitutional principles which seated the present illustrious family upon the throne, without exultation, pride, and confidence. Gentlemen, you seem to have formed a just estimate of the present awful crisis. You feel yourselves called upon to arm in defence of that Constitution under which this great, free, and powerful Empire has so long flourished; in defence of our much beloved King, whose long reign has been one uninterrupted stream of bounty to the Irish nation; in defence of our native land, and of all those fond endearing ties which bind us to our homes – and against whom? Against a gloomy and implacable Tyrant, inflated with success, and exulting in the prosperity of his crimes – who proclaims through the world that the ruling and burning passion of his soul is to let loose upon us the horrors of his all-devouring revolution, and to blot the British Empire from the map of Europe. The question, then, at issue, is no less than the very existence of the British Empire. Whether this nursery of heroes, sages, and patriots, the general asylum of fallen greatness, and of persecuted religion, the last refuge in Europe of expiring liberty, morality, the law, shall still maintain her paramount rank among nations; shall continue to move in her own spacious and proud orbit in the system of the world? Or whether we too are to be hurled from our sphere, degraded into the abject class of French satellites, shorn of our native lustre, and chained down in all our future motions, and eternal destiny, to the sovereign laws of the Great Nation; to the iron domination of a remorseless enemy, whose overwhelming ambition we alone have hitherto controuled? Surely, Gentlemen, the struggle which fate has cast upon us, though awful, presents a sublime and proud spectacle. These little islands, trusting in that gracious Being who hath so often made our cause his own, and crowned it with triumph, now hurl defiance at the blood-stained Colossus that bestrides the Continent, and stand forward "single-handed" the intrepid champion of freedom, of Christianity, of a benumbed and stupefied world, against the most ferocious power that ever scourged the human race.

Whatever shallow speculators might heretofore have dreamed upon the French Revolution, there can be now but one opinion upon it; dire experience, and the frank acknowledgments of treason itself, now stamp it as one tremendous tissue of tyranny, infidelity, rapacity, and blood. Look at all those ill-fated nations who have been subdued or seduced one by one into French fraternity; look at the mouldering ruins of Europe parcelled out, and carved, and crumbled, as the rancour or caprice of the spoiler have pronounced their doom; but, above all, look at the last sad victim to French perfidy, brutality, and ravage at Hanover, desolated in vengeance to our Sovereign, and in violation of a solemn treaty, before the wax had well cooled; then ask yourselves, my countrymen, what will be your lot should the happy shores of Ireland be successfully assailed by this horde of merciless banditti? What better treatment can Ireland expect than the continental conquests of France? If this declared enemy of human happiness were to triumph over your virtue and valour, Ireland were then doomed to unutterable calamity through all her orders, ranks, and sects; the rich of every sect would be beggared; the poor of every sect would be trampled into dust; your women dishonoured; your youth, by conscription, recruited into foreign ranks; and Ireland become one hideous scene of indiscriminate plunder, poverty, slavery, and death.

If there be yet an individual amongst you haunted by French illusion, so besotted and so base as still to balance between infamy and honour, between the invader and his country, let him hear the last injunctions of our late young Cataline: "If the French come as a foreign enemy," mark Emmet's own words, "meet them, oh, my countrymen, on the shore, with a torch in one hand and a sword in the other: receive them with all the destruction of war, immolate them in their boats, before our native soil shall be polluted by a foreign foe. If they succeed in landing, fight them on the strand – burn every blade of grass before them – rase every house – collect your provisions, property, wives, and daughters – fight whilst two men are left; and when but one remains, let that man set fire to the pile, and release himself and the families of his fallen countrymen from the tyranny of France." O, si sic omnia !

Such, Gentlemen, is the dying legacy of that ill-fated youth to his deluded followers – such the best atonement that could be made for his enormous crimes by one whom nature had endowed with no mean talents; satis eloquentiae, sapientiae parum! And who, had he taken a virtuous direction, might have been an ornament, and not the parricide of his country.

Gentlemen, you cannot, perhaps, render a more solid service to your counties at this juncture than by an active and general circulation of that Paper, the last solemn act of a dying Christian, who had recently arrived from France, was deep in the French councils, and knew well the flagitious purposes which inspired the threatened enterprise, and the disastrous consequences to Ireland of its ultimate success. That desperate enterprise we can have no doubt of their undertaking: we know it is the Golden Expedition with which the Usurper has long amused his bankrupt, licentious followers. Demonstrations at the same time will be made upon our sister island –

> "That fortress built by Nature for herself,
> Against infection and the hand of war,
> Against the envy of less happier lands –"

not in the silly hope of storming that impregnable fortress of loyalty, gallantry, and public spirit, but with the view of masking their main design upon us – their design to conquer Great Britain in Ireland. We know that here they look for co-operation; but, Gentlemen, I do not so despair of the Commonwealth; on the contrary, I doubt not that the glorious opportunity which will then present itself to our people of redeeming their tarnished character, will be eagerly and universally embraced, and that we shall see the good old loyalty of Ireland replaced upon its former elevated and proud pedestal. The higher order from end to end of the island are enthusiastic in the cause of their King, and their country, and their God. They laugh at the Tyrant of Europe offering liberty to freemen. And if a great portion of our peasantry have unhappily been seduced by our self-convicted traitors from their primitive loyalty and innocence into a foul rebellion, is it unreasonable to hope that bitter experience, time, and reflection, have opened their eyes to a just sense of their own true interests, and to the base views of their flagitious leaders? Is it too sanguine to hope that the loyal, pious, and persuasive exhortations of the Titular Dignitaries of the Church have not been thrown away upon their flocks; have exposed to their view in all its native deformity the horrid features of French fraternity, and renewed in their minds the sacred and inseparable obligations of religion and allegiance? Even from the atrocious but despicable rising in our capital, quelled by a handful of spirited yeomen and the Poddle-guard, it is no violence to infer the present impotence of treason, and a happy revolution in the minds of its former votaries; and I cannot but hail the late instantaneous burst of loyalty in the Mayo peasantry, upon the alarm of a French descent, (the more alert, perhaps, for the visit with which that country was already favoured from France) as the first fruits of that happy change of sentiment, and a promising presage of a general and abundant harvest.

Meantime it would be wise to improve and cherish this returning virtue of our deluded countrymen. It would be wise to promote a spirit of conciliation and harmony amongst all our sects and classes; and to abstain from all those irritating discussions which have led to incalculable mischiefs, which fierceness and pride only generate, and are utterly repugnant to the charities and genuine character of Christianity.

If the views from without be gloomy and alarming, it is the more necessary for us to avoid all collision and animosity at home. When the vessel is labouring in a storm, shall the mariners separate into adverse parties, instead of employing their joint efforts for the common safety? Nothing has been wanting to us on the part of the crown. We have a brave and powerful army, commanded by an officer selected for the defence of Ireland by the King himself, for his military reputation and great talents. We have a government firm, but yet temperate, conciliatory, and constitutional, who conducted the late state trials with equal energy and moderation, and thus have asserted the empire of the laws, and restored general confidence, without straining the principle of the Constitution.

But vain would be the best institutions, and fatal the most flattering appearances were they to induce any indolence or relaxation in the exertions of those who possess any influence or authority amongst us. The times demand a multiplied vigilance on the part of our magistrates or executive power through all its gradations, to watch and stifle every murmur of that malignant spirit which has so long afflicted Ireland, before it swells into a storm; to quench every rising spark, which, if neglected, nothing can extinguish but the blood of our fellow-subjects. This is a duty which peculiarly belongs to you, Gentlemen of the Grand Inquest of your respective bailiwicks. You have sworn to make diligent inquiry after all offences which tend to violate the public peace. I have no doubt that you will, through the whole of this awful and momentous Term, pay a diligent and peculiar attention to this part of your duty; and you may expect that the Court will not be wanting to give full effect to all your proceedings.

1. William Downes was appointed Chief-Justice after the assassination of Arthur Wolfe, Lord Kilwarden, by the followers of Robert Emmet. Downes does not appear to have enjoyed great health, which may explain why Day on more than one occasion over the years replace him to give an important address. Passages in this one are similar to the charge which he delivered some weeks earlier to the Co. Cork grand jury, when the memory of the Emmet rebellion was very fresh, (Ed).

2. *Kerry Evening Post 24 July 1880.* Rev. Arthur Blennerhassett Rowan, *Tralee and its Provosts Sixty Years On, with introduction by The Last of its Provosts* (private collection, only 24 copies printed, p.2).

3. PRONI, Redesdale Papers, photocopy 3030/9/13, Day, Limerick, to Redesdale, 10 August, 1803.

4. Pamphlet footnote: Lord Kilwarden's dying words were: "I forgive my aggressors - let them have a fair trial."

5. 4 November, birthday of King William of Orange (Ed.).

Exonerating the Sheriff of Tipperary: Sentencing Potter, 1804

Thomas Judkin FitzGerald, the cruel and notorious High Sheriff of Tipperary, was prosecuted by Robert Potter for a libel in 1798. Potter won the case with damages, but despite this, and seeing FitzGerald at the fair in Ballinasloe in October 1803, he summoned a number of witnesses to hear him pronounce FitzGerald a liar. In 1798 Thomas Judkin FitzGerald operated under the protection of the Indemnity act of 1796; the following sentence on Robert Potter by Day includes a justification of FitzGerald's actions in the pacification of Tipperary in 1798. Other judges were not as quick as Day to provide this justification: William Fletcher, cited elsewhere in this book, endeared himself to the defeated where Day failed. This report is taken from the Freeman's Journal, 6 December, 1804.

Robert Potter – You are brought up this day to receive the sentence of the Court for having uttered gross and opprobrious language to Sir Thomas Judkin FitzGerald, Bart., with an intent to provoke him to send you a challenge. The report of the learned Judge who tried the information at the last Assizes for the county of Galway has just been read, and it states shortly that at the fair of Ballinasloe, in October 1803, you rode up to the prosecutor, attended by a number of persons attracted by the occasion, and with a loud voice exclaimed, 'that you were come to insult him publicly, and to tell him that he was a liar'. The crime of which you stand convicted, professing, as it does, to seek deliberately the life of a fellow-creature, and which of course in the abstract is a crime of the first magnitude, in your case is attended with circumstances of peculiar aggravation. It appears upon recurring to the affidavits, that in the year 1798, a year which called forth all the virtues as well as all the crimes of our unfortunate country, that the prosecutor, in his capacity of High Sheriff of the county of Tipperary, had exerted himself with singular energy and effect in stemming the progress of rebellion in that county; that he had in the discharge of his official duty unadvisedly and unwarrantably indulged himself in strong reflections upon your loyalty; that you had, as became a man conscious of his own innocence and sensible of what you owed to and might well expect from the laws of the land, resorted to them for redress; and that you obtained a verdict and damages from the present prosecutor. Thus far, Sir, your conduct was not only correct, but commendable. One might have hoped that this triumph over your aggressor would have contented you; that having vindicated yourself against those aspersions, and asserted your innocence by that best criterion of truth, the verdict of a Jury, all further irritation would have subsided, and that you would have discharged your mind of any hostility to the individual whom you had thus publicly confuted and punished by due course of law. One might have hoped that having thus obtained full redress from the laws, they had acquired a new title to your respect; and that you would have been the last man in the community to trample upon that equal and admirable system of jurisprudence which had so recently cast a shield of protection round your own person. Nor would it have been very unreasonable to hope that a well-affected and loyal gentleman (such as I am bound to take you, grounding myself upon that verdict) would have made some allowance even for the excesses of an over-heated and impetuous loyalty, for the unavoidable irregularities of that awful period of general confusion and dismay, when in the discharge of an arduous official duty the best intentioned must inevitably have confounded some innocent with the guilty; and that having vindicated your character in the face and by the voice of your country, you would have consigned all personal petty feelings to everlasting oblivion. – Such, Sir, should have been your conduct. But, Sir, what has been your conduct?

At an interval of near five years, no pretence or colour for intermediate irritation (none at least appearing in proof), in a public fair and in the presence probably of the greatest concourse of people known to assemble upon commercial occasions in Ireland, and that from every corner of the country, as if to communicate by an electric shock at once through the land the outrage you intended, you ride up to the prosecutor, and without the ordinary courtesy of preliminary conversation, with a loud voice and a ferocious manner, your address those insulting and opprobrious expressions to him of which your were convicted. Perhaps an instance of more deadly or malignant rancour hardly occurs in the annals of murder; for, give it what specious name you please, it is not fashion, it is not a false and absurd sense of honour, it is not the cry or babble of the idle, the giddy, or the profligate, that can change the immutable nature of the deed; I tell you, Sir, that the law of the land, as well as the law of God, pronounce a homicide committed in a cold-blooded duel to be a wilful, premeditated murder. A verdict and damages could not satisfy or soothe your irritated feelings; time and reflection, which assuage and subdue the fiercest passions, seem to have lost their physical power upon you, and instead of calming to have inflamed and exasperated your mind; and at the end of near five years you proclaim an inextinguishable warfare; you avow a settled and implacable thirst for the blood of the prosecutor. Good God, is there to be no limitation to animosity? Are hostility and hatred to be immortal, and benevolence and good will only to be of short duration? And what marks the inveteracy of this outrage still more strongly is, that so far from being followed by any expression of remorse or sorrow on your part, the character of the prosecutor is maligned, and your own conduct attempted to be vindicated by your affidavit.

God Knows, Sir, if you do possess courage, as I doubt not but you do, many beneficial and honourable occasions for displaying that useful quality present themselves at this gloomy crisis, without turning it upon the defenders of our country; upon a gentleman who never manifested more true courage than in treating that foul indignity with a calm and contemptuous moderation.

Sir, it is necessary to chastise those of turbulent and unbridled temper for their own good, and, what is much more important, for the protection of the amenable and well-regulated in society.

Sir, it is necessary to teach you, and through you to teach all other duellists by profession, to teach the country at large, whose characteristic stain is a propensity to this barbarous crime, that it cannot be tolerated in any state pretending to civilisation, but must be beat down by the strong arm of the law.

The Defendant having undertaken in open Court to pay the costs of the prosecution, amounting to near £300, the Court sentenced him only to be fined one mark, and imprisoned three months, and to find security to be of the peace and good behaviour.

4

Summer 1807 on the North-East Circuit and a change in the Ministry

The Whig 'Ministry of All the Talents', led by Grenville, Fox and Grey and which fell from power in March 1807, is blamed by Day for the poor prosecution of the war against Napoleon. Prussia was defeated (Jena, October 1806) after the 'Talents' cut off subsidies. Napoleon's Continental System against British trade is in force since November 1806. Russia has been recently defeated (Friedland, June 1807), and the terms of the treaty finalised by Napoleon and Alexander on the barge at Tilsit on July 7 have just been received.

The Whigs are also lukewarm in their support for the Established Church and the Monarchy. The 'Talents' fell on the rejection of their Catholic Officers bill, a measure which would ordinarily find Day in support, except that George III was against, and Day supported the King.

Monaghan, Armagh and Carrigfergus ...

Tuesday 14th July. Leave town with only five horses and three servants. Poor old Purcell who had been my faithful companion for many years and through some thousand miles is suddenly seized with the farsy, and I am forced to leave him and the footman behind. Dine at Man of War[1] and sleep at Drogheda, 23 miles.

Wednesday 15th Breakfast at Ardee. Meet McCartney at Castleblaney and dine and sleep there. This far a more interesting ride than by Dundalk, passing by Buxton Filgate's Louth Hall etc. and in general through an interesting corn country. Mac and I saunter into Lord Blaney's[2] picturesque demesne wch his Lordship has quitted (captus amore famae) to accompany General Whitelock to the Rio de la Plata with a fair prospect, I think, of chastising the fanatical perfidy of the Bishops and Monks of Buenos Ayres to the gallant Beresford[3] and Home Popham.[4]

But how their perfidy dwindles in juxtaposition with the malignity of the ex-ministry (Lords Grenville, Howick, St. Vincent &c.) who, instead of hailing and rewarding the conqueror of South America, brought him to trial and procured him to be 'severely censured' (the words of the sentence) by a court-martial.[5]

Why not impeach those insufficient men for their gross mismanagement of public affairs during their (fortunately) short-lived administration? For not making a powerful descent in Pomerania to aid the heroic descendant of Charles 12th and of Gustavus Vasa[6] in raising the north of Germany and making a diversion so formidable in the rear of Buonaparte's as might have relieved Danzig and forced the Usurper to fall back from the Vistula? For not combining with the Allies and urging their joint and concentrated force against the heart of the common enemy, instead of frittering away our strength in detached and feeble expeditions-against the Dardanelles, against Egypt, and where our military character has been tarnished by defeat as our political and moral character has been by drawing the sword upon an ally in profound peace, and where success could have produced no benefit?[7]

In short, the contribution of those trusty guardians of British interests and honour to the common cause was the mighty sum of £80,000 lent to the King of Prussia to redeem his Capital, a sum wch many a private gentleman in England has borrowed upon his estate![8] Hence the late disastrous termination of the war in Poland, and the separate armistice wch the magnanimous Alexander has entered into with France, indignantly and in disgust omitting us, so that by and bye we shall again have the honour and happiness after this prostration and wreck of the rest of the continent to prosecute the contest 'single-handed' with the Great Nation![9] Oh for a Pitt to bring those traitors to the block!

Meantime, while vengeance is preparing for us, while such a storm is brewing against these islands as all our former storms were but whispers to it, our great men, instead of uniting to meet it with the combined energies of the Empire are wasting the precious moments in mutual recrimination, in scolding and billingsgate and scrambling for power and places.[10] So it was with Carthage, torn to pieces by internal divisions and factions, when Scipio walked in one day and settled all differences among them by kindly relieving both parties of all further care and trouble about the government. Does not Gibbon also describe the Greek Empire distracted by petty intestine feuds, the Blues and the Greens fighting and cutting each other's throats in the hippodrome of Constantinople when Solymam took the liberty of interrupting them and without a struggle subjugated the successors of the mighty Roman Empire! -28 miles

Thursday 16th Breakfast where I slept, at Castleblaney. Reach Monaghan about 12 where I find that my associate, Baron McClelland,[11] who arrived last night, has very kindly taken up the Common Court as being considered heavier duty than the Civil. Dine as usual with Mr. Blaney Mitchell. 12 miles.

Friday 17th Both courts rise early and the Baron and I take a delightful ride to Ballyleck, once the beautiful seat of my poor old friend Jack Montgomery,[12] many years the popular and hereditary (for his father had also been) representative of this county.

Saturday 18th Finish all the records, viz. 7 in all.

Sund. 19th We go to prayers wch were given at the Meeting house (the Church being un-roofed) and afterwards proceed to Armagh where we are very politely and

Armagh Cathedral, from Daniel Grose, The Antiquities of Ireland, Roger Stalley Ed. Dublin 1991 (courtesy of Lord Rossmore and the Irish Architectural Archive).

agreeably entertained at dinner at Dr. and Mrs. Carpendale's[13] in company with General and Mrs. Kerr, Sir George and Lady Leith &c. 12 m. On our return home we find cards of invitation from the Primate, being the first instance of his notice of any judges by His Grace.[14] I had, however, on a former occasion received the honour of apology from him for not asking me to dinner as Mrs.Stuart's accouchement was expected every hour. All this is explained by an English recommendation of me to His Grace, who by the bye is a strange eccentric character but a highly educated virtuous gentleman.[15]

Tuesday 20th[16] Spent yesterday and today in the Crown Court - mortified by a long trial wch keeps one in court till 9 and forces me to send an excuse to the Primate. I had a great mind to hang all the prisoners in order to get away at the dining hour, but it is only the Jury who have that privilege and not the Judge: 'And culprits hang that Jurymen may dine'.

Wednesday 21st Get away from Armagh at 5 p.m. after visiting at the Primate's and at Dean Hamilton's.[17] Ride by Hamilton's Bawn, the old seat of the Acheson[18] family immortalized by Swift. Draper's Lodge, long the place of Swift's residence in his parish of Mullabrack, is hard by. Stop for the night at the nice cleanly little inn at Portadown where between 9 and 10 there comes on one of those extraordinary thunder storms wch are so familiar in England and so rare in Ireland. The lightening filled and illuminated the house, the thunder rolled over our heads and the rain descended in torrents.

Thursday 22nd Breakfast at the wretched inn at the wretched town of Moira. Ride after to the Maize Races where I pass four or five hours very pleasantly. Ride round the course (a four mile course). A red sandy soil, very heavy and guttery from the late rains. Piper (called the best horse now in Ireland) belonging to Mr. T. Callwell,[19] Abbot - lately purchased from Lord Donegal[20] by Mr. Joyce, and Little Harry- Mr. Wm. Whaley's - started - 5 to 1 & 6 to 1 on Piper against the field. I get up into the Lady's Box and take 5 to 1 twice. The knowing ones taken in, two very fine heats, each won by Abbot to the mortification of many and the joy of more and the astonishment of all. Piper gave 7 lb 4 in a distance weight for age to Abbot, beat the first heat by 2 or 3 lengths but the 2nd by not quite a whole length. Drive to Belfast where I dine and sleep at the Donegall Arms, an excellent hotel - 30 miles from Armagh.

Friday 23rd July. Breakfast at Carrigfergus[21] (where I find the Baron who had arrived the night before) with the Graveses. Try Records to a late hour. 10 miles.

Saturday 24th Go early to court & call on Lecky against McNaughton[22] wch had been prefixed by me for this day for the accommodation of Plunket who comes down at 150 guineas specially for Petitioner. Array challenged for Defendant by McCartney, for that the Coroner, to whom the writ and distring[23] as had been delivered, returned a panel at the nomination of Petitioner's attorney. The challenge allowed by Plunket[24] and thus a trial of great expectation wch had attracted a crowded auditory, and was likely to employ me to a late hour of evening, fortunately for me goes off. A most audacious, corrupt practice of the attorney and coroner, and proper to be inquired into above.[25]

Sunday 25th We go to prayers and hear an excellent sermon from the Dean of Connor, Graves.[26] The Baron and I ride after prayers to his very respectable friend,

Mr. Kerr's of Red Hall,[27] a very interesting ride of four miles on the road to Larne and an elegant seat. Pass a very agreeable day and return under the seasonable shelter of a chaise.

Monday 26th Wind up the light business of the Assizes. We dine at the Dean's and meet Captain O'Neill,[28] a very honest and deservedly popular fellow knight of the shire. Maraguite, the agreeable little Creole whom the Col. Graves[29] married in Trinidad, amuses us not a little by her naivete. Mrs. Dawson, Lady Asgill, the most wise and sagacious and valiant Genl. Sir Charles Asgill.[30] The Baron leaves us and we join the ladies and have agreeable music from the good-humoured Puffin, Anne. O' Neill at 9 sets off on horseback for home - 21 miles. I send my cavalry to Belfast.

Belfast, Downpatrick and Donaghadee

Tuesday 28th July. I perceive I have been mistaking the day of the month since this day sen'night wch was the 21st but wch I erroneously dated the 20th. The Sheriff, McNaughten, accompanied by his brother, the Member for the county, takes us in his handsome barouche and four English bays to Belfast to breakfast. The Baron and I ride to Johnny Couther's, the Halfway House - 12 miles. Here it was that poor brother Finucane walked into a room in Spring 1798 and seeing it crowded with a large party sitting round a table and paper and ink before them retreated very much disconcerted at his own abrupt intrusion and begging a thousand pardons. The party too retreated pretty precipitately by the back door, and on the Judge's mentioning the adventure and his own rudeness by and bye to the Sheriff, "Good God (exclaimed the latter) that is the committee of United Irishmen whom I have been for some days looking for," and ran into the house with his bailiffs. But by this time the committee were long dispersed in various directions. Proceed under cover of heavy rain to Down and dine with Mr. Thompson, the Sheriff, and the Grand Jury.

Wedn. 29th July. Charge the Grand Jury, Mr. Savage M.P. Foreman. Commend them for the improved state of the circuit road and "lowering the Hills of the county Down" (alluding to a popular toast once in this county among the opponents of Hill, the Marquis of Downshire)[31] and I recommend to them as a better expedient "to circumvent the Hills" i.e. to carry their roads where possible round the base pursuant to the Statute. Try four Records for the Baron.

Th. 30th Finish the Crown business & rule the book Maiden Assizes,[32] & what is more grateful a Maiden circuit hitherto.

Fr. 31st The Baron is enabled by my assistance to leave town this morning for his house near Dundalk a day sooner than he expected, & in return he very kindly undertakes to do all the business civil and criminal of Dundalk and Drogheda,[33] leaving me at liberty to proceed from hence to Donaghadee (25 m.) & and thus save above 100 miles of ground to my horses and about a week of time to myself

Breakfast with Mat. Franks & wife[34]; engage them to dine. Spend 3 or 4 dull hours at presentments. Intelligence arrives of an action between the Leopard (Captain Humphreys) & an American frigate, the Chesapeak, who refuses to deliver up deserters or to be searched. After a number of Americans kill'd she strikes and after the deserters are taken out she is dismiss'd.[35] Will this involve us with America? the Universe against poor old England! But poor old England in a righteous cause defies the Universe. Independence or annihilation! This is another of the favours wch we owe to the "Talents" who made such pusillanimous concessions in negotiating with the Yankees as have intoxicated and inflated into insufferable insolence those upstart bullies. Nothing but primness, temperd and regulated by moderation, will control their incroaching & arrogant spirit. The Navigation Laws alas ! are given up.[36]

Sat. 1st Augt. Drive out to my friend Ward[37] at Castleward - 5 miles - & spend the day with him. The lunatic Lord Bangor, his brother, dines with us, so decent and correct in his manners and appearance that it could never occur to a stranger that he is lunatic.[38] Ward presses me to visit Lady Arabella[39] at their house - Holyhill Fareham (Hampshire) - before I return from England, and promises she shall show me the dockyard and all the lions, and so I will if I can spare time.

Sund.2nd Aug. Ride to Castlewellan to meet my dear little wife who arrives this morning by appointment safe and well from Dublin. But before her arrival I call on my old friend Lord Annesley[40] who takes me to see his charming grounds wch in truth combine great variety of beauty: a mountain wooded mostly with holly, at the base of wch stands his elegant ground-floor Lodge surrounded by an highly-polished lawn & fronting a beautiful lake. The old Grange built by his father looks more like a town than a collection of offices, and without exaggeration would accommodate a regiment. The garden containing seven acres is inclosed by a Castle wall ten feet high and lined with brick, another great performance by the late Earl who had projected also a Chateau upon a suitable scale. The well-dressed lads and lasses are suffered by my benevolent friend to pass through his gates along of the lake and even by the walks under his windows to prayers of a Sunday, & give gaiety and animation to the landscape. After this ramble of about 2 hours we return to the town, and, finding Mrs. Day arrived, his Lordship takes us to breakfast at his present house, wch when he gets into the Lodge will answer very well for a respectable inn. Receive a very friendly and pressing letter of invitation from Mat. Forde for us both to pass the day and night at his house, but am forced to decline it and I return with Mrs. Day to Downpatrick on our way to Donaghadee.

M.3d Send back the postilion with two of my horses to Loughlinstown[41] and proceed with the other three and Thomas and Terence to Donaghadee by Cumber- 25 miles. Dine & sleep there.

1. An inn about six miles north of Swords *(The Post-Chaise Companion, or Traveller's Directory of Ireland,* 3rd edn., Dublin 1803).

2. Andrew Thomas Blayney (1770-1834), 11th Lord Blayney, the builder of the modern town of Castleblaney. A famous soldier, he commanded the 89th Regiment of Foot during the war in the Peninsula.

3. General William Carr Beresford (1768-1854). Illegitimate son of George de la Poer Beresford, first Marquess of Waterford. At Buenos Aires with Sir Home Popham, 1806, where he was forced to capitulate, was imprisoned, but escaped to England.

4. Sir Home Popham (1762-1820), Rear-Admiral, left the Cape of Good Hope unguarded in order to attack Buenos Aires with troops under the command of William Carr Beresford. They captured

Buenos Aires in early July of 1806 but lost it some days later and became prisoners. The government sent John Whitelocke at the head of an expeditionary force to the Plate, but Whitelocke took and then lost (12 September) Buenos Aires and returned to a court marshal where he was sentenced to be cashiered.

5. Though the city of London considered him a hero, Home Popham was tried in March 1807 and 'severely reprimanded'. Howick is Charles Grey, 2nd Earl; St. Vincent is John Jervis, First Lord of the Admiralty under the Addington administration when his reforms in the navy drew strong criticism from Pitt among others, and Commander of the Fleet under the 'Talents'.

6. Gustavus IV of Sweden. The royal house of Sweden (Vasa) was related by marriage to that of Prussia (Hohenzollern), both, together with Britain, standard bearers of the Reformation in northern Europe. Gustavus's father, Gustavus III, was assassinated in 1792 coming from a masked ball (subject of the Verdi opera). Day saw the slain monarch in heroic light for having reduced the powers of the Swedish nobility.

7. In late 1806 the 'Talents' sent a squadron under Admiral Duckworth to force a passage through the Dardanelles. The Turks resisted successfully. 6000 men occupied Alexandria to prevent another French attack on Egypt, but they were eventually forced to withdraw after much bloodshed.

8. British assistance to Prussia had amounted to only £80,000.

9. The Treaty of Tilsit, July 1807, between Napoleon and Emperor Alexander of Russia was, in Day's view, the product of the failures of the 'Talents'. It meant the defeat of the allies and the isolation of Britain. It permitted a division of the French army to invade Swedish Pomerania, and Russia to invade Finland. Danzig surrendered to the French some weeks previously in May.

10. The Tories remained divided between those who joined Pitt to support Addington's lacklustre administration in 1804, and hawks such as Canning who remained aloof. This difference first emerged after the Peace of Amiens.

11. Baron Mc Clelland (1768-1831). Of Millmount, Co. Down. BA, Trinity, 1787, Middle Temple, Irish bar 1790. MP Randalstown 1790. Supported the Act of Union. Solicitor General 1801, Baron of the Court of Exchequer 1803.

12. John Montgomery, MP County Monaghan in the parliaments of 1783-1790 and 1790-1797.

13. Thomas Carpendale MA was appointed headmaster of Armagh Royal School 1786 by Archbishop Robinson. Vicar Choral 1804; died in the fever epidemic on 18 October 1817 while still headmaster.

14. William Stuart (1755-1822), Archbishop of Armagh 1800-1822, previously Canon of Christchurch, Oxford, thereafter Bishop of St David's. He was son of the 3rd Earl of Bute. The Archbishop's wife (m. 1796) was Margaret Juliana, daughter of Thomas Penn of Stoke Poges *(Debret's Peerage)*.

15. Primate Stuart opposed a Union engagement to appoint the son of John Beresford, Chief Commissioner of the Revenue, bishop of Kilmore. His opposition – unsuccessful - was on grounds of personal unsuitability. Cf. Michael MacDonagh, *The Viceroy's Post-Bag*, London 1904, pp. 98-119. Stuart was hostile to Catholic emancipation.

16. He errs in the date, but recovers below.

17. Rev James Archibald Hamilton (1748-1815), Prebend of Tynan 1790, Archdeacon of Ross and Prebend of Mullabrack 1790-1804, Dean of Cloyne 1804-15. Primate Robinson appointed him first astronomer of Armagh Observatory (James Blennerhassett Leslie, *Armagh Clergy and Parishes*, Dundalk 1911, p. 62).

18. Acheson, earls of Gosford, Armagh magnates. Jonathan Swift's satirical poem *The Grand Question*

Debated considered the dilemma of Sir Arthur Acheson (1688-1749) on what to do with his property at Hamilton's Bawn: whether to convert it to a government barracks or to a malt-house for making beer.

19. Caldwells of Ballymoney?

20. The Chichesters, marquesses of Donegal, controlled Belfast corporation.

21. Carrickfergus held the assizes for both the town and the county of Antrim. It was also the residence of Rev. Thomas Graves, Dean of Connor.

22. John Gage Lecky Esq., a magistrate, plaintiff, Edmond Alexander MacNaghten, MP for Antrim, defendant. This was an action for defamation, plaintiff alleging that McNaghten had removed him unfairly from the commission of the peace. See *Freeman's Journal,* 30 July, 1807.

23. distringas (L) 'thou shalt distrain': writ directing a sheriff to distrain, in this case to empannel a jury.

24. William Conygham Plunket (1764-1854), Solicitor-General 1803, Attorney-General 1805; resigned rather than serve under the Tories who were returned to power by this time in 1807. His successor as AG was the Huguenot William Saurin, who leads the prosecution of the Catholic delegates and the editor John Magee in the later years of this book.

25. As McNaghten's brother was Sheriff the nomination of jury men was made by the Coroner; but his choice was dictated by the plaintiff's attorney, causing Macartney, counsel for McNaghten, to challenge the array on the basis that 'the fountain of justice had been polluted'. Plunket allowed the challenge. (*Freeman's Journal,* 30 July, 1807.)

26. Rev. Thomas Graves, 1745-1828; 1771 Rector of Ballymacelligott and Nohaval, 1785 Dean of Ardfert, 1802 Dean of Connor, 1811-1828 Rector of Rincurran (Kinsale). His father was Rector of Kilfinane and Darragh in Co. Limerick. Elsewhere Day states that he and Graves are relatives.

27. Red Hall, the seat of Richard Gervase Ker, in the parish of Broadisland overlooking Larne Lough.

28. Major John Bruce Richard O'Neill, MP County Antrim 1807.

29. Major-General James William Graves, Col. Commanding the 18th Royal Irish Regiment. Son of Rev. Thomas. Born 1774, m. Marie Victoire Black in Trinidad, 1802. The Duke of Wellington recommended their son, John Crosbie Graves, for the Bombay Cavalry in 1836, (British Library, India and Oriental Room, *Cadet Papers* L/mil/9/184/595.)

30. Gen. Sir Charles Asgill (1762 or 3-1823). Soldiered in America and was taken prisoner at Yorktown. Helped suppress the Rebellion of 1798. He m. (1788) Sophia, daughter of Admiral Sir Charles Ogle.

31. Arthur Blundell Sandys Trumbull Hill (1788-1845), 3rd Marquess of Downshire; succeeded in 1803.

32. Assizes were 'maiden' when no capital sentence was passed.

33. Assizes were held for the town of Drogheda, and for County Louth at Dundalk.

34. Matthew Franks, 1768-1853, of Jerpoint Co. Kilkenny and 17 York St. Dublin. Son of Thomas Franks of Ballymagooly Co.Cork and his wife, Judge Day's sister Catherine. Matthew was Judge Day's 'register' on circuit.

35. Britain responded to Napoleon's continental blockade with the Orders in Council, which placed restrictions on neutral trade with Europe and affected American trade in particular. The British

claim to search neutral vessels enabled *HMS Leopard* to take off a deserter and three others of ambiguous citizenship from the *USS Chesapeake* ten miles off Cape Henry.

36. The Navigation Laws confined the imports of the American colonies to goods carried in British vessels. In Ireland the achievement of 'Free Trade' in 1779 by the Volunteer campaign admitted Ireland to the trade with the West Indies. Day may have sympathised with America's predicament, but the same Navigation Laws commenced the difficulties with the mother country, and now the circumstances of war with Napoleon warranted restrictions on the movements of foreign vessels.

37. Edward Ward (1753-1812) MP.

38. Nicholas, 2nd Viscount Bangor, (dunm. 1827), elder brother of Edward Ward. He was the subject of a statute in 1785 to vest the leasing of the estate in his brother and other trustees (see *Journals of the Irish House of Commons,* vol xi, 30 May, 1785).

39. Arabella Crosbie of Ardfert Abbey, County Kerry, sister to John, 2nd Earl Glandore, m. Edward Ward in 1783.

40. Richard Annesley 2nd Earl of Annesley (1745-1824). Member of the Irish Parliament for various places. His mother was daughter of Beresford, first Earl of Tyrone, a powerful parliamentary interest.

41. The owners of Loughlinstown House were the Domville family. Day leased it from 1798, the year of his elevation to the court of King's Bench, and resided there to his death in 1841 (Registry of Deeds, Dublin, Book 515, page 405, no. 335669).

In Scotland

Georgian philanthropy expected little from the state but much from private individuals and the parish. In Scotland there is much to admire in the educational system of the Kirk and in the frugal life style of the Presbyterian ministers. An obvious contrast is drawn with the neglect and non-residency of ministers of the Established church in England and Ireland.

Port Patrick, Stranraer, Glenluce, Newtown Stewart

Tuesd. 4th The packets are all detained at the other side so I prevail, not without difficulty, on Mrs. Day to commit herself with me to a comfortable Trader full of horses, and we make a very fine passage of 5 hours. But I confess I can never apply the epithet fine to a passage by water, unless it be very fine to be very miserable the whole way. In fact we were as sick as dogs. But let me not be insensible to the goodness of Providence: if there was no pleasure there was no danger, and sea sickness even has its votaries. On landing we found Collector and Lady Harriet Skeffington,[1] Mrs.

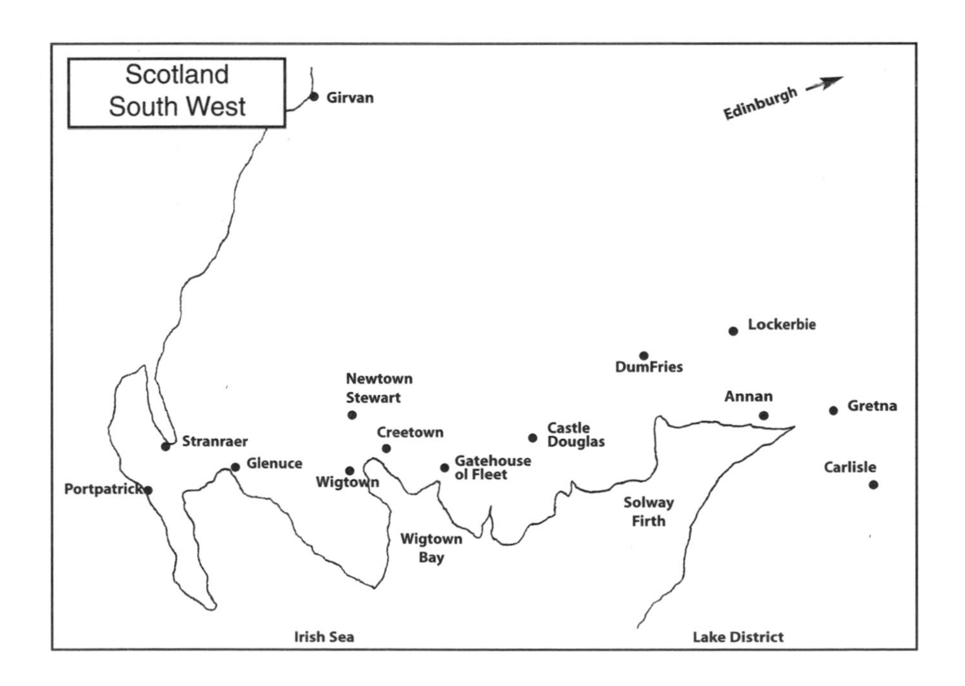

Lawlor and her son, Mr. Crumpe[2] with others waiting for the wind-bound packet. The little inn being occupied, we proceed over the rugged wretched road to Stranraer - 6 miles - & are very comfortably accommodated at the King's Arms. N.B. there is a new line of road carrying on 2 miles round, but through a less irregular country, & therefore the present very absurdly is neglected.

W.5th Visit at an early hour the strand - some thousand mazes of herrings taken last night, 500 to the maze - the like not known there 20 years before. Lord Stair[3] the Lord of the soil much complained of. Visits this country for one month in the year in the shooting season, and that without a single companion. Reserved and selfish, thrown out of the representation of the Scotch peerage at the late election "for voting (to use the words of a braa cheeld of the north to me this morning) for the Papists". [4] Drive over a charming road through his fine plantation and am prevented by the envious bad weather from riding into his demesne & taking a nearer view of the ruins of Castle Kennedy. Stop at Glenluce - 10 m. - for the night.

Th. 5th Well accommodated by the boozy Scott, McCrae, at the Maxwell Arms. Sir John Hay the proprietor of this town and estate. I get on horseback and ride through a very dreary country, for the most part of moss and moor, but over a very fine road save for the first 6 miles wch are not yet finished.

Newtown Stewart

Approaching Newtown Stewart the country softens and improves. Mr. Boyd within 2 miles of the town is planting and reclaiming. The town situated on the Cree, a handsome river in the bottom of a well-planted amphitheatre where Sir John Maxwell's house and woods appear to great advantage. Stop to breakfast at the Golden Lion - 16 m. from Glenluce.

Visit the little parish school. Education universal in Scotland, so much so that a parent would be discarded as an alien and an outcast of society who did not send his children to school. All are taught to read, write and generally some elementary smattering of arithmetic, hence no idler known, no offence ever committed, but all are disciplined from the shell. (Quaere, if this tends not to lift them above their condition and tempts them upon emigration & adventure.)

The ordinary tillage & layout of the country are mostly executed by travelling Irish, who, overflowing in their own country, are employed in these thinly-inhabited regions at a very advanced price. This neat town the property of Lord Galloway whose possessions are very extensive. The character of this young Peer not yet understood, but the late Earl was idolized. In the American war cattle bore no price and the tenantry would have been ruined but that he bought up every man's stock, so that instead of receiving rent his Lordship had money to pay to every tenant. Being asked by an English gentleman how much a square acre did he generally let his grounds at, "Square acre! (replied he), Square mile is the measurement that I give my claim".

The bridge was carried away last December, so we cross the Cree in a very good ferry-boat, & I ride under Sir John Maxwell's woods etc. till we reach Cree Town - 8 m.- the property of Mr. McCullach, where we feed & from thence 11 m. more to Gatehouse.[5] If the ride before breakfast was dreary & desolate, the rest of the day's journey made ample amends. A more beautiful and picturesque country I have seldom travelled than the 19 miles from New Town Stewart, but particularly the last 11 wch conduct the traveller over a very fine road with the Wigton Bay on one side and Mr. Hannay's, Sir David Maxwell's & other luxuriant woods hanging over the road on the other. Pass by some handsome seats: W.M Kenzie's whose place reminds one of Glinn, but a much more highly-finished scene; another M McCulloch. But towering above all is Murray of Broughton.[6]

The Gatehouse of Fleet, Castle Douglas

The town commands the Bay & stands in the foreground of a bold but well-dress'd & planted Country. N.B. Not at all fatigued by a ride of 35 miles.

Fr. 7 Aug. Sleep at Sloan's, the King's Arms. Clean and comfortable in the highest degree. One who knows nothing but what he reads of Scotland would scarcely believe that cleanliness is the universal striking feature of the people. Their towns are neat & cleanly, their houses are cleanly, their persons cleanly. Either Johnson[7] was a foul libeller, or the people are much improved since his day. We rise early & stroll into Cally, the fine seat of Murray Laird of Broughton within a mile of the town. The footman by order of his Mistress invites us in & shows us the principal apartments of the noble mansion. Among the pictures of the great saloon, Pilate Questioning Our Saviour deserves particular notice. In our progress we picked up a little domestic scandal. The late Laird who built the house had been married to Lady Catherine Stewart, sister of the late Earl of Galloway. After some years cohabitation he eloped with a Miss Johnstone, who tho' Governess of his daughter was a young lady of respectable Scots family, & rambled thro' England & the Continent with her under a concealed character. His daughter at length died & a formal separation then taking

Castle Howard

place between him and his Lady, he and his Mistress returned to Cally where they resided until 1793 when he died leaving 2 sons now living. His great possessions belong to the eldest, a promising youth of 18 upon the point of entering in Cambridge. Their Mother (who is called the Widow of Murray though Lady Catherine still lives) is represented to be most amiable, exemplary & religious. She had assumed the name of Murray, but her Ladyship upon her husband's death remonstrated in a correspondence with her upon this liberty, in consequence of wch she immediately dropped the name & resumed her own, and even her sons' letters to her are always directed to Mrs. Johnstone.

Proceed after breakfast to a very fine country diversified by verdant hills & hollows. Nothing through this journey more striking after passing through the crowded population of Ulster than the uninhabited and undivided state of the county of Wigton and even of the Stewarty, or Shire, of Kirkcudbright wch we have been in since we left Newton Stewart. The whole country is stocked with Moyleys, i.e. hornless cattle of all colours but mostly black and a large proportion of them white-faced like the Hereford breed. They seem a beautiful breed of cattle, very light about the head & neck & heavy in the hind quarters, soft and sleek skin, & as it would seem more inclined to flesh than milk.

Cross the fine river Dee & ride into Castle-Douglas (a stage of 14 miles). Neat & clean like every other where we have seen, upon the margin of a pretty loch. The estate of Sir William Douglas,[8] Laird of Douglas Castle, an old money-making bachelor who, not contented with the rents and produce of his large estates, has a finger in a cotton manufactory in this village and in a bank and other establishments. He pushed at the late election to bring in his nephew for the county, but finding that nail would not drive he united with Lord Galloway's interest against Lord Selkirk, & Mr. Montgomery Stewart, brother of the former, was returned.

Another family anecdote. John Anderson the purchaser of the Forward estate & the Barrymore estate, the founder of Fermoy, last year the High Sheriff of the Co. of Cork, was son of the Jailer of Dumfries.[9] His bror. was a chaise driver from this town but died early. This I have from Douglas, the father of the Inn-keeper of this town, who was his school-fellow. I state this to show what a clear head and enterprising spirit regulated by good manners and & an excellent heart can accomplish. Such is the benevolence of this little man that in his ascent he has reached out his hand to several & raised them to independence & comfort. He established Mail coaches amongst us, gave us roads excelled only by the great avenues into London, built the most elegant town that any individual in either Island can boast of, and, in short, while advancing himself, this little son of a Jailer has been a benefactor and a blessing to the country to wch he has emigrated.

Dumfries, Annan.

Sat. 8 August. Rise with the lark. Back for half an hour at the turnpike. Ride for 2 miles by the side of a handsome sheet of water. Pass by a romantic well-wooded Glen in our descent into the plain where Dumfries lies. Arrive at the King's Arms to breakfast - 19 m. from Castle Douglas. A spacious, handsome town situated on the river Nith. Visit the Jail (where I found but 2 prisoners) & the Court-house constructed with form of an Amphitheatre. The two judges sit together & beside them the Minister who opens the court always by prayers. It is still more formal in England, for there the Judges of Assize are conducted by the Sheriff, Lord Lieut. & other considerable personages of the Court in solemn procession upon their arrival in the Town to Church, where prayers & an Assize Sermon are delivered. It is only in Ireland that all grave and venerable Solemnities are despised & the Sacred Institutions of old times are trampled upon. An active spirit of building seems to progress this town, favoured no doubt by the fine quarries in the neighbourhood of red free-stone; & Buccleuch-Street connecting the new bridge with the old town promises when finished to be a handsome street. All the cottages round the town are constructed of that stone wch with the decent dispositions of the people gives an air of neatness & comfort to the whole country.

Travel forward in the evening to Annan - 16 m - of wch we walk about 3 miles till we reach the summit of the acclivity from whence we survey with great delight the magnificent Solway Firth bounded on the side of England by the sublime Cumberland Mountains. Stop for the night at Mrs. Rickard's Inn upon the road having travelled this day 35 miles. The country improving rapidly. Lime imported from Whitehaven sold from 1s. to 1.6d. The Winchester Bushel[10] is drawn... 30 miles into the interior of the country & laid out at the rate of 50 bushels to the Scotch acre.

Sund. 9 Augt. Resolve to lie by and indulge ourselves & cavalcade at this good Inn during the Sabbath, but are awakened by the clattering of horses so loud in the stable-yard that I conceived it must have been the arrival of a troop of dragoons. On looking into the yard it turns out to be only Lord Abercorn[11] & suite with 24 horses 24 Servants & 4 carriages on their route to Ireland.

After breakfast we repair to Kirk wch was full even to overflowing. It was too suffocating to attempt to press in so we content ourselves with taking our post with many others at one of the doors, in full view & hearing however of the minister who canted away very much in the accent & with the lungs of my good Lord Bishop of Elphin[12] who by the bye was bred & born at Carlisle in the next county & was son to the late worthy Bishop of Carlisle.[13] He[14] married a very amicable woman, the widow Tomlinson, his present wife, mother of a gentleman of large estate & handsome seat near Carlisle.

I said "with the accent & lungs of Law", but alas! not with his talents or good sense. Yet the congregation seemed much impressed with the zeal of their pastor & joined universally & devoutly in singing the psalms & listened with great attention to the discourse composed of trite unconnected observations & crowded with numerous extracts from Scripture. But the fair way of judging of a tree is by its fruit. Not a human being was to be seen in the street from 11 to 2, or from 4 to 6 - for all were at morning & evening prayers. It was not like the Popish congregation who retire from devotion to the dramshop & give up the evening of their Sabbath to drunkenness, debauchery & riot. It was not like the Protestant church, attended only by women & a few quizzical men, while the majority are walking up and down the street in front of the Church cracking vapid jokes upon religion, or scatter'd thro' the country on parties of pleasure, or engaged in professional or other worldly occupation, forgetting altogether that "this is the Lord's Day". After prayers we find them walking in cheerful groups along the banks of the beautiful Annan in nice & gay attire & content & comfort in their ruddy countenances.

What is the reason why the Scotch peasantry are the most moral, amenable, sober, exemplary & honest of H.M.'s subjects? This is a political problem of the greatest importance to resolve. The only cause that I can discover is education, the Universality of Education in Scotland, & that in its commencement always religious. Accordingly, it was pleasing to see every one of the congregation down to the humblest produce a pocket Bible, or at least reading out of a neighbour's, when references were made by the Minister to Scripture. A well-dressed young man with chestnut locks a sun-burnt face & the rugged hands of a plowman seeing me without a Bible invited me to participate in his, & turned over from extract to extract with the celerity of the best-educated reader, & it is known that on the Sabbath evenings the young ones of every family read large portions of both Testaments with great avidity. Here then is an object wch their education however limited enables them to attain - for wch from early habits they acquire a taste & in wch they take great delight - an object wch interests their curiosity & improves their hearts. The tippling houses, therefore, wch in England & still more in Ireland are crowded on Sundays by illiterate peasantry for want of other means of occupation, in Scotland have but scanty custom. Those hot-beds of riot, immorality and disaffection & all manner of crime boast but a few plants of Scottish growth. In the late debate on Mr. Whitbread's bill for establishing parochial schools it was hardly to be believed that a man of the talents and literature of Mr. Wyndham[15] would have opposed and profess'd himself hostile to the education of the poor. But if Mr. Windham be one of the most ingenious, he is also one of the most eccentric of mankind. With a heart of great tenderness & sensibility he professed himself a friend to bull-beating & an enemy to the abolition of the slave trade. With a mind well stored with various learning & drawing much solid benefits from his solid acquirements, he denies that education will enlighten, soften or civilize![16]...dedicisse fidiliter artes...mores...[17]

But I do not want any refinement of education. I wish that some may learn to write and cypher according to the aptitude and capacity they may display for learning, but let all be taught to read, & let the book they are taught in be, not Guy Earl of Warwick or Don Belianos of Greece or any such trash, but the Bible. But in Ireland it is objected that as the two Religions are not agreed in their version of the Old Testament the Protestant Bible will not answer universally. Then I answer let both Religions be instructed from infancy in the New Testament about wch. they agree; & as to the Old Testament let each thumb away his own version of it - nocturna versate manu versate diurna. I laugh at the pretty subtleties & metaphysical distinctions wch are raised between the two Persuasions. The hostility is kept up by priest-craft, avarice & ambition for wordly & not spiritual purposes, but for the clergy the priests & politicians of both persuasions it would be easy to bring them both to a fair & friendly understanding.

Besides the universality of a religious education the conduct and example of the clergy have considerable effect upon the general morals of the Scotch. The Catholic Priest receives the private confession of his parishioners, inflicts a penance, grants absolution for the past, & leaves them to open a fresh account of offences & sins. The

Protestant Parson fattens in luxury & laziness upon his rich benefices, a non-resident, pluralist & voluptuary at Bath or some other fashionable haunt of profligacy, leaving the souls of his fleeced flock to the care of a half-starved, contemptible curate who gabbles through the service one day in the week while through the remainder he exhibits an example the contrast of his doctrine. But the Presbyterian minister always resides & never acts by deputy, not contented with dedicating the Sabbath to devotion & prayers (I speak of Scotland) he visits his parishoners through the week & looks into their general conduct – the progress of the young in religious education, & the perseverance of the aged in a moral & exemplary course of life, instructing reproving or comforting them as occasion requires. By this system of constant visitation he becomes instantly acquainted with any immorality or lapse from virtue, & by refusing all quarter or compromise he rebukes & shames the sinner back to the right path.

In short, my panacea for England & Ireland would be parochial religious education, not forgetting a Sunday School in every church & chapel; to raise the Income of small livings and curacies at the expence of the overgrown, & thus nearly level all to a moderate but respectable independence; disallow pluralities & enforce residence, & further in Ireland to commute Tithes for their full equivalent, out of wch the Protestant clergy may continue to enjoy their present income but distributed more nearly to equality, & a decent provision might also be furnished for the Catholic Clergy to be in the patronage of Government. This in its effects as well as principle would resemble the Regium Donum or Parliamentary provision in Ireland for the Presbyterian clergy, who thereby have been converted from a Republican, disaffected faction into the warmest stick-law for H.M.'s government & the Monarchy.

N. B. From Portpatrick to Longtown 118 miles - of wch I rode 84. The indefatigable Doctor Duigenan[18] seems to have bit me. But the worthy old Doctor's familiar airing on horseback is from Holyhead to London & back again, so that I must not be named in one day with him.

1. Chichester Skeffington, Collector of the Revenue for the port of Belfast, previously MP for County Antrim in the Irish parliament. Married Harriet Jocelyn, daughter of the first Earl of Roden, (*The Gentleman's and Citizen's Almanac, 1808*).

2. Crump was a well known medical family in Judge Day's native town, Tralee.

3. John Dalrymple 6th Earl of Stair, one of the Representative Peers of Scotland 1790-1807 and 1820-1821. British Ambassador to the court of Prussia. D.S.P. June 1 1821.

4. The 'Catholic Officers' bill caused the collapse of the 'Talents' ministry. It was an uncomfortable situation for the writer who, though a Tory, was sympathetic to the bill. The same ministry passed the anti-slavery legislation which banned slave transport from Africa to the New World, a subject on which he was also in agreement.

5. The Gate House of Fleet.

6. James Murray had come from Ireland where his family owned a huge estate in Donegal. He built Cally House and the village, Gatehouse of Fleet, beginning in 1759. He married the sister of the Earl of Galloway.

7. Dr Samuel Johnson visited Scotland in 1773 while the writer was a student at the Middle Temple. Accounts of the opening night of the new play, *She Stoops to Conquer*, by Oliver Goldsmith, in 1774 place Johnson in the audience on the opening night; a letter from the retired Judge Day to Goldsmith's biographer, Prior, places the young Robert Day in the pit during the same performance where he acted as security against the anticipated danger of audience disruption (see Appendix 5). In the event there was no trouble and the play proved an immediate success.

8. Sir William Douglas made a fortune in the Virginia trade having begun his career as the 'Pedlar of Penninghame'. He bought Carlingwark and surrounding land for 2000 pounds. The town was made a Burgh of Barony in 1792 and renamed Castle Douglas.

9. Day had an additional interest in Fermoy: it was home to his sister-in-law, Barbara Forward, wife of his brother, Rev. Archdeacon Edward Day of Beaufort.

10. The Winchester Bushel, described as a measure used in England from the time of Henry the Eighth.

11. John James Hamilton (1756-1818) 9th Earl of Abercor. (op. cit.)

12. John Law became Archdeacon of Carlisle, later Bishop of Clonfert from 1782, Killala 1787 and Elphin 1795-1810. His wife was Anne Thomlinson, a widow. They had no family. Like Day, the Bishop of Killala gave parliamentary support to the Catholic relief legislation of 1792-3, occasioning an attack on him from Chancellor Fitzgibbon, Lord Clare. At Killala his distribution of Catholic literature in the interests of moral improvement was an acceptance of the failure of his own church's mission among the majority. He defied the rebels in 1798.

13. Edmund Law (1703-1787), Bishop of Carlisle 1768-1787, father of the Bishop of Elphin. Previously Master of Peterhouse, Cambridge, where he was a leading representative of heteredox opinion within anglicanism; published anonymously his *Considerations on the Propriety of Requiring Subscriptions to Articles of Faith* in 1774 during the Non-Conformist campaign agains subscription to the Thirty-Nine Articles of the Church of England.

14. John Law, Bishop of Elphin, op. cit.

15. William Windham (1750-1810), Chief Secretary in Ireland under Northington in 1783. Joined Pitt in 1794 and advocated a vigorous prosecution of the war, opposing the preliminary peace terms of October 1801.

16. The Whitbread bill provided an entitlment to two years free education for children from seven to fourteen whose parents were unable to pay. In addition to opposing the Parochial Schools Act, Windham opposed the abolition of the slave trade for its detrimental effect on English commerce, also because he believed that the French and other powers would take up England's portion of the trade, and because he considered the measure to be ill-advised while Britain was at war. Day was an enthusiastic supporter of the Militia Transfer bill which Windham opposed during the parliamentary debates that August.

17. 'to have studied faithfully the arts ... manners ...'

18. Patrick Duigenan (1735-1816). Born a Catholic in Co. Leitrim, conformed to Anglicanism and followed a brilliant career in Dublin University. Called to the Irish bar 1767, King's Counsel 1784. MP Old Leighlin 1791, Armagh 1798. Supported the Union. Was vehemently anti-Catholic in parliaments before and after the Union.

England: her Northern Magnates and the Jails of Northumberland

The time he devotes to visiting the prisons in the north of England is consistent with his record on prison and penal reform in Ireland. He is also something of a historian and antiquarian. William Howard, Earl of Carlisle, was son of the executed 4th Duke of Norfolk who was connected with the Northern Rebellion against Queen Elizabeth in 1569. The son remained true to the old religion whose standard was raised by the Rebellion and which enjoyed the allegiance of the house of Norfolk. It is likely that his admiration for the son is equally founded on William's creation of a northern outpost for what Day often called 'the arts of peace and civilization'. Day had great admiration for the great Tudor law giver, Henry VII, while he preferred the moderate Protestantism of the Tudors to the later excesses of the Puritans during the reigns of the Stuarts. But first, as he prepares to cross the border into England, he passes through Gretna, where he bears reluctant witness to the phenomenon of civil marriages for runaway English couples.

M 10th Augt. Quit Mrs. Rickard's & the comfortable inn at an early hour & ride to the Longtown (10m.) in Cumberland having entered England at the turnpike a mile before you reach the town. Cross the Solway Moss, called here the "Solway Floo", famous for having travelled some 20 or 30 years ago (qu. if not in 1771) from its primaeval station forward carrying hedges & even houses in its progress till it entered the Solway Firth. A similar phenomenon took place not many years since in the Co. Limerick. The bog got bloated with obstructed water, wch at length, bursting "its cearments",[1] with great impetuosity wasted the loosened bog upon its surface down the side of an inclined plain until the water got disengaged &, finding vent, worked out a channel for itself.

Pass thro' Gretna Green & Springfield, a village on the Scotch side of the marsh (i.e. bounds), & there see Jo. Paisley[2] the famous matrimonial artist, the Tinker who solders together the impatient runaway inamoratos from England & Ireland. Upon inquiry there seem some doubts entertained whether this cobbled operation, this scandalous farce, amounts in Scotland to a valid marriage. For if valid there, it must be valid every where.[3] A marriage performed according to the ceremonies & ordinances of any country in wch it is performed is valid in every other. The regular and accustomed form of marriage in Scotland is similar to that of the England and Irish church: the Banns are published on three succeeding Sundays, & the Minister either in Church or at any private house joins the pair in wedlock in presence of witnesses, without, however, the use of a ring. But it is admitted that a marriage performed in presence & by the mediation of a magistrate is precisely as valid & therefore not infrequent, the Minister however, refusing to admit the parties to the rites of the church till they shall express their sorrow & be rebuked in open church. Marriage, in short, in Scotland is a mere civil contract, & even those who deny the validity of Jo Paisley's performance as a marriage admit its obligation as a contract. The parties covenanting in presence of witnesses to cohabit for ever as man & wife are bound by such agreement. They can not after separate. Or if he put her away he is bound to support her, & neither can ever enter into any matrimonial contract during the life of the other. But the children (say they) are spurious & and can not inherit, unless the parents after marry in due form wch legitimates the prior children born out of wedlock.

On the other hand, it is contended that the contract thus entered into in presence & by the ministry of the Tinker, however revolting to every sentiment of delicacy propriety and decorum, enures[4] in Scotland, & consequently, if performed in Scotland all over the world as a perfect legal & valid marriage, that the parties not only are inseparable, but that the issue are legitimate, & that in all its effects and consequences it possesses all the obligation & quality of the most formal marriage. The only inconvenience suffered is what is also inflicted on parties married before a magistrate, that the Minister will not recognise them as married, will not baptize their children, church the wife, or admit them to any of the rites (quaere rights) of the church until rebuked. And this they insist is an assumption & usurpation of the Ministry who for the purpose of giving greater publicity & solemnity to the most important contract that can be enter'd into in society (no one will insinuate that it can be for engrossing to themselves a source of great profit!) inculcate the necessity & duty of publication by Banns. And to this opinion I incline. If marriage be but a civil contract among the Presbyterians, it should seem that all that was necessary to its validity (as to that of all other contracts) was the free consent & concurrence of both parties; that for its security & the facility of proof the contract ought to be enter'd into coram lestes, & that the Minister, the Magistrate or the Tinker are alike competent to the function of witness.

Longtown consists of two wide, neat, brick streets intersecting at right angles, the estate of Sir James Graham. Here we call a council upon the advisable line to London & resolve to decline the direct & shorter road by Carlisle (having taken that route in 1801) to proceed across the narrow neck of England to Newcastle & so descend by the eastern side of the island upon London. Accordingly, at the turnpike we quit the Carlisle road & turn into the bye-road across the river Line wch conducts us through a poor mossy country 12 m. to Brampton. Here I see for the first time the extraordinary convenience of the Rail-way or Iron Roads for the conveyance of coals. With the slightest declivity or even on an horizontal surface one horse draws ten ton coals with little or no exertion. At Brampton two roads to Newcastle contend for preference, one through Hexham wch the stage coach travels & is the more frequented, the other by Chollerford through an open-field naked country; both good roads but the latter shorter by a mile. I prefer the latter because I learn that the Roman wall accompanies a great part of it.

Three miles from the town I alight & prevail upon my little fellow traveller to walk down to Naworth Castle,[5] the Earl of Carlisle's, of wch we take a rapid view. It encloses a Square or Court into wch several doors open like a college quodrangle. Enter the great Hall occupying one of the four sides ninety long & finely proportioned; pass on through two rooms hung with tapestry in fine preservation. Queen Mary's portrait, wch from its tawdry drapery, full-puffed ruff & stays from chin downwards, I mistook for Elizabeth's till I perceived the crucifix in her right hand, the sceptre in her left. Proceed to Lord William Howard's old bedroom, the original bed wth plaid curtains still standing, & up by a narrow spiral staircase to his Library containing all the musty monkish works of his day scattered in great & blameable negligence on the shelves, all coverd with mould & dust. Cross the Court & visit the Chapel wch occupies another side of the Court. Here also are great marks of neglect & decay. The armour of Lord William Howard are also shown flung negligently in the long Gallery on a chest, & beside them his cradle, both evidencing his gigantic stature even from infancy up to maturity. Alas, how fallen off in the petit-maitre person of his present representative![6] My good Lord of Carisle! I humbly move your Lordship to put together this heavy coat of armour, clasp them upon some colossal statue, either equestrian or pedestrian (as in the Tower), & let this illustrious ancestor of yours be stationed at the end of this fine Gallery if on a pedestal, or in the centre of the Court if on a horse. Again I would with great humility recommend Gothic massive furniture in place of nice finnikin[7] ...camp-beds, cane-back chairs & such like modern furniture wch form a ridiculous contrast with the antique character of this venerable structure. His Lordship spends but a month or two in the shooting season at this seat, contenting himself with the contracted accommodation (augusto limiti) of Castle Howard[8] for such part of the rest of the year as his talents can be spared from Parliament.

Thomas Howard, 4th Duke of Norfolk, executed 1572, by Holbein

Proceed in the carriage for the first time these three days the remainder of the stage, 11 m., to Glennhelt (a single house sunk in a deep valley), where we spend the night. A sorry auberge, yet who that is familiar with Irish inns will think any of this route sorry?

Hadrian's Wall, Newcastle

Tuesd. 11 Aug. We walk up the hill & set out for Chollerford 17 m. On the way a jolly farmer saluting me observed that this was fine weather for the hay. Availing myself of this civility as an invitation to a little chat, I asked where the line was of the Roman wall.

"Come with me (says he) & I will show you the Wall in perfection. There is my name (pointing at the words "Mathew Magna" painted on a cart) & I hold here above 2000 acres in my own hands."

"I presume from your name, wch. is Roman, that you trace your pedigree from the founders of the wall, & your ancestors were a very great family in this country in old times, & have been settled here since the days of Agricola." [9]

"Lord Sir (says he) it must be so, for my poor Jo who goes to the Free School at Heydon-Bridge always calls me Agricola."

So saying, he took my mare by the reins & led me along a rugged path till we reached the summit of the Grampian Hills, above his house along wch the Wall runs distinctly & in considerable preservation. The stones appear to have been piled upon one another without any regularity of masonry but cemented grouted by the infusion of hot liquid lime mortar. Here the hills look down on the north side of the wall into an abrupt cliff & formed an insurmountable barrier to the Picts; but where the Wall in its progress towards Newcastle descended into the plain the Romans found it necessary to run a deep fosse along the Wall & that fosse in general is the only trace that remains along the low & improved country of that Imperial work. After taking a grateful & affectionate leave of my friend Mathew Magna, or as he said he was vulgarly called, Mat. Macnay, I ride several miles through a country resembling much in its appearance & character the southern or western parts of Ireland: a great deal of heath or moss diversified sometimes with fine limestone verdure without a single tree to the horizon, divided by dry stone walls, & stocked with sheep & horn cattle in great numbers. My friend Mathew assured me he had upon that single farm above 2000 sheep & many hundreds of highland kyloes i.e. heifers wch he generally picked up travelling at hazard along the road.[10] They cost him, one with another, from £5 to £6, & after a winter's keep upon his grassy hills & giving among them but very little of hay, the butchers were glad to come to the ground for them from September to Christmas & drove them off fat & the most delicate of all beef at about £121 four years old & abt. 3 cwt. Great command of lime through all this country, & most abundant & most spirited use made of it; so that the Derwentwater Forfeitures, through wch this road passes & wch were perhaps the most extensive possessions in the Co. Northumberland, are from unproductive moor converting fast into finely-cultivated and well-inclosed farms.

This deviation brings me late into Chollerford, so I get hacks to our carriage &, leaving our horses behind, we drive 21 miles to Newcastle. A more hilly & irregular road I never travelled than from Brampton to Newcastle though certainly extremely fine under foot. It is curious to see how studiously the road everywhere declines the valley or low ground & climbs the sharpest summit of every Hill.

After having been repulsed from one or two of the inns on account of the great Fair wch begins this day & has filled the town we are at last provided with a comfortable lodging at Ainsley's in Moseley Street. Chollerford is an humble but clean inn at the foot of the Bridge upon the Tyne commanding an interesting reach of that noble river & a very fine picturesque country. Mr. Clayton the Town Clerk of Newcastle has a very handsome seat in the neighbourhood.

Wednesday 12th August. A foul Fair day - the first rain in my route since this day three weeks at Portadown. The great Fair of Newcastle began yesterday &, as a reasonable old dame expressed herself, is allowed to last no longer than eight days more. Immense herds of beautiful short-horned cattle of the Holderness species pass through the town all day to the fair-green about two miles off. Horses & sheep also in great numbers, many of the former from Ireland. The short-horned cattle about 5 ct., the prevailing kind universally throu' this county.

We visit St. Nicholas's Church,[11] a venerable piece of Gothic architecture, the spire very striking, fitted up in the style of a Cathedral, being in the diocese of Durham, furnished with some handsome monuments. One in particular struck me, erected "to the memory of Henry & Dorothy Askew the protectors of 12 orphan nephews & nieces in gratitude to the best of guardians by G.A. Askew in 1801". Two medallions are embraced by a beautiful female figure representing Benevolence, while on the other side stands Gratitude inspiring a fine boy who gazes on the medallions. Another is created to the uncle of Lord Collingwood[12] whom this town boasts of as a native.

Newcastle scene c. 1800 (Newcastle City Library)

Alderman Clayton, brother of the Town Clerk, very obligingly shows us the Exchange & conducts us up a handsome flight of steps into the Town Court - the Hall a very handsome well-proportioned room of great length. At one end is the Court of Assize where the Judge tries the criminal & civil causes for the county of the town of Newcastle. It should be separated & cut off from the Hall by a screen, as the noise of that crowded hall must drown the voices of those in the court. Against the wall behind the bench are whole-length portraits of Charles 2nd & of the unfortunate James 2nd. I don't remember to have met before in any public building with a portrait of the latter. By what accident it escaped the revolutionary rage of 1688 is not easy to conjecture; perhaps the populace thought they had done enough in plunging into the river a very fine equestrian statue of James wch then stood in a conspicuous part of this town.

From thence we climbed up a numerous flight of steps called the Castle Stairs & visited the County Courts wch are held fronting each other in the Moat-Hall. They are too near to one another & the voice of a loud-lunged barrister might very distinctly be heard in the other. I see no peculiar convenience in the construction of these courts. An elevated box is provided for the Witnesses to deliver their evidence from facing the Bench & the Jury Box wch is close to the bench, so that both the Judge & Jury have a full command of the voice &, what is no less material, of the countenance of every witness. The approach for carriages to the court -house is under a low gate through a narrow ill-paved passage & indeed that & the area in front of the principal door are shabby & scandalous in the extreme. My lords the Judges (who by the bye are always conveyed here as at every other assize town in England by the High Sheriff in his carriage to court accompanied by a numerous train of attendants) must have half the powder shaken out of their periwigs before they reach the bench.

But the great & indelible stain upon this town, or rather upon the county of Northumberland, is the County Prison. Upon descending a few squalid steps Mr. Lockit called to his pert daughter to fetch a lighted candle, but upon opening the ponderous door wch creaked with the voice of thunder upon its hinges, & seeing "darkness visible" within, I begged a second light, & thus furnished we entered the most dreary dungeon that fancy could imagine.

"This to be sure (said I) is the condemned cell".

"No Sir, this is the whole of our Jail".

In this single undivided apartment are confined men & women, prisoners before trial & convicts after. Felons & trespassers - all are immured indiscriminately, well supplied with straw, but without a ray of light to grope their way save when the door is opened; but the walls are very thick so that we never have any escapes, & the vault is very dry & cool so that no one ever dies with us."

Thus, according to this tender-hearted gentleman, the only quality essential to a good jail is security, & the only favour wch a prisoner has a right to expect is that he shall not perish by cold & damp before trial. What deducts however from the gross amount & quantum of the shame is that the great County Jail of Northumberland lies in Morpeth, as being more central, & that the prisoners who are always lodged there in the first instance are only removed to this hideous depot of living carcasses a few days before the Assizes, here to take their trial. But many are taken up & confined upon suspicion. Many who are falsely charged through malice or mistake are acquitted, & the benign principle of our law presumes every man innocent until legally convicted. Yet here is the most afflicting punishment little short of death inflicted before trial, wch no crime after trial could justify or palliate short of capital.

"The prisoner is confined here only for a few days." But why for one hour?

Indeed Newgate, the town prison, is, by comparison only with the County Jail, to be endured. It was one of the numerous Towers wch were built on the walls of this town & contributed much to its strength before the invention of gunpowder, & under it stood one of the town gates through wch Percy Street passes. It possesses, it is true, the only requisite wch seems here to be wanted for a jail, solidity of wall & strength, but none of those accommodations wch Howard was so unreasonable as to claim for his fellow-men: no yard for prisoners, no water for drinking or washing. In short, let Newcastle boast of a Thornton[13] & a Blackett[14] - two distinguished philanthropists of this town - but commend me to Howard[15] who travelled through the world to visit prisoners & captives, to purge the dungeon of its pestilential vapour, to ameliorate prisons, & to show mercy to the most forlorn & desolate outcasts of the human species!

"Pray sir what is that handsome building of cut stone & two wings?"

"That, Sir (answered the gentleman as he passed by) is the Assembly Room. I am a subscriber. Give me leave to show it to you."

Upon wch, without waiting for a reply, he stept on before us to the door, called the waiter & conducted us through a most beautiful suite of apartments, the principal wch is a Ball Room lighted by seven large glass chandeliers suspended from the ceiling, a double cube of 90 feet long.

"I am going, Sir, (said Colonel Dennis, for by this time we had exchanged addresses) your way, & allow me to conduct you both to your door."

However, passing on, he took us into he Mansion House very much upon the seal & in the style of that of Dublin.

"Here I did hope to introduce you to Mr. Read, the Mayor, one of the most hospitable & generous men living & who could never consent to your quitting his jurisdiction without dining with him."

But upon ringing I find he is gone out on a shooting party, this being the first day of the moor-game season.

The judges reside with the Mayor during the Assizes & are handsomely entertained, & if there happen a day to spare they are taken by the Mayor in his barge up & down this fine river upon wch the Mansion House stands. Sometimes between morning & evening prayers on the Sunday in the Assises week - for the Judges come in here always on a Saturday - go to Church twice, & leave it on Friday when they dine & sleep at Mr. Clayton the Town Clerk's fine house & proceed next day, Saturday, to Carlisle. A very alarming but as it happily turned out a very ludicrous accident befell my friend Baron Thompson here at the last Summer assizes. Stepping rather negligently from one boat into another he actually plunged head foremost into the river & disappeared, & must certainly have perished but that soon to the joy of the dismayed & horror-struck Mayor & his company the poor Baron emerged striking away both legs & arms with all the skill & vigour of a Newcastle keel-man & reached the bank in perfect safety & as cheerful & collected as if he had only been bathing. This incident not having been attended with any serious consequence has exercised the wit of ballad-mongers & other merry wags, but to no man's amusement more than the Baron's.

The Colonel pressed earnestly for permission to conduct us through the rest of the town & shew us all the lions,[16] but declining positively & with sincere expressions of gratitude to give him further trouble he saw us to our door & made his bow. The Colonel I understand is upon the staff here, being Barrack Master of the District.

Th. 13 Augt. Project a ride to Tynemouth & Shields at the embouchure of the Tyne, but postpone on account of the rain. Stroll with Mr. Ainsley through Pilgrim St, Northumberland St., Percy St, Saville Row &c, & acquire a competent knowledge of the outline of this large & populous town. It seems to be much more considerable than York & vastly better built. The Corporation enjoy a large estate - at least £30,000 a year - but their application of it is enlarged & liberal: they pave the streets, defray the salaries of the Rector of four Parishes, as well as of the Mayor whose allowance is £1500, & the other officers of the Corporation & of other public establishments.

This City boasts of being the birth-place of some illustrious living characters. Lord Collingwood is a native of whom they are justly very proud. So also are the two Scots, Sir John Scott, Lord Eldon[17] the present Chancellor, & Sir Willaim Scott the Judge of the Admiralty. They are a singular & splendid instance of the towering growth of talents regulated by integrity & perseverance under the cherishing influence of our happy Constitution. The grandfather of these Adelphi was a common carter in Newcastle. His son arrived at the condition of a coal-fitter, that is a person whom the captains of coal ships employ to fit them out with cargoes - a very humble situation in wch however some money has now & then been put together. He sent his sons to the Free-School here for education at 2s.6 a quarter for each; from thence they proceeded to college, & so on till they arrived respectively at their present eminence, beloved for their virtues as much as admired for their learning & abilities. But there is no case however prosperous & apparently enviable without its countervailing cares & suffering. The Chancellor when a young & volatile fellow received his wife, Miss Surtees,[18] then a pretty girl, out of a window. She was the daughter of a banker & thought too good for the son of an humble coal-fitter. But the father has failed & is now a bankrupt in the King's Bench; the daughter who has a strain of madness by her mother is become the most tormenting oddity that ever hen-pecked & afflicted a poor Jerry, & their only son has lately died. The poor Chancellor's only comfort now is in his grandson, the issue of that deceased son by the daughter of Sir Mat. White Ridley, M.P. for Newcastle. It is to the credit of the Chancellor that he forgot not his old master Dr. Moyses[19] but provided hansomely for him upon coming into office.

Fr.14 Augt. Rise early & sally forth, notwithstanding the heavy rain, to visit Sir Walter Blackett's celebrated house in Pilgrim St. where the unfortunate Charles had been confin'd for six or eight months in 1646 by the Scotch who then sold him (as Judas did our Saviour) for a sum of money, £400,000. They claimed large arrears of pay for their army employed by the Parliament, & made use of the scandalous expedient of surrendering for their wages to his open enemies their King who had fled to them for protection.

1. A cerement, or the cloth soaked in melted wax used to wrap an embalmed body.

2. Joseph Pasley, or Paisley op. cit.

3. Lord Hardwicke's Marriage Act of 1754 required the publication of banns and made secret weddings illegal in England. They could still be performed in Scotland, so couples flocked to Gretna Green, just over the border.

4. inures, i.e. comes into operation.

5. Naworth was part of the (Cumbrian) Dacre inheritance which became united with that of the Howards, dukes of Norfolk, on the marriage of Thomas, 4th Duke of Norfolk, and his son, William, to Dacre heiresses. The son, William (1563-1640), married Elizabeth Dacre in 1577. Naworth was restored to him after his father's execution in 1572. He thereafter restored the Castle. Day undoubtedly admires him for his antiquarian interests (books, manuscripts, Roman artefacts) and for having reigned patriarchally for many decades as a representative of civilisation in a wild border region.

6. Frederick Howard, fifth Earl of Carlisle (1748-1825), Lord Lieutenant of Ireland from 1780-82 (just before Day entered parliament) and supported the grant of legislative independence. Judge Day's criticism appears founded on Carlisle's Whig politics and dissolute early life: at age nineteen he travelled in Europe with Charles James Fox and after they returned home paid Fox's gambling debts. Carlisle was an ally of Lord Fitzwilliam, whose brief viceroyalty of 1795 removed Day's party at Dublin Castle; more recently he supported Lord Grenville's administration of 'All the Talents' of 1806-7. (See Carlisle Papers, BL, Add. Ms. 50830, Dropmore Papers, Ms.58992.)

7. Perhaps finical, over-nice.

8. Castle Howard, Yorkshire, like Blenheim, designed by Sir John Vanbrugh.

9. Agricola, a leading figure from the Roman conquest of Britain.

10. kyloe, or kylie: a small breed of cattle with long horns reared in the Highlands and western islands of Scotland.

11. St Nicholas' became the cathedral of a new diocese when Newcastle divided from Durham in 1882. The spire dates from about 1470. The monument of the Askews remains in place today.

12. Cuthbert Collingwood, Lord Collingwood (1750-1810). Served with Nelson in the West Indies and at Trafalgar. At Trafalgar he took command on Nelson's death, succeeding to his command in the Meditteranean.

13. Roger Thornton (? – 1429), eight times mayor of Newcastle and Member of Parliament.

14. Blackett St. in Newcastle commemmorates Sir William Blackett (? -1680), a coal and lead merchant, who was elected Mayor of Newcastle on a number of occasions during the 1660s. His son Edward was also Mayor of Newcastle.

15. John Howard (1726-1790), prison reformer. He wrote *The State of Prisons in England and Wales,* published in 1777, having investigated prisons in England, Ireland and Europe.

16. A 'lion', or person of outstanding interest, verb 'lionise'.

17. John Scott, first Earl of Eldon (1751-1838), Lord Chancellor. on the retirement of Pitt as prime minister in 1801, serving almost continually to 1827. Defender of the Test and Corporation Acts and Catholic exclusion.

18. Elizabeth Surtees eloped with Eldon in 1772 'by an upper story window' (Dictionary of National Biography).

19. Rev. Hugh Moises taught Eldon and Lord Collingwood in the same class at Newcastle Grammar School. On becoming chancellor Eldon made Moises one of his chaplains. (Dictionary of National Biography).

The Prince-Bishopric of Durham and the pleasures of North Yorkshire

The Industrial Revolution appears in the district of the rivers Tyne and Wear (and later in the collieries of Birmingham and Wolverhampton). He anticipates no matching revolution in the spheres of politics, yet criticises the Prince Bishop of Durham for neglecting to found alms houses and schools. The wild natural scenery of Durham offers an escape – it is 'romantic', like the novels and poems he collected – those of Walter Scott and the Irish song writer Thomas Moore.

Durham, Bishop Auckland, Raby Castle, Richmond, Harrowgate and Leeds

One might well employ many days in exploring the curiosities of Newcastle & its environs. But Richmond is our object, & we can afford no more time to the Tyne. As soon as the rain abates about 2 o'clock we set off for Sunderland quitting the direct road to Durham in order to see the celebrated Iron Bridge wch crosses the Wear & unites Wearmouth with Sunderland. All the country between the Tyne & the Wear, a district of 12 miles, is excavated by collieries, the source of immense wealth to England & a fruitful nursery of sea-men. Some of the pits are known to pass under the Tyne & to communicate by a subterraneous passage with both sides of the river to a depth exceeding in some instances 200 fathoms.

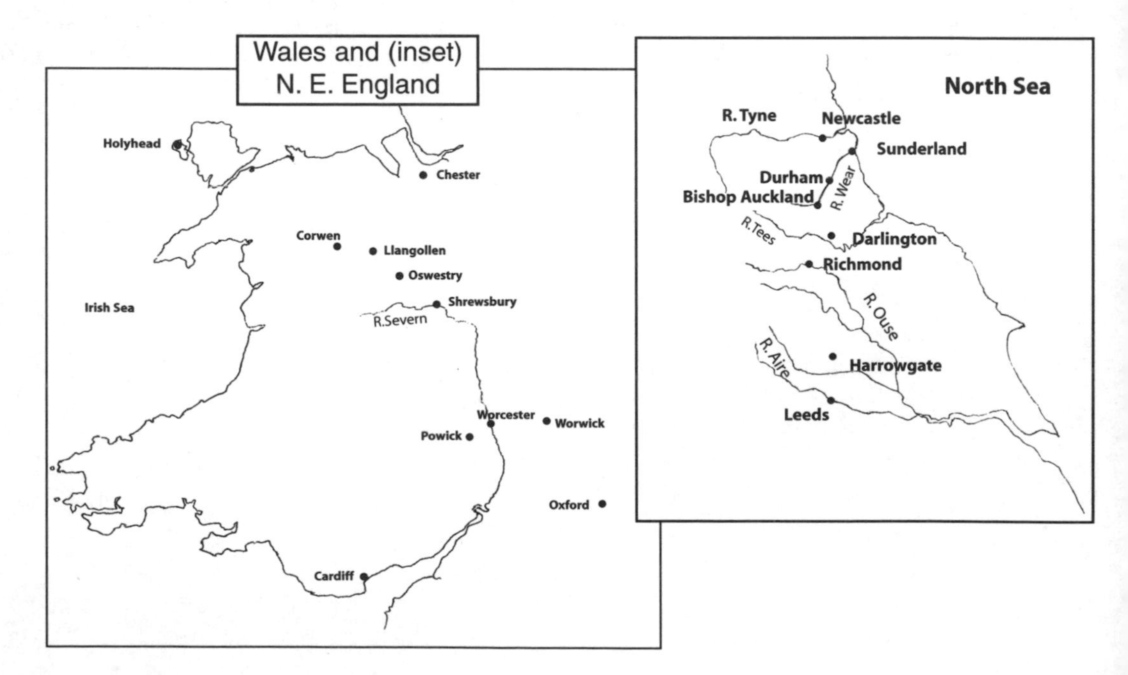

Durham Cathedral 1809 (the Cathedral Library, Durham)

Visit the Bridge, a stupendous work! We are conducted through one of the toll houses & are shewn its mechanism. Its span 236 feet & its height above low water 100, admitting vessels of 2 or 300 tons to pass without lowering their masts. It was constructed in one year, 1796, upon a plan & nearly at the expence of Rowland Burdon Esq. then M.P.[1] for this county, Durham. But he has shared the fate of many a public-spirited enterpriser: he since then has failed & at the late election was rejected by the county while the public enjoy incalculable benefit from this noble offspring of his patriotism & talents, particularly Sunderland wch lying on the south side of the Wear communicated precariously by ferryboats with Newcastle, Shields & the rest of the country to the northward of the Wear. Two years ago the abutment on the north side yielded considerably & of course created great alarm & it now very perceptibly overhangs & projects beyond its base to the eastward, but this settlement has not since encreased & the public confidence is restored. Wearmouth is an irregular wretched town, good enough, no doubt, for the Colliers & Keelmen, its inhabitants. Sunderland is a great deal better & more respectably inhabited. But who would go a yard out of his way to see either but for the bridge?

Dine & sleep at the Bridge Inn (Darling's) where I do not intend to put up on my next visit to Sunderland.

Durham

Sat. 15th Augt. Breakfast at Durham 15m. A country finely cultivated & thickly inhabited. Abundance of coal-shafts. It would seem as if this entire peninsula of

England consisting of Cumberland, Durham & the south of Northumberland were at bottom a stratum of coal & lead. I speak of the tract of country between Newcastle & Sunderland to the eastward on the North Sea, & Whitehaven & Workington to the westward on the Irish Sea. The ordinary price of coal through this county is 5 shillings for as much as the three horse cart will contain. Stop at the City Tavern in the Market Place. A close-built, ordinary city. As I descended into, it brought to mind Downpatrick, built in the bottom of a Punch-bowl. However, upon further acquaintance with it, here is a noble river, magnificent antiquities &, what is better, great comfort & cleanliness; there the Cathedral, though very respectable, might be stolen out of this without being missed, no river, some comfort if comfort can exist without cleanliness.

We visit the Abbey,[2] once the depot of previous offerings & great wealth presented to Cuthbert the parton Saint, but stript by indignant Reformers who thought it more for the public benefit that the good things there found should be put in a course of use & circulation than remain enshrined & loaded up for tantalized spectators to gaze upon. Ascending to the great area in front of the Abbey, you come unexpectedly upon it & are struck with astonishment with the grandeur & magnificence of the Pile. Next to the Cathedrals of York & Westminster this is the finest piece of antique architecture wch we have to boast of. Upon entering it, however solemn & noble the three isles, there is a striking inferiority here to those two Minsters: the architecture is Saxon, that is, the arches are not angular but perfect segments of circles, & the columns are gross & clumsy in the extreme, very inferior to the light Gothic architecture wch succeeded. The windows are very fine but no stained glass nor are there any monuments. The Cloisters are very fine & in high preservation. From thence we were conducted into the College consisting of twelve houses or buildings for the twelve Prebendaries, in wch scarcely one is found to reside.

The next object of our curiosity was the Palace where I had the satisfaction of learning that the judges, their clerks & marshals are still better accommodated during the Assizes than even at Newcastle. They come in here on Tuesday about 4, drive to the Cathedral & after proceed to Court to open merely the Commission; & they stay till Friday. On Wednesday His Lordship entertains the judges, nobility, grand jury, magistrates, clergy &c in the White Hall, a mob from 80 to 100! But Thursday is a quiet day.

The Bishop's income exceeds £30,000 a year, & the Prebendaries enjoy, the lowest not so little as £1000 a year, & a few beyond £2000. His Lordship's patronage is beyond any other in the kingdom. I then desired to see some of the charitable institutions founded by the Bishop of this diocese & his clergy.

"What institutions Sir?"said our conductor with a vacant stare?

"Why, the Alms-houses, the Hospitals the Diocesan charter schools & other eleemosynary establishments largely & munificently endowed by this most pious, most charitable, most beneficent clerical body out of the vast possessions vested in them by law ad pios usus."

"Oh Sir", replied he after a short pause, "I suppose you mean that Alms-house founded about 200 years ago for four decayed men & as many decayed women?"

But seeing I was not to be put off by a single instance & that so small & so remote, the man went on & added:

"I protest I have been about this Cathedral & Palace man & boy for many years & I never heard of a single act that deserved the name of charity that the Bishop or the Dean & Chapter of Durham were ever guilty of. The Bishop hardly ever comes among us save at the Assizes wch is but once a year when he is obliged to be here to entertain the judges."

I turned away with disgust & shame & called another subject. Here then is a lamentable exemplification of the total & absolute inefficiency of a bloated & pampered ecclesiastical establishment to any good works or virtuous & beneficial purpose. The great riches & celibacy of the Popish clergy naturally led to the gross immoralities & profligacy wch scandalized that body, & finally produced the Reformation.

Bishop Auckland

We decline the direct road by Darlington in order to see the Bishop's second Palace at Auckland 10 m.[3] Drive through his fine park, a fine indulgence accorded by his Lordship to gentlemen's carriages. Struck by the venerable Chapel seated upon a bold eminence, & (riding on) no less by the grandeur of the Palace itself. Passing through the gate into the town of Bishop - Auckland am required to leave my name. Stop for the night at Williamson's King's Head, a very cleanly civil house.[4]

Sund. 16 Augt. Send forward my horses early this morning to Staindrop, 9 m., while we wait to attend prayers at the Bishop's Chapel. All the domestics, Mr. Em...[5] the Steward, &c in mourning for Mrs. Barington who died the week before last. She was a benevolent charitable lady, clothed & sent to school many poor children of this town & is much regretted.[6] The Bishop[7] attends & gives the concluding blessing. A mild, venerable-looking old man. The Clegryman, having from the Altar given notice of the Sacrament for next Sunday, proceeded to the pulpit & before Sermon pronounced in a very impressive manner from the prayerbook the exhortation to the flock to prepare themselves diligently for receiving it. This struck me to be very proper but I don't remember to have heard it before. A beautiful Chapel in the Gothic style of architecture. The Altarpiece the Ascension. In the Antichapel is a handsome statue as large as the life of Bishop Trevor[8] seated in a nitch. The Castle (for I find it is not called the Palace, that name being applied only to Durham) is not shewn on Sundays. I do not wonder the Bishop prefers Auckland for his residence to Durham. The house & offices are said to be much more commodious but this beautiful Park thro' wch the Wear flows in full pride is an appendage of great attraction & such as few seats can boast of.

Raby Castle

Take posthorses for Staindrop for the purpose of visiting Raby Castle,[9] Earl of Darlington's famous seat. Drive through the Park wch, though more extensive & more crowded with plantation, is not so interesting as Bishop Auckland - it is flat & tame and the attempt at water wretched, while the other is bold irregular & full of romantic glens & cliffs, & watered as I said by a fine River stocked with abundance of deer. Our chaise drives through two gateways, the outward over a fosse & secured apparently by a portcullis, & rattles on over broad pavement actually into the great Hall. The Prince on his visit here last Summer was very much struck by the novelty of that circumstance & grandeur of that fine Gothic Hall sustained by four rows of pillars. To produce a more striking effect it was lighted up in great splendour as His Royal Highness did not arrive until after nightfall. I own myself disappointed here: no pictures of any merit, save three of the other day by Marshal[10] - the Earl & his horses, hounds & servants of the field the subject & very well executed. Probably now that Stubbs[11] & Gilpin[12] are gone Marshal may be our best painter of animals. A very few pictures & not a single statue or marble, but to supply this want you are shewn the Chinese Drawing-room & Bed Chamber! fitted up for the reception of the Prince of Wales & Duke of Clarence by the artist & precisely upon the model adopted by the Prince himself at the Pavilion - this I suppose that His Royal Highness may believe himself at home. Above-stairs a noble Hall is shewn where many a baron bold has heretofore revelled - 90 feet long & proportionately wide & lofty but not a single article of furniture in it modern or antique. Lord Pembroke of Witton or Marq. of Exeter, late of Burleigh-Castle, would have contrived to furnish this magnificent shell with feudal armoury - massive oak chairs tables chimney pieces &c - or with statues & other monuments of the fine arts wch though not in character would want no apology. The stairs painted white, a miserable mockery of stone - so at Durham Palace the floor of the Tapestry Room & the Stairs are painted black, a paltry imitation of oak.

Snack at the Queen's Head in Staindrop where Terence is harnishing[13] our refreshed cavalry. The chain having broke down we cobble it up with stops with the help of Mr Ingram's servant who seeing our distress most kindly runs out to bear a hand. In consequence I am forced much to my mortification to resign the mare to Thomas. Immure myself to the chaise for this stage.

Richmond, Yorkshire

Drive to Richmond 15 m.,[14] rather a hilly road from the time we advance three miles over the Wear[15] into Yorkshire, particularly within a mile of the town where the road is long steep & rugged. An extremely rich, highly cultivated extended view from <u>this</u> Richmond Hill as well as from that of Surrey - whether you look to the south-ward down upon the town, or to the northward on Dundas's fine seat. But where is the liquid mirror here to reflect, refresh, diversify the scene? Where are the barges & boats to glide perpetually upon the bosom of a noble sheet of water & give life & spirit to the whole lanskip? [16]

Mond. 17th Augt. Ramble before breakfast. Send in every direction to find out Mr. & Mrs. Powell. No tidings to be had of any such persons. The Postmaster refers us to Lawyer Hog "who knows some Mr. Powell". Beat up his quarter & find him in the suds yielding up his bristles without a grunt. I have heard of a learned Hog but certainly this is the first <u>polite</u> Hog I have met with.[17] After shewing us into the ladies he dispatch'd his toilette, gave us to understand that there had not been a gentleman or lady of that name for twenty years in Richmond except poor Powell the conveyancer who lately died & his mother who on his death went to settle in London.

But to console us for this disappointment who should walk in upon us to our great surprise & delight but my old friend Mrs. Cross with a sweet grand-daughter in each hand whom she presented to us, Miss Mayor & Miss Caroline Mayor.

"For God's sake, what propitious gale blew you both to Richmond? Caroline passing by the inn was told that carriage belonged to a Judge from Ireland, & ran back to announce that it certainly must be my friend who was come. Upon that chance I posted down from the Hill & have the happiness to find her conjecture verified."

"We came in last night on our way through Harrowgate to London & are detained here by the breaking down of our coachman's chair, an accident wch we felt as a misfortune but wch turns out to be most fortunate as to that we are indebted for this most unexpected gratification."

It seems my amiable old friend resides here with her son-in-law & daughter who live on Richmond Hill at what is called the Hill-House & have a fine blooming family of three sons & four daughters. They pressed us to pass the day with them, but failing in that they dragged me out to see the lions. Our first visit was to Mr. York's beautiful grounds situate on the Swale tumbling over a rugged bed along the base of a very abrupt finely wooded precipice. On our return from the grounds was presented to Mrs. Yorke, a very interesting, polite old lady, who apologized for the absence of Mr. York on account of indisposition. This couple are idolised through this neighbourhood: his income is about £7000 a year, & having no children he thinks he ought not to hoard but spends his whole income in beneficence & charity. He is proud of the antiquity of his family & disclaims any connexion with the Hardwickes.

The principal part of the town is his Estate but the borough belongs to Lord Dundas who has a fine estate here, a fine estate in Ireland & a fine estate in Scotland - the Hebrides principally. His Lordship[18] we all know is son to Dundas the Contractor,

Richmond (Yorkshire): 'A View of the town', 1798 (Yorkshire County Record Office)

who, a mere Scotch adventurer, made half a million in the German war under Prince Ferdinand & would have spent it in hospitality & dissipation had he not - fortunately for his family - been soon cut off. The son, a more prudent man, married Lord FizWilliam's sister, & their daughter last year married her cousin-german Lord Milton.[19] Thus it is that Lord Dundas & his two sons take so warm a part in Parliament with the Foxites. This family assisted naturally in returning Lord Milton at the late election, but corruption too was very busy for him while Lascelles fell a victim to confidence & indolence. It was even whispered that his own agent, to whom he had committed the circulation of his letters, betrayed him & kept them back.[20]

Our next visit was to the ruins of Richmond Castle, the birth-place & residence of Henry 7th, from whence he transferred the name of Richmond to Sheane, now Richmond, in Surrey, where he built a palace on the Green (a wing of wch is now inhabited by my friend Dundas the King's surgeon) in wch he resided some years & died. From thence to the famous Tower in Mr. Robertson's ground, wch, though in high preservation, is all that remains of a very extensive & considerable abbey, according to tradition. And finally, Mrs. Day & I visited Mrs. Mayor at her beautiful residence of Hill-House where we were most cordially received. It commands a prospect wch Lord Dundas prefers to the more polished lanskip of the other Richmond Hill, & I observe from hence what escaped me yesterday evening - the Swale meandering at the foot of the hill in great beauty.

At length, & not indeed till a late hour, we tear ourselves from our kind friends who part us with great regret, Miss Mayor presenting Mrs. Day with a very elegant workbag, the painting of wch was very neat & executed by herself.

Visit Easby[21] ruins upon the river a mile below the town & taking post horses proceed to Leaming Lane, the Royal Oak Couldwell's - 15 m.- where I had sent Terence & the horses this morning to wait for us. Take a snack at this nice & comfortable house & in the evening proceed with my own horses 10m. to Rippon - the weather intensely hot & propitious to the harvest -saw this day the first corn reaping.

Harrowgate Spa and Leeds

Tuesd. 18th Augt. Breakfast at Lower Harrowgate (10 m.) at the Swan. Walk after breakfast to the Spa - not come here for health. A ride of near 200 miles on my route from Portpatrick is some evidence that God has spared me as much health & strength as might be expected at my age, & my Fellow-traveller, thank God, stands as little in need of it - & if we are come for <u>pleasure</u> I think we have mistaken the road; for I see no pleasure in making or even seeing others making wry faces over this saline stinking water, & from the specimen we have had the accommodation is but indifferent - our bed-room no longer than a sentry box where in this hot weather we should suffocate in a night - & the company at <u>this</u> house appear but shabby. I understand, however, things are better at <u>High</u> Harrowgate, a mile farther on. After dinner, proceed to Harewood - 8 m., [22] walk into his Lordship's fine park containing between 4 & 500 acres & inclosed with the finest wall of chizzled stone. Harewood Castle is to be seen but on Saturdays. <u>Outside</u> it appears no great thing: a regular front of cut stone whose centre and pavilions contain two floors. The entrance & gate into the Park very

Harewood House, by Turner. Courtesy of the Earl and Countess of Harewood, and the Trustees of the Harewood House Trust

striking. His village elegantly designed & executed.

Creep on over a hilly sandy road to Leeds, 10 m., where we stop at the Bull & Mouth in the street called Briggate (i.e. Bridge-Gate) & are very well accommodated.

Wednesday 19 Augt. Walk through this very considerable town before breakfast. Fortunately it dont return members, & therefore no electioneering or its invariable companions, venality idleness & riot. I was surprised to see Masted Vessels of some burden at the Bridge over the Ayre, wch after joining the Ouze below York falls into the Humber. Leeds & its vicinity are the principal district for weaving woollen cloth. The inexhaustible collieries in the neighbourhood have attracted a manufacturing population. The awful state of the continent, & still more the irritated state of America have injured much the manufacture here as probably everywhere else in the British Islands. Trade & manufacture we know are of a nervous & sensitive quality, shrinking from (though perhaps ultimately not injured by) the slightest touch.

Impatient to reach London, not only to see our friends there in its neighbourhood but to receive our letters from Ireland, we resolve to fling ourselves into one of the coaches from hence to London. So I take seats in the rockingham for tomorrow, & we proceed in our own carriage to Ferrybridge, 16 m., thence to be taken up at 7 a.m., our own cavalcade to follow us at their leisure. On the way from Leeds I join some farmers & discourse wth them on the striking difference between making hay in England & in Ireland. Supposing no rain, here the hay is tossed & turned for two or three days & drawn off from the windrows & rick'd in the haggard. With us it is in three or four days made up in damp cocks & not three or four weeks after brought into the haggard. The consequence is that the English hay necessarily heats & sweats, becomes moist & ugly & loses its colour; the Irish is put up perfectly seasoned &dry & retains its fresh & green colour. Each course has its advocates who contend strenuously for the advantage & superiority of their favourite. But possibly both are right. The heated hay becomes sweeter & more palatable by the English process, & the sluggish cart horses & the horned cattle are found to eat more of it & to fill themselves abundantly with it; the latter therefore thrive the faster upon it, whether it be for the pail or for the butcher, while the former work the keener upon a full stomach. But for active service, whether it be for the road, the chaise or the turf, there can be no doubt that the well-seasoned hay, being the dryer food, is far preferable. A chaise-horse, a hunter or racer would immediately burst his wind upon such foggy food as hay saved in the usual way in England & therefore you see horses of this description limited here to the smallest imaginable allowance of hay.

Neither could I avoid animadverting upon what struck me as being a most wasteful & slovenly mode of saving oats & barley in universal practice throughout this country. The corn is mow'd. After remaining a short time in the ledge or sweath[23] it is turned over on the other side; then shortly, instead of being bound in sheaves, it is raked into very small cocks & next day carted from the field into the haggard & made up immediately into stacks or ricks. In short oats & barley are saved very nearly in the same manner as hay. The farmers whom I talked with admitted this course to be extremely wasteful & ineligible if it could be avoided, & defended it on the ground of necessity resulting from the dearness of labour - where an able-bodied labourer could not be had under half a crown a day & his victuals in harvest. "Besides (said they) all the grain thus scatter'd is not wasted, for the neighbourhood turn in their pigs upon the stubble at so much a head & by & bye leave not a grain of it." The wheat however is reaped & bound & then carted off.

View of Leeds, engraved by J. Cousen from a drawing by Charles Cope, published by Robinson and Hernaman, Leeds

Cross the noble bridge wch has been finished since my former visit to this county in 1801 over the Ouze at Ferrybridge & stop at the Greyhound in the heart of the town, a very cleanly comfortable house where we are taken good care of. The principal & more elegant Inn is at the north side of the river situated beautifully on its bank. I forget its sign.

1. Rowland Burdon (1756-1838), MP 1790-1807.

2. The Abbey, to which he refers, must be Durham Cathedral. The Abbey was suppressed in 1539 but refounded in 1541 as the Cathedral Church of Christ and the Blessed Virgin Mary. It contains the tombs of St. Cuthbert and the Venerable Bede.

3. The town is Bishop Auckland. Auckland Castle has been principal country residence of the bishops of Durham since Norman times.

4. This inn in Bishop Auckland continued as The King's Arms until recent times. It now trades as 'The Posthouse'.

5. unclear

6. The Bishop's second wife (m. 1770) took an active interest in popular education.

7. Bishop Shute Barrington, born 1734, Bishop of Durham from 1791 to his death, 1826.

8. Richard Trevor, Bishop of Durham 1752-1771. The statue (still to be seen there) is by Nollekens. Among the items which the visitor failed to see because of the closure of Auckland Castle were the paintings of Jacob and his Twelve Sons by Zurbaran which Bishop Trevor bought in 1756. The Zurbaran portraits are still on view at Auckland Castle.

9. Raby Castle in Durham, a mile from Staindrop. Seat of the Nevilles and birth place of Cicely Neville, the 'Rose of Raby', mother of King Edward IV and Richard III. It has been home to Lord Barnard's family, Earls of Darlington and Dukes of Cleveland, for over 350 years.

10. Benjamin Marshall (1768-1835), a painter of hunting and racing scenes. From 1812 his studio was at Newmarket.

11. George Stubbs (1724-1806), artist who depicted horses and sports.

12. Sawyer Gilpin (1733-1807), overshadowed by Stubbs from the 1760s; he illustrated animal scenes from Swift's 'Gulliver's Travels' and Shakespeare 'Macbeth', among others.

13. harnessing

14. His destination is the other Richmond, the one near London.

15. Day is mis-informed about the name of this river. One crosses the Tees, not the Wear, to enter Yorkshire,.

16. landscape

17. Tristram Hogg was a prominent lawyer of Richmond at this time.

18. Sir Thomas Dundas (1741-1820), Baron Dundas of Aske, Co. York, m. Charlotte, dau. of William 3rd Earl Fitzwilliam. His father, Lawrence Dundas, was Commissary-General and Contractor to the army.

19. Mary m. (8 July 1806) Viscount Milton.

20. Henry Lascelles, second Earl of Harewood (1767-1841). He contested the general election in 1807

to represent Yorkshire in the Tory interest, the first contested election in sixty-six years. The poll opened on May 20 and lasted fifteen days with huge expense on both sides. He lost but was returned for Westbury in July of the same year. Day's Tory preference is evident here.

21.Easby is a Premonstratensian foundation of the middle 12th century. The founder of the order was St Norbert.

22. The seat of Henry Lascelles, second Earl of Harewood (1767-1841).

23. swethe, Old English for swathe.

London: an Indian debt, protests against war and a sick Irish Judge

Percival Pott, the writer's father-in-law was the eminent surgeon of St. Bartholomew's Hospital. One day Percival fell from his horse and broke his ankle, later directing the operation to save the limb which gave to posterity the procedure known as 'Pott's Fracture'. Day makes his base once again with his friends at Richmond-on-Thames and Hampstead.

Th. 20th Augt. We are taken up by the Post - Coach abt. 7 a.m., travel all day & night & arrive at the Saracen's Head, New Snow Hill (off Skinner-Street) abt. 3p.m. on Friday 21st , having found it so commodious & safe a conveyance that even Mrs. Day's original fears soon vanished & she became quite reconciled to it. Indeed the night was the most agreeable period of the journey, for we had a brilliant moon & a refreshing breeze, whereas Friday was intensely hot & dusty, particularly as we approach'd the immense & still - increasing capital.

Skinner-Street (so call'd in honour of our much to be honoured friend the poor Alderman[1]) an erection since our last to London in 1801, not more important & beneficial by the spacious, direct & mild communication wch it furnishes between the West & East ends of the Town than beautiful in its execution.

After brushing off the dust of the road & dispatching a snack we call a chaise & drive down to Richmond where we are received with open arms & warm hearts by our longing & delighted friends.

Sat. 22nd Visit several of our Richmond friends, but first my poor friend Sir John Day[2] whom I find but little altered in appearance & plight, but alas ! in spirits & in mind, depress'd, hypocondriac, wild, yet with an effort at his old good humour.

"Ah, Bob (said he) you see "non sum qualis a ram". Poor Lady Day[3] with streaming eyes informs me this malady has been stealing upon him for three years & that he will ask or follow no advice. He raves perpetually upon his claim upon the Nabob of Arcot,[4] forgeries, conspiracies against his property & life & such stuff. In short, while the instrument in general is in tolerable tune this thing vibrates sad discord. I confute & laugh at those chimaeras, change the subject, entreat him to turn his thoughts to more cheering objects e.g. his elevation to rank honour & wealth from abject obscurity & bless the benignity of Providence instead of brooding thus incessantly & intensely upon imaginary or even upon real ills.[5]

Sund. 23 Go to Church & hear a good sermon from Mr. Young, the Curate of W. Savage, the Rector of this Union. He succeeded Mr. Thomas Wakefield who died a few years ago - very much lamented by his parishoners, if we are to believe a stone Tablet erected to him against the wall in this Church.[6] But, according to some in

Fountain Court, Middle Temple. By kind permission of the Masters of the Bench of the Honourable Society of the Middle Temple

whom I confide, it overates extremely his pretensions. He was certainly a man of charity & great sensibility, but he was dogged in temper, coarse in manner & tinctured strongly with the democratic principles of his brother, the famous Gilbert Wakefield.[7] The good old King having crossed the Green one day on foot from the gardens to visit his old favourite, Lord Onslow, was hailed & greeted by the crowd who assembled to receive him, the populace rending the air with acclamations while all stood up with uncovered heads. Mr. Wakefield, however, whom chance brought right across His Majesty, knew nothing in <u>his</u> character particularly, or in the Kingly character in general, that called upon him to pay any compliment upon the occasion & he proceeded sturdily under the King's nose without deigning so much as to touch his hat.

But what was more censurable was the tablet wch he erected in Richmond Church recording in very inflated terms the virtues of his brother Gilbert & ascribing the prosecution & conviction of that renowned champion of democracy for his libel on the Bishop of Llandaff to the persecuting and oppressive spirit of administration, thus perpetuating an acknowledged lye upon the sacred walls of the House of God.

Mon.24th Breakfast in London. Take lodgings at No.11 Bury St. Saunter about. No acquaintance in town. Go to the Haymarket. See & greatly admire Young in Sir Edward Mortimer in the Iron Chest – Quaere if he be not the first tragedian now extant?[8]

Tu. 25th Visit my good old friends John Watts & his wife at Hampstead. Find him at 71 scarcely altered from what I had first known him in 1769 when he was 38. She, however, miserably haggard & broken. Never was the physical effect of temper upon the human constitution more perfectly exemplified than in the case of this worthy couple. Stay to dine.

26th Return to Richmond, dine with poor Sir John. I undertake for him the conduct of his Arcot claim before the Carnatic Commissioners, Mess Hobhouse, Cobourne & Horner, for wch he professes much gratitude. He minds – offers- to assign me his claim, then his ring, but I good- humouredly put him off.[9]

Th.27th Ride to Bushy Park & leave my ticket at the Duke of Clarence's who is from home reviewing his Volunteer corps. Sit half an hour with his R. H.'s Chaplain, my old friend Loyd "of Cardigan", as we called him at Alma Mater. Proceed to Lord Glenbervie at the Pheasantry whom I find at home & also her Ladyship - oh how like the poor father Lord North![10] Almost as pleasant & almost as ugly. Decline to stay & dine but promise to come & stay a few days with them.

Illness and Relapse

W.9th Sept. Nothing memorable to this day. Receive much polite attention from many in Richmond. Invitations to dinner from Sir Cha' Rice, Mr. Ward, Mr. Dundas &c. - cards to tea innumerable. The Wattses one day dine with us from Hampstead. Take Mrs. B. Watts up the river as far as Twickenham. Saunter again for 2 or 3 days to London. Received a day by Lord & Lady Redesdale[11] with great kindness. Refused to dine with them for I saw they were busy & bustling to set off next day for Cheltenham. Lord Carleton[12] out of town, Lord Chichester[13] out of town - everybody out of town. A more stupid place than London in September does not exist: no Parliament, Courthouse, Opera, Vauxhall - nothing but Bartholomew Fair & Exeter Change & the Little Theatre. The only friend I met was Downes.[14] In short, London in September stands high among "the miseries of human life". Oh yes, my good friend Lord Glandore[15] is in town & he thinks September & October are the best of the 12 months to spend in London for he is sure not to be interrupted in those months at his studies. Having return'd to Richmond on Tues. the 8th I take Mrs. Day next day & her sister Miss Potts to Hampstead to dine with John Watts - on our way we call at Dr. Nicholas's School at Eling to see little John Watts, grand-nephew of the other John. Above 200 boys here! Quae. - Shall I send Bobby there?[16] I fear it is too crowded. Sleep very comfortably at Bob Watts's, father of my little fag John.

Th.10th Stroll after breakfast with Watts &c to the Heath. Visit the elegant Public Rooms lately finished here. Many nice villas scattered through the Heath. Lord Erskine[17] has got a very handsome piece of ground, commanding a most extensive prospect, but he chooses to build away from the prospect within five feet of the Spaniard (an old public House of great resort). A very cold day. We dine with Bob Watts & in the evening I find myself a good deal indisposed. Take 3 James's Pills.

Fr. 11th Rise early & ride to breakfast with Mrs. Patterson, York Place, the Ladies coming in the Chaise. Dine with her & stay to sleep. A very comfortable house.

Sat.12th Spend a feverish night & rise this morning much out of order. Shorten our visit & return to Richmond. Send for Dundas who pronounces that I have got a fever. He orders James's Powders, warm water for bathing my feet &c.

Sund.13th James's Powders repeated. Nothing can exceed the kind & affectionate assiduity of my Richmond friends during my confinement, wch continues about a fortnight. Dundas with great judgment & attention under Providence conducts me safe through a fever wch threatened in its commencement to be more serious. Take the air some days.

Wed.30th Lord Glandore pursuant to notice very kindly calls to take me first to see Hampton Court & after to dine at the Toy with him, Henry Herbert & a very interesting gentleman, Mr. Hamilton O Hara. I run the risk, though not sufficiently convalescent, & attend him. On our way we visit Lord Glenbervie whom we find not quite recovered from an erisypelas.[18] He claims my promise but am too limited in time to perform it. I decline accompanying the party through this truly Royal Palace, finding myself unequal to the undertaking. Who does not know that it was built by that son of a butcher with a princely spirit, Cardinal Wolsey, who was forced by Henry 8 to change it with him for Richmond Palace built by Henry 7. But it was greatly enlarged & improved by William 3d. N.B. The Royal Arms over the entrance are supported by a Lion & Griffin (dragon); the Unicorn was afterwards introduced from Scotland by James 1. Pleasant day.

F.2 Oct. We go to London to prepare for Ireland.

Sund. 4th Dine at Hampstead with the Wattses.

M.5th The Richmond Ladies visit us & we promise to spend next day with them on our way to Ireland.

Tu. 6th Send off the servants & equipage by Parkgate while we proceed on our way to Holyhead as far as Richmond, where I relapse & take to my bed for a week. Meantime the kindest invitations come to me from my friends Lord Chichester (at Stanmore Lewes, Sussex) & from Sir Jon. Lovett,[19] aggravating not a little the sufferings of sickness. My dear friends of Ireland are greatly shocked by a report of my death, but with the help of God I shall soon in person satisfy them of its falsehood.

W.14th Oct. Leave Richmond, the Sisterhood with streaming eyes & sorrowful hearts embracing & pouring out cordial prayers for mutual happiness. Drive to Colebrook 12 m. a 15d per mile, from thence to Henley -18 m.- at do., from thence to Benson 11m.at 14d p m Oh, beautiful Maidenhead bridge! Oh, divine Vale of Henley-Upon-Thames! Oh, celestial weather!

1. Thomas Skinner, elected Lord Mayor in 1794. (op. cit.)

2. Sir John Day (1738-1808), retired Advocate-General of Bengal, opt. cit.

3. Benedicta Day

4. See *'Report from the Committee on the Petition of the Creditors of the Nabobs of Arcot'*, Parliamentary Papers: Report, 1806.

5. In March 1805 Judge Day asked the Knight of Kerry to press with Castlereagh the claim of Sir John concerning 'a bond debt of some thousands contracted by the Nabob of Arcot with Day for professional services, and for payment of which with many others the Nabob several years since deposited ample funds in the Company's treasury at Madras' (NLI, photocopies of the FitzGerald papers, Day, Loughlinstown House, to Mce. FitzGerald, Knight of Kerry, 11 March, 1805).

6. The Church of Mary Magdalene, Richmond. The Wakefield tablet can still be seen there.

7. Scholar and philanthropist, Gilbert Wakefield was jailed in 1799. He had replied to Richard Watson the Bishop of Llandaff's defence of Pitt's war policy and the new income tax, simultaneously attacking Llandaff as an absentee and pluralist. Wakefield spent two years in Dorchester prison and died shortly after release.

8. Charles Mayne Young (1777-1856). Sir Edward Mortimer in the *Iron Chest* was one of Young's roles after he came to London in 1807 to play at the Haymarket. He became accepted as the leading English tragedian after Kemble (DNB).

9. Day's letter to Maurice FitzGerald of 11 March 1805 (quoted above) implies a personal interest on the part of Judge Day in Sir John Day's Arcot claim ('It may be of importance to me, and this I hint to excite you the more').

10. Sylvester Douglas, Baron Glenbervie (1743-1823), op. cit. His wife was the daughter of Lord North, PM.

11. Sir John Mitford, first Baron Redesdale (1746-1830), Lord Chancellor of Ireland 1802-1806. Day had an easy relationship with Redesdale though Redesdale was hostile to further Catholic relief.

12. Hugh Carleton (1739-1826), Chief Justice of the Common Pleas (Ireland) 1787-1800, op.cit.

13. Thomas Pelham, second Earl of Chichester (1756-1826).

14. Probably William Downes (1752-1826), Chief Justice of Day's court, the King's Bench Ireland, where he succeeded Lord Kilwarden who was killed in the Emmet rebellion in 1803. His Dublin residence was Melville, Booterstown, on the route to Day's at Loughlinstown.

15. John Crosbie, 2nd Earl of Glandore, of Ardfert Abbey, Day's cousin and the leading representative of the Dublin Castle interest in Kerry politics.

16. Probably the writer's grandson, Robert Day Denny (b. 1800).

17. Thomas Erskine, first Baron Erskine (1750-1823), English Lord Chancellor during the 'Ministry of All the Talents' in 1806.

18. Erysipelas is a skin infection which can affect all the layers of the skin.

19. Jonathan Lovett (d. 1812) of Liscombe House, Bucks. and Kingswell, Co. Tipperary, was a contemporary of Day at the Middle Temple and appears in Day's marriage settlement. Lovett's sisters appear to have married Irishmen. Jane married John Bennet, justice of the Court of King's Bench, Ireland, and Susanna married William Henn of Paradise Hill, Co Clare, Master of the Irish Court of Chancery. Day wrote: 'I imported very nice Jane Lovet in 1774 with my late poor wife' (RIA, Day papers, Ms. 12w17, dated December 1838) .

Oxford and Warwick: the mystique of the Stuarts, the Wars of the Roses

Oxford was a centre of Royalist resistance during the English Civil War. Christ Church Oxford and Warwick Castle display portraits of the Stuart kings, to whose tragic end and loss of the throne Day is clearly sympathetic. The executed Charles 1 is seen as the victim of English anarchy and Scots betrayal. Regional magnates, such as the family of Beauchamp, earls of Warwick, were prominent during the Hundred Years War with France and the civil wars (Wars of the 'Roses') that followed.

Middle Temple Hall, showing the old benches and the royal portraits which would have hung in the same position in Robert Day's time. By kind permission of the Masters of the Bench of the Honourable Society of the Middle Temple

Th.15th Dine & sleep at Benson. Find myself much refreshed. Very good beds, but the dearest house I have met with in England. Mary FitzGerald,[1] whom we had the good fortune to pick up in London and bring with us, reports that our Hostess was as jolly & loud in the Tap-room as any of the wagoners & that she could not sleep all night for the uproar & disorder in the room under her. Friends of mine, avoid sleeping at Benson!

12 m. to Oxford. Breakfast this morning at Blue Boar, Oxford. Visit Christ Church. Turn into the beautiful Hall. Admire the fine old oak roof not inferior to that of the Middle Temple Hall. Among the numerous portraits recognise the great old Lord Mansfield[2] and the little old Lord Mansfield,[3] the munificent Primate Robinson,[4] Cleaver Bishop of Ferns,[5] Agar Archbishop of Dublin,[6] who are neither great nor munificent, Chief Baron Mc Donald,[7] Speaker Abbot, the best of Speakers,[8] Lord Grenville, Chief of "All the Talents",[9] Mr. George Grenville his father, who severed America from us,[10] Bishop Dolben[11] great-grandfather of Sir William Dolben & permanent member for the University, an excellent picture by Reynolds of old Markham Archbishop of York, now 90 years of age,[13] Cardinal Wolsey, the founder, & Henry 8th (by Holben) the pretended founder "who spared neither man in his wrath nor woman in his lust" &c. At the end of the Hall stands the bust of our good King. Take a glimpse of the Chapel abounding in beautiful stained glass. Proceed through the Radcliffe Quadrangle to see the building erected "munifcaentia alumnorum praecipue ... Ricardi Robinson Arciep Armach". Great Tom strikes 11 & warns us away so we run to our chaise & drive off through Woodstock to Enstone, 14 m. at 1s a mile.

N.B. The Blue Boar a civil house & cheap e.g.1s. a m. for posting. From Enstone to Shipston 14 m. at 1 s a mile. From Shipston, instead of proceeding to Stalford 11 m. and from thence to Birmingham 22 m., we turn off to Warwick 17 m. (at 14d.a m milc), a line I never took before, in order to see the famous Castle, & here we dine and sleep at Hudson's Black Swan. Travel 57 m. this day, somewhat too much for me, but 40 m. yesterday.

Fr.16th Dress & breakfast. Visit the fine Church – Templum Beatae Maria Mariae Collegiatum.[14] The great curiosity here is the Earl of Warwick's little Chapel[15] wch

Ambrose Dudley, Earl of Warwick. Led the suppression of the Northern Rebellion of 1569, and assisted at the trial of the Queen of Scots

being roofed with a most curious stone roof escaped two conflagrations. On one side lodged in the wall is a splendid monument of Elizabeth's famous Earl of Leicester,[16] & on the floor between is one of his younger brother Dudley[17] created by Elizabeth Earl of Warwick upon the extinction of that title in the Beauchamp family. In the centre of the Chapel stands under a brass canopy the monument[18] of Beauchamp Earl of Warwick, the founder, who built this elegant Chapel in the reign of Henry 6. Beside the wall is the monument of the 2nd Earl of Warwick of the Dudley family, on whose death without issue, the title becoming again extinct, it was conferred by James 1st upon Fulke Greville[19] in whose house it has continued ever since. From the Chapel we were conducted by a short flight of worn-out stairs to the confessional where the penitents whispered their offences through a hole in the wall to the Priest who could not see them seated in a chair in an outer room. The great eastern window over the Communion table was a gift of the present Earl. Warwick was once a bishopric & this church the cathedral; but it is united now with Worcester.

James Graham, Marquess of Montrose, by Vandyke. Scottish Royalist. Executed in Edinburgh 1650

Warwick Castle

From the Church we proceed to the Castle[20] said to be the largest & in the highest preservation of any in England - situate upon the beautiful Avon & commanding a finely-planted park 9 miles in circumference. You enter a noble Hall furnished with old armour & two moose deer heads & horns. From thence into the Cedar-Room, a finely-proportioned drawing-room wainscoted with cedar & furnished among others with a fine portrait of Charles 1st, another of his faithful adherent the unfortunate Duke of Montrose,[21] & a third of the still more unfortunate Earl of Strafford,[22] all by Vandyke; two heads by Guido as fresh as if drawn but yesterday, while a portrait by Reynolds had lost all its carnation & become as white as statuary marble. Over the chimney is a good portrait by Romney of Wortley Montague[23] in his Turkish habit & bushy beard. Beyond this is the small drawing room once the billiard room wch boasts of an inestimable portrait of Machiavel by Titian. There is also a very fine Portrait of the Earl of Arundel who presented Oxford with the Arundelian Marbles, one of the ancestors of the Duke of Norfolk who offered 1500 guineas for it. Next to this is Queen Anne's bedchamber in wch stands the elegant velvet bed in wch Her Majesty

Thomas Wentworth, Earl of Strafford, by Vandyke. Royalist Lord Deputy of Ireland. Executed London 1641

State Dining Room, Warwick Castle, with equestrian portrait of Charles I and his equerry. Courtesy Warwick Castle.

slept. Over the chimney hangs a whole length portrait of some Duchess of Parma by Titian dressed precisely in the modern female costume. The room is hung with a correct representation of Versailles & the Garden in fine tapestry.[24] Next is a small apartment crowded with small portraits, among wch the most attractive is Charles 2nd's beautiful Duchess of Cleveland.[25] Anna Bullein & her sister also are interesting; Martin Luther, another head of Chas.1st & one of his Queen,[26] &c. There are very few wch remain upon my memory of a very considerable & select collection. In one of those rooms is a whole-length of Ignatius Loyola[27] in his vestments by Rubens, a very striking portrait of the painter Ricard by Vandyke &c &c.

At right angles with this suite of apartments you turn into a narrow gallery, quarried, as it were, out of the massive walls of the Castle, at the end of wch stands an equestrian portrait of Charles 1st, with his Equerry on foot, the counterpart of the portrait in Hampton Court & the Temple Hall, all of wch dispute for originality; but the Prince of Wales on seeing this portrait lately has decided the doubt and against probability insisted the 3 were originals by Vandyke & that none of them could be a copy. But credat Judaeus appellam how improbable that Vandyke was so enamoured of this subject or that Charles had such predilection for that equestrian character that

His Majesty selected it for 3 portraits!

(N.B. the Prince wished to rent this princely Castle: the poor Earl's imprudences have forced him away from it & Lord Brooke, his son,[28] has the Estate. Who was Guy Earl of Warwick? I only remember that powerful & rebellious Baron in Edward 2d 's reign.)[29]

Beyond the Gallery, or rather in the continuation of it, lies the Armoury, crowded with coats of mail, shields, helmets, matchlock, guns, cross-bows, Guy E. of Warwick's huge spur & a vast variety of ancient arms. We find there also in very odd company & most strangely misplaced: an antique bust of Demosthenes & 2 or 3 other smaller antiques. There is indeed a much finer Parian marble bust of Minerva Galeata[30] in one of the other apartments & these as I recollect are the only antique sculptures in the Castle. From the Armoury we were conducted to the Chapel, scarcely worth visiting, & from wch the damp & cold soon banished us, & lastly from thence back through the Great Hall to the eating parlour, furnished, among other good pictures, with a very striking one of two lions by Rubens. Such is the substance of the lesson taught us by the civil House-keeper, & who will say that it was not worth a crown? In the Garden they show standing in the Green House a Vase of immense magnitude embossed with bunches of grapes wch the pedestal tells was raised by Sir Wm. Hamilton in the Emperor Adrian's Gardens at Tibur.[31]

Feasted with this luscious banquet we return to the Inn & post off to Knowle, 10m, at 15d per mile where they shew you at the Mermaid kept by Marshall, the portrait of Slaney, a gentleman of fortune in that neighbourhood who presided with great good humour for many years at the Club held at that house. At 35 he weighd 46 stone, &, being then unable to sustain any longer his own weight, resigned in due form the Chain of the Club, first, however, at their desire, sitting for this picture, & took to his bed where he lived only for 2 years longer, still encreasing in corpulency. Part of the wall was taken down for his coffin & corpse to pass thro'. The Club revere so much his memory that they have refused to part with the portrait to his devisee who press'd anxiously to have it . But what was Slaney to the present Llambert who last summer weighed 52 stone & walkd very firmly under the pressure of that immense mass?[32]

From Knowle to Birmingham 10m. at 14d pm, & from Birmingham Castle Inn to Wolverhampton 14 m. at 14 d.pm. N. B. Castle Inn 14d pm. Every other inn in Birmingham charges 15d. But from hence to Holyhead we are assured the rate of posting is 15d a mile invariably. But 34 miles this day. What population from Birmingham to Wolverhampton! 14 miles of almost one uninterrupted street ! & travelling after nightfall it seem'd to us as if the whole country was on fire.

Sat.17th Rise early. A dear & saucy house I believe the Lion. Breakfast at Shiffnall, 12 m. Change horses at Watling St., 7 m, in the neighbourhood of the great Iron Works of Ketley & Oaken Gates and the Iron Bridge Coalbrookdale, & almost suffocated by the Vesuvian vapour of the forges & furnaces.

From Shrewsbury through Wales to Holyhead

Proceed to Shrewsbury 11m. crossing the noble Severn for the first time & passing by Lord Berwick's fine seat[33] upon its banks. From thence to Oswestry 18 m, the last of the English towns, & from thence to Llangollen 12 m., taking leave of England in the valley of Chirk where the great Aqueduct is conducted across the Valley upon 10 tall arches; & at Llangollen (having lost the beauties of the Vale & having narrowly escaped being overset in consequence of travelling after nightfall) we stable our horses for the night - & Lord knows it is an inn scarcely fit for horses to stable in. On entering the House we are told by the boozy old snuffy Bill-dame that we can have no accommodation, that it was a fine night & we may proceed to Corwen but 10 miles off. With some coaxing, however, we obtain first a room wth 2 beds & at last a closet inside that room wth a bed in it; our dinner too, after waiting beyond all patience, is served up smoked & burn'd but not dress'd - & next morning after all the neglect of the night before we have to encounter the laziness of the Waiter & the scurrility of the Ostler, & not without much exertion are we able to extricate ourselves before 8 o'clock. 60 m. this day.

Sund.18th Breakfast at Corwen - 10 m.- wch we drove in one hour. The Welsh Post Boys are famous; but really it is awful to rattle down those hills so furiously where the stumble of a horse or the breaking down of a wheel may chuck the carriage & all over the precipice into eternity. Change horses at Craniog, 13 m.; & from thence proceed by the new road (instead of turning to the right by the old road to Llangwryst & Conway) to Capelcarrig -15 m.[34] A more beautiful, romantic & picturesque scene I never travelled - sometimes thro' a soft wooded valley water'd by smooth reaches of the Conway river, sometimes working our way along the sides of perpendicular mountains over abrupt precipices stunn'd with the roaring of the river in the Valley beneath tumbling in foaming torrents now, & anon in headlong cataracts down its rugged bed - it seems in short to combine all the various & contrasted beauty of the Dargle, the Gap of Dunloe & Lord Bantry's charming Vale, what do you call it?[35]

Yet it must be confessed that one pays some price for the magnificent scenery in the nervous sensations excited by the rapid rate of rushing down a steep declivity near half a mile long, winding continually round projecting cliffs & guarded from the precipice by a very frail, flimsy battlement. It is to be hoped however that Lord Penrhyn,[36] to whom the public are indebted for this great work, will not find it difficult to correct those awful portions of the road & so make perfect what already does his Lordship such honour. The history of this road is whimsical. Lord Penrhyn, having canvassed at Conway upon a General Election, was received with hisses & hootings & all manner of insult, his carriage even pelted & the panels broke. This as was natural gave his Lordship such rooted offence that he declared he would make the grass grow in the streets of Conway; & thereupon he set surveyors to work who struck out this new line beginning two miles from Bangor on the old post-road & falling into the Llangwryst road about three miles west of Craniog, in all above 13 miles, shortening the Holyhead road to London above 10 miles & avoiding Conway ferry; so that the old road by Conway is now wholly deserted save by the Chester Mail Coach; & this too, it is expected, as soon as the new road is connected & those acclivities softened, will proceed by this line to Corwen & from thence turn off by Ruthvin to Chester wch will exceed the present line to Chester not more than a mile.

19th The new Inn of Capelcarrig is very handsome & upon a great scale.

Bonniface, whom I discovered to be an Irishman spite of all his pains to pass for English, is civil & attentive; but the appointments & establishment of the house are very poor & but ill-proportiond to so long a house. A dear bill & what is worse a bad chaise & horses to convey us a stage of seventeen rugged miles.

The beauties of this road did not end yesterday. After traversing about 5 miles of dreary turf-bog we approach a fine lake in the bosom of an amphitheatre of the most savage mountains wch appear to close upon the traveller & block up his egress. Advancing however along the margin of the lake you at length discover a narrow passage thro' wch a very good road makes its way under a still border & more craggy mountain than any that yesterday presented to us. Westward of the Half-way House you at last arrive at Lord Penrhyn's celebrated Slate Quarries[37] wch he has connected with the commodious creek at Bangor by a Rail-way 7 miles long. What a contrast between this delightful region, crowded with hundreds of the prettiest cottages so nice & clean that none of them would soil the cambric handkerchief of Lady Penrhyn & parcell'd out into meadows & gardens, & the infernal regions wch surround Wolverhampton in Staffordsh, & Kessley in Shropshire where every house appears a forge & every human being a Cyclop!

Breakfast at the best of all houses, Jackson's at Bangor-ferry - cross the ferry without alarming even Mrs. Day, & finding no chaise to be had at the other side we gladly secure seats in the Stage Coach & arrive safe & well at Holyhead about 5 p.m.

"No birth to be had, all are engaged", are the first notes we hear on our arrival, & that from the best authority - the Steward - adding "this to be sure is unfortunate for the wind is a fine South-west & no packet will sail tomorrow, Tuesday".

From this state of mortification however we are soon relieved by our dear friends, Stephen & Mrs. Rice, whom Providence had just sent before us in the morning time enough to secure for themselves the state cabin & who generously insist upon sharing with us. About 10 we embark & after a fine rough passage of about 12 hours on board Jones's Packet

Tu. 20th Oct. we arrive all safe but all sick as dogs at the Pigeon House -

> Now let us sing Long live the King
> & the Uxbridge long live She
> Who brought us safe to Ireland green
> Our loving friends to see.

1. Mary FitzGerald of Bandon, the writer's second wife.

2. Willian Murray, 1st Earl of Mansfield (1705-1793). Lord Chief Justice of the Court of King's Bench from 1756 to 1788. Accused of Jacobite leanings, was in general favourable to Catholc relief legislation.

3. Sir James Mansfield (1733-1821), Lord Chief Justice of the English Court of Common Pleas 1804-1814.

4. Richard Robinson, first Baron Rokeby, Archbishop of Armagh 1765 to his death in 1794. Was responsible for the building of the Royal School, the Observatory, the Bishop's Palace and much more.

5. Euseby Cleaver (1746-1819). He accompanied the Marquis of Buckingham to Ireland as his chaplain. 1789 Bishop of Cork and Ross, Ferns and Leighlin later the same year. Became Archbishop of Dublin 1809.

6. Charles Agar, Archbishop of Cashel 1779-1801, Dublin 1801-9. Opposed Catholic relief legislation.

7. Sir Archibald MacDonald (1747-1826), Chief Baron of the Exchequer 1793-1813.

8. Charles Abbot (1757-1829), Chief Secretary of Ireland February 1801 to January 1802 when he succeeded Sir John Mitford as Speaker of the House of Commons. Remained as Speaker to 1817.

9. William Wyndham Grenville (1759-1834) formed the 'Ministry of All the Talents' in early 1806 following the death of Pitt. It lasted to March 1807.

10. George Grenville was responsible for the famous Stamp Act of the 1760s which contributed to the American War of Independence.

11. Probably the Royalist John Dolben (1625-1686), Archbishop of York 1683-6.

12. Sir William Dolben, 3rd Bart., MP Oxford University (1768, 1780-1806), a Protestant Evangelical.

13. Day exaggerates a little. The dates of William Markham are 1719-1807. He died in November. Born in Cork, became Headmaster of Westminster School 1753, Dean of Christ Church, Oxford 1767, Bishop of Chester 1771, Archbishop of York 1777. Friend and collaborator with Edmund Burke (DNB).

14. The Collegiate Church of St Mary, Warwick.

15. The Beauchamp Chantry in St Mary Collegiate Church.

16. Robert Dudley, Earl of Leicester, lover of Queen Elizabeth.

17. Robert's younger brother was Ambrose Dudley. The Warwick title had been granted to their father, the Duke of Northumberland, powerful member of the Protectorate.

18. The tomb of Richard Beauchamp (d.1439), a magnificent masterpiece of medieval art. Earl of Warwick, Richard Beauchamp was Captain of Calais and Custodian of Rouen Castle during the imprisonment of Joan of Arc.

19. Sir Fulke Greville, (1554-1628), Chancelor of the Exchequer to King James 1, was granted the ruined castle of Warwick by James, in 1604. He spent at least £20,000 on its restoration. He was not granted the earldom of Warwick but became the first Baron Brooke.

20. Warwick Castle was successively the seat of the Beauchamps, Nevilles, Dudleys, and Grevilles (Barons Brooke, recovering the Earldom of Warwick from 1759).

21. James Graham, Marquis of Montrose (1612-1650) raised Scotland for Charles, using Irish troops who had supported Charles's cause in Ireland. The portrait mentioned here continues on display at Warwick Castle.

22. Thomas Wentworth, 1st Earl of Strafford (1593-1641), Lord Deputy of Ireland, executed in 1641 following trial on charges of raising an Irish army to fight for Charles 1 in the English Civil War.

23. Edward Wortley Montagu, husband of the more famous Lady Mary (1689-1762), writer of the 'Letters'. In 1716 Montagu was appointed ambassador to the Porte.

24. The tapestry continues to hang in Warwick Castle, but the portrait over the fire place is Queen Anne, after Kneller.

25. Day in a footnote: "Mrs. Palmer, a woman prodigal, rapacious, dissolute, violent, revengeful." Barbara Palmer, nee Villiers, Countess of Castlemaine and Duchess of Cleveland, was mistress of Charles the Second.

26. Henrietta Maria de Bourbon, wife of Charles 1. Elsewhere Day uses the epithets 'the Great' and 'the Immortal' for her father Henry IV. Henry's conversion to Catholicism during the wars of religion, together with the attributed remark that Paris was 'worth a Mass,' has earned him a reputation for narrow pragmatism among some historians. But Day's politics are majoritarian. As Queen of England Henrietta Maria's retention of her Catholic faith, and her influence on both of her sons' conversions to Catholicism, made her the object of Day's condemnation (RIA, Day Papers, Ms. SR 24n13, History of England).

27. Founder of the Jesuit order.

28. George Greville (1773-1816), who emulated some of his father's extravagances and in 1804 was forced to sell part of the estate following expensive improvements.

29. Day's recollection is correct. Guy de Beauchamp, Earl of Warwick, was one of the 'Ordainers' a group of earls who opposed the influence of favourites around King Edward II (1307-27); in 1312 Guy had the leading favourite and lover of the the King, the Gascon knight Piers Gaveston, seized and beheaded near Warwick.

30. Galea (L. helmet). The bust of Minerva Galeata continues on display at Warwick Castle. The island of Paros was famous for its white marble.

31. Sir William Hamilton (1730-1803), diplomat and archaeologist, British envoy at the court of Naples. The 'Warwick Vase' in the Greenhouse at Warwick Castle was purchased by Hamilton and donated in 1774 by him to the Earl of Warwick. Hamilton's wife, Emma, formed a romantic relationship with Admiral Lord Nelson.

32. Daniel Lambert (1770-1809) of Leicester, who exhibited himself in London in 1807. He was 'the most corpulent man of whom authentic record exists' (DNB 1938).

33. Noel-Hill, raised to the peerage as barons Berwick in 1784. Residence at Attingham, near Shrewsbury.

34. Capel Curig was an old staging post on the road from London to Holyhead.

35. The word Glengariff is written in the Ms at this point.

36. Richard Pennant (1737?- 1808) was a West Indian sugar plantation owner, becoming MP for Liverpool in 1767. He developed his Carnarvonshire estate and the Welsh slate industry, building many cart roads and erecting a quay on the river Cegin for shipping the slates from his estate by means of a tramroad.

37. Still in operation, the slate quarries overlook the village of Bethesda and are visible from Penrhyn's castle.

Loughlinstown House, Co. Dublin, reproduced from Ella B. Day, Mr Justice Robert Day of Kerry, Exeter 1938

5

In Ireland: illness and recovery at Loughlinstown; the Leinster Circuit, Spring 1808

Judge Day suffers a relapse after returning from England. After some months of recuperation at Loughlinstown he undertakes the Leinster Circuit, which then included Tipperary. Tipperary has been the scene of a rural war conducted by the Caravats and Shanavests. The choice of Day to tackle rural crime in Tipperary and Kilkenny is a recognition of his experience, as well as his popularity.
He is increasingly reluctant to travel the Munster circuit because of the clash of personal interests with his judicial role.

2nd Novr. After spending a few days in sequestered relaxation at Loughlinstown I am again seized with little or no provocation with the Hernia Humoralis wch herries[1] us all to town.

Alas! I am confined always to my house & sometimes to my bed with repeated relapses of this alarming complaint thro' the whole of Michaelmas Term, the first default I have ever made even for a day thro' my judicial life. Macklin [2] my surgeon & Murphy my Apothecary.

Hartigan & Hamilton are called in to a Consultation wth Macklin who proscribe a Mercurial medicine wch on consulting Dr. Percival[3] he fortunately forbids. Thro' my unfortunate confinement my greatest comfort is the benevolent assiduity of my worthy friend the Chief Justice[4] who sits with me 3 or 4 hours every week.

January 1808

23rd January. I decline going to Court, being a day only of form.

25th I join my brethren who greet my return to Court with hearty congratulation.

On this day my poor dear brother the Archdeacon and Vicar Genl. of Ardfert died in Tralee after an illness of 3 days - a man of fine parts and great erudition, and of benevolence unbounded.[5]

multis flebilis, mihi ab imo corde carus.[6]

Discharge my steward John Neill for drunkenness and total negligence of my business in my absence, if not worse, after a service of nine years.

12 February. Attend Court through the whole term without any suffering, so that with reasoned prudence and caution I trust in God I shall hear no more of the Hernia Humoralis. Boldly undertake the Leinster circuit, and consent to the design of Saurin, Attorney-General,[7] to begin at Clonmel on 7th March.

Otherwise the overflowing Jail of that Town and disturbed state of Co. Tipperary would make a special commission necessary.

Lent Circuit in Leinster

Thurs. 3 d. March. Leave Loughlinstown House at 8 a.m for Dublin on my way to Clonmell with £100 viaticum. Call upon Lord Manners, Chancellor & conferred with reference to the source & foundation of his high character.[8] Receive some useful hints derived from English practice. Sorrowful Thursday with poor Ned who having been with us since Saturday returns this day to School.[9] My new purchase Cobb is seized with an inflammation just as I order the carriage to the door. I look about for Mat. Franks whom we at last find, & borrow a horse from him. Send Cobb to Watts the veterinary Surgeon. Vexatious question among judges: " Is it best to travel circuit with one's own horses or with cobbs?" The former the more respectable, the latter the more prudent & frugal. I have always & invariably practised the former course.

Frid.4th Breakfast at Johnstown. Drive 4 in hand attended by 3 servants; 2 in the chaise & 1 on horseback. Bate at the blackguard 19 mile House. Stop for the night at Ballytore, 28 m. from Dublin. Tough rabbit & blunt knives! But Ledbeater is a Quaker & I respect the whole Society.[10]

Sat. 5th March. Breakfast at Carlow & drive & sleep at Kilkenny, 30 m.

Sun. 6th Breakfast at Maher's Nine Mile House. Drive for first time by the New Line through the Glen by Mr. Elliot's improvements, capable of rivalling (if planted) the Welsh vales. Dinner at Clonmel. At 8 Smith, Baron[11] arrives.

Mon. 7th Open the Assizes with charge of an hour upon the unhappy state attributable to the supineness of the magistrates. The Grand Jury beg to publish the charge. Two convicted of a murder & arson & robbery.[12]

Tues. 8th Two more convicted of murder.

Wed. 9. One man convicted of a rape. Dine with the bar. The two first, Ryan & Keaty, hanged, & on

Th. 10th the next 2 hanged – Lyons.[13]

Fr. Sentence two Caravats & 2 Shanavests to be flogged three times, & to be imprisoned, 1 of each for 2 years & 1 of each for 1 year & security &c. [14]

Sat. 12th Several convicted of misdemeanours under the Whiteboy Act & sentenced as yesterday.

Sund.13 Mar. Go to church, wch is a very respectal one. Walk with Bagwell to the handsome Glebehouse lately built by May the Rector.[15] From thence to Cary's school, almost a ruin,[16] & so on through this very thriving town. We dine with Bagwell at his handsome seat of Marlfield[17] & return late after a pleasant day.

Mond.14th Try…for murder & convicted.

Tuesd. 15th W. Power, a magistrate tried for murder & acquitted. He should have been convicted of manslaughter.[18] Write to the Chancellor to supersede him & McCarthy of Springhouse & Mr. William FitzGerald of the commission of the peace. The Baron also complains of the magistrate Mr. Geo Shaw - all broke, wch I take to be an excellent example.

W.16th Close the severest Assizes I ever was engaged in for criminal matters since 1798 & proceed to Kilkenny with a heavy cough.

Th. 17th The Baron gives the Co. Grand Jury an excellent charge. I preside in the city.

Sund. 20th Take a late breakfast with Col. James Butler (who I predict will be Earl of Wandesford) at Knocktopher, Langrishe's place, 10m.[19] Travel the following 14 m. through heavy rain over a dreary country to Waterford.

Mon.21st Mar. Swear & charge the County Grand Jury. Decline Dean Lee's[20] invitation to dinner & feel at home on mutton broth.

Tu. 22 M. Wilson acquitted of a barbarous murder wch he committed. Two men capitally convicted of mail robbery. Spend an agreeable day with Power Trench, Bishop of Waterford, and entertained most handsomely. A very good-natured, well-bred gentleman.[21]

23rd. Two young men convicted of burglary. Recommended by the grand and petty juries, wch I back to Government.

Thursday 24th Proceed on our way to Wexford to Ross, 10 m. to Mr. Charles Tottenham's, where we are very politely entertained at bed & board.[22] The approach to the town over the fine Barrow beautiful. The town well paved & flagged, the direct contrast of Waterford whose pavement is abominable. The Corporation ought to be roasted. I had like to have forgot that I breakfasted very comfortably this morning with my friends Collector May & wife at their beautiful Villa May-farm on this fine river Suir below Waterford.

Fr. 25th Mar. Very heavy snow all night & all the whole day. This prevents my visiting the town where the famous Battle of Ross was fought 5 June 1798, in wch poor Lord Mountjoy fell,[23] & General. Johnson fought gallantly, & wch about 1200 men finally prevailed against 3000 rebels. Beauchamp Bagenal Harvey commanded them & kept at such respectful distance that the rebels deposed him & substituted General Roche, an excommunicated priest of great courage & some talent.[24] Bate at Foukes's Mill[25] and drive in the evening into Wexford, 20 m from Ross. Travel all day over classic ground but covered with snow.

Sat. 26. The Baron charges the Grand Jury with his well-known talent. We had agreed to urge to every grand jury the necessity of economy, wch we accordingly inforce in every county.

Sund.27th Dine with Mr. Meadows the Sheriff[26] two miles out of town: Lord Ely,[27] Lord Valentia, &c. Lord V, whom I now meet for the first time, a very interesting polished gentleman.[28]

M 28th The Baron taken up the whole day with the long-expected trial of Alcock for the murder of Colclough in a duel.[29] All Waterford & Wexford counties pour into Wexford to attend the trial. Several come from Kilkenny, Tipperary, Wicklow & Dublin. It closes about 9 in the evening when the jury, after a most ingenious & elegant charge from the little Baron, acquitted him with the approbation of the whole court. No judge in the United Kingdom probably could have conducted the charge with such address as the Baron, who without compromising the law yet flung out such grounds by insinuation as quieted their consciences touching the pious perjury wch they were predetermined to commit. Yet quaere, whether the correct course for the judge in such cases be not distinctly to lay down the law viz. that homicide committed in Rencounter or where the passions have not had time to subside or cool, is manslaughter, but in a deliberate duel is murder. All the circumstances wch in a court martial or a court of honour may be taken into consideration to palliate the offence should be left to the jury to take up of themselves; & the judge, knowing that in point of law they are of no value to vary the quality of the crime, is bound to tell the jury so. If there be any favourable facts, such as e.g. as abundantly appeared in Alcock's case, those belong to the Crown to appreciate and to act upon. But the Irish judges enter into the chivalrous temper of the country & we are beginning to consider the case of a duellist as an exception in the law of murder.[30]

Tues.29th Mar. Dine with Capt. Lefroy.[31] I wish he would keep better fires.

W.30th Breakfast on my way to Wicklow at Edward's of Oulart, facing the house where parson Burrowes & family[32] were inhumanly butchered in the Rebellion. In the rear lies the Hill where 101 of the North Cork Militia were cut to pieces with poor Major Lombard at their head. Their confidence & contempt of the Rebels were their destruction. Instead of firing from a safe distance they actually flung away their shoes & stockings to overtake & charge them & when arrived on the top of a bank up started thousands of the enemy & instantly surrounded & dispatched them. Col. Foote valiantly fled to fight another day & with him a drummer boy, the only survivors of the party. 10 m. Proceed to Mr. Beauman's Hyde Park by invitation. 14m. The Baron arrives at 9. Very politely & handsomely entertained.

Th. 31st After breakfast we proceed to Arklow, 2 m. beyond the bounds, bate, & proceed along the shore to Wicklow, 10 m. where I swear & charge the grand jury.

Fr. 1 April. Finish the Crown business in one day. Two men (... & Nowlan) convicted of burglary. The former I recommend.

Sat. 2. Breakfast with my amiable friends the Fosberrys at Bray, & surprise agreeably my dear little woman at dinner who did not expect me till tomorrow.

& here endeth this journal.

1. herry i.e. to harry.

2. Gerard Macklin Esq., State Surgeon (*Gentleman's and Citizen's Almanac 1810*).

3. Possibly Dr. Joseph Perceval (1756-1839), first professor of Chemistry at Dublin University; associated with the opening of Sir Patrick Dunn's Hospital in 1808.

4. William Downes (1752-1826) succeeded Arthur Wolfe, Lord Kilwarden, as Chief Justice of the King's Bench.

5. Rev. Edward Day (1738 –1808). Rector of the union of Kiltallagh, Killorglin and Knockane (Beaufort) 1771, Archdeacon of Ardfert 1802, Vicar General diocese of Ardfert. Residence Beaufort. Many travel writers of the period record meeting 'Dr. (Archdeacon) Day'.

6. Approxiate translation 'Very sorrowful, dear from (the/his/my) innermost heart'.

7. William Saurin, Attorney General 1807-22. Commanded a high profile in the trials of the Catholic delegates in 1811 and 1812, and in those of the editor of the Dublin Evening Post, John Magee, in 1813 and 1814, in all of which trials Day presided with the other judges of the King's Bench.

8. The Chancellor from 1807 to 1827 was Thomas Manners Sutton, Lord Manners, (1756-1842), formerly Solicitor General of England during the administration of Addington. There is some scribbling of the text at this point and a reference (perhaps from their conversation) to Nelson's victory at the Nile and Duncan's at Camperdown.

9. His grandson Edward Denny (name written above 'Ned' in the ms.) was nicknamed 'The Hymn-Writer'. He attended Eton.

10. Ballitore, a Quaker settlement. Burke attended the school of Abraham Shackleton there. It was the home of Shackleton's granddaughter Mary Leadbeater (1758-1826), poet and diarist *(The Leadbeater Papers, Mss. and Correspodence of Mary Leadbeater,* 2 vols., London 1862. Vol.1 is 'The Annals of Ballitore', where on page 344 she reports the visit of Judge Day while on circuit in 1814).

11. Baron Sir William Cusac Smith, b. 1766, Lincoln's Inn 1784, called to the bar 1788, supported the Union strongly in parliament; Solicitor-General 1800; Baron of the Court of Exchequer 1801; died 1836.

12. Day arrived at Clonmel 'escorted by a strong party of dragoons', and Baron Smith 'attended in a similar manner arrived at a later hour', Day later presiding in the criminal court (*Freeman's Journal,* March 12, 1808). See the contemporary press for the trials of Caravats and Shanavests at these assizes. The regions affected in this phase of rural agitation were the South Tipperary, Kilkenny and West Waterford.

13. *The Limerick Gazette and General Advertiser* of March 18 1808 gives Thursday morning for the execution of John Ryan and Matthew Keaty. They were executed at Gallows Hill ('The Sheriff was attended by the Grand Jury and a vast assemblage of Magistrates and Gentlemen'). Patrick Lyons and Patrick Feeny were executed on Friday for the murder of Patrick English of Ballynavin during an attack on his house: 'they said it was for taking the grass of a field from Barrett, the stewart of Dr. Greene'. Ibid.

14. These were cases of 'tumultuous assembly' in Cahir and Tipperary. Such assemblies often involved the tendering of oaths. Day 'expatiated on the enormous mischief of these audacious assemblages which are the root and foundation of all the confusion in the country'. Ibid.

15. Rev. Thomas May, Rector of St. Mary's 1795-1811.

16. Rev. Richard Cary was headmaster of Clonmel Grammar School from 1777 to 1821.

17. Marlfield, the seat of John Bagwell MP is near Clonmel. He was foremen of the county Tipperary Grand Jury.

18. Edmond Power, a magistrate, was tried for the murder of Joseph Lonergan. The trial heard that Power shot him in the back.

19. Mount Pleasant in Limerick. See pedigrees at back of this book for the connection of Wandesforde of Castlecomer with Rose of Morgans in Limerick.

20. Ussher Lee, Dean of Waterford 1804.

21. Power Le Poer Trench (1770-1839). Bishop of Waterford 1802-1810, Kilmore 1810-1819, Archbishop of Tuam 1819. The Trench family seat was Galbally, Ballinasloe. His father was William Power Keating Trench, Lord Kilconnel, Viscount Dunlo 1801and earl of Clancarty 1803. The son's appointment to Waterford was the reward for his father's support for the Union in the Irish House of Lords, but Day's admiration for him may have owed more to the bishop's record on church reform.

22. Charles Tottenham (1743-1823) MP, of Tottenham Green. He was 'Tottenham in his Boots', after a hurried appearance in parliament for a vote on the Treasury surplus. In 1798 he commanded the Yeomen at New Ross.

23. Luke Gardiner, 1st Viscount Mountjoy, killed on the bridge of Ross 1798.

24. Fr Philip Roche was appointed to lead the South Wexford rebels in 1798.

25. Foulkesmills.

26. Arthur Meadows of Hermitage, Sheriff of Wexford in 1808.

27. John Tottenham, later Loftus (1770-1845), 2nd Marquess of Ely, of Loftus Hall, Co. Wexford.

28. Arthur Annesley (1744-1816), 8th Viscount of Valentia and 1st Earl of Mountnorris, sometime Governor of Wexford. His estate was near Camolin in the north of County Wexford.

29. The duel took place during the general election of 1807. Richard Brindsley Sheridan, running mate of John Colclough, made a strong speech against the Insurrection Act and this excited the Catholic tenants of Mrs Cholmondeley's estate to declare that they would not abide by her pledge to vote for the Tory candidate, William Congreve Alcock. Alcock demanded the votes, challenged Colclough and killed him with a ball to the heart. Barrington saw the duel as the snuffing out of the independent interest in Wexford by the forces of the Marquess of Ely.

30. Baron Smith found that some of the prosecutors 'have themselves been present aiding and assisting at the perpetration of what they now represent to have been a murder'; Smith also spoke of 'that mild sentiment of mercy which softens and pervades our law', and he appeared to take into account the traditional resort to duels and the present tensions during the continuing international war. Alcock was found not guilty (*Faulkner's Dublin Journal*, 14 April, 1808).

31. A Captain Anthony Lefroy (1777-1857) , 65th Regt, was brother of the more famous Thomas Langlois Lefroy, the future chief justice of the Court of Queen's Bench. The family was Huguenot, its seat Carriglass near Longford.

32. Rev. Richard Burrowes lived at Kyle Glebe, near Oulart. It was 'an important repository for surrendered arms'. It was attacked in May 1798. He was piked in front of his residence during some confusion about an apparent attempt on his part to negotiate (Daniel Gahan, *The People's Rising, Wexford in 1798,* Dublin 1995, p. 20.).

The Charge
delivered to the Grand Jury of the County of Tipperary on Monday 7th of March 1808 by the Hon. Mr. Justice Day

and now published at their request.
Dublin.

Printed by Graisberry and Campbell, Back Lane, 1808

Gentlemen of the Grand Jury,

The peculiar circumstances under which the Leinster Circuit commences, as well as the unprecedented difficulties in which the Judges find the County Tipperary unfortunately involved, make it my duty to trouble you with some observations before you retire to the Grand Jury Room.

If the present Circuit has gone out at an earlier period of the Spring than is usual, or perhaps convenient to Country gentlemen, if it commences at the town of Clonmel, where a circuit never before commenced, the occasion of this novelty is but too well known. The unhappy state of your county, the lawless and turbulent spirit which has so long and so notoriously rioted uncontrouled through the greater part of it, made it an object of public concern that the Judges of Assize should proceed to deliver your overflowing gaol, and administer justice among you with as much celerity after the Term as might consist with due solemnity and the legal and necessary notices. – Such was the wish of our firm and vigilant government as communicated to the Judges; it was some object to avoid the expence of a Special Commission, and still more important to save you the serious inconvenience of two Assizes instead of one; and, to this just and reasonable desire, the Judges, not balancing, for a moment, between their own convenience and the public interest, have without hesitation conformed.

Upon looking through your Calendar, I perceive, with infinite regret and pain, that the afflicting reports from hence appear to have been in no wise exaggerated. If the Calendar (as I have sometimes heard it called), the criminal barometer of its bailiwicke, if the state of the gaol, be no unfaithful symptom of the moral and civil condition of the country at large, then is the state of civil society in your county deplorable in the extreme. I hold in my hand a paper, which for its size and quantity of matter resembles more the chart of a county than Calendar of its gaol; an affecting catalogue of 148 of our unfortunate fellow creatures, incarcerated since the last assizes, under charges for the deepest atrocity! In truth, it is a downright misnomer, a gross abuse and perversion of language to say that civil society exists in a county so inundated with crime. Gentlemen, it is vain to deny, that in no other county in the United Kingdom is to be found so inveterate a relaxation of all order, so habitual and confirmed a contempt of all law, both human and divine, as have characterised the peasantry of the county of Tipperary. I allude not to the Rebellion; of that disastrous visitation God knows you had your full proportion. But you then only shared in the general infatuation and criminality of the land. I refer to the dismal records of your Crown Office for half a century. I refer you to the memorable era of the White Boys, and of the enormities which followed that stubborn and unhappy commotion. I refer to those halcyon days when land was recovered amongst you, not by the slow and vulgar process of ejectment, but by beat of drum, when the still calm voice of the law was drowned amidst the roar and thunder of cannon; when lawsuits were conducted "with all the pride, pomp and circumstance of glorious war." To the county of Tipperary, Ireland stands indebted for a peculiar criminal code, written like the laws of Draco, in blood, the Laws against tumultuous risings, commencing with the 15th and 16th G.3 called the *Whiteboy Act;* a statute whose provisions are unknown in England, because the crimes which it seeks to depress are unknown there; a statute whose sanctions, however severe and vindictive, are not disproportionate to the familiar crimes of our country.

The crimes which I allude to, and which, having originated in this county, have, with an eager and fatal emulation been propagated from time to time through various other counties of Ireland, are lawless confederacies of the peasantry against property; and tumultuous risings, chiefly in the night time; sometimes in large bodies, and sometimes in gangs and banditties, to effect by terror, the guilty purpose of such confederacy. The object of these offenders have varied at various times. Sometimes their entire vengeance has been levelled at Tythes: a species of property of property of sacred and indefeasible tenure, consecrated by Divine institution, and the immemorial usage of Christendom to the maintenance of the church. From thence, as might well be expected, they have sometimes proceeded to the regulation of lay property, and modification of rents, and I understand that lately these Sovereign Legislators have promulgated a law amongst you, whereby, after reciting "that it is an intolerable grievance, and an arrogant encroachment upon the Rights of Man, for any owner of land to choose his own tenantry, it is enacted by the authority aforesaid, that it shall not be lawful for any person to take ground, or enter into the possession of any farm, or habitation, without the special license of the association him thereunto authorising, and, in case any persons shall be found offending in the premises, he shall, for the first offence suffer penalties of carding, roasting, or house burning, in the discretion, of the Association; and for the second offence, he shall suffer death as in cases of felony, without benefit of Clergy."

The professed purpose of these associations has always been a redress of grievances. But, gentlemen, the Constitution knows no course of proceeding for the redress of grievances, but by petition of any one or all of the three branches of the Legislature, conducted in a peaceable, orderly, and respectful manner; a right unequivocally asserted at the Glorious Revolution in the famous Bill of Rights. Whether these confederacies do suffer any real grievances, it belongs not to us to inquire; but if one might judge from the quality and character of the specific redress which they prefer, it is plain that the most galling grievances which they feel, are the fetters of civil society – those restraints which Religion and Law impose on man in the social state for the protection of persons and property. The grievance which oppresses them is that inequality of condition and property which necessarily and physically results from the inequality of human faculties and capacity; a grievance, for which these virtuous declaimers would no doubt suggest, as the best specific, an Agrarian Law, in other words, a general scramble, out of which a new inequality much more to the palate of these gentlemen would instantly arise, namely, the ascendancy of brutal strength and ferocity over talent and virtue.

Associations formed for purposes so daring and so desperate necessarily generate in their sweeping progress the foulest enormities. The first step of the flagitious leaders, is to deliver their deluded followers from every trace of religion and of an avenging God; a task, facilitated by the total neglect of parents and pastors to inculcate early morality among the lower order. – Their bloody rites are gravely opened with a solemn oath of fidelity to this infernal cause, an oath in its effect to commit every crime; to that oath, and to that alone, the unfortunate men are found to adhere with a scrupulous punctuality. – Then follows, in rapid succession, a black and mournful train of the most hideous and savage crimes: burglaries, house-burning, abductions, robberies, rapes, torture, murder; in short all the revolting atrocities which crowd this disgusting Calendar. Crimes the most enormous, in truth, are now so frequent among us, "so familiar to our slaughterous thoughts," that they no longer excite in our minds the slightest shock or emotion. These daily occurrences have hardened the public heart; they have brutalised the national spirit; they have tarnished the national character; and the good old name of Irishman, once another word for every thing gallant, generous, and humane, is become almost as opprobrious even as the name of Frenchman.

To redeem the national character, and to stem the tide of national crime, the Legislature has interposed with this vindictive and energetic statute; and as you are likely, if I may judge from the Calendar, to be called upon to act upon it, in many of the cases which are to go before you, and as it is of the utmost public importance that this crowded auditory, and through them the whole country, should be clearly and distinctly impressed with the law, I feel it not foreign to my duty to detain you with a brief abstract of the principal provisions of one of the best considered acts in the statute book.

The Statute begins with the mere act of assembling in arms, or under any usual denomination or dress, in terrorum populi, though the insurgents proceed to no actual violence, a high misdemeanour, punishable by pillory, whipping or other corporal punishment, besides fine and imprisonment, at the discretion of the court. But every act, or even threat or violence committed in furtherance of the guilty purpose of the association is punished with death; as sending threatening letters, procuring another, whether by threats or promises, to become a member of such criminal confederacy; compelling or by threats attempting to compel, any person to quit his habitation, farm, or place of employment after nightfall, assaulting any person, or injuring his habitation, offices, haggard, or other property; taking away, after nightfall against the will of the owner any horse, arms ammunition, money, or any goods, or by threats causing the same to be delivered; abetting, succouring, or concealing any of the offenders; administering seditious oaths – in short, every imaginable act or threat of violence, or in prosecution of the general purpose of the association, is punishable by death. But the legislature has not contented itself with denouncing the crime. It has armed the magistrates with abundant means to detect and bring to justice the criminal. Two magistrates are empowered to summon any person whom they suspect to have been, or of intending to be, in any such unlawful assembly, and one is authorised to summon and examine any person capable of giving evidence of any offence against the Statute, and to bind both over to the ensuing Assizes; the one to answer such charges as shall be exhibited against him, the other to prosecute ; and if both or either refuse to enter into the recognizance, the magistrates have full power to commit for such contumacy. And in case of any disturbance they are invested with power proportioned to the emergency.

They are in such case clothed with extraordinary power, limited before to Sheriffs, of commanding the *Posse Comitatus* (or to use the language of the statute, "all his Majesty's subjects of age and ability within his bailiwick") to assist in apprehending and dispersing, and, for that purpose to resort to such force, tho' death ensue, as the necessity of the case shall require. And if in such a conflict, any offender be killed, the magistrate and those acting under his command shall be excused and indemnified; and if any of his party be wounded or killed, besides the capital consequence to the offenders, the Grand Jury are required (and if such a case shall now come before it will be your duty) to present liberally for the wounded sufferer, or in case of death, still more liberally for his personal representative.

When the law is thus arrayed in all the terror of death, and the Magistrates are armed with the most efficient powers, it is natural to ask how it happens that, while the rest of the island enjoys a profound peace, there should be in the county of Tipperary so little security for persons or property? In this county, where all the materials for human happiness have by a bounteous Providence been so profusely scattered! Where the Palatinate of the loyal, brave, and generous Ormonde, in a former century, dispensed justice and civilization to a willing and contented people! In this fine county, where our Great Deliverer,[1] as he surveyed from one of your heights the Golden Plain that stretched beneath him even to the utmost verge of the horizon, exclaimed with rapture, "This is indeed a country worth fighting for!." Such, Gentlemen, should be the language of us all: "this is a country worth fighting for!" For, will you tamely surrender this fine county to felons and banditties? Will you resign your property to the spoiler, and your throats to the midnight murderer? Is this a county that shall relapse without a struggle into its ancient barbarism, and become once more a wilderness of wolves, or of human beings worse than wolves? The infatuation and curse of our first parents are surely still upon us; and I fear it is not in the nature of man to be happy even in Paradise. Gentlemen, the source of the evil is obvious. It would be unbecoming the high commission which I most unworthily bear to palliate your disease.

The source of the evil is the indolence, the inactivity, the reprehensible supineness of your magistracy. Hic fonte derivata clades. The laws are not executed but are suffered to repose in your statute book. If the magistrates to whom the constitution commits the execution of the laws, would step out with activity and courage, if they discharged their duties with the alacrity and vigour to which they virtually pledged themselves when they solicited and obtained the commission of the peace, if the higher orders in general would exert the authority and influence, which condition, education and property universally confer in society, then would the lower orders be amenable, and submissive to the discipline of the law. The proud boast of England is, that a constable's staff executes the law. There the humblest individual in the community (and an humbler cannot be easily imagined than a petty constable) clothed with legal authority is himself a host. And why? Because the magistrate, sustained by every man of influence and power in his neighbourhood, executes, and if necessary inforces, a due obedience to the laws of the land. But why do I appeal from your own county for instances of the most active public spirited and courageous magistrates? Can we so soon forget that in the late Rebellion the fiercest mobs have crouched and tremble in the presence of a single magistrate, armed only with the law, but inspired by a deep sense of duty and by a generous zeal for the honour and interests of his country? Have you not seen in the course of last winter a magistrate of the highest rank braving the frosts and snow of that inclement season, scorning the indulgencies which infirmity might well claim, and which rank and property too often claim, exhibiting a noble example to his fellow magistrates and upper orders of the county, of courage, activity, and public spirit, and by the personal exertions of himself and of those associated with him, at the most unseasonable hours of the night and the most merciless season in our memory, maintaining a profound tranquillity and a perfect reverence for the law through the district of his Lordship's residence?

I forbear to detain you with other instances of magistrates whose spirited and meritorious conduct entitles them to the respect and gratitude of their country. Indeed I doubt not that several virtuous and worthy gentlemen are to be found among your magistrates. But, give me leave to say, that at a season like the present, it is not enough that a magistrate lead a virtuous and blameless course of life, or even act with ordinary diligence, or discharge the meer ordinary duties of his office. When the restless and wicked spirit of insurgency is abroad, magistrates must not fancy that they fulfil their functions by merely receiving informations or granting warrants. If the law has invested them with extraordinary powers to meet the emergency, and fully commensurate to the evil, the law also expects and enjoins that, instead of suffering such powers to languish, and for want of wholesome exercise to expire, the magistrates when the occasion demands shall call them forth into life and active animation. The law commits the peace of the county to the High Sheriff and other magistrates, and the court of King's Bench will hold them responsible for the preservation of it. As one of the Judges of that Court I have no hesitation to say, if it appeared to us that a magistrate suffered a portion of country within his neighbourhood, or within his reach, to be disturbed or annoyed without an active effort to apprehend and disperse the insurgents, the Court would have no difficulty to lay him by the heels and punish him in an exemplary manner. The case of

Alderman Kennet is well known. He was Lord Mayor of London in 1780, the year of the memorable riots;[2] and because he presented a feeble and unavailing opposition to the popular torrent which overflowed and disgraced the capital at that period, he was made a signal example by the Court of King's Bench. If there be amongst you associations of the peasantry, formidable for their numbers and ferocity, linked together by the accursed obligation of blasphemous oaths and the all-powerful magic of certain senseless names, it behoves the magistracy to form counter associations. "When wicked men conspire (says an eloquent statesman) the virtuous should associate."

But, Gentlemen, while I lay before you the law, as applicable to the cases likely to employ your attention, and, while I raise my feeble voice to awaken one and all to a sense of the prostrate and deplorable state of society in your county, God forbid that I should have excited a single exasperated sentiment against an individual in this Calendar. It is indeed a great relief and comfort to my mind under the awful duties of the present Assizes to see so respectable a Grand Jury before me, gentlemen so well acquainted with the important duty you have undertaken, so well disposed to discharge it, and whose stake and character afford the best guarantee to your country for your good conduct. Whatever the crimes of your country may be, you will give to the prisoners the full benefit of the British constitution, presuming every man innocent till he shall be proved by satisfactory evidence to be guilty; that unrivalled constitution which protects alike the peasant and the peer, under whose fostering influence, active and virtuous industry leads infallibly to virtue, to independence and honour. You will not transfer your honest detestation of the crime to any prisoner merely charged with it; in considering every case you will divest yourself of all prejudice and favour, carrying an even mind between the prisoner and the public, erasing from your memory every thing you have heard or read without doors upon the subject, and governing yourselves altogether by the evidence before you. And upon the subject of evidence, I am warranted by the unanimous opinion of the twelve Judges to acquaint you that the only legal evidence to ground a bill of indictment is the personal viva voce examination of some one or more of the witnesses for the Crown. This is the uniform practice in England, a practice which in justice to the prisoner as well as to the public I seriously recommend to your adoption.

Gentlemen, a word or two upon your statutable province of taxation. From the well applied and temperate use of this jurisdiction, it is certain that very essential benefit has resulted to Ireland. No man will deny the importance of numerous roads to the execution of the law, to commercial and social intercourse, and the improvement of the soil; and I doubt if there be in the world an equal proportion of territory intersected and traversed by so many and such well-constructed roads as our island. But it is as certain that no institution ever degenerated into grosser abuse. In the mode of levying this tax some of the most important principles of the constitution are violated. The fundamental principle of all taxation, one which enters into every scheme of finance, is that every man shall pay in proportion to his property. But this tax, by the covenants and management of the lessors of land, devolves, not upon property or income, but upon agricultural industry; not upon the land-owner (like the English land tax), but upon the already overburdened land-holder. So also by this dexterity, the Grand Juror who imposes the tax shares little or nothing in the burden of it, which if he did would afford abundant security against his abuse of the power. The consequence is what may be expected. This tax, from its misapplication and overwhelming magnitude, is become the most oppressive burden which the Irish farmer labours under. After exhausting all his meagre means to discharge the exorbitant Rack Rent, then comes this second rent upon which he had never calculated, and the encreasing enormity of which he could never have foreseen. This recollection, I doubt not will excite you to economy. You are, in truth, in the exercise of this function but the trustees of the purse of your tenantry, and should hold its strings as strictly drawn as shall be consistent with the public interest: selecting from the numerous demands which will crowd upon you, such only as are of acknowledged and general advantage.

But, Gentlemen, a still more powerful argument for economy arises out of the unprecedented state of the British Empire and the awful aspect of human affairs. The present awful crisis calls with a commanding voice upon all the Grand Juries of Ireland, to exercise the severest frugality and thus to preserve unimpaired the resources of the people for the weighty demands of national defence; for the heavy burdens, which our very existence as a free and independent people must necessarily induce. For the question now at issue is no less than the very existence of the British Empire; whether this nursery of heroes, sages and patriots, the asylum of fallen creatures and of persecuted religion, the last refuge in Europe of expiring liberty, morality and law, shall maintain the paramount rank among the nations – shall continue her triumphant career under the mild and constitutional sway of a Brunswick, of George the 3rd, whose long reign has been one uninterrupted stream of bounty to his Irish subjects, particularly to those of the Catholic persuasion? Or whether we too are to be bruised down into a French province and consigned to the iron domination of some brother or cousin, or other vile instrument of an unrelenting usurper. Surely, Gentlemen, the struggle which fate has cast upon us, though awful, presents a sublime and proud spectacle; these pigmy islands inspired by the heroic courage and ardent love for the free constitution to which they owe greatness, launching defiance at the blood-stained Colossus that bestrides the continent, standing single handed, the intrepid champion of Freedom, of Christianity, of a benumbed and stupefied world! What the final issue of this awful conflict will be it would be blasphemy to doubt, mean time at such a crisis it would be wise to promote a spirit of conciliation and harmony amongst all our sects and classes, and to abstain from all these irritating discussions which pride and fierceness only generate, and which have led the country into incalculable end.

It would be the part of the wisdom of an enlightened and Christian policy to forego those paltry religious and political squabbles which disgrace and distract us, to deposit them upon the public altar, and offer them up an acceptable sacrifice to our struggling country. If the views from without be gloomy and alarming, it behoves us the more to avoid all collusion and animosity at home. When the vessel is labouring in a storm, shall the mariners separate into parties instead of employing their joint efforts for the common safety? Give us but unanimity at home, and under that

Gracious Being who hath so often made our cause his own we may bid defiance to a confederate world.

1. King William of Orange.

2. The Gordon Riots in London, 1780.

At leisure in Wicklow

Nothing memorable during these two Terms. (Trinity Term sat Friday 17 June & ended Wednesday 5 July). The Duke of Richmond[1] gives me a pair of colours for John Day,[2] son of the Revd. James, to my very great pleasure.

Tuesd. 12 July. A party of 11 set out upon an excursion through the beauties of Co. Wicklow, first meeting by invitation at Master Henn's nice & sequesterd Lodge (hired for the season) near Killeancarrig.[3] From thence we proceed through the noble seats of Bellview[4] & Mount Kennedy to Dunrann where we alight & with the help of a silver key we open an entrance contrary to the injunctions of the wretched money-hoarding owner Grogan Knox, one of the two surviving brothers of Cornelius Grogan hang'd at Wexford with Beauchamp Bagenal Harvey for treason.[5] Walk through this beautiful valley, as beautiful as it could be without water. Having spent here a couple of hours we proceed by Ashford Bridge to the still-more romantic Devil's Glen, passing under Synge's castellated mansion. Here indeed is abundance of all the materials of picturesque beauty – rock, wood & water - disposed in the boldest & happiest manner. Stroll on under a sweltering sun for 2 miles till we reach the waterfall, lamenting only that the valley ended so soon. From thence drove off to Newrath-Bridge where we refreshed our famished appetites with a good dinner & good beds.[6]

W.13th July Drive through Mr. Tighe's respectable seat of Rosanna, & in sight of extensive oakwoods, to breakfast at Rathdrum, then through the beautiful but neglected Avondale, the lovely child of my late poor friend Sam Hayes,[7] along the enchanting banks of the Avon & Avoca, down the noble scenery of the Vale of Arklow where we lunch, then visit Shelton[8] wch the lordly owner has not condescended to do for several years, preferring the stews & public houses of London, & late in the evening return to Rathdrum to dine & sleep.

Th.14th Breakfast at the Seven Churches having provided ourselves with the necessary materials at Rathdrum. Then traverse a dreary country till we suddenly descend into the paradise of Luggilaw where we are received by order of the benevolent owner Peter La Touche with the most hospitable attention. Boat for an hour on the lake after dinner & catch a couple of dozen trout for supper. Sleep luxuriously for the first time.

Fr.15th St Swithen's Day. "The morning lowers & heavily brings on the day." The first rain since we left home, but after breakfast the sun breaks out and with the help of 12 or 16 of the Redshank natives we get our carriages up the zig-zag steep that guides you into the Sally-Gap pass, & from thence upon the Military Road where after travelling without meeting a pebble to obstruct us for 5 or 6 miles we turned off by Glencree Barrack to Enniskerry where our party separated & withdrew to their several homes, sighing that the excursion ended so soon. But pray who were the party? Mrs. Fosberry, her two sons & two lovely daughters,[9] Mr. Aubrey Hunt[10] & his sweet little wife; John Day Collis,[11] Judge Day & Mrs. Day & their grandson Edward Denny. And a pleasanter expedition or a happier party could not exist.

Inn, Newrath Bridge, Co. Wicklow. The place where Day stayed remains an Inn

Sund. 17th The party rendezvous at dinner at Loughlinstown to talk over the charms of our excursion. The Leylands meet them.

Fr. 29th The Robertses (4) Col.& Mrs. Brown & Mr. & Mrs. Aubrey Hunt dine with us, & who should arrive unexpectedly at dinner-time but Sir Edward Denny & Mr. John Purcell from Cork !

1. Charles Lennox, fourth Duke of Richmond (1764-1819), Lord Lieutenant of Ireland 1807-1813. Governor of Canada 1818-19.

2. Capt John Day was son of the writer's first-cousin, Rev. James Day, Rector of Tralee. Subsequent career: Ensign 13th Sept. 1808 in the 87th Irish Regiment of Foot (Prince of Wales' Royal Irish, later the Royal Irish Fusiliers), Lieutenant 11 April 1811, Captain 18th May 1823 (The Royal Irish Fusiliers Regimental Museum, Armagh). He died unmarried (Mary Agnes Hickson, *Kerry Evening Post,* 28 August, 1880). The regiment's inclusion of many Catholics in the rank and file reflected the outlook of its founder, Sir John Doyle, who was a friend of Day. Historian M. A. Hickson has written: '…my maternal uncle, Captain John Day, served in it (the 87th) throughout the whole of the Peninsular war from Talavera to the battle of Toulouse, when he went with part of it to India to encounter even greater dangers in the Burmese war, after which he returned home invalided to die…'. (*K.E.P.,* 2 November, 1892). His promotion to lieutenant was reported in the contemporary press, together with the suggestion that it was his reward for being one of 'the Barossa Heroes', a battle near Cadiz fought on 5 March 1811 in which the 87th under Lord Gough was prominent, and in which the French eagle was captured by one of the regiment, Sergeant Masterman.

3. William Henn, of Paradise Hill in Clare, Master of the Irish Court of Chancery.

4. The seat of Peter la Touche.

5. Cornelius Grogan and Bagenal Harvey were hanged on the bridge at Wexford on 28 June 1798.

6. Hunter's Hotel, Newrath Bridge, Rathnew, is the modern name of the old coach inn where the party spent the night.

7. Samuel Hayes (1743-1795) MP Wicklow and later Maryborough. Lover of trees and horticulture. Of Hayesville, renamed Avondale, which was inherited by the Parnells.

8. Howards, earls of Wicklow.

9. The Fosberrys of Kildimo in Limerick were connected by marriage with the Godfreys of Kerry and the Spring-Rices of Mount Trenchard.

10. Sir Aubrey de Vere Hunt of Curragh Chase, son of Sir Vere Hunt and Eleanor Pery, sister of the 1st Earl of Limerick, m. 1807 Mary Spring Rice, sister of Lord Monteagle.

11. John Day Collis (d.s.p.) was the son of Judge Day's first-cousin, John FitzGerald Collis (see FitzGerald pedigree) Deputy Keeper of the Records, of York St., Dublin and his wife Margaret (a niece of Day), daughter of John Day ('of Sunday's Well', Cork), presumably Judge Robert's brother, the 'Alderman'; see remarriage of Margaret in *Hibernian Chronicle,* 5 February, 1795. In December 1808 John Day Collis was approved for his fourth voyage as ship's mate to India-China (British Library, Ms. L/mar/c/vol. 776, *Description of Masters and Mates approved for the Extra Ships of the Season 1810*). He may be the Admiral Collis (a nick name?) mentioned elsewhere in these diaries; alternatively Admiral Collis may refer to Major John Collis of Kent Lodge.

Summer Circuit 1808:
the Mansions of Leinster, new Jail at Kilkenny

Mon.1 Aug. J. Osborne[1] (my Associate for the first time) came to Loughlinstown yesterday through very heavy rain to dinner. This morning we proceed at 6 to Wicklow where we arrive at half after 9 to breakfast. £165 viaticum. Dine with the Grand Jury. Recommend to them the idea of an address to His Majesty upon the Spanish Insurrection, wch they readily resolve upon & frame. Osborne J. finishes early & drives off to Emmavale, Col. Christmas's.

Tues.2d. Finish the Crown business. Maiden assizes.

Wednes 3rd Certify £13.13 to be due allowance for lodgings including maid servant. Send off my equipage by the direct route to Arklow while I go in Sheriff Blackford's landaunet open through Rathdrum to Ballyarthur to breakfast with Mr Symes. A place of uncommon beauty. His new Octagon hanging upon the brow over the sweet Vale of Arklow! One could sit there enjoying the enchanting scene till closed by night. After breakfast ride with Mr. Symes & the Sheriff through the Vale of Arklow, about 6 miles, & thence to Col. Christmas where I join Osborne & dine & sleep.

Th.4th Rose early & we breakfast at the poor inn of Gorey. Abel Ram has rebuilt his house, but Stephen Ram after squeezing about £1000 from the Commissioners has left his fine old seat still in ruins.[2] Meet & walk up & down with Dean Bond who tells me a most curious anecdote. Arrive about three at Wexford where Osborne swears the Grand Jury.

Fr. 5th Aug. Try 6 Records -

Sat.6th August. Finish the business early. Osborne proceeds to Mr. Christmas's Emma-Vale 4 m. beyond Waterford. We have allowed too much time for Wexford Assizes. The course should be to arrive here on Thursday at or before 1, proceed forthwith into business & continue through Friday & Saturday, & Sunday after prayers to set off as far as Ross for Waterford, & Monday morning at 10 o'clock to open the commission in Waterford.

Sund. 7th Hear an excellent sermon from the excellent & exemplary Mr. Dunne. After prayers the Sheriff attends me to see Lyster at Belmont (Frank Hutchinson's handsome Seat) just convalescent from a bilious fever; from thence across the romantic bridge of Ferrycarrig to Castle Saunders[3] the noble Seat of Lord Arran,[4] stripping fast of its fine plantations & verging rapidly to decay; from thence to Mr. Le Hunte's elegant seat of Ardtramont[5] exhibiting in its high state of preservation a perfect contrast to his neighbour Lord Arran; and so on over the Long Bridge back to Wexford. Voila, done the circular ride, from 8 to 10 m. long.

M.8th Visit with the Sheriff & Clerk of the Peace the new jail erecting out of the town by Morrison upon a contract at £11903.6.7 including the Infirmary.[6] A large sum indeed where there are but 18 cells for felons! I can not say I admire much the design. The airing ground is indeed ample & spacious & the masonry seems executing very well & of very good materials. But 'twould have been more provident to purchase the ground before the work was begun & to employ the architect at the usual percentage of 5 p cent than by contract.

Tu. 9th Breakfast at Fowke's Mill, famous for a hand-fought battle in the Rebellion, & drive after to Ross where I meet Edward Murphy Esq. & Driscol who conduct me to Mr. Murphy's noble seat a mile below Ross. Here I & my servants are most hospitably & liberally received at bed & board. Next morning

W.10 after breakfast I ride to Waterford, 9 m., where I meet Osborne & we proceed about 3 to open our commissions & swear our Grand Juries.

Th.11 Dine with the Mays at their handsome Villa upon the noble river with a party of fashionables.

Fr. 12th Dine with Sir John Newport[7] at the Kilkenny side of the river. After dinner Osborne & I proceed to Miss Linwood's Promenade & celebrated Exhibition of beautiful pictures.[8] But it is hard to do justice to beautiful pictures when one is surrounded by living beauty. Presented by her brother to Mrs. Christmas who presents me a polite invitation from her husband, wch on

Sat. 13th Augt. I accept, & meet at dinner among others Lord Carysford[9] whom I had not known before, & the amiable & fascinating Mrs. Scott daughter of my dear friend poor Gervaise Bushe & niece of my dearer friend Henry Grattan.

Sund. 14th After breakfast Col Kane (the Sheriff) & I proceed for prayers to Portlaw Church but don't discover that we having missed the turn to till we arrive through the magnificent woods & demesne of Curraghmore at the Marquis of Waterford's gate.[10] I do not recollect anything in England, taking the extent of the grounds & the grandeur & boldness of the scenery, much finer than this princely seat. Lady Waterford, daughter of Lord Delaval, brought £30 or 40,000; & about £12,000 a year after Lady Delaval's death comes to the Marchioness for her life, reverting to her 2d son if she shall have any. So that the Marquis must work hard in his shirt to secure that fine estate in his family.

M.15th Break ground at 6 & pursue a very pleasant drive through the Park, & under the wooded hills over the Suir to Carrick where the Sheriff Co. Tipperary receives me, & we proceed to breakfast at Clonmell. Formidable Calendars: 114 prisoners & 32 records! I forget in its place to mention that at Waterford there were but 3 records, & 14 criminal numbers, one of whom was convicted of burglary, but I recommend him; one also was capitally convicted before Bror. Osborne.

Sund. 21st A most laborious & harassing week! Dined however pleasantly one day at Sir T. Osborne's[11] with only his brother & sister & brother-in-law Carysford, & another day with the Bar, the only dinners I made during the week. Ride to the Nine-Mile -House where I meet my old acquaintance Jack Johnson[12] who, though an Englishman, is the best Irishman I ever saw upon the stage – and I have seen Moody[13] and Sparks.[14] He made me laugh at the story of poor Paddy in Italy. A shew-man who had amused many a village with a dancing bear worked him into a fever & the poor animal died. Just as he had done skinning the bear a savage-looking fellow asked for alms, but the shew-man thought it better that the fellow should earn his bread, so he seized him & sewed him up in the bear's skin. In this garb he danced the poor human bear very much to the entertainment of the spectators & to his own profit for many a long & hot day. When Father O' Leary happening to pass by one day, & hearing the bear say to his master in notes with wch the honest priest fancied himself pretty well acquainted, "By Jasus! Paddy dances better nor any bear you ever had before," begged permission of the keeper to speak with the bear, upon wch he found that his ear had not deceived him & that sure enough his poor countryman had nolens volens been personating & made a grand progress in the character & habit of a bear - & it was not without much address & expense he could purchase from his keeper the release of poor Paddy from the bear-skin. Proceed to dinner at Kilkenny.

M.22 Aug. Charge the Grand Jury of the County & finish on

Wedny. 24th Visit the new Jail with the local inspector Dr. Duffey & the architect Mr. Robertson[15] - a splendid monument of the well-placed liberality of the county & of the talents judgment & integrity of the architect. I consider it a model in point of security, accommodation & excellence of design.

1. Charles Osborne (1759-1817). Voted for the Union and was appointed to the court of King's Bench in 1802. Connected to the Christmas family of Co. Waterford through his mother and wife. Died of typhus fever 1817.

2. Ramsfort, the seat of Stephen Ram, MP Gorey 1789, greatly damaged in the rebellion of 1798. Rev. Thomas Ram came to Ireland in 1599 as chaplain to the Earl of Essex and was made Bishop of Ferns and Leighlin in 1615.

3. Saunderscourt. Col. Robert Saunders received 3,750 acres in the barony of Shelmalier in 1666.

4. Arthur Saunders Gore, 2nd Earl of Arran (1734-1809). He possessed large estates in counties Mayo, Donegal and Wexford. Represented Donegal borough and County Wexford in the Irish parliament. Resided chiefly in Dublin and London. A founder of the Irish Whig Club (1789). His father had acquired Saunderscourt in 1730 on his marriage to Jane Saunders. The Gores descended from a Cromwellian officer, Sir Arthur Gore.

5. George Le Hunte.

6. Sir Richard Morrison (1767-1849), pupil of James Gandon. From 1800 he lived near Bray, not far from Day's home.

7. Sir John Newport (1756-1843). MP in the Whig interest for Waterford from 1803 to 1832. Strong supporter of Catholic emancipation. Irish Chancellor of the Exchequer in the 'Ministry of all the Talents', 1806-1807.

8. Mary Linwood (1755-1845). Her 'clever imitation of pictures in worsted embroidery' appeared in London, later in the 'Edinburgh, Dublin, and the chief provincial towns' (DNB).

9. Carysford, family name Proby, whose seat was Glenart Castle, Arklow, Co. Wicklow.

10. Henry de la Poer Beresford, 2nd Marquess of Waterford (1772-1826), Governor and Custos Rotulorum of the County of Waterford and Colonel of the Militia.

11. Sir Thomas Osborne, 9th Bart., lived at Newtown Anner, the family seat, two miles east of Clonmel.

12. Some authorities give the birthplace of John Henry Johnstone (1749-1828, not Johnson), as Tipperary, others the barracks of Kilkenny where his father was in a dragoon regiment. Day appears clear that his family was English. Johnstone became well known on the London stage for numerous Irish roles.

13. John Moody (1727?-1812) was from Cork. He gained fame with Garrick at Drury Lane theatre. Day may have seen him as Major O'Flaherty in Cumberland's *The West Indian* in 1771, or as Sir Patrick O' Neale in *The Irish Widow*, an adaption of Moliere by Garrick, in 1772, or as Conolly in *School for Wives* by Kelly in 1773. (DNB).

14. Sparks was a comic actor and, like Moody, is mentioned in Churchill's *Rosciad.*

15. William Robertson (1770-1850) the architect of Kilkenny jail (1805) and courthouse (1815).

Autumn in Kerry: public man, private fortune

In 1773 his father, Rev. Day, made Robert a grant of property near the Maine river in mid Kerry. From this beginning his estate grew. Away from these farms, in the northern baronies of Kerry, 1808 saw the worst of the whiteboy campaign, which may explain why Day avoided the Munster circuit. This is his first journey to Kerry since the loss of his brother, the Archdeacon of Beaufort, in January.

Fr.26th Aug 1808. Send my chaise with a pair of horses and two servants forward to Dublin and home, while I take the route back in my curricle by Clonmell and Mallow to Killarney and Kerry.

Sleep at Clogheen at Magrath's who gives me a very interesting account of the rapid progress in the improvement of this county wrought principally by Lord Lismore and Mr Anderson.[1] The former at the head of £26,000 a year has already built offices that cost £5,000 and is proceeding with a mansion the estimate of wch is £55,000 in the midst of a park and demesne of 1500 acres.[2] Rigid economy however is his character; while that of Anderson is confounded generosity and benevolence.

I just learn that the Dennys passd yesterday thro' Mitchelstown and Cahir to Clonmell from whence they were to proceed this morning to Waterford on their way to Cheltenham; so that I was so unlucky as to miss them today at Clonmel only by a few hours.

Sat. 27th The bleak dreary Kilworth Mountain is disappearing, and a cheerful uninterrupted corn country is succeeding. But if there be a human creation upon earth it is the present Fermoy; a mud-wall filthy village metamorphosed by its present public-spirited owner into a splendid bustling city ! worthy of its charming site.[3]

Sund. 28th Aug. Drive to Milstreet, 17m., a very interesting ride and for the most part a very good road.

M.29th Three miles from Milstreet such a storm of wind and rain arises as I don't remember to have ever before been exposed to continues without interruption for four hours till I reach Killarney drenched as if I had fallen into a lake. Plunge mother naked between the blankets at Moll Coffee's, take copiously of spirits inwardly and outwardly, and rub and chafe all my limbs as hard as possible. N.B. Dr. Moriarty approves of all this process as excellent for keeping up the circulation and natural heat; save the external application of spirits wch he says evaporate and abstracts instead of promoting heat. But (said he) "the friction of the limbs counteracted any evil effect that might proceed from the application of spirit".[4]

Tu. 30th Rise in as good health (bless'd be God), and as fresh as if I had sufferd nothing yesterday. Ride to Muckruss and Cahirnane,[5] and dine wth Tom Garvey.[6]

W. 31th. Dine wth J. McDonagh[7] after settling accts. Present him wth twelve spoons, twelve teaspoons and fish.

Th. 1st Sept. Ride (accompd. by J McD.) to Donman'een,[8] Phil Fowlue and Orpen building clever houses. Dine and sleep at Kilburne.[9] Meet there Mrs. Day my poor brother's widow for the first time since our misfortune - much affected.[10]

F.2d. We visit Rockfield where Thompson is building a clever house and Almon has built one.[11] Dine and sleep by invitation at Jack Duggan's.

Sat. 3d. After breakfast visit Clonmelane. Fix upon a situation for J. McDonagh's intended house. N.B. Necessary to charge him about taking strict care of the plantations, repairing the walls etc. Return to dine and sleep at Poulouragh.

Sund. 4. Drive to Tralee. Breakfast wth Jas Day.[12] Go to prayers. The excellent condition of the Church does great honour to James, who from a ruin has by stimulation and working at Vestry upon the parishoners converted it into one of the nicest country churches I know. I dine with him.

M.5 dine with Robin Hickson.[13]
Tu.6th with D Connell.[14]
W. 7th with Stephen H. Rice.[15]
Th. 8th with Will Rowan![16]
Friday 9th with John Rowan.[17]
Sat.10th with Jas Connor
S. 11. with Zeb Mac.[18]
M. 12th dine again with James Day
Tu. 13th dine with Wilson[19]

W.14th Leave Tralee for Dublin -

Never before experienced more affectionate or flattering attention in Kerry, yet never enjoyed myself less. In every ride I miss my constant and attached companion. Every company appears insipid and flat without his cheerful and enlightened conversation. His image haunts all my steps. Even in the stillness of night within the walls of this dreary Castle, whose gloom my poor dear Betsy is wanting to enliven, I often play the whimpering girl in recollecting how abruptly my beloved brother was snatched from me, and therefore I confess I quit a scene without regret where every object serves but to recall the memory of my irreparable loss.[20]

Day Place, Tralee, c. 1900. Lawrence Collection.

Elm Hill, Rathkeale, from the Encumbered Estates Rental, lithograph 1850-60 (NLI)

Breakfast at O. Stokes.[21] Walk to Grogeen and Ballynruddery.[22] Return to dinner. Find the Alderman[23] in high preservation.

Th 15th Assemble the magistrates in and about Listowel and give them a serious lecture about the disturbed state of the country owing to their supineness. Dine at Grogeen. Returning at night see the telegraphic communications by short and sudden lights from hill to hill among the insurgents.[24]

F.16th Travel by Atea and Ardagh to Rathkeal, calling on my way at Studdert's Elmhill.[25] A very good carriage road, but eighteen long miles and some hills wch. the road might avoid. Sleep in Limerick at Gills, an indifferent house.

Sat.17th Breakfast at Sir R. Harte's.[26] Sleep at Nenagh.

18th Breakfast with poor P. Bayly, mother of 12 living children, 4 more who died & just ready to fall to pieces of a 17th - preserves her sweet expression of countenance - a fine family.[27]

Sleep at the best inn on the road, Fallon Black Bull, Maryboro.

Oh what a magnificent road from Limerick to Dublin! Very fine weather all the way - W.21st Sept. Reach home - find my poor impatient wife very well & happy to receive me after an absence of near 2 lunar months - her companion John Collis & darlings Dizy & Lumpkin whom I had found wild & turned out to grass in Kerry & packed them off to Loughlinstown to take them in with the calves & foals for the winter.

1. John Anderson builder of Fermoy and promoter of the mail coach roads (op.cit.).

2. Cornelius O'Callaghan, created 1st Viscount Lismore of Shanbally 1806. John Nash built Shanbally

Castle, Clogheen, Co. Tipperary. It was demolished in 1957.

3. The Viceroy Hardwicke, writing in 1803, noted John Anderson's Fermoy achievements: 'two handsome streets, with a Market Place, two considerable breweries, and an excellent inn'; 'a very fine Barrack for the accommodation of a thousand infantry and a hundred cavalry is now nearly completed' (B. L. Hardwicke Mss. Add. Ms. 35708, Hardwicke to Pelham, 26 March 1803).

4. Dr Patrick Moriarty of Killarney. In 1804 Day presided, according to *The Freeman's Journal,* at a case involving Dr Moriarty and Nicholas Connolly Hussey after the latter had 'posted' the doctor in Killarney and invited a duel over a medical bill which he had refused to pay. Connolly Hussey was fined and imprisoned (The *Freeman's Journal,* December 6 1804).

5. Muckross was the seat of Henry Arthur Herbert MP. Cahirnane was the seat of Richard Townshend Herbert, Day's cousin.

6. Unidentified.

7. According to Griffith's Valuation Thomas McDonagh held the largest farm, 64 acres, in Cloonmealane townland, civil parish of Kilnanare. Elsewhere Day writes of instructing 'John McDonogh' to compel his (Day's) freeholders to vote for the Knight of Kerry in the 1807 election, or earn his personal enmity. Lands in Clonmelane and Gortnagloch and in Knockglass West were assigned to Day by his father in a deed of 1773: (Registry of Deeds, book 296, 459 197 718.)

8. Dunmaniheen, Killorglin parish. This townland is mentioned in Day's marriage agreement of 1774. Property in Dunmaniheen was the subject of litigation over many years between Day and the Blennerhassett family. See the later pages of this diary.

9. Kilburn townland was part of the Kilcoleman (Godfrey) estate near Miltown. Rev. William Godfrey was curate there from 1807 before becoming Rector of Kenmare. Rev. Wm's wife was Lucy, daughterof Arch. Day.

10. Barbara Forward, widow of Archdeacon Day. Her son, who succeeded his father as Rector of Kiltallagh, died near the end of the same year, 1808. (The diary is silent on his death, but see his obituary, with 'after a few days illness', in the *Cork Mercantile Chronicle,* 9 Dec. 1808.)

11. The owner of Rockfield East is given in the important contemporary source, John O'Donovan's Name Books, as Judge Day.

12. Rev. James Day, Rector of Tralee 1805-1818 was Day's first cousin. He was married to Margaret, a sister of McGillicuddy of the Reeks. He died in 1818.

13. Robert Conway Hickson was High Sheriff of Kerry in 1811. His father, Robert Christopher Hickson (obit 1813 in these diaries), converted to Catholicism having embraced the Established church as a young man. Day observed to Glandore: 'a convert from Popery relapsing again to his first religion stands as the Papist of old under all the disabilities of the statutes of Anne', and 'I should not wonder if George Hickson were malignant enough to take some steps against his cousin upon that ground.' Daniel O'Connell also noted Hickson's conversion: Hickson had 'publicly converted', an event which 'has given some amusement to the talkative inhabitants of Tralee'. Probably it is the son, Robert Conway Hickson, who is featured throughout this diary. Mary Agnes Hickson wrote of him: 'His elder brother James having been disinherited for marrying a Roman Catholic, Robert Hickson was heir to a good estate, and had no need to follow a profession; but the more agreeable training he received at the Chancellor's card table and at the card tables at Ardfert House made him a confirmed gambler to his life's end. He was High Sheriff in 1811, and died unmarried circa 1825.' See Talbot-Crosbie Mss., NLI, Judge Day, Loughlinstown House, 27 February 1810, to Lord Glandore; O'Connell's

Correspondence, vol. 1, 18 January 1810; Mary Agnes Hickson, *Kerry Evening Post,* 20 October 1880, *KEP,* 21 June, 1882.

14. This could be Daniel O' Connell (1775-1847), 'The Liberator', more likely Dr Rickard O'Connell (infra 208, 210n).

15. Stephen Henry Rice, Assistant Barrister for Kerry 1799-1829, not to be confused with Stephen Edward Rice of Mount Trenchard in these diaries. The former was a sometime resident of No. 5, Day Place. As Assistant Barrister he succeeded Tom Rice, probably Judge Day's aunt's husband.

16. Counsellor William Rowan, Provost of Tralee 1807, 1808, 1809, 1810 and 1811(*Kerry Evening Post,* June 20, 1888, list of Tralee's provosts). He married Letitia Denny, dau. of Sir Barry Denny 1st. Bart.

17. Sheriff of County Kerry in 1805. His daughter Harriet married Rev. Edward Day, son of Archdeacon Day.

18. This is probably Eusebius McGillacuddy, referred to subsequently as Zeb Mac, and in the *Limerick General Advertiser,* 3 November 1809, as a sub-sheriff of Kerry. B. 1754.

19. William Wilson, a Tralee attorney, appears on Kerry property deeds of around this time.

20. The Castle is Tralee Castle. The Archdeacon lived at Beaufort House.

21. Oliver Stokes, Lieutenant in the Feale Yeomanry; married to Elizabeth, daughter of 'the Alderman' (John Day of Cork). First Barrack-Master of Tralee, ancestor of Stokeses of Mounthawk.

22. Ballinruddery was the seat of the Knight of Kerry, at this time Maurice FitzGerald the 18th Knight (1774-1849). Day was the head tenant of Grogeen townland, parish of Finuge, part of the Knight's estate. Roseland Cottage appears on the first Ordnance Survey map at Grogeen, and this was probably where they walked.

23. It is difficult to establish this individual with certainty, but Day's brother John Day of Cork, Mayor of the city in 1807 and referred to elsewhere as an alderman there, seems the most likely candidate. Alderman Day's wife was his first-cousin Margaret Hewson of Ennismore. He died at the Barrack House Tralee in 1819 (see *K. E.P.* January 28 1913).

24. The year 1808 saw widespread violence in the two northern baronies of Kerry.

25. Maurice Studdert of Elm Hill, near Rathkeale, m. Dorothea dau.of William Minchin of Greenhills, Co. Tipperary. His sister, Agnes Elizabeth Anne, m. 1778 Ulick FitzMaurice of Duagh, whose mother was Judge Day's first cousin.

26. Sir Richard Harte, Mayor of Limerick 1806.

27. In an 1802 diary entry Day describes a stay in Nenagh with Harry and Pen Bayly 'at their sweet little cottage, Violet Bank' (lost diary, quoted in Ella B. Day, *Mr Justice Day of Kerry*).

1809 Summer Circuit, Munster, and with the Lord Lieutenant at Killarney's Lakes

Before leaving Dublin and after he returns, Day presses the Lord Lieutenant, the Duke of Richmond, to make appointments which favour his relatives. During Richmond's tour of the south Judge Day presides at his reception in Tralee Castle

Tu. 11th April. See the Duke of Richmond & solicit one of the Kenmare livings, vacated by the inhuman murder of poor Tisdall, for William Godfrey, in wch I have happily succeeded.[1]

Sat. 15th Mary Fosberry married to William Henn,[2] an amiable couple & likely to be very happy. Both families assemble at Bray where the ceremony is performed by Mr John Rowley. Dine & pass a pleasant day at Mrs Fosberry's. The Henns remain till Monday.

The Chief Baron[3] & I having chosen this circuit we appoint it to begin at Ennis so early as Tuesd. Morning 11th July -

N.B. the Judges some terms back resolved to adopt the immemorial practice of the English Judges, viz. to open invariably the circuit at the first town not earlier than the Monday fortnight not later than the Monday 3 weeks after the last day of term.

Fri. 6th July. I leave town this morning & breakfast at Johnstown whither (as usual) I dispatched my equipage & servants last night. Take with me about £150 viaticum. The Chief Baron set out yesterday for Mt. Prospect[4] having agreed to meet me on Monday next p.m. at Ennis so as each of us to enter early on business the next day. Sup & sleep at Judge Johnson's nice thatched cottage, Herbert Hill,[5] on the road's side between Munstereven & Emo.

Sat. 8th After breakfast Johnson J. conveys me to Emo where I sent my horses &c last night. Dine at Mountrath & sleep at Smallman's comfortable house Roscrea.

S.9th Sleep at the little Bird Hill House[6] & am very civilly accommodated.

Mon. 10th July. Take up Killen & proceed by Callaghan's Mills to Ennis,10 miles shorter than by Limerick, & thro' an interesting country.

Tu.11th Dash into business - 28 Records entered. Dispose of seven & we dine with Daxon Treasurer.[7]

Sat. 15th Rise at 4 after a severe week. The Chief Baron tries 4 & I the rest of 28 Records mostly important & difficult. Drive out to Kilcishin to the Sheriff's Mr. Studdard[8] married to my friend Ashworth's daughter the fair Melusina where I don't arrive till 9

Mon. 17th at Kilkishin spend 2 nights & a day very pleasantly - an excellent House, fine water scenery & great capability thro' Mr. Studdert's extensive grounds - proceed this morning at 5 to Limerick where I arrive before 9 - swear in & charge the Grd. Jury - the criminal & civil business of the county too much for one Judge - 20 Records besides a weighty Crown Calendar. Madden, convicted of Horse-stealing, the only capital conviction.

Dine with the Rev. Harty, the Bishop,[9] the Collector & with my good old friend Hill;[10] God grant it has not been a farewell dinner. One of the most grateful events at Limerick was the receipt of a letter from my dear wife announcing her safe arrival at Holyhead on Friday a.m. to breakfast after a famous passage without a qualm - another letter received on Friday 21 from her at Worcester.

Sund. 23rd Breakfast at Askeaton. Ride thro' the beautiful approach to Cappa, now Mt. Trenchard, with Stephen Rice,[11] just opend, and snack and dine and sleep very comfortably at Capt. Leslie's Tarbert House.[12]

Mon.24th Breakfast as usual at Oliver Stokes' in Listowel where I wait for the Chief Baron, from whence we proceed under protection of Townsend Gun H. Sheriff to Tralee. Try ten records. Dine with Stephen Rice, with Connor, and three days with Zeb Mac. Receive the presentments and try sundry traversers for the C. Baron who leaves Tralee for Killarney on Thursday to see the lake.

Sat. 29th I follow and catch him at Killarney. Proceed together over the cursed road to Milstreet where we meet the High- and Sub- Sheriffs (both Justin McCarthy), who entertain us.

Sun. 30th Proceed by the new line to Macromp where we breakfast at the Castle with Mr. Hedges. Arrive in the evening at Cork.

Cork M. 31st Swear and charge the Grand Jury. Edwd. Eagar, grand-nephew of Rowly Hassett, capitally convicted of forgery.[13] C.B. sixteen Records.

Wed. 2d. Aug. The Chief Baron yesterday opened the Commission in the County; but 42 nos. in his calendar. Proceed this morning into the County Record Court where I am presented mirabile dictu with a Bill of fare of 75 Records ! The City Limerick Fishery Case & L. Limerick and Uniacke[14] employ each 2 days.

Sund. 6th The Chief Baron decamps after giving me a day & half. I dine with Tom Cuthbert & sleep-

Frid. 11th Finish the unprecedented labours of these Assizes at 5 this evening - dine wth Pope.

Sat. 12th Ride to see my poor friend Falkland crossing at Passage & dine & sleep at Cuthberts[15] - delighted to find Falkland so much better than he had been represented to me.

Sund. 13th Dine again at Woodview.[16]

14th Decamp at 6 for Fermoy.

Tuesd. Arrive at home after an absence of 6 weeks.

1. The Kenmare vacancy arose on the murder of its incumbent, Rev. Tisdall, at Priest's Leap on the road from Bantry to Kenmare on March 23, 1809. Day makes no mention of the trial of Michael Murphy for this crime, or his execution on July 29 1809, the day Day left Tralee for Cork (*The Freeman's Journal,* 4 August, 1809).

2. The bride's parents were George Fosberry of Kildimo and Christina Rice of Mount Trenchard in

Limerick, the writer's cousin.

3. Standish O'Grady (1766-1840), 1st Viscount Cahir Guillamore and Baron Rockbarton. Appointed Chief Baron of the court of Exchequer in 1805. Presided with Baron Denis George at a special commission in Limerick and Tralee in January 1809.

4. Mount Prospect, residence of Standish O'Grady

5. Robert Johnson was appointed Justice of the Common Pleas in 1801 but lost his position following libels on the Irish government written by him and published in 1803 under the pseudonym *Juverna.* Day was one of only two judges who voted against Johnson's extradition to stand trial in London.

6. Bird Hill House, residence of Robert Twiss and his wife, Elizabeth Atkins of Firville, Co. Cork. Twiss's father, George, of Cordal House (near Castleisland) m. Honoria Meredith, dau. of Day's aunt, Marian FitzGerald and her husband William Meredith of Dicksgrove, near Castleisland (*A Genealogical and Heraldic History of the Landed Gentry of Great Britain and Ireland,* 2 vols, London 1894, Vol. 2, Twiss).

7. Giles Daxon of Stamer Park, Co. Clare.

8. Thomas Studdert (c 1780-1873) of Kilkishen House, High Sheriff 1809, m. 1807 Melicina, daughter of Robert Ashworth.

Robert FitzGerald, 17th Knight of Kerry

9. Charles Morgan Warburton, Bishop of Limerick 1806-1820. Elsewhere Day notes that his real name was Mungovan and that he was a convert from Catholicism.

10. Possibly Rev. Archdeacon Hill, described as 'Treasurer to the Fever and Lock Hospital' (*Limerick General Advertiser,* 28 July 1809).

11. Stephen Edward Rice was Day's first-cousin, their mothers being sisters of Robert FitzGerald the 17th Knight of Kerry. He was the father of Thos Spring Rice, 1st Lord Monteagle.

12. Sir Edward Leslie, Captain of the Tarbert Cavalry of Yeomen, 1796, raised by him.

13. A sister of Sir Rowland Blennerhassett married John Eagar of Ardrinane: Rosemary Ffolliott (ed.), *Biographical notices principally relating to counties Cork and Kerry collected from newspapers 1756-1827 with a few references 1749-55.*

14. An action to establish the inheritance of James Uniacke of Mount Uniacke, near Youghal. The jury not agreeing, a new trial was necessary (see below).

15. Tom Cuthbert m. (1791) Lucy, daughter of Day's sister, Catherine Day, and Thomas Franks of Ballymagooly, near Mallow.

16. Tom Cuthbert's house (*Directory to the Market Towns, Villages, Gentleman's Seats and Other Noted Places,* Dublin 1814).

The Mansion House Ardfert, referred to as 'Ardfert Abbey,' home of Lord Glandore. (Collection D. Cameron.)

Memorial Sept 1809: Ewd. Day 23rd Regiment Native Infantry Bengal Establishment. Admitted 22 August 1801, Lieutent. in 1805.[1]
Let the Shambles & Houses
Write to Mr Newenham about the site for Barracks.
Promote Infirmary
Promote Steeple

Q Would it be possible to get the inhabitants to flag light & cleanse Tralee?[2]

Q. Can any plan be adopted to redeem Ralph Marshall's affairs from destruction?[3]

N.B. Bidet, horse, wardrobe, long dressing-glass, 2 bason stands, basons and bottles, carpet round the bed and before the peer-table, hearth-rug, carpet along the gallery, firescreen.

Settle with the Yieldings.

Cows for Talbot -

Speak to Hare about conveying the legal estate of Ballybrack[4] ....discovery in trust for Mat Hare.

For having eggs in winter: get a coop in your kitchen near the fire with a constant supply of clean hay. Put in the hens for a few nights successively. They will at last go in of themselves and range themselves like well- drill'd soldiers in the ranks. The warmth will bring them to lay as in cabins. It would be well also to grate some boil'd liver into their oats.

6th Sept. 1809 -
Leave Town for Tralee with £70 in notes. Sleep at Johnstown.
7th Sleep at Backlane.[5] Violent rain at night.
8th Fri. —— at Roscrea
Sat. and Sunday—— Peterfield.[6]
11th M. Limerickk ——Harte's.
12th T. Tarbert.
13th W. Listowel - Stokes
14th Th. Ardfert and Tralee. Dine at Frank Mac's.[7]
15th Fr. Dine at Robin Hickson's.
16th Sat.———at Dr. Connell's.
17th Sund. Dine and sleep at Ardfert Abbey.
18th M. Dine at Jas. Day's.
19th Tu. ——at Zeb. Mac's.
20 W. ———at James Day's.
21st Th. breakfast in Killarney and pay my respects to the Duke and Duchess or Richmond. Return in the evening and dine at the Tavern[8], the first time there ten years. Their Graces promise to stop and refresh with me next Tuesday 26th at the Castle.

The best mode of using salt herrings is, to tarboil potatoes, then skin them. Let them then and the herrings be boil'd together and serv'd up together. Some take out the bones and mash them together wch makes an excellent meal.

Frid. 22nd Spend the day at Ardfert.

26th Tuesday. At 2.00 their Graces arrive at Tralee Castle from Killarney. The Provost (Mr. Rowan) & Corporation wait upon His Grace, address him by Judge Day, their Recorder, & present him with his Freedom in a gold box. Sit down to a cold collation "consisting of all the delicacies of the Season". The company the Duke & Dutchess,[9] Lady Mary Lennox & Lord March,[10] Lady Edwd. Somerset,[11] Major Loftus, Captn. Ready & Sir Chas. Vernon,[12] Lady Glandore, Mrs Bateman,[13] Provost & Mrs. Rowan, Major & Mrs. Ponsonby,[14] Sir W. Godfrey[15] Sir Rowld. Blenerhassett, Col. & Mrs. Godfrey,[16] Major & Mrs. Langton,[17] Mr. Stoughton, Mr. Talbot etc, etc.

26th 27th Dine each day wth Their Graces at Lord Glandore's, and come home each night.

Th. 28th Dine at R. Hickson's -

Fr. 29th — at Lord Glandore's, being Corporation Day[18] in Tralee swear in Rowan Provost. Corporation resolve to move the Market from the Square to the new Shambles

Sat. 30th Proceed by the short road to John Day's Kiltalla.[19]

Sund. 1 Oct. Go to Church and receive sacrament -

Mon. 2d. Ride wth John Day to Kilburn & thro' Donmaniheen -

Tues. 3rd Ride to Rockfield and Clonmelane -

4th. Ride again to Clonmelane and dine wth Duggan

Th.5th Giles Ray[20] and I ride back the short road to Tralee. Vestry for repair of streets

Diana Sackville, Countess of Glandore, wife of John Crosbie, 2nd Earl.

Sat. 7th. Take James Day in the curricle to breakfast with Maurice Hewson , & to dinner to Knockglass - a nice place !

Sund. 8th Go to Church, return to Tralee & dine with Frank Mac.

M.9th Dine at Dr Connell's.[21]

Tu. 10th Ride with Mr. Purcell over Baltygarron. Dine & sleep at Barrow.

11th Attend Vestry - proceed wth Purcell to dine at Churchill - return at night

Th. 12th Dine at Maurice Copinger's.[22] 23 at table .

Fr. 13th Dine & sleep at Ardfert - & return -

Sat. 14th to breakfast. Dine at Frank Mac's.

Sund. 15th Dine at J. Rowan's Arbella -

16th - dine (for the first time of my life) at Rowley Bateman's -

Tuesd. 17th. —— at Sam Collis's[23]

18th ——— at Jas. Day's

Th. 19th. —— at Sir Rowld Blennerhassett's[24]
Fr. 20th ——at R. Hickson's.
Sat. 21st. Dine & sleep at the Peer's.[25] Forwarded in his Chaise & four to Listowel on Sund. 22d. Send off curricle to Cappa.

Devine's Bill[26] & Cook 2.19.8 half-penny

Fr.27th Oct. Visit the Lord. Lieutenant's in the Park but he was out on horseback. Proceeded to Loughlinstown.

Mon 30th Came to town

Tuesd. 31st Had audience from the Duke who promises to serve Lord Glandore on the first occasion. Ask for Postmaster, previous to recommend. In the evening stepping (in a hurry home) into my curricle I missed my footing and fell backwards upon the flags - carried in by the chaiseman senseless and remained so about twenty minutes till awakened by Macklin's launcet - no fracture but a concussion apprehended - copiously bled.

Frid.11th Nov. Return to Loughlinstown for the sake of solitude and silence - where I am directed to live low and pass the month of November.

Mon.21st Visit the Duke in the Park to return thanks for his inquiries and to know Lord Glandore's fate - mortified to hear Lord Rosse is appointed Postmaster - alas! What's to be done?

Absent myself the whole of Michaelmas Term from Court. N. B. Did the like M. T. 1807 for the Hernia Humoralis.

Memorandum to speak to the Archb. to obtain clause for legalizing Blennerville Church & such like -

Surely no consideration of Mail Coaches roads bridges or jobs of any sort can justify a dire want of attention to the urgent necessity for a new Jail, an object for wch humanity so loudly plead

1. Second son of Alderman John Day of Cork and Margaret Hewson; a Colonel in the Indian Army; m. Mary, daughter of Patrick Trant of Dingle (Mary Agnes Hickson, *Old Kerry Records*, vol. 2, p.234).
2. Elsewhere, near 30 July 1810 in the ms. of this diary: subscription to Prince's Quay £1.2.9, to Zeb. Mac's footpath £1.2.9, to railing Day Place £4.0.0
3. Ralph Marshall was Day's nephew, son of his sister Lucy and John Marshall of Callinafersy, Sheriff of Kerry in 1799. He disappeared in 1809 having joined the Spanish army in the Peninsular war. There was a court case over an insurance policy on Marshall's life, when Judge Day appeared as a witness and conceded that his nephew was a vain man, and, though the owner of a great estate in Kerry, financially embarrassed (see *The Limerick Gazette and General Advertiser*, 16 July 1811).
4. O'Donovan's *Name Books* give Judge Day as the owner of Ballybrack in the parish of Aglish.
5. In the diary of 1829 Judge Day places this inn near Monasterevin, its owners 'the Graves family whom I remember here and at Maryborough for 70 years back.'
6. Holmes residence near Lough Derg at Puckane, Co. Tipperary. Peter Holmes was MP for Banagher and a leading advocate of prison reform (the Holmes act of 1782, Prisons Act of 1784).
7. Possibly Francis McGillycuddy (1751-1827), 3rd son of Cornelius and Catherine (nee Chute) McGillycuddy op. cit, and the same (?) as 'Francis Chute McGillycuddy of Tralee, gentleman attorney' in National Archives, deed no. 1025/3/12/30.
8. Unidentified.
9. The Duchess of Richmond was Charlotte Huntly, eldest daughter of the 4th Duke of Gordon, hostess of a famous ball before Waterloo.
10. Lord March was Richmond's eldest son and 5th Duke. Mary, Richmond's eldest daughter, m. 1820 Sir Charles Augustus Fitzroy.

11. The wife of Lord Edward Somerset (1776-1842), son of the 5th Duke of Beaufort, was Louisa Augusta, sister of William, 3rd Viscount Courtenay (Irish estate near Newcastlewest, Limerick). See below.
12. Described elsewhere as Chamberlain of the Castle (i.e. Dublin Castle).
13. Arabella Denny, m. Rowland Bateman Jr.
14. Major William Carrique Ponsonby of Crotta. A political rival of Day. Appears in correspondence with Sir Arthur Wellesley in Wellesley's *Civil Despatches.*
15. Sir William Godfrey 1738-1817, of Kilcoleman Abbey, Miltown, m. Agnes Blennerhassett.
16. Lieutenant Colonel John Godfrey, son or Rev. Luke who was brother of Sir William; m. Letitia King.
17. Major Langton was commander of the South Cork Regiment of Militia, then stationed in Tralee. (*Limerick General Advertiser,* 3 November, 1809.)
18. The Provost was elected 'on the Nativity of St. John' and installed on the feast day of St. Michael. (*British Parliamentary Papers,* 'Reports from Commissioners on Municipal Corporations in Ireland 1833', Vol. 27.)
19. Rev. John succeeded his first-cousin Rev. Edward Day Jnr. as Rector of Kiltallagh in 1809 after Edward died in December of the same year as his father Archdeacon, 1808. The Chief Secretary, Arthur Wellesley, the future Duke of Wellington, wrote to the Lord Lieutenant, the Duke of Richmond on December 14, 1808 suggesting the division of the union of Kiltallagh: (Judge)'Day's nephew' i.e. Rev. John Day, should be given Kiltallagh, (which included Currans, Kilcoleman and Killgarrylander), and 'the better half of the living (Killorglin and Knockane) be given to 'Mr. Hyde'. Judge Day, who told Sir Robert Peel (Chief Secretary 1812 to 1818) that 'I possess a considerable estate in the parish of Kiltalla', would appear to have secured the appointment of each nephew following representations to the Marquis of Cornwallis and the Duke of Richmond respectively. He survived both, John dying in 1817. (*Civil Dispatches of the Duke of Wellington,* quoted in the *Kerry Evening Post,* March 20, 1860; Peel Correspondence, British Library, Add Ms. 40266, Dublin, 31 May, 1817, Day to Peel.)
20. Giles Ray of Anna, 1st Lieutenant of the Miltown Corps of Yeomanry.
21. Dr Rickard O'Connell, No. 3, Day Place, Tralee.
22. Maurice Coppinger was possibly son of Maurice Coppinger, later a judge, many times MP for Ardfert in the 1760s and 70s, who m. a sister of Sir Maurice Crosbie.
23. Rev. Sam Collis of Fortwilliam m. Anne, dau. Edward Rae of Keel and his wife Anna Langford. They had a son Rev. Sam Collis, Royal Navy, who m. Cherry, dau. Maurice Leyne, MD, Tralee. The death of a Rev. Samuel Collis, chaplain on board the *Berwick,* 'and late of Fort William, Co. Kerry', is reported in the *Limerick Gazette,* 3 May 1811; Rev. Collis's elder brother and heir to Fort William was William Collis, who m. Deborah dau. Dr William Crumpe, M.D. Tralee. The ruined house, Fort William, had the date 1790 and the initials S.C. above the doorway. (*The Tralee Chronicle,* 18 September 1866; the house, R. McMorran; see also a number of references to (one?) Samuel Collis of Barrow and/or Fortwilliam in Rosemary Ffolliott's *Biographical Notices.*)
24. Sir Rowland Blennerhassett (1741-1821), 1st Bart., the builder of Blennerville. Created baronet September 22 1809 after representations from James Crosbie of Ballyheigue.
25. 'The Peer' is John Crosbie of Ardfert Abbey, 2nd Earl of Glandore.
26. *Pigots Directory* of 1824 gives Pat Devine of the Crosbie Arms, Castle St. Tralee. The King's Jubilee celebrations in late October appear to have taken place at Devine's hotel (*Limerick General Advertiser,* November 3 1809). By then Day had returned to Dublin.

A Charge delivered to the Grand Juries of the City and County of Dublin in the Court of King's Bench, on the 23d of January, 1810, by the Hon. Mr. Justice Day.

Published at the Request of the Grand Jury of the County. Dublin.

Published by Graisberry and Campbell, Back Lane, 1810

A complete version of this charge appears in the Freeman's Journal of 10 February 1810. The charge reveals an extraordinary commitment on the part of Day to the humdrum business of prison reform. His inspiration included the Italian Cesare Beccaria and the Englishman John Howard, as well as Day's friend, fellow MP Peter Holmes.

Gentlemen, of both Grand Juries,

Having been confined to my house through the whole of last Term by a severe accident,[1] I have had no opportunity till now of addressing the Grand Juries (in discharge of my peculiar duty in this Court) upon a subject of great importance, which had been referred to us by command of the Lord Lieutenant, and which was brought before them by the Court, in the course of that Term. I allude to the prisons and other places of confinement within your respective jurisdictions. Upon looking into both boxes, I can have no fear that the present Grand Juries will content themselves with a meer formal or cold discharge of the sacred duty which we owe to the most unfortunate of our fellow creatures; but that you will enter upon it with the feelings of men and of Christians – with a generous and sympathetic sensibility the true characteristic of our country.

But, before I proceed, allow me to advert for a moment to certain papers with which some of the late City Grand Jury waited upon my Lord Chief Justice, and which his Lordship has just put into my hands. One is a printed pamphlet professing to exculpate the City Grand Juries from certain observations of the Court. For what purpose this pamphlet (which, by the bye we all had before seen published in the newspapers) was handed to the Chief Justice, I am utterly at a loss to conjecture. I shall only say, that it is not the course of the court to reply to newspaper publications or pamphlets; nor can I approve of any component part of a court of justice making appeals to the public touching any proceedings in the court through newspapers or other publications. The intercourse between the bench and the Grand Jury is always open and free, such as the public interest indispensably requires; and the court never performs a more pleasing duty than in receiving any communication from the Grand Juries, with all the attention to which so proud a member of our criminal jurisprudence is peculiarly intitled. The other paper is a writing purporting to be a defence of themselves against the report of the jail commissioners, and the evidence of the local inspector; a perfectly legitimate and justifiable paper. Some of the charges insinuated against certain members of the former grand jury are well repelled in that paper. The blanket contract, indeed, though extenuated a good deal by the extreme pressure of the occasion, appears to have been very defectively executed. But the flippant insinuation touching the bread contract is fully answered, I will not say, by the established reputation of Alderman Manders, to whom it alludes, but by the subsequent part of the local inspector's own evidence.

Gentlemen, if the jails of any part of Ireland have been neglected, the blame does not lie at the door of our present government. Early in the Duke of Richmond's viceroyalty his Grace's commands were communicated to each of the twelve judges in an official letter, requiring us to call the attention of the several grand juries at the then approaching circuits, to the state of their respective prisons, and to impress upon them as an imperious duty in point of moral obligation and of public policy the amelioration of the prison system of Ireland. In point of fact, the Judges did bring the subject specifically and pointedly before the Grand Juries throughout the Circuits; and there is great reason to hope, that a sanguine spirit, in favour of that interesting object, is at this moment in full activity through the country. – The same benevolent sirit, alive to the interest and credit of this great city, issued last year, a commission of five gentlemen, eminently qualified to execute that high trust, authorizing them to institute an inquiry into the state and condition of the prisons in and about Dublin; and those commissioners, after a solemn investigation, have made an elaborate Report full of important and valuable matter, exposing the gross and inveterate abuse in many of the prisons, and submitting some judicious observations and remedies for the evils complained of.

The Report addresses itself partly to the Court of King's Banch, partly to the Term Grand Juries, and partly to the Government and Legislature. In other words, the report enumerates existing evils; some within the summary controul of the Court, some to be redressed by the presentment of Grand Juries, and some beyond the competence of both.

With respect to this last class of abuses, it would be injustice to pass over the active and unremitting exertions of the Secretary, to forward an efficient and substantial correction of all such evils as lie within the reach of Government. Newgate has already been relieved of its overflow by a transfer of 50 or 60 female convicts from thence to the Penitentiary at Smithfield under the 22nd of the king. Bridewell too, that long neglected mansion of misery, has not escaped his inspection. Employment, instruction, food and raiment have been provided for both those houses and it is expected that the half-famished, naked and squalid inmates will resume their natural plight and condition, and be restored one day to the world, reclaimed from vicious habits and useful members of society. There is reason also to hope that a national penitentiary upon a suitable scale is in contemplation wherein confinement at industrious employment may be substituted at the discretion of the court for transportation: a punishment illusory or burdensome in practice, and in my mind, most vicious in principle. For I own, I do not understand that political morality which colonises another country with the outcasts of our own. It is not a change of climate that will work a change of mind, or render him reformed and useful at the antipodes who is too profligate to be indured at home. In short, government, I have authority to say, is prepared to resort to Parliament for such further powers as are yet wanted to the full accomplishment of its benevolent purposes.

As to that class of abuses which lie within the correction of the Court of King's Bench, and which for the first time have been brought under its observations by this report: the Court has lost no time in directing its most serious attention to them; and it will afford general satisfaction to know that all have either been already corrected, or put in a train of immediate amendment. Gentlemen, we shall hear no more of the Jailer of Newgate being saddled at the price of half his salary with a rider. We shall hear no more of the Keeper of the Sheriff's prison, built by public presentment, paying an annual rent as for private property to the City Sheriffs; a corrupt practice, which (though prohibited under the heavy penalty of £500 by the 3d of the King), has been in use ever since the erection of that prison, till discontinued by the present very worthy Sheriffs[2]; a practice which licenses the Keeper to indemnify himself by unfeeling exaction upon the wretched debtors. We shall hear no more of chambers in the prisons set up to the highest bidders or let without reference to sex, condition or seniority, as best suited to the caprice or rapacity of a Keeper, or for the purpose of underletting at arbitrary and exorbitant rents. The prisoners will henceforth know what accommodations to demand, for they will read their own rights posted up, and, conspicuously displayed in every prison, pursuant to the merciful provisions of Holmes's Act[3]: a statute, in every line of which it is easy to trace the presiding genius of Howard guiding the pen of its benevolent author. The prisoners too will see a table of fees placed before their eyes, beyond which no jailor can exact; a table which had been approved of by the court so long since as Lord Clonmel's time, though the report erroneously states that no table had yet been adopted or approved of. In short, Gentlemen, the greater part of the last vacation was devoted by the Chief Justice to the framing such orders and regulations with the concurrence of his brethren, as seem best calculated to correct and prevent a recurrence of all such evils as lie within the summary control of the court.

It remains now to see what the evils are within the power and province of the term Grand Juries, which call for correction. And in touching upon this part of the subject, I shall have very little to address to you, Gentlemen of the County, and that little in the language of congratulation and praise. Kilmainham jail in truth exhibits a proud monument of the humanity and munificence of the county of Dublin, and the architectural skill of the late Sir John Trail who built it. Middlesex, that reservoir of wealth and of crime, can boast of nothing like it. The Newgate of London, which is the county jail of Middlesex, is in size and structure, confessedly inadequate to the purposes of its appropriation. But your county jail embraces all the prime desideranda to a perfect prison - security against escape and abundant space most judiciously distributed for all the great purposes of health, classification, solitude and labour. It is satisfactory also to perceive that the prison is not more commodious in its construction, than well administered by its Keeper. And as to the several wants of the prison and its prisoners, some of which are stated by the Report to be very serious, I understand they were provided for by the last Grand Jury with their usual liberality. I am happy, then, to close this part of the case with the following flattering extract from the Report: "That as soon as certain impediments to improvement shall be removed by the Legislature, we hope to see the Jail of Kilmainham under the auspices of the Grand Jury, who have already evinced a most laudable and exemplary zeal for its improvement, and, under the government of the present Jailer, a pattern to the other prisons of Ireland."

I now turn, with very different emotions indeed, to the Prisons of the Metropolis, which, though under the double guardianship of the Corporation and Grand Jury of the City, exhibit a painful and affecting spectacle. "Newgate," says the Report, "is a disgrace to the capital." In its construction Newgate wants the necessary accommodations for health and separation, and in its execution and materials is miserably insecure. The space which it incloses is too contracted and scanty, for its average number of prisoners: and yet, of the scanty, and contracted space several cells are made no use of, while the rest are so crowded and crammed with inmates as to rival the Black Hole of Calcutta. This inhuman and scandalous abuse the local Inspector has never thought proper to bring before the court, who for the first time were apprised of the fact by the Report, an omission the more accountable as that Officer seems very anxious to do his duty and I believe is a very benevolent man. From 8 to 14 prisoners compressed into a cell 12 feet by 8 in the heat of summer – and this to keep them warm ! Why gentlemen, the sufferings in the Slave Trade could hardly exceed this; that unchristian traffic in human flesh, which has disgraced Christendom so long, and whose abolition constitutes one of the brightest gems in our good King's diadem. I say the deck of a slave ship exhibits no bad parallel to the floor of one of these cells by night; where the frugal distribution of space, and the ingenious contrivance to accommodate so many heads and hands, bodies and legs, must be no less curious than horrific. But we need not go so far as to Africa for a counterpart. If we are to credit a late Sheriff of London,[4] (and upon less authority tha fact would be incredible,) the Newgate of that city is not an atom better. Perhaps, indeed, Dublin waits for London to take the lead, and it might be thought not respectful for the second Corporation in the Empire to pass by in the road of benevolence the Metropolis of the world. I remember a jail fever which broke out here several years ago in a crowded and illventilated prison, and which, after several prisoners had fallen victims to it, was communicated to the Commission Court, and swept away some Barristers and Jurors. In 1807, a malignant distemper raged in every prison in Dublin. When prisoners are thus condensed and huddled together – some ulcerated, some diseased, all squalid in the extreme – they must necessarily contaminate the mass, and generate a pestilential atmosphere. Every cell thus tenanted becomes a focus of infection.

But revolting as this may be, it is not the worst. The mental contagion communicated by indiscriminate confinement without any classification of crimes, is more pernicious and of more extensive public mischief than the most pestiferous jail distemper could be. A more copious source of general immorality hardly exists than this defective system of imprisonment. The object of imprisonment is not to punish only but to reform; but if the object were not to reform the imprisoned, but to send them back upon society thoroughly schooled in depravity, a more successful course could not be taken than the present; than yoking infamy with innocence, the victims of folly and misfortune with criminals, helf corrupted wavering youth with hardened callous age, mere culprits with convicted felons. Prisoners thus prepared, when let loose again upon the world, only serve, like foxes enlarged by sportsmen, to keep up and multiply the species. Hence it is that, notwithstanding the numerous victims offered up here and at the Old Bailey, after every session, to offended justice, the malignity of the moral infection countervails the force and beneficial effect of so much awful example, and the prisons are kept constantly overflowing with fresh recruits. The common defence (if defence it can be called) of Transportation is, that better it is to dispose of convicts even in that way, than thin the human ranks by numerous and incessant executions. But better at once in my mind to withdraw the plea of clergy, and rid society of such nuisance, than to train and ripen convicts thus by evil and corrupt communication for new crimes; for a new, a more expert, and more successful career of profligacy.

Against this gigantic evil there is but one resource – to get rid altogether of this incorrigible irremediable pile, and to build another Newgate. To the expence of this, if to be employed as a National depot for the reception of transports from the several counties of Ireland, it is fair that the nation should be called upon to contribute. Great Britain has advanced far in this noble work of humanity. Who has not heard the Jails of Gloucester and Cornwall, the Castle of York, the Bridewell of Edinburgh? We too have some excellent prisons. Kilkenny boasts of a prison which Howard himself might approve of, a prison which does honour to that enlightened county, and to the talents and integrity of Mr Robinson who studied the best English models upon the spot, and finished that great work within the limited time and the estimate originally furnished by himself. Shall Dublin, then, so famed for her numerous charitable establishments and expanded benevolence, hesitate or delay to rear so indispensable an Edifice, at the loud call not only of humanity and justice to the prisoner, but of her own best and most precious interests? A prison upon such a scale, as shall suit the abundant and increasing depravity inseparable from so affluent, large, and increasing a population; a prison which shall combine security with accommodation; wherein not only the sexes shall be separated, and the offences classed, but ample provision be made for solitary confinemen and industrious occupation.

Meantime, Gentlemen, as this Pandemonium cannot rise like Milton's, we must till a better be constructed provide for the one we have as well as we can. I understand from my Lord Chief Justice, that the last Term Grand Jury, presented largely towards the numerous wants of the several prisons, as set forth in the Report of the Commissioners. But you will not take that report, however respectable, for evidence, but personally visit your Jails. In your Inquisatorial capacity, there is no duty more imperative upon you; painful no doubt in the execution, but clear to humanity, and such as upon reflexion will reward your finest feelings. See the several prisons with your own eyes, *occulis subjecta fidelibus,* and judge then for yourselves, what wants to be provided for, and you will provide accordingly. But in God's name, let us not provide grudgingly. Let us not weigh out in standing beam-scales the bounties of Parliament to the most wretched of our fellow-creatures. Let us display our frugality on worthier objects than the scanty rights of the unhappy. Waste not your hours and days in cold-blooded discussion, whether a pauper prisoner shall have four-pence a day for bread, or whether he could not exist uon three-pence; like the surgeon's torturing experiment how long an animal could live under an exhausted receiver! After all, what could your utmost liberality amount to, but a few shillings, more or less, extracted from the superfluity of each of us, for the relief of pining penury, and half-starved human beings? I want not to make a prison a place of comfort; but by imprisonment the law means only a restraint of personal liberty, and every suffering beyond such restraint is extra judicial punishment and therefore illegal.

Among the wants to be provided for, I trust that Hositals and Chapels were not overlooked. A separate, well ventilated apartment for medical patients, with suitable furniture and such other necessaries as their situation requires, is indispensable in every prison. And still more, a secret place of worship where the consolations of religion may be administered by a virtuous and feeling Pastor, such as the present Ordinary, Mr. Gamble. And here allow me to express deep regret (in answer to a memorial from a multitude of Roman Catholic prisoners) that the law does not yet warrant me to give in charge to you a provision for a Chaplain of that persuasion. The great mass of prisoners we know to be Roman Catholic, for whose accommodation it would surely be reasonable, that the Grand Jury had power to appoint, with the approbation of Government, a loyal and pious Pastor at a competent salary, who, co-operating with the Protestant Clergyman, might, by religious instruction and admonition, contribute essentially to that moral amendment through prisons, which is one of the prime purposes of imprisonment. Few subjects call in my mind, more strongly for the consideration of an enlightened Legislature.

In your progress through the prisons, you will feel it a paramount duty to examine the prisoners, strictly and apart, as to the treatment which they receive from their keepers; and also into the conduct of the several officers attached, at liberal salaries or emoluments, to the jails of Dublin. As far as their conduct in general has come under my observation, it has been attentive and humane. I allude to the Inspector-General, Mr. Archer, a very laborious and intelligent Officer, the accuracy and candour of whose Reports, as far as I have followed them, I can testify, the Local Inspector, the Chaplain, and the Physician, Dr. Mills, whom I consider an important acquisition to your prisons. I am sorry to exclude from this commendation the Surgeon and Apothecary. The latter candidly avows, that he visits the jails for the most part by proxy, by his apprentices, and that he conceives himself not bound to personal attendance. But the statute speaks a very different language. The 26th of the King distinctly and expressly requires him to attend the Physician in all his visits to the prisons; and I do not see how he can make affidavit (as the statute requires) that all the medicines charged in his account were delivered in the prisons, unless he himself be the bearer, or see them administered. Indeed a skilful Apothecary, by a feeling and assiduous attention to poor patients, may be of more general use than even the Physician. With respect to the Surgeon, it appears that between him and his apprentices, a great number of the surgical patients are utterly neglected, upon this curious distinction, that he is not bound to prescribe for country transports, transmitted to Newgate. The man who, amidst those scenes of woe, where all the sympatioes of our nature are perpetually solicited, can coldly calculate the limits of his duty, who can circumscribe it by any line short of his utmost power of doing good, who is not alive to human suffering, and ever ready to overdo the letter of his duty - that man I pronounce utterly unfit for the sacred trust confided to him. Why shall not so productive a customer as Newgate be attended with the same assiduity as you or I, or any other individual patient? Gentlemen, this system of deputation must be cut up by the roots. These are not offices which can be executed by deputy. No man can impart his professional skill to a deputy. No man's personal and assiduous attendance can be dispensed with, where the critical nature of the duty, the law of the land, and the best feelings of our nature, loudly demand it.

Gentlemen, I have trespassed too long upon your indulgent attention. I shall now release you; trusting that you will by an earnest and diligent application, through the Term, to the affecting and interesting subjects given to you in charge, lay the foundations, conformable to the beneficent views of Government, not only of a radical reform of the prisons, and a substantial amelioration in the condition of the prisoners of Dublin, but of that important part of the National Police, the entire Prison system of Ireland.

1. See diary entry of 31 Oct. 1809 (op. cit.).

2. Sir John Riddal and Sir Edward Stanley (printed footnote).

3. 26 Geo. 3, c. 27 is the footnote in the collected charges. The Act's principal provisions included the appointment of jail inspectors, including an Inspector General, and the enforcement of existing legislation on sanitation and the separation of offenders. Peter Holmes (MP Banagher) was associated with many pieces of jail legislation.

4. See Sir John Philip's letter to the Livery of London in 1808 (printed footnote).

6

1810: Munster for Spring Circuit, the Viceroy in Wicklow

With Co. Clare magnate John Crofton Vandeleur he discusses the failed expedition to the Scheldt and the island of Walcheren under the command of Chatham in September and October 1809. In October 1809 Spencer Perceval became prime minister of 'this virtuous but tottering administration' which lacked the talents of Canning and Castlereagh, both lost to the government after they fought a duel on Putney Heath.

Th. 8th March leave town at half 3 for Johnstown - with £180 viaticum.

Wretched weather - young horse's eye inflamed as well as my own - indeed a heavy cold about me, sometimes in the shape of hoarseness, sometimes of oppressed lungs, sometimes of partial rheumatism, ever since my recovery from the severe accident of 31st last Oct.

Fr. 9th Breakfast at Kildare- morning fair & drive cool & refreshing -

the weather breaks & becomes desperate to Backlane where I stop for the night. Alas, the poor horses! The servants are well covered.

John Ormsby Vandeleur[1] pops in & joins me for the evening . We deplore the infatuation of Lord Chatham[2] & the feebleness of this virtuous but tottering Ministry.[3]

We expatiate on the mischief of Middlemen who are not known in the North or in Scotland, & I rejoice that this race of vermin are disappearing fast thro' Ireland & with them long leases & extended farms. We admit however that small farms can not be favourable to tillage, for who would be at the expense of a heavy establishment of horses, carts, implements of husbandry, barns & stables, so indispensable to agriculture, where the space is contracted.

A life & 21 years (or 31 years at most) is the proper term, & that life had better be one of the Royal Family or some notorious person.

We doubt the wisdom of this new measure of reducing the size of Whiskey Stills wch of late had been advancing greatly the duty & concur in the injustice of putting down the qual (quality?) stills to the capitalists who built them on the faith of Parliament

- & we concluded with a volley at the abominable Grand Jury system of taxation wch is conducted more corruptly perhaps in the Co.Clare than in any other in Ireland; £26,000 raised last Spring at 3s per acre, when in Co. Dublin it did not exceed above £6,000 at 1s per acre - he who rides my horse with his own spurs won't spare him as he would his own.

Backlane continues to be an excellent house.

Sat. 10th - a bright morning & a pleasant drive to breakfast at Borros - the new Inn a good house - the day holds up famously & proceed (stopping to feed at Dunkerron) to Nenagh, 34m this day.

Sund. 11th Send on my equipage to Bird-hill & take a hack to breakfast with the Bayleys. Oh with what joy & delight am I received by all the family! The amiable Pen has transmitted to all her children her own fascinating goodness & has inspired them all with her own affection for her old friend -console poor Jane on the recent marriage of her late unfeeling unmanly admirer with an assurance that she has had a fortunate escape from him. Present her with some pretty music; but 'tis Sunday & I can't expect a song.

Drive away to Bird-hill & the weather coming on heavily & the road reported bad I suddenly resolve to bilk[4] Molony of Kiltannon,[5] with whom I was engaged to dine & sleep, & took the safer though longer route to Limerick where I stop at Swinbourne's excellent though dear house.

In the evening baron Sir Wm Cusack Smith my associate arrives.

12th Breakfast at Newmarket & arrive about 3 at Ennis. Glorious weather. Open the Commission. The Baron arrives, & we proceed to dinner together at the hospitable Giles Daxon's, the Treasurer.

Tuesd. 13th Swear the Grand Jury & charge them.

14th March. I drive with my old friend Archdeacon Kenny & family.

Th.15th Dine with my very worthy & excellent old friend the Ex-Judge Finucane who spends his latter life in hospitality, benevolence & seeking for every occasion of doing good.

Fr.16th Jas. McCarthy[6] capitally convicted - spend 12 hours this day in Court.

Sat. 17th The whole day employed in presentments. The Grand Jury (Vandeleur Foreman) exercise a most laudable rigour & economy - the demand this year amounts (in round numbers) to £57000; the grants last Spring were £21000; & the amount of this Assizes falls short of £10000! Co Clare may by persevering in this course of frugality redeem its blighted character.

Sund.18th Ride to breakfast at Newmarket. Drive from thence to the Sheriff Scott in his nice landaulet to within 5 m of Limerick where the City & Co. Limerick Sheriffs meet us & I ride in with them to Limerick. What an astonishing population is drawn out this fine Sabbath, well-dressed & well-looking, to stare at a human creature with three tails! Dine at Tervoe.[7]

M.19th Mar. Limerick - Open Commission in City & charge G.Jury, Vereker foreman. Visit the Ordnance Stores wch tho' on a small scale are worth seeing - the horses kept in the best condition - allowance for each per day : 16lbs Hay in 2 divisions of 12 & 4, & 12 lbs Oats in 3 equal feeds - a feed of moisten'd bran 2 or 3 times a week in lieu of the middle feed.

Dine with my old friend Sir R. Harte.

Tu.20th Dine with Mayor Loyd.

21st Dine no where but fag to late hour.

Th. 22 Dine at home.

Fr.23rd Dine with Collector Bolton Waller[8] & the pleasantest party I have yet met. Col Vereker[9] & his fair bride, a nice interesting girl, very like Arthur of Glenomera,[10] Lady Massey &c.

John Crosbie, 2nd Earl Glandore, the writer's cousin and political patron

Sat. Dine with the Bishop.

Sund.25th Breakfast with Tom Connor on the first goose egg this season - & meet the Baron[11] at dinner at Mt. Trenchard where we are entertain'd by Stephen Rice at bed & board with his usual hospitality.

M.26th Ride to Listowel 16m where I breakfast at Stokes's. My old friend Lord Glandore comes to meet me with John Talbot.[12] After breakfast he takes me in his chaise to Odorney where we part, & I proceed to Tralee where I open the Commission. Baron & I dine with Zeb Mac Subshff.

Tu. 27th Mar. We dine again with Zeb. Mac.

W.28th I dine with Barrister Rice.[13]

Th.29th Dine with Wm FitzGerald, Barrister.

Fr. 30th Dine at Robin Hickson's.

Sat. 31st Dine at Frank Mac's & after dinner receive the presentments before 12.00.

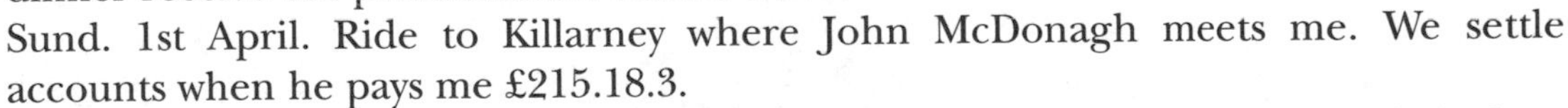

Sund. 1st April. Ride to Killarney where John McDonagh meets me. We settle accounts when he pays me £215.18.3.

Ride from thence to Milstreet over the worst circuit road now in Ireland, & dont arrive for two hours after nightfall. The equipage arrives in an hour after, providentially without accident. Meet here the Co. Cork Sheriff, Adams, & Sub., Lawless, over their battle with the little Baron who having slept last night at Killarney arrived at Milstreet from thence early this day. Never was I upon any former 1st. April made as such a fool as this day upon this cursed road.

M.2nd Breakfast wth Hedges at Macromp in his respectable castle, 10m., & after drive to Cork, 18m., without bating. The Commission for the City Cork opend by the Baron.

Tuesd. 3rd Ap. Enter upon & dine with the High Sheriff (Wagget Recorder against Johnson Mayor).[14]

W.4th Wagget & Johnson continued. Dine late at home.

Thurs. 5th This morning I charge the Jury who find for plaintiffs with nominal damages. Yesterday I had opened & charged the Grand Jury of the County of Cork - Dean Freeman Foreman.[15]

I bring home to dinner Burton,[16] Quin, Goold[17] & Franks. Baron dines with Jones.

N.B. I received from John Talbot for Lord Glandore at Tralee £6 to hand to Miss Margt. Crosbie No.18 Usher's Quay.

Fr.6th Breakfast & dine with the Cuthberts: Patrick, Lucy & her children Jane, Catherine, Lucy, Margaret John Maryanne a nice group. My sister in high health.[18]

Sat.7th Breakfast with the Alderman.[19] Spend the whole day till 9 in the Crown Court & forced to send excuse to Genl. Floyd & Lady Denny.[20]

S.8th Baron & I go to the cathedral & dine with the honest Bishop.[21] His daughter Mrs. Leslie a pretty woman, Mrs. Lawrence a well-bred unaffected Lady.

M.9th Breakfast & dine with the Cuthberts

Tu. 10th April Breakfast & dine with the Alderman.

W.11th Dine no where. Baron begins Uniacke @ Uniacke. Plaintiff goes thro' his case about 11 o'clock p.m.

Th.12th Baron continues Uniacke a Uniacke @ Defendant closes his case about 3 in the morning.

Fr. 13th Baron charges the Jury for 2 hours with great brilliancy, who found for the Defendant! Minor - concludes his business

Sat. 14th Baron sets out to sleep at Fermoy. I finish 17 very troublesome records in the City, pass sentence of death upon 2, close the Circuit about 8, & bring home to dinner Quin, Burton, Goold & Hitchcock.

Sund. 15th April Breakfast at the poor House at Watergrass Hill, being forced to take shelter from the pelting of the pitiless Elements -

Stop to dine sleep at Ballyporeen where I am agreeably surprised by Serj McMahon & Goold.

16th They take the Clonmel road & I the Cashel. Breakfast at Cahir 11 m, Cashel 11m & stop for the night at Littleton 9 m -

Tuesday 17th Breakfast at Castle Durrow, 16m. On this line are 3 ruins worth visiting - Cahir Castle, the Rock of Cashel, & the Round Tower near Johnstown (wch by the bye can scarcely be called a ruin having suffered but little from the tooth of time).

Abbey Leix, Daniel Grose, The Antiquities of Ireland, Irish Architectural Archive

Bate at Ballyroan having passed in view of Sir R. Staples's & Lord De Vesci's[22] fine seats - not forgetting the beautiful water castle of my late poor friend Lyon - whose is it now? - 8m - drive to Emo, 9 miles, where I leave my servants & equipage & take a hack to Judge Johnson's cottage where I spend the evening very agreeably - his eldest daughter an amiable accomplished girl famous for drawing likenesses from memory - shewed me an excellent Braham drawn in a fortnight after her last view of him - even in paper she cuts excellent likenesses - her scenes from Marmion in cut paper executed with great spirit & precision.

Easter Sunday 22 Ap. Return to Loughlinstown after an absence of more than six weeks & a laborious circuit, yet (blessed be God) much better in general health than on going out -

Fr. 27th Ap. This evening the first Cuckoo favoured us with his hooping notes -

Thursday 3rd May - & this evening the first Landrail[23] croaked thro the meadow .
Friday 4th & this morning the first swallow flitted by my window
W.9th Term sits - later by - weeks than last year

Tu.5th June Term ends.

The festivities of Mount Kennedy[24] take place during this vacation - I drive there from town & after spending a very agreeable night (as agreeable as the sight of lively dancing & pretty women & the enjoyment of a good supper & cheerful society could make it) I return to Loughlinstown at 6 a.m. & after two and a half hours rest go back to town. The Duke danced all night. Duchess of Gordon a dame of strong head & coarse manners.[25]

Fr.22 Trin. Term sits.

Work hard thro this term to get out of arrear. Downes absent several days towards the end thro' deafness. The famous trial of L. Hussey against Lord Sydney Osborne was tried by the four judges of King's Bench in the last vacation as a quasi trial at Bar. After a sitting of three and a half days the jury could not agree & no verdict found.[26]

Th.12 July. The Pattersons visit us. The Shaws have been with us a month. Harriett Day visits us twice, the first time last term for a week, the second time for 10 days this vacation.

Sat. 21st July. Lord & Lady Lorton[27] & the fine old Col. King dine with us, Knight Kerry, Mr. & Mrs. Ormsby &c. Make some pleasant excursions with the Pattersons, one particularly to visit the Guns and the beauties of Mount Kennedy.[28] Return through Belview & spend a pleasant day in spite of the envious weather.

Fr. 27th The Pattersons quit us for Malahide.

1. John Ormsby Vandeleur of Kilrush, son of Crofton Vandeleur. Commissioner of Customs in Ireland, Foreman of the Co. Clare Grand Jury.

2. Lord Chatham led the Walchern expedition in the autumn of 1809 which ended in retreat and heavy losses of men through typhus. The press carried Chatham's exculpation in February.

3. The ministry was formed by Spenser Perceval after the resignation of the Duke of Portland in October 1809. Canning and Castlereagh had fought a duel and were not included, causing Day to worry that the war would not now be pursued vigorously.

4. bilk: to avoid or escape.

5. Moloney, Kiltannon, near Tulla, Co. Clare.

6. James McCarthy, 'found guilty of burglary and robbery in the house of Michael Marsh, of Kielmore, Co. Clare', 'to be hanged on the 14th of April next' (*Limerick Chronicle*, 17; 21March, 1810).

7. Tervoe was the residence of Col William Thomas Monsell (1754-1836), MP Dunleer 1776-1783, Dingle 1798-1800.

8. Bolton Waller of Castletown Waller, aka Castletown Manor, near Ballysteen, Co. Limerick.

9. Charles Vereker, 2nd Viscount Gort (1768-1842), residence Roxborough. Distinguished himself in 1798 as Lieutenant Colonel of the Limerick Militia at the battle of Colooney against the French under Humbert. Opposed the Act of Union and supported Catholic emancipation. MP in the Irish parliament for the borough of Limerick from 1790; MP at Westminster to 1817. He m. secondly, March 5 1810, Elizabeth dau. of John Palliser of Derryluskin Co. Tipperary.

10. Glenomera was the Arthur residence, between Limerick City and Broadford, Co. Clare

11. Baron Sir William Cusac Smith, b. 1766, Lincoln's Inn 1784, called to the bar 1788. He made a famous speech in parliament in support of the Union. Solicitor-General 1800, Baron of the Court of Exchequer 1801. In 1834 Daniel O'Connell persuaded parliament to investigate his conduct as a judge, but the investigation was not proceeded with. He died in 1836.

12. John Talbot of Mt. Talbot, Co. Roscommon, succeeded Ld. Glandore in the Crosbie estate and assumed the name of Crosbie. His mother was Ann Crosbie, Glendore's sister.

13. Possibly Dominic Rice of Bushmount, Co. Kerry. He was prominent in the Catholic campaign. A Dominis Rice sponsored Daniel O'Connell's call to the bar in King's Inns, Dublin, in 1798.

14. The Recorder was claiming the right to a seat on the council and to compensation of £5000. 'for injury sustained by not being admitted to the full privileges of the recordership'. He won the case and received 'nominal damages'. His counsel were Wilmot and Goold (*Freeman's Journal,* 10 April 1810).

15. Edward Deane Freeman, inheritor of the Freeman estate at Castle Cor, barony of Duhallow, about five miles north-east of Kanturk.

16. Probably Charles Burton, 'the little Englishman'. Second in reputation only to J.P. Curran on the Munster circuit.

17. Possibly Sir Francis Goold, pro-Catholic barrister, or Thomas Goold, later Sergeant at Law.

18. Mrs. Franks (nee Catherine Day).

19. Probably Alderman John Day, formerly Mayor of Cork, brother of the writer.

20. Anne Morgel, widow of Sir Barry Denny (2nd Bart.) m. Genl. Floyd.

21. Thomas St. Lawrence, Bishop of Cork from 1807. Son of the Earl of Howth. Died 1831.

22. John De Vesey (1771-1855) 2nd Viscount de Vesci, of Abbey Leix, Co. Laois, m. (1800) Frances Letitia, daughter of William Broowow of Lurgan, Co. Armagh.

23. landrail or corncrake

24. Mount Kennedy was, until his death in 1801, the residence of George Cuninghame. Warner William Westenra inherited the property and the title Lord Rossmore from Cuninghame. In 1826 George Gun of Kerry inherited Mount Kennedy on Westenra's death. Here took place the reception which was the highlight of Lord Lieutenant the Duke of Richmond's tour of Wicklow in June 1810.

25. The Duchess of Gordon was the mother-in-law of the Duke of Richmond.
26. His heir at law, Hussey, challenged Lord Beaulieu's will devising his Irish estate to Lord Sidney Godolphin Osborne 'on the ground of his lordship's having died a relapsed Catholic'. (Talbot-Crosbie Mss., Day to Glandore, 27 February, 1810.)

27. General Robert Edward King, 1st Viscount Lorton (1773-1854), the builder of Rockingham, near Lough Key, county Roscommon. He m (1799) his first-cousin Frances Harman. See the writer's visit to Rockingham elsewhere in this diary.

28. George Gun of Kilmorna and Gunsboro in Kerry m. Jane or Jean Gordon, niece to General Cuninghame whose property, Newtown, Mount Kennedy, he inherited. The Guns were also connected by marriage with Day's political rival in Kerry, Lord Ventry, of Burnham near Dingle; anticipating difficulties at the general election of 1802 Day wrote of 'the combined treasury of Burnham and Mount Kennedy.' (PRONI, FitzGerald papers. Merrion Square, Day to Glandore, 5 December 1801).

Wellington's Victories in the Peninsula reach the Connaught Circuit 1810

The good news from the Peninsula reaches the Connaught circuit. Napoleon poured 100,000 men into Spain but has neglected his supply lines. Wellington, preparing to break out of Portugal, will constructed the Lines of Torres Vedras, and wait.
Sligo and Roscommon are home to family connections of the writer: the Mahons of Strokestown are relatives, the Talbots of Mount Talbot relatives of the Ardfert Crosbies. A plaque in Sligo Abbey reveals a connection with his ancestors the Earls of Desmond.

30th July. Set out after breakfast with Bob Franks, three servants in livery & the crier - take viaticum £202. Stop to bate at Maynooth where George B.[1] my associate breakfasted. He takes the Longford road, I the Athlone, the inns on both roads being in general insufficient for the accommodation of two judges & their suites. A beautiful rich English country from Dublin to Maynooth!

Duke of Leinster just 19. Hamilton his agent (next brother to Hans M. P. for Co. Dublin) rents Carton Demesne - the Duke is said to be very promising - so indeed is every young Nobleman - but pray, wait!

Tu.31st July dined & slept yesterday at Moyvalley Inn - an admirable house. Change my mind & instead of going by Kilbeggan follow the Baron (who slept last night at Kinnegad) & pass him on the road. Breakfast together at Mullingar. Ride 10m to Rathowen. Stop at Longford for the night - no bed for me at the inn, but Mr. Barber, attorney, very kindly accommodates Bob Franks & me with excellent beds.

W.1st August. Ride after breakfast 16 miles through Lanesboro to Roscommon. Commission opened by George (Baron) at Roscommon.

Thursday 2nd Half a fine buck sent to the judges by Sir E. Crofton. Genl. Mahon Foreman. Eleven Records entered, eight tried. The lightest assize town I ever remember. An intelligent, candid, well-conducted though punctilious bar (i.e. fond of making points). Two of the bar with our registers dine each day with us.

Sat.4th Certificate of £20. Dine and sup at my old friend and kinsman Lord Hartland's at Strokestown,[2] a fine demesne of 800 acres and a most comfortable place, 10 miles from Roscommon.

Sunday 5 August. Lie by at the polite old Peer's. Go to church with him and his very courteous old lady.[3] Ride through this fine demesne before dinner.

Mon. 6th After spending two days in clover we break ground at 6 a.m. and breakfast at Carrick. Swear and charge the Grand Jury, Clements Foreman.

Tuesday 7th Kept in court till 11 at night by the trial of a riot between a corps of Orange Yeomen and a ferocious mob of the suffering people. Cause and cross cause, both parties being indicted, and I try both (as in the Equity courts) together, and send the issues together to the jury who convicted five of the countrymen out of twenty indicted, and acquitted the Yeomen.

Wednesday 8th Ride to the magnificent seat of Rockingham[4] to breakfast (six miles from Carrick) where we find the good old Col. King had arrived the night before to receive us in the absence of Lord and Lady Lorton. Ride for an hour over this noble demesne through both parks and along the picturesque lakes studded with wooded islands. Stop to examine the foundation of the magnificent chateau now in rapid progress under the auspices of the celebrated Nash of England, to be finished by Christmas 1812. Estimate about £40,000. When finished, that Rockingham, take it all in all, will be the grandest seat in Ireland not excepting Curraghmore. From Rockingham we ride through Boyle to the top of the Curlew mountains where the storm forces me to take shelter in the chaise. Proceed to Marcrea House by invitation of Mr. Cooper,[5] and dine in this very handsome, castellated mansion erected by the late Mr. Cooper his father, under Johnson of Dublin. A very fine demesne. Some old but very extensive young plantations, but no water save a small river. This I think might be swelled into a handsome lake in front of the house. A very interesting, courteous, unaffected Lady Mrs. Cooper,[6] rather handsome and certainly very pleasing, from Yorkshire. Three fine boys. Cooper is the second brother; occupies occasionally this fine mansion in the absence of his poor elder brother the owner who still remains with Willis and probably never will recover. The second brother also represents now the county. Drive in after dinner six miles to Sligo where Baron opens the commission at 9 p.m. This day's journey on the whole for water, scenery, is perhaps the most interesting on any of the circuits.

Thursday 9th August. Go into the civil court for little more than form. Remain for half an hour and come away after finishing all the Civil business of the assizes. Probably the consequence of the universal depression of credit and the consequent difficulty of getting money upon paper, perhaps too the increasing stamp duty and other expences of law, make men more cautious of experiments at litigation. What a charming walk has Boyd taken me to Belvoir[7] along the hills through Mr. Martin's pretty grounds hanging over the river, and looking down over the splendid and picturesque scenery of Hazelwood, the lake, the bay, Benbulben, Knocknaree and all the grand features of the neighbourhood of Sligo!

On our return visit the Abbey of Sligo. Three sides of the cloister in perfect preservation. Here you are shown the monument of a Countess of Desmond, the wife of Sligiae Domini.[8] For want of my glass I could not command distinctly the inscription, being a little too elevated, and therefore shall endeavour before my departure to pay the Abbey a second visit.

Friday 10th Repeat my visit to the Abbey, and here follows the inscription wch yesterday I was unable to read :

Hic iacet famosissimus miles Donatus Cornalianus Comitatus Sligiae Dominus cum sua uxore illustrissima Dna Elinora Butler Comitissa Desmoniae.

The monument is no contemptible piece of church sculpture of 200 years old. It stands flat against the wall, and over the inscription are the Lord of Sligo (who appears, by an inscription over his head wch I was unable, on account of its distance, to do more than pick out a word here and there, to have been of the name of Connor) in armour, and the Countess with her proper coronet, kneeling vis-a-vis each other. Over each is an appropriate inscription wch I could not reach for want of a ladder. I have just learned from Whitestone that an elevation of the monument is to be found in the Anthilogia Hibernica. Beside the monument under the eastern window stands the Altar, in decay but very capable of easy repair. Indeed it is much to be lamented that this fine ruin the Abbey is not repaired into a minster as Downpatrick church was by the Marquis of Downshire. And so it will if Lord Palmerston the owner be possessed of the Marquis' public spirit. Lord P. who is now Secretary at War is a young nobleman of promise.[9]

Sligo Abbey: tomb of Dir Donough O'Connor and the Countess of Desmond, from Daniel Grose, The Antiquities of Ireland, Irish Architectural Archive.

George B. closes his business this day about 6, and we drive to the splendid seat of Hazelwood to dinner. A very handsome establishment ; the dessert of forced and natural fruit particularly abundant and fine. Lady Sarah (sister of Lord Enniskillen) very unaffected and courteous, and Mr. Wynne,[10] a highly respectable gentleman in his various relations of life. His demesne exquisite and in the highest condition. His cattle, wch are the long-horned Leicestershire, very fine. His Suffolk punches great patterns. Last year he imported nine Merino ewes and four rams wch have given him this year nine fine lambs. He has crossed his South Down with the Merino, and the fleeces are thicker and longer a good deal than the South Down. His brother the Revd. Richard Wynne dines with us, a sensible, worthy gentleman. Hazlewood possesses some hails of Killarney. The demesne, like Muckruss, divides the lake into two, not unlike Muckruss Lake and the Lower Lake, and facing the tongue of land composing the demesne are bold and black mountains resembling in shape Mangerton and Tomies, but all upon a dwarfish scale in reference to Killarney.

Saturday 11th Start from Sligo. Breakfast at Col. Irwin's, eight miles from Sligo, where I recognise my poor brother Chamberlain's daughter married to Revd. Mr. Crinus Irwin.[11] Bate at Hillas's father's ten miles farther, and drive on seventeen miles more to Ballina, the mansion of the excellent Col. King. A charming day's journey all along the coast and in view of the ocean till as we approach Ballina we turned up along the banks of the Moy. Here we saw across that fine river the Round tower of Killalla, and below it a mile or two the landing-place of the French in 1798.

Sunday 12th Go to church. Prevented by the envious rain from paying our intended visit to Dr. Verschoyle, the Bishop of Killalla,[12] six miles below Ballina.

Monday 13th Take an early breakfast with our truly respectable host, whose unremitting and cordial hospitality can not be exceeded. All the horses and servants, save the Baron's hacks, are entertained here. Over the chimney hangs a conspicuous medallion forbidding every person from giving vales to the servants. At the age of seventy-six he is the first up and the last in bed in his house, and with his own eyes sees that each guest wants nothing. Every Monday morning a large sum is distributed in charity. At Dinner he sets the laudable example of limiting his table to two soups and a single course. In short, I know not a more striking instance of the union of benevolence, liberality and economy in the same person. The affecting intelligence of the death of his little favourite great-grand niece, Lord Lorton's eldest daughter (about seven years old), arrived this morning but was not to be communicated till after our departure.

Ride to the wretched village of Foxford, the estate of Lord Clanmorris[13] (11 miles), sad evidence of the unfeeling heart of its owner; where amidst the crowd who surrounded the judges stalked a strapping lunatic in his birthday suit, no more noticed by the lads and lasses than the statues of Priapus were by the Roman matrons. The exhibition indeed was familiar to the town for his hide was literally tanned. We, however, thinking the display as indecorous as inhuman, ordered the Sheriff to remove the unfortunate man to the county infirmary. Proceed to Castlebar, 11 miles.

Tuesday 14th Poor Collier gets sick. Borrow a horse from the obliging sub-sheriff. Arrive to dinner at Ballinrobe where Lord and Lady Tyrawley and their son Col. Cuff[14] receive and lodge us for the Assizes with great cordiality and comfort. George (Baron) opens Commission.

Wednesday 15th A pleasant dinner party. Col. Dillon (Lord Dillon's son and Member for the county) a very civilized, interesting young man.[15] He had raised a regiment, the 102nd wch he left in Jamaica. Last year he served as a volunteer in the Spanish army and was present at the famous battle of Ocana in wch the Spaniards out of an army of 56,000 lost above 20,000 and the French of about 45,000 lost above 10,000. Since then the regular army of Spain has been unable to rally. Col. Dillon's account and anecdotes of Spain are inexhaustible and entertaining. According to him, the Spaniards, so far from being à jealous people are the most indulgent husbands, taking and giving the utmost latitude. The women are very beautiful and very licentious. They marry at 12; after a child or two the fond couple go as fancy leads them respectively; at 28 or 30 she becomes old and haggard and then becomes religious and a devotee. Theatricals and all amusements are forbidden, but bullfights.

The church in consequence becomes everywhere a scene of amusement. The music, vocal and instrumental, is exquisite. On the great altar at Seville on a certain Saint's Day, David dancing before the Ark was the subject of representation, and this was displayed by an elegant Ballet upon the altar. The processions and draperies are splendid: all is addressed to the senses. The atrocities of the French exceed all conception. The women are[16]...to death, the nuns particularly, but sodomy is the familiar and favourite crime of the French. Their prisoners are butchered in cold blood. If through fatigue or wounds or other accident they are found to lag on a march the general order is to dispatch them, an order most religiously honoured. Of all the generals Messena is the first, the first in cruelty as well as courage and skill. Lannes was the second in both. Augereau is a poltroon, but in the other indispensable quality of barbarity not inferior to any of his fellow assassins. Bernadotte and Berthier gentlemen, Junot a robber. Pity Dillon has not as much ballast as sail.

Thursday 16th and Friday 17th Spend in clover with our friend Lord Tyrawley. Lady Tyrawley, the ci-devant Wewitzer,[17] famous formerly for Rosetta, Polly and such like characters; heretofore the mistress, now the wife of our hospitable host, a more amiable woman scarcely to be found; exemplary in the highest degree in all the domestic relations, as wife, mother, mistress: a well-bred gentlewoman intoxicated by elevation, but becoming thoroughly her situation.

Saturday 18th Leave our cordial friends after breakfast for Galway where we each open our commission.

Sunday 19th Go to church. Very handsome and respectable. The incumbent is styled Warden of Galway; it is an extra-diocesan or peculiar jurisdiction independent of the bishop, about £600 a year, capable of being £1600.

Mrs. Day left Dublin shortly after me with the Shaws for Galway where she has been ever since. I find her here in high health with Mrs. Shaw where I dine this day. A very worthy, reputable family. Mrs. Currie, the daughter, very handsome, well-bred, unaffected and amiable; a handsome likeness of Miss Walstein, wife of Major Currie, Aide-de Camp to the gallant General Hill, now reaping laurels under that first of commanders, Lord Wellington in Portugal, where by his Fabian system he seems to be wearing out and mouldering down the great French army under the butcher Massena. Hill commanding the right wing down towards the Tagus keeps Regnier in check and prevents him from advancing upon Abrantes and turning our flank, while our left wing leans upon Almeida and the high ground towards the Douro. The world knew the gallantry of Wellington, but his profound skill as a general or commander of an army was never so tried or established before. 'The darling Child of Fortune' (as Bonaparte stiled his favourite Massena) at the head of 100,000 men dares not to advance upon Wellington with an army not exceding 60,000 !

Friday 24th August. Assizes end. Business light. The heaviest work was Eyre-Hedges against Perse, when, after spending a whole day in the trial the jury could not agree and a juror withdrawn.

Remain Saturday and Sunday.

1. Denis George (d. 1821), Baron of the Court of Exchequer. Of Stephen's Green, Dublin. Irish bar 1776. Became Recorder of Dublin in 1785 while Day served still at Kilmainham. Baron of the

Exchequer 1794 to his retirement in the year of his death.

2. Maurice Mahon (1738-1819) of Strokestown, created Baron Hartland of Strokestown in 1800, was Day's second cousin.

3. The wife of Maurice Mahon was Catherine, daughter of the first Viscount Mountcashel. They married in 1765. She died in 1834.

4. Lord Lorton commissioned John Nash to build Rockingham in 1809 on a site overlooking Lough Key. Nash was recalled in 1820 to add a third storey. (Anthony Lawrence King-Harmon, T*he Kings of King House,* A.L. King –Harman, 1996. P46.)

5. Edward Synge Cooper of Markrea Castle, MP Sligo 1806-1830.

6. The wife of Edward Synge Cooper was Anne dau. of Gov. Harry Varelst of Bengal whose seat was at Sheffield.

7. Belvoir, the seat of George Ormsby Esq. (*The Post-Chaise Companion*).

8. Eleanor, Countess of Desmond, nee Butler (1545- ?), widow of Gerald, 'Rebel Earl' of Desmond (obit. 1583), married Donogh O'Connor Sligo about 1597 and lived the remainder of her life in Sligo. He died in 1609 and her will is dated 1638, though she may have lived many years more. (Anne Chambers, *Eleanor Countess of Desmond.* Dublin 1986. P.200, 224, 229).

9. Henry John Temple, 3rd Viscount Palmerston (1784-1865), Secretary at War 1809-27, Foreign Secretary 1830-41, 1846-51, Prime Minister 1855-58, 1859 to his death. Seat was Broadlands, at Romsey in Hampshire. Irish estate in Sligo. In the tradition of Canning and the liberal wing of the Tories where Day found his political home: supported Catholic relief when expediency permitted (such as the bill of 1825); 'mediated' abroad in support of liberals in Belgium, Spain and Portugal, and to promote British interests including those of free trade. Earlier members of his family included Sir John Temple, Master of the Rolls in the reign of Charles 1, who wrote an account of the Catholic rebellion of 1641 later used to justify the campaign of Cromwell in Ireland.

10. Owen Wynne MP Sligo 1801, High Sheriff 1819 and 1833. He m. 1790 Lady Sarah Cole, sister of the 2nd earl of Enniskillen, John Willoughby Cole.

11. Amy, daughter of William Tankerville Chamberlain, judge of the King's Bench 1794 to his death in 1802, married Rev. Crinus Irwin of Tanragoe, Co Sligo in 1807 (Burke's *Landed Gentry of Ireland,* 1958).

12. Rt. Rev. James Verschoyle (1750-1834) of Kilberry, Co Kildare. Dean of St Patrick's 1794, Bishop of Killala and Achonry 1810. His family came from the Netherlands to Ireland in the sixteenth century (Burke's *Irish Family Records* 1976).

13. John Bingham (1762-1821) of Newbrook was created Baron Clanmorris of Newbrook, Co. Mayo, in July 1800. The stain glass window in the church in Foxford is inscribed as the gift of the fifth Viscount Clanmorris.

14. James Cuffe, illegitimate son of James, 1st Baron Tyrawley of Castle Lacken by Miss Wewitzer, his long time mistress and later wife. The father was MP Mayo from 1768 to 1797, in which capacity Day would have known him; after 1774 he was an opponent of further Catholic relief, also opposing parliamentary reform. The son, Col. James Cuffe (above), later represented Tralee in the Imperial Parliament from 1819 to 1828. The Cuffes were related to the Gores, lords Arran.

15. Henry Augustus Dillon of Costello-Gallen, MP county Mayo 1802-1814 when he succeeded as 13th Viscount Dillon. In parliament he spoke in favour of the Catholic petition of 1805. His father, Lord

Charles Dillon, 12th Viscount (1745-1813), referred to in this passage, was nephew of Arthur Dillon, Col. of Dillon's regiment, guillotined during the Reign of Terror in 1794; Col. Arthur's sister, Charlotte, was the first wife (m 1777) of Valentine Browne, 1st earl of Kenmare. The family descended from Theobald Dillon from the Pale, a Collector of Composition rent in Connaught, who in the 1580s acquired the entire barony of Costello (Ballyhaunis), native patrimony of the MacCostellos.

16. Word unclear.

17. Miss Wewitzer was a London actress.

A Judge Compromised:
Autumn 1810 in Kerry, and Munster Circuit, Spring 1811

A growing rift with sections of the magistracy in the northern baronies of Kerry marks Judge Day's return to the Munster circuit in 1811. A separate development is a case brought against him arising out of a property deal in the county. The press will refer to 'Judge Day's Great Equity Cause'. News from the War in the Peninsula continues good: a young cousin is a hero at Barossa.

Monday 27th Leave Galway where we experienced much kindness from Mrs. Shaw and family, and arrive to dinner at Dean Foster's, Gort, 17 miles. Entertained very hospitably by him and our old friend Mrs. Foster. Lord Kiltartan[1] drops in and presses us hard to give him next day at his fine lake, but we resist.

Tuesday 28th Proceed to Crusheen where we bait. A remarkable house to breakfast at. Visit the Abbey of Quin, the most beautiful and the highest preservation of any in Ireland. Sleep in Limerick, about 35 miles from Gort, passing by Quin and Sixmile Bridge.

Wednesday 29th Reach Mount Trenchard to dinner. Send next day for Massey, coachmaker, to Limerick, who for £50 contracts to metamorphose my old chaise into a new one pursuant to the instructions of Stephen Rice.

Friday 31st Proceed in the chaise brought by Massey to Listowel where we find the Alderman and wife at Oliver Stokes'. Sunday after prayers we dine at Ballinruddery where the Knight, having no wife to help him, yet entertained us very comfortably. We sleep there.

Monday 3rd September. After breakfast proceed to Tralee. In Tralee I am detained till the middle of October by a tormenting Commission issued by the petitioners in Blennerhassett against Day.[2] During this long period we lodge in the Castle, and nothing can exceed the friendly hospitality and attention of all the inhabitants to Mrs. Day and me. Sometimes I visit Killarney, often my tenants, often Lord Glandore. I bestow also much time on the paving and flagging of the town wch the inhabitants take up and prosecute with great alacrity and liberality. The Spa also I frequent, and quaff copiously, and having Baltygarron in my hands to let for forming a fund for Sir Edward's young children, I have it in contemplation to erect a neat building over the well, and dress an acre of ground behind it, and to let lots for building and improving in the neighbourhood; and thus, by providing abundant accommodation and dressing the whole face of that quarter, to bring the Tralee Spa into fashion and demand.

10th October. Mrs. Day with Robert Day proceed for Dublin, and in Limerick take up my chaise in respect of wch Mr. Massey has fulfilled his promise and admirably executed his contract.

20th I follow in Robert Day's gig, and touching at Listowel and Mount Trenchard as usual arrive in Dublin on 26th and at Loughlinstown the 27th in perfect health after three months, and grateful to God for protecting me throughout against the slightest accident.

Munster Circuit, Spring 1811

Monday 18th March. Open the Commission this morning in the city, Col. Vereker Foreman.

Saturday 23rd After a light week and getting fringed gloves,[3] John Franks[4] and I ride to Glin where we find excellent accommodation for man and horse.

Sunday 24th. Breakfast at Oliver Stokes', dine with Maurice FitzGerald and sleep at Stokes'.

Monday 25th John Franks and I resume our ride and proceed on horseback to Tralee, having rode from Limerick (54 miles). Not bad at 64, but what is this to Dr. Duigenan who rides from Holyhead to London at 76 ?

Tuesday 26th Charge the Grand Jury and give the magistracy and gentry round Listowel a severe jobation[5] for the lawless state of the country (Lord Castlerosse[6] Foreman).

Saturday 30th Pass sentence of death on five for acts of Whiteboyism, of whom can recommend only one. A laborious week.

Sunday 31st Go to church and dine with Stephen Rice. The Baron proceeded to Killarney Friday.

Monday 1st April I breakfast at Frank Murphy's, taking Robert Day with me. Bate at Killarney and take an excellent luncheon at Galwey's.[7] Sit an hour with Lord Kenmare.[8] Sir T. and Lady Maryanne Gage[9] on a visit to his Lordship; so also the Knight. Ride to Milstreet.

Tuesday 2nd Breakfast as usual with my friend Eyre Hedges at Macroom. Bate at the Ovens, a very clean, comfortable house. N.B. The woman of the house English. The kitchen so furnished with bacon that it may well be called the Land of Ham.

Dispose of ten Records in the city. In the county try many capital cases. Four convicted, of whom one was hanged for a cruel murder at Mitchelstown Monday 8th. Another, Captain Rowser, was left to be hanged, and the other two pardoned. A most laborious and oppressive fortnight.

To comfort us arrive tidings of the glorious battle of Barossa, 5th March - and on same day the retreat of Massena. During the Assizes of Cork Master Ponsonby prevails on five or six magistrates dupes or delinquents to placard me for my lecture to the indolent gentry and corrupt or cowardly magistrates in the neighbourhood of Listowel. However, the Grand Jury very spiritedly defend me by an address, and two of these delinquents turned accusers, viz William Richard Hilliard and John Sandes Esquires. I shall get the Chancellor to break of the Commission for infamous practices, as well as William Twiss and Thomas Giles Esquires.[10] While at Cork I received very distinguished attention from General Floyd and Lady Denny.[11]

Saturday 20th Dine with my dear and longing wife at Loughlinstown where everything looks very well after six weeks absence. N.B. The Chancellor dismisses said four magistrates.

1. John Prendergast Smyth (1741-1817). Baron Kiltartan 1810, Viscount Gort 1816. The Prendergast Smyth - Charles Vereker control of Limerick City politics lasted from the 1770s to 1841.

2. This was the long-running litigation between Judge Day, as defendant, and the sons of Rev. John Blennerhassett about land in Dunmaniheen, Killorglin parish. See later chapters.

3. The Limerick sheriffs presented him with 'gold fringed gloves' in March 1816, when an assizes proved 'maiden', i.e. had no capital sentences (*Ennis Chronicle,* 27, March, 1816); Mary Leadbeater reports Day being wished 'a pair of white gloves' when he visited Ballitore (Quaker) school during the Leinster circuit (*Leadbeater Papers* (Vol. 1 p 344.)

4. Sir John Franks (1770-1852) Day's nephew. Bar 1791 and went the Munster circuit. 1825 appointed Judge of the Supreme Court of Calcutta.

5. A rebuke or reprove; derivation biblical: Jobe, the object of lengthy reproofs by his friends.

Crotta House, home of William Ponsonby, later Julian and Kitchener.
Neale, Views of the Seats of Noblemen and Gentlemen.

6. Valentine Browne (1788-1853), Viscount Castlerosse 1801-1812, later (1812) second Earl of Kenmare.

7. Possibly Christopher Gallwey, agent of Lord Kenmare. The *Gentleman's and Citizen's Almanac for 1815* gives a Christopher Gallwey as Barrack Master of Killarney.

8. Valentine Browne (1754-1812), Viscount Kenmare; created Earl of Kenmare 1801.

9. Sir Thomas Gage was married to Marianne daughter of Lord Kenmare.

10. The *Limerick General Advertiser,* 23 April 1811, carries a report of Day's dispute with the North Kerry magistrates. The Chancellor of the day (1807-1827) was Thomas Manners Sutton, Lord Manners.

11. Anne Morgell (Lady Denny) was widowed at age sixteen by the death of her husband Barry Denny, 2nd Bart. in a duel at Oakpark with John Gustavus Crosbie on October 20 1794. She was the daughter of Crosbie Morgell of Rathkeale. She maried (1805) General Sir John Floyd, Bart.

Charge to the Grand Jury of the County of Kerry, Spring Assizes 1811.[1]

Gentlemen of the Grand Jury,

It is with sincere and deep regret that I cannot congratulate you on the present state of a certain portion of our common county. I understand from the Sheriff and some magistrates, that a wide district of your northern barony, lying principally between the town of Listowel and the frontier of the county, continues to be agitated, and that all the blood which has been shed has produced no durable effect upon the lawless and stubborn spirit which has so long disgraced that quarter of the country. This is the more observable when we recollect that in the Rebellion of 1798 this county stood unshaken by the storm which raged at that disastrous period, a proud and almost solitary exception to the then general state of Ireland. No county had in former times been more famed through all its parts for loyalty, love of order and respect for the laws, than the county of Kerry. In those happy days the progress of the judges was but an excursion of pleasure. The whole population of your county poured forth to hail their arrival with all the joy of conscious innocence; and the judges had but the grateful task of flinging wide open the prison gates, and of proclaiming a general jail delivery. Alas! Gentlemen, what an iron age has succeeded to those golden days! Look at this Calendar: 53 numbers written in characters of blood. Is this the modern reception which the county of Kerry, once the pattern county of Ireland, is pleased to give to their judges of assize? Must your judges at every assize wade through blood and carnage to give peace to those who will make no effort towards that great object for themselves? Are the judges to turn executioners? Are we, whose sacred and prime duty it is to administer justice in mercy, to become the butchers of our own species, to restore tranquillity to an indolent gentry and to corrupt or cowardly magistracy?

But God forbid that I should involve all within that quarter in an indiscriminate censure. Several there are among them whose qualities and services do honour to their country. Of the meritorious magistrates amongst you I happen to see two in court whose activity and courage I am happy to record, the Rev. Mr. Neilan[2] and Mr. Stokes. Happily, too, this turbulent spirit is confined to comparatively narrow limits. – Southward of the disturbed district there would seem to be a broad line of demarcation, beyond which, throughout the whole of this extensive county, all is peace, tranquillity and good order. Gentlemen, it is beside the bound of my duty, and indeed of my time, to enter into a discussion upon the causes of this sad contrast. But thus far on behalf of the criminal peasantry I may be allowed to observe, that they want the counsel and protection of the feeling and sympathetic gentry, and the exertions of an active and efficient magistracy, to check their excesses and inforce a respect for the law. On the contrary there are magistrates in the county who compound felonies, screen their delinquent followers and purveyors, trade upon their commissions and administer justice by sale. They want amongst them the hereditary virtues of the house of Kenmare, spreading like a guardian angel its fostering wings over a contented country, cherishing civilizing, blessing all within the happy range of its extensive influence. 'Go (I would say to the great Lords of the soil) go, and do thou likewise;' and instantly, as if by magic, the great work of peace, good order and happiness is accomplished. Here at once disclosed and exemplified is the great Arcanum for governing the Irish peasant. It is false as libellous to say that the Irish peasant is an impracticable, perverse animal.

Believe me, Gentlemen, the whole mystery consists in a due mixture of conciliation and firmness. On the one hand an ear ever open to the distresses of the people, and an heart ever ready to relieve them; on the other hand a strict and parental controul over their excesses, and an unbending execution of the law without respect to religious sect or political party – such a course would insure a full ascendancy over the ardent and inflammable, but generous and flexible minds of the Irish peasantry, and win from them a willing submission to the discipline of the law. It is in vain to look to special commissions, to military force, or any other aid that a vigorous and willing government can afford you. – Such are but short-lived puny palliatives. It is in yourselves after all that you must expect to find a permanent and radical remedy for the evil.

From this point the report reverts to indirect speech and covers the proceedings, unsatisfactorily. What follows is taken from The Freeman's Journal, 5 April, 1811. Ed.

This, (the break-down in law and order in the northern baronies of the county-Ed.) his Lordship declared with much energy and warmth, was to be ascribed to an indolent and cowardly gentry, and to a corrupt and inefficient magistracy, who compromised felony and bartered their commissions. But God forbid, his Lordship said, that he should be unable to distinguish between that degraded portion and those upright and fearless espousers of the laws of whom our county could boast – he would instance Mr. Neilan and Mr. Stokes.

His Lordship next directed the attention of the Grand Jury to the grants which should be called for towards forwarding the new line of road intended for a mail coach between this town and the city of Limerick. The benefit of a like measure was already seen in the southern part of the County, and the expediency of such in the proposed quarter was plainly evident. The learned Judge was aware that a skilful gentleman had been deputed by the Post Office to repair to this country, to hasten the undertaking, and he did hope that the Grand Jury would, by pecuniary assistance, accelerate the measure, in as far as might be compatible with that commendable parsimony they should deem necessary to accompany their grants. His Lordship next argued very forcibly the necessity of erecting a new county gaol. He said, that there should be laid before them a representation made by the highly valued and respected local inspector (the Rev. James Day), his near relation and very esteemed friend, expressive of the total unfitness and insufficiency of the existing prison. His Lordship observed that in consequence of its being confined, and having other irremediable disadvantages, its filthiness equalled that of a pound, and that as to any idea of classification of the prisoners, which the law very humanely required, it was out of the question. His Lordship produced the act of Parliament which has reference to the government of prisons, and which enforces the erection of county gaols according to a specific plan, for the comfort of the prisoners, and expressed his confidence, that even if the law had not made it imperative on them, they would on duly weighing the matter, spontaneously offer the necessary supplies. But, he said although the law does compel the execution of the work, it does so leniently, as government will advance the sum required, which need only be paid by half yearly instalments without interest. The learned Judge concluded by reminding the Jury of the Act of Parliament which enabled them to appoint for the service of the prisoners chaplains of their respective persuasions, and it would be ill-directed parsimony to curtail the allowances which were permitted to be devoted to that purpose. His Lordship here bestowed a highly judicious and elegant encomium on the Roman Catholic Clergyman (the Rev. Michael O'Sullivan, P.P. of this town), on whom the duty would devolve, begging the Gentlemen of the Jury might be assured that his Lordship conceived him a bright ornament to his profession, and a person peculiarly capable of performing the object here in view, viz. the reformation of that vicious assemblage which there always presents itself.

1. *Limerick Gazette and General Advertiser,* 23 April 1811.

2. Rev. Nicholas Neilan, Parish Priest and magistrate, Causeway, Co. Kerry.

Robert Day to the county of Kerry Grand Jury, 26 September 1798. [1]

Gentlemen of the Grand Jury,

I am not aware on looking into the Calendar of your prisoners that any Bill of Indictment is likely to be sent up to you of an unusual nature or that calls for any observation from me. It is equally unnecessary for me to trouble Gentlemen of your experience with any general discussion on the duties of a Grand Juror.

But before I dismiss you allow me to congratulate you and all good men upon the present flattering and happy aspect of public affairs. Insurrection black and unnatural has been succeeded by an alarming invasion, and both have effectively been crushed. Whatever mischiefs both may have produced amongst us, they have served ultimately and in effect but to prove the steadiness of Irish loyalty and Irish valour.

But, Gentlemen, however consoling the present appearance may be, I trust we shall not be deluded into any fatal security by this calm. To the eternal honour of your county (of which it is my greatest pride to be a native) it has preserved itself pure and untainted through the whole of this trying and perilous crisis. The seeds of treason have been scattered among you, but they don't vegetate or strike root in your soil. The steady loyalty of the county of Kerry has been the theme of universal admiration. But, Gentlemen, a late tragical transaction[2] in this country proves that some secret and malignant enemies to your repose and honour have been busy among your peasantry. I allude, you perceive, to the sudden ebullition of Treason, the smothered fire which burst out at Castleisland and might have wrapt in flames and desolated your whole county, like another Wexford, but for the prompt spirit and active energy of our Yeomen. – Let that horrid transaction awaken you to an increased vigilance and activity. Watch and take up all suspected strangers. Messrs. Arthur O'Connor, Emmet and their fellow conspirators now own that the peasantry while left to themselves were loyal, virtuous and innocent, that they deluded our credulous gulls by assurances of an agrarian

distribution and other prospects of plunder, and that by Reform and Emancipation and other such cant terms which sicken with disgust the heart of virtue and honour, they meant nothing but the subversion of the state – mere watchwords for insurrection and rebellion. Let us but open the eyes of our misguided people to the criminal views of their betrayers; let us by an equal and contrary activity on our part encounter the diabolical machinations of those Fiends; let us by benevolent, sympathetic and conciliatory conduct win the affections and confidence of the lower orders and we shall thus early bend them to the yoke and discipline of the law. Cherish the bees which collect the honey on which the whole hive must be subsisted. There is as little of good sense and policy as there is of virtue and humanity in rack-rents, grand jury jobs and all that short-sighted spirit of rapacity, which characterizes unfortunately too great a part of our Kingdom, exhausting the sources of general subsistence; grinding the people who are the sinews, substance, arms and strength of every country. Let the lower orders feel the full benefit and protection of our excellent Law and they will respect and love it. Let it not be said that the Laws are but cobwebs; too weak for the strong, and too strong only for the weak – Laws which speak a mild and equal language to every subject, but which serve as instruments of oppression in the hands of bad magistrates and bad men.
But, Gentlemen, I beg pardon for this digression from the immediate line of our duties. The awful times and critical state of our country must be my apology.

1. Day papers, RIA Ms 12w11.

2. Three Protestant Yeomen were inhumanly butchered in August 1798 in the dead of night in the barracks of that town. The rest of the corps had gone the day before to the races of Tralee and imprudently left to those unfortunate men the charge of all the arms and ammunition which they lost with their lives. (See *Kerry Evening Post*, 20 March 1833, Ed.)

Summer of Catholic Discontent: 1811 on the Home Circuit

A government proclamation has banned a Catholic convention. The proclamation will be defied, and cases arising will come before Day in Dublin. For now he enjoys one of his favourite circuits. The Home circuit proceeds through Carlow, Athy (for Kildare), Portlaoise (called Maryborough, for Laois, or Queen's County), Dangan (called Philipstown, for Offaly, or King's County), Mullingar, (Westmeath), and Trim (Meath).

Saturday 27th July. Start with Mat Franks for Johnstown with £130 viaticum and find my kind-hearted associate Lord Norbury[1] and his register Mr. Jackson at dinner before us.

Sunday 28th Breakfast at Ballytore. Proceed to Castledermot where I wait for Lord Norbury, and from thence proceed together to Carlow. Knot Sheriff, our registers Espinasse and Meredith dine with us and Rochfort.

Monday 29th His Lordship opens the judicial campaign in the Crown court. I gallop through seven records. Spanish Brown, Jebb[2] and Wolfe dine with us.

Tuesday 30th I stick the whole day in a cursed usury record against McCartney, Carlow banker, who obtains verdict. Our registers and Wallace, Ridgeway, Vezey and Tickell dine with us.

Wednesday 1st August. We take a pleasant ride to Brown-Hill and walk with Brown and his comely daughter into their garden. A very respectable mansion. Return to breakfast. Go into court to try eight records, but have the satisfaction to find two submitted to arbitration, and remanets at the desire of both parties entered on the other six.

"Plaze your Honour, I am a poor dissolute woman whose premisses is contagious to your Lordship's backside at the lodgings and was yesterday injected by that thief Paddy Kennedy and am ruinated if your Lordship's honour and glory won't take my concerns into your hands."

"What can I do, my good woman? You must speak to some lawyer or attorney to bring your case regularly before me."

"Ah, my Lord, my Lord, I know myself and all I have under your Lordship."

"Lord Barrington,[3] you are the most studious man alive. You read pamphlets even coming down to the house in your carriage."

"I protest (said his Lordship) I am so occupied with the War Office that I have not a moment for study. I have not, except in my carriage, dipped into a book these twelve months."

'What! (replied Charles Townshend) not dipped even into Harrington's Oceana?'[4] N.B. Lady Harrington could explain that allusion.

Lord Lucan, who was a strong and vain Irishman,[5] had borrowed one night from the soldier his sentry-box in stable-yard for himself and her Ladyship. On returning he handed a guinea to the sentinel, but her Ladyship rebuked this extravagance assuring his Lordship that she never paid more than half a crown.

Lord North had tender eyes and closed them generally during a debate. Sir Joseph Mawby in a long speech complained much of the inactivity and indolence of the Administration, and asked what vigilance could be expected from the minister when, like another Palinarus in a most interesting debate he actually fell asleep. 'Would to God (said his Lordship, leaning forward) I were now asleep'.

Lord Bacon,[6] speaking somewhere of the folly of prosecutions and libels, said they reminded him of schoolboys attempting to tread out a bonfire whereby instead of being extinguished the sparks flew up in their own faces.

The Duke of Marlboro (then Captain Churchill) had been the handsomest fellow in the Guards with nothing but his commission. The Duchess of Cleveland, one of Charles the Second's mistresses, had received £5000 from one whom she despised for a night's lodging. The act of infidelity having lain heavy on her conscience, she prevailed on the handsome Churchill to relieve her scruples by succeeding her former bed-fellow the following night and accepting the £5000. This sum he gave to Lord Halifax for an annuity of £500 a year, and that was the first income the Duke had that he could call his own.[7]

Epitaph by Jack Selinger upon his jockey :

'Here lies Paddy Murphy who died of a galloping consumption.'

Another upon an Irishman who was hanged:

'Here lies the corpse of Paddy Fagan, who died in the full enjoyment of his health by a fall from the scaffold.'

Old Langrishe,[8] having sent to the foot of the table for some beef, and being asked wch side of the sirloin he preferred, answered that he always stuck to the side that was uppermost.

A fat, clumsy ...[9] was produced upon the table in a trial at Philipstown before Lord Norbury. 'Pray Sir, who and what are you?' ' I am, plaze your Lordship, the postmaster of this town.' 'Yes, Sir, (replied the learned Lord) I see you are well qualified to dispatch a mail (meal).'

Mr.P. the celebrated hay-maker, having fitted a pair of stays one day on a Mrs. J-n, she complained of the great length of the peck. 'Ma'am (said he) it is very complete, it is as near the thing as possible'.

Price of lodging in Carlow £18.4.0.

Wednesday. Leave Carlow about two, and ride through the beautiful country along the Barrow to Athy (9 miles). Lord Norbury remains behind.

Athy

Thursday 1st August. Charge shortly the Grand Jury. Two men capitally convicted for robbing Flynn. Dine with us Jebb, Adair and Furlong.

Friday 2nd Another capitally convicted for uttering forged notes. Blackburn,

Ferrall and Darcy dine with us.

Saturday 3rd Ride 15 miles by Kelly's, Pigot's, Sir Alan Johnson's, Vicarstown and Dean Trench's to dine and sup at Judge Johnson's. Beautiful ride.

Sunday 4th Spend the day at the ex-judge's. Dine with us Wallace of the bar, Mr. Smith and Mr. Adair. Proceed in the evening to Maryboro.

Monday 5th Dine with the Bar. Delightful singing from Blackburn and Hussey; excellent imitation by Bethal; and a most devout exhortation by Charles Ball.

Tuesday 6th R. Staples and co. dine with us.

Wednesday 7th Depart certifying £20 for the house, and dine at Mr. Warburton's respectable seat Garryhinch where we meet Parnell and a large party of ladies and gentlemen. Warburton has eight sons and never had a daughter. Drive in after nightfall to Philipstown.

Philipstown

Thursday 8th August. Charge the Grand Jury (Bernard Foreman).

Saturday 10th After very light business discharge the Grand Jury, but too late to accompany Lord Norbury to dinner at Charleville Forrest.[10]

Sunday 11th The judges are entertained in this wretched town in high style at Mr. Smith's, tenant of Lord Ponsonby,[11] who is seized of this one-third share of the Molesworth estate in right of his mother, and by his patent is bound to entertain the judges. But they have got rid of the horses and servants whom I conceive them bound to provide accommodation for no less than for the judges. Ride to Mullingar, 17 miles, passing near McCan's, Usher's, Rochfort's and other fine seats. In general an excellent country. Lord Norbury arrives from Lord Charleville's full of admiration of the splendid style of that splendid place.

Wednesday 14th Finish seven long records.

Thursday 15th Breakfast with Mr. Purdon at his pretty house in the garden near Killucan. Visit Mr. Wynne's elegant glebe-house and grounds: does great credit indeed to his taste, and still more does his interesting, amiable English wife.[12] Scamper off to the Handcock's in that neighbourhood. From thence we ride through the beautiful farm of Purdon's brother. Several handsome habitations of the Purdon family through this morning's line. Lord Longford is landlord of all this sweet country, and is supposed to possess about £15,000 a year. A better landlord or a better or more respectable gentleman is hardly to be found. We ride forward attended by Purdon, Handcock and others to the bounds in the bog where we meet the Sheriff, and alighting get into my carriage having rode about 20 miles this day. Drive about 6 miles to

Trim

Visit the old Castle, once the rendezvous of the Irish parliament in the early periods of the English connection.

Saturday 17thTry for Lord Norbury the action of Ogle against the renowned O' Connor. Damages for assault upon the person by this man of the people, a man held in such abhorrence in this county that no one visits him.[13]

Sunday 18th Invited by many respectable gentlemen to their houses: by Lord

Cunyngham,[14] Sir Marcus Somerville,[15] Mr. Bligh etc. Certify for lodgings £20. Bate at Black Bull. Visit the Urial family, a very substantial family of farmers consisting of a father and nine sons, all perfect masters of every kind of country business. Take Lord Norbury with me to his house Cabra where we dine.

The subject wch chiefly engrosses Dublin is Downes Chief Justice's warrant, 8 August 1811, arresting Dr. Sheridan for acting as delegate, and four or five others for acting as electors of delegates to the Catholic Committee. In contemplating the proceedings of the Catholic meetings it may be asked why do they not confine themselves to the professed object of the meeting, the petitioning Parliament? Because that is not their real object, because they would control and not petition; because they would intimidate (and overawe) the Legislature. Who fetters (who presumes to restrain) their inestimable and undoubted right to petition? Have they not petitioned session after session? Are not the doors of Parliament as open to them as to every other sect or class of subjects? But they must not disguise rebellion or revolution under the cloak of petition. It is other things they want and not Catholic emancipation - repeal of the Union, Popish Parliament, separation from Great Britain and connection more with France - these if possible are their objects, nay their avowed objects. Government though firm have been temperate. They gave warning and practised forbearance, but instead of waiting quietly for a legal decision they (mean time) try to stir up tumult. Look at their publications. Is that the language of man desiring only the rights and privileges of the constitution, or the inflammatory language of men desiring to destroy it? See Dublin Evening Post, their organ, about 15th August. Notwithstanding the high legal authorities who are ready to risk their professional reputations, I incline still to think that the assembling a body of delegates, a permanent Catholic or Popish Parliament, is in direct violation of the Convention Act (wch is but a declaration of the common law). Were petitioning the sole object, we have shown that such a meeting is unnecessary. (The doors of Parliament are wide open to all sects and have been entered by none more oftener than by this sect.) They do not resort to such meetings (or expedients) in England (where the precious right is well understood and guarded with a jealous care). Delegated meetings are liable to be perverted by designing and desperate men to the worst purposes, to purposes far beyond the professed object. It is absurd to say that the right of petitioning is infringed when the Roman Catholics have every mode and channel of complaint open to them that Protestants or Englishmen have. The House of Commons would not receive a petition from a delegation - and therefore fair to infer that delegation is illegal. It has been said that the statute does not affect committees appointed bona fide to prepare petitions, but only such as make petition a pretence for delegation. But such was not the construction of those who opposed the Bill at the time, much less of those who supported it. Watchman of the constitution in those days held a different language.

1. John Toler, Lord Norbury (1739-1831), the 'Hanging Judge' of folk history. MP for Tralee 1776, later Philipstown (Dangan) and Gorey. Attorney-General 1798. Chief Justice Court of Common Pleas 1800. Presided at the trial of Robert Emmet in 1803. From Beechwood in Co. Tipperary.

2. Richard Jebb (1766-1834), Justice of the King's Bench from 1818. The Jebbs, originally from

Nottinghamshire, lived in Drogheda, where their father was Alderman. King's Counsel 1806, third serjeant 1817, Justice of the King's Bench 1818. Richard's brother John was Bishop of Limerick from 1822.

3. William Barrington (1717-1793), Secretary at War 1755-61, 1765-78.

4. James Harrington (1661-1677), political theorist His 'Oceana,' 1656, concerns a mythical commonwealth.

5. Patrick Sarsfield (d. 1693), Lord Lucan?

6. Francis Bacon (1561-1626), Lord Chancellof of England.

7. This is a well-recounted episode from the affair of the Duchess of Cleveland (Barbara Palmer, op cit.) and John Churchill, later Duke of Marlborough, hero of Blenheim.

8. Possibly Sir Hercules Langrishe (1731-1811) who changed sides to the government support during the 1780s.

9. illegible, appears too be 'witness'

10. Charleville Forest, the seat at this time of Charles William Bury (1764-1835). Created, 1806, 1st Earl of Charleville. He married (1798) Catherine Maria daughter and sole heiress of Thomas Townley Dawson, Dublin. His paternal ancestry was Bury of Shannon Grove in Limerick.

11. John Ponsonby, 2nd Lord Ponsonby of Imokilly. His mother was Louisa Molesworth.

12. Rev Henry Wynne, Rector of Killucan, Co. Westmeath. He was brother of Owen Wynne, MP Sligo. He m Katherine, daughter of John Eckersall, of Clarerton House nr Bath.

13. This is probably Roger O'Connor, originally from west Cork. He rented Dangan Castle which burnt down after he had insured it. His brother was Arthur O'Connor of the Press, imprisoned in Margate in 1798. Roger's son was Fergus O'Connor the Chartist leader in England.

14. Conyngham, Slane Castle.

15. Sir Marcus Somerville, of Somerville House on the banks of the Boyne at Athlumney, Navan.

Autumn 1811: loss of the County vote, protecting the Urban oligarchy

A deal has allowed Lord Ventry's candidate, Col. James Crosbie of Ballyheigue, to share the county representation in the forthcoming general election of 1812. But Day's cousin, Maurice FitzGerald, Knight of Kerry, is the great hope of the party as a supporter at Westminster of the campaign to win unqualified Emancipation. Day must play his cards very carefully. In public and in private he adheres to the Veto policy, which would give the government a say in appointments to the Hierarchy. The Knight's espousal of Emancipation will help smooth relations between the judge and O'Connell.

Sunday 8th September. Drive from Limerick through Adare and Rathkeale (both much improved) to Elm Hill[1] to dine with Mr. Maurice Studdert, who was denied at dinner hour though at home. He had frequently solicited me to stop and dine with him on my way to Kerry. Feed at Alpin's at Ardagh, and turn down in the evening two miles to Newcastle. The honest George Hilliard and his wife seize me and insist on my spending the night with them, where I experience a warmth of treatment that fully compensates for the repulse at Elm Hill. Mr. and Mrs. Chute very kindly contend for me with the Hilliards but in vain.

Monday 9th September. Visit before breakfast the Castle of the disgusting Sodomite Lord Courtenay,[2] a very respectable mansion. Locke, his agent, is dismissed by Lord Courtenay (who is as respectable as his cousin is the contrary), and leaves Newcastle tomorrow to make room for Mr. Carte his successor. Drive Mrs. Hilliard to her brother's John Upton, Ashgrove to breakfast, and then Hilliard and I proceed by the Ardagh road to Listowel (8 miles), calling at Springmount[3] and Ballinruddery on the way. Dine and sleep as usual at Oliver Stokes'. Maurice FitzGerald of the party,

William, 3rd Viscount Courtenay

Tuesday 10th who calls for me and after riding about spend the day together happily at Ballinruddery. How delightful to hear that the county is settled for the next election, Lord Ventry supporting Col. Crosbie, and Lord Kenmare the Knight of Kerry singly. Thus my old friend Lord Glandore, who heretofore so influenced our elections is made Scapegoat of the Alliance. I am sorry that Herbert, who is a very respectable member with all his eccentricities and failings, should be forced to give way to that illiterate, unprincipled Moon's Calf Col. Crosbie. And I think Lord Kenmare has much to answer for in deserting his old friend Lord Glandore and his relation, neighbour and friend Herbert.[4] Herbert too, who voted zealously for every Roman Catholic question in Parliament - but nothing will now go down with the Roman Catholics but[5] ...soul and body. If you give a vote, a single vote, to Perceval, to the 'No Popery' administration, all your servitude to their cause merges and disappears, and you are rejected with scorn. So also Lord Ventry has treated Herbert like a tailor and a blackguard. He does not actually in terms promise, but he deludes by specious professions and equivocal half-promises, so that Herbert obtains for him a promise of step in the peerage, declining to solicit favours for any other friend; and now he suddenly throws him off and sets up Crosbie and will return him. Much however as all this is to be regretted, I expect how happy it is for this county of cousins and consanguinity that we shall have no contest.

Wednesday 11th September. Drive to Ardfert Abbey and ride about and spend an agreeable tete-a-tete with the Peer. Lady Glandore confined with the gout (though she denies it), and Mrs. Dean Crosbie[6] only dining with us .

Thursday 12th. Drive to Tralee and breakfast and dine with Stephen Rice.
Friday 13th. with Francis McGillicuddy.
Saturday 14th. with James O'Connor.
Sunday 15th. with George Rowan[7]
Monday 16th. with ex-Treasurer Blennerhassett.
Tuesday 17th. ith Robert Hickson.
Wednesday 18th. with Admiral John Collis.
Thursday 19th. with Doc. Connell.[8]
Friday 20th. with Treasurer Thompson.
Saturday 21st. with James Day.

Thus overwhelmed with the hospitality and kindness of Tralee, and never dining two days at any one house. Tralee improves. The Barrack advances rapidly. A temple is to be erected over the Spa by Graham. The northern mailcoach road in great forwardness - the southern indeed in great backwardness - but still the county is getting on. And I predict that our Spa in another year, and indeed our whole county, will become a place of great fashion and resort.

I never remember more intense heat in Ireland than for ten days or a fortnight of this month. Tuesday and Wednesday, the 3rd and 4th, I had a fire, but the weather then became suddenly so scorching that my lips blistered for the first time in my life. The crops in consequence have ripened everywhere southward of Dublin in great luxuriance, while eastward the potatoes and aftergrass suffer severely.

The comet appears in awful splendour every starlight night,[9] sometimes presenting the appearance of a great lustre suspended in the firmament to lighten and astonish the benighted traveller, sometimes that of a volcano vomiting up a flaming exhalation. Through a telescope it appears like a small moon surrounded with a luminous atmosphere. The comet of 1807[10] presented, if I recollect right, a long horizontal tail like a fuze issuing from a bush. But from the present rises somewhat obliquely an inflamed vapour diffused like hair, much wider than the dish of a planet. Comet comes, I suppose, from coma, the brilliant hair wch issues from it.

Mulcahy, Henneberry, Clune and Craven were recommended by me last Spring assizes from Ennis for enlisting. The two former were admitted to enlist, but the two latter still remain in jail under transportation. Quaere at the Castle why. See Thomas Arthur Esquire's letter 8 Sept. 1811. Robert FitzGerald, Tralee Jail, offers to enlist. Is strong and active, I hear. Quaere of jail Inspector.

Maurice Fitzgerald, 18th Knight of Kerry (1772-1849), painted by John Wood, 1836, possibly in Cork (collection of Sir A. Fitzgerald, Bt.).
MP Kerry 1795-1831, Irish Treasury Board 1801, resigned 1807 on the fall of the pro-Catholic Whig administration, out of office to 1827 when he came in under Canning as a Lord of the English Treasury

Sunday 22d September. Weather suddenly breaks down and the equinoctal gale breaks out with great force. Drive, however, to Listowel and dine with the Stokeses.

Monday 23rd. Weather-bound. My kind host bestows me a fine bay mare, six years old.

Tuesday 24th Drive to Mount Trenchard taking Maurice FitzGerald with me in the curricle. The worthy Stephen as usual in mortar and dirt. Visit his ...,[11] wch will hereafter, I predict, form a striking feature of the excursions from Dublin to Killarney.

Wednesday 25th A tremendous gale last night. Lie by for the day in excellent quarters. A more civilized or better-bred being exists not than the little hostess.[12]

Thursday 26th Set off in brighter weather for home, and forced to make short journeys

Thursday 1st October. Arrive in good health and spirits, blessed be God, at Loughlinstown, where I find my dear wife with Robert very well and impatient to receive me.

Wednesday 6th November. Term sitting. A challenge is taken on the part of the five Catholic delegates to a grand juror. Debated. Court differ, Day J holding the challenge lay, the other three holding it does not lie, to a Grand Juror. County Grand

Jury sworn.

Thursday 7th The Grand Jury for City sworn. Day J charges both grand juries (on second day of term quod nota) and animadverts strongly on the seditious 'orators, scribblers and printers' who have been agitating the public this long vacation upon Catholic emancipation.

Friday 8th Indictment found against Kirwan &c five delegates.

Monday 11th Delegates traverse and plead in abatement that foreman Hone holds place removal at pleasure. Attorney General demurs. Refuses to join in pleading.

Saturday 16th Court unanimously over-rule plea in abatement and allow demurrer (Downes Chief Justice long hesitating).

Thursday 21st Dr. Sheridan's trial. After two days' trial the Court construe the statute to apply against delegation in general.

Friday 22d The jury about 9 p.m. find traverser not guilty ' in consequence of insufficiency in the evidence'. Great and indecent acclamations.

1. Maurice Studdert of Elm Hill, near Rathkeale, m. Dorothea dau.of William Minchin of Greenhills, Co. Tipperary.

2. William, 3rd Viscount Courtenay (1768-1835), of Powderham Castle, Devon, was the juvenile party in a sexual scandal with William Beckford. The scandal broke in 1784 when charges were brought against Beckford, writer of the Gothic novel *Vathek*. Courtenay died unmarried and the earldom devolved on his cousin (Sir Bernard Burke *Peerage and Baronetage* London 1887).

3. Springmount, or Duagh House, home of the Fitzmaurice family. Day's aunt, Anne FitzGerald, married John Stack of Ballyconry, whose daughter Margaret married John Fitzmaurice of Duagh House. See Appendix 4 for Judge Day's letter to the grand-son of John and Margaret, Major-Gen. John Fitzmaurice.

4. Henry Arthur Herbert of Muckross, brother-in-law of Lord Glandore and Member for Kerry after the general elections of 1806 and 1807.

5. Words unclear in ms.

6. Dean Maurice Crosbie, uncle of the second earl of Glandore, was Dean of Limerick for 37 years to 1809. His second wife was Pyne Cavendish.

7. George Rowan of Rathanny, Collector of Excise, Tralee area, c. 1805-17, cousin of William, Provost.

8. Dr. Rickard O' Connell: occupant of Number 3 Day Place, later Physician and Surgeon to the county jail, Tralee, predecessor to Dr. Francis Crumpe who replaced him in 1830.

9. First reported on 11 April, it was known as 'The Great Comet of 1811' due to its brightness and its unprecedented period of visibility to the naked eye, 260 days.

10. Visible for 90 days and about a quarter as bright as the comet of 1811.

11. The words written here appear to be 'Pinman-maur'.

12. The wife of Stephen Edward Rice (m. 1785) was Catherine Spring of Castlemaine. Their son was the eminent Thomas Spring-Rice, first Lord Monteagle; their daughter Mary married Sir Aubrey de Vere.

'Judge Day's Great Equity Cause' comes to trial, December 1811

A private property acquisition in Killorglin led to accusations of corrupt practices against Judge Day, and eventually to a long-running court action. In 1778 Day acted for a client to dispute a land inheritance in Killorglin. In what appears an obvious clash of interests he later acted as one of the appointed arbitrators in the case, at which proceedings his client was awarded the property. Day subsequently obtained the land for himself when his client died and on foot of an arrangement made during the legal proceedings; in the case brought against Day he was also accused of using his brother, Archdeacon Day, as trustee to conceal his ownership. The case may have had some political motivation. The disappointed party in the land inheritance dispute was the Rev. Blennerhassett, Rector of Tralee for many years to 1805 and related by marriage to Lord Ventry. The case was brought against Day by Rev. Blennerhassett's sons. Here it reaches the Chancery court

Tuesday 3rd December. Blennerhassett against Judge Day. Saurin, Attorney-General states for Plaintiffs. Makes strong and deep impression. Betts 5 to 4 on Sharper.

Wednesday 4th Proofs read for plaintiffs.

Thursday 5th Solicitor-General states for Defendant, a most eloquent, spirited and powerful statement.

Proofs read. Bets 2 to 1 on Judge.

Friday 6th Sergeant Ball speaks to evidence. Answered by Plunket[1] in one of the most impressive, ardent and able speeches ever heard at the bar. Chancellor declares all ground of fraud imputed to Defendant has been completely removed, that his conduct throughout the transaction was fair, honourable and generous, and contrasts it with the unclear, ungrateful and fraudulent conduct of plaintiffs. Bets 5 to 1 on Judge.

Saturday 7th Serjt. McMahon[2] for Plaintiffs, and Burton for Defendant. Chancellor closes the whole argument by repeating his former observations on the contrasted conduct of the parties.

Monday 9th Townsend for Plaintiffs abandons all charge or insinuation of fraud against Defendant, and confines himself to the single point of the irregularity of Defendant's proceedings in the ... [3] of Trinity Term 1786, laying the demise in name of Lord Milton though he had executed deed of sale to Defendant the year before. His able and ingenious argument makes great impression on the Chancellor. Answered by John Franks with great learning. Dwyer[4] and O' Connell at large into the pretended frauds and slanderous charges of the Bill, though the Chancellor desired they would confine themselves to the above single point. Excited by this course of argument, the Chancellor repeats his entire approbation of Defendant's conduct, that no foundation whatever appeared for the scandalous charges of

Plaintiffs, and disapproved of the line of observation taken by counsel.

Saturday 14th Chancellor gives notice of decree next Monday.

Monday 16th Chancellor goes at large into the case. Dwells with eloquence and the feelings of a gentleman upon the purity, integrity and generosity of Defendant throughout, and the unfounded and scandalous attacks on his character by Plaintiffs whose conduct was unclear and fraudulent; that were he now at liberty to decide upon the merits he would dismiss the Bill with full costs, but that the legal objection urged by Townsend he would send to a legal court to decide, and pronounced an Interlocutory Decree that a case should be framed with the concurrence of counsel for Court of Common Pleas. Plunkett then stated that if Defendant's counsel had an opportunity given them of answering Townsend, that he had no doubt he could satisfy the court that the point ought to have no influence on His Lordship in his decision, and proposed to have that point spoken to by one counsel on each side. Chancellor : "I shall be very happy to hear you, but the sittings are now too short, and let that point be argued early next term." The court crowded to over-flowing throughout the whole hearing. Bar unanimously of opinion with Defendant and come to him in crowds, with pleasure sparkling in their eyes, to congratulate him.[5]

Tuesday 17th Join my family at Loughlinstown viz. Mrs. Day and Mrs. Sandes lately arrived from Dawlish.

Monday 23rd Sister Franks and Margaret and Catherine Franks join us. Bob Day dined with us yesterday but left us this morning.

Monday 30th The Lawlesses and family dine with us. Bob Franks came yesterday and Tuesday 31st leaves us. John succeeds him.

1. William Conygham Plunket (1764-1854).
2. Possibly William McMahon, called to the Irish bar 1799, becoming Third Serjeant in 1806 and Second Serjeant 1813, master of the rolls 1814. Died 1837. (The words Dwyer and O'Connell are crossed out after the word McMahon.)
3. some words unclear, but in 1786 Day served an ejectment on the tenants of this property for non-payment of rent.
4. A number of barristers by the name of O'Dwyer served during this period. The O'Connell referred to is Daniel.
5. The coverage of the verdict in the press is poor but it appears to contradict the impressiom of euphoria for Judge Day conveyed by this diary. The fact that aspects of the case were subsequently considered in another court appears to confirm the tenuous nature of Day's victory in this one. To be considered was an ejectment by Day for non-payment of rent served on the tenants in the name of the owner of this Kerry property, Lord Milton, on Milton's death in 1786: it was alleged that Day was by then the owner but that he had failed to register the fact. The *Cork Mercantile Chronicle* reported, 'The Chancellor yesterday pronounced judgement in this case. It is against the Honourable Judge. We have forborne for obvious motives to speak upon this subject, or even to mention the admirable speeches of Messrs. Plunkett and Burke in favour of Mr. Day, and the still more conclusive and unanswerable arguments of Mr. O' Connell'. The *Limerick General Advertiser* carried this brief report: 'By this decision Mr Blennerhassett comes into possession of a very considerable part of the landed property in the county of Kerry enjoyed by the Honourable Judge.' *Freeman's Journal* 17 December; *Cork Mercantile Chronicle,* 18 December 1811; *Limerick General Advertiser* 20 December 1811. This case is reported in Thomas Ball and Francis Beatty, *Report of Cases Argued and Determined in the High Court of Chancery in Ireland during the time of Lord Chancellor Manners* (2 vols. London 1813 and 1824), vol. 2 pp. 104-139.

7

Sentencing Thomas Kirwan, Catholic delegate:
'Proceedings against Thomas Kirwan, Merchant, for a Misdemeanor.'[1]

The second half of 1811 witnessed a widening rift between Judge Day and the press. Sections of the press, including the Freeman's Journal, broke free of government control and prepared to ride the democratic surge alongside the Catholic Committee. In May, Day sentenced the newspaper editor Watty Cox for a libel on the government. Meanwhile the Chief Secretary, William Wellesley Pole (one of the Wellesley brothers), issued a proclamation to ban, under the terms of the 1793 Convention Act, meetings of the Catholics leading to a representative assembly. When Catholics delegates appeared for trial before Day and the other judges in the Court of King's Bench in November the defence charged that the jury was packed. Day tried to be even-handed in this matter, but he attacked the campaign for Emancipation as prejudicial to the state and to the Empire. He drew contrasting responses. His remarks won him the admiration of some, but also the degree of personal animosity which only a feeling of betrayal could evoke. Day was again the sentencing judge in February after the conviction of Thomas Kirwan, one of the Catholic leaders. Kirwan was to be treated with leniency in a final effort to dissuade the movement from further political activity.

Thomas Kirwan,
You have been tried on an indictment founded upon a statute the 33rd of the King, commonly called the Convention act, for having voted and acted at an election of delegates, to represent the Roman Catholic inhabitants of the parish of St. Mary's in this city, in a general committee of the Catholics of Ireland. After a patient and dispassionate hearing, you have been convicted upon a clear, conclusive, and uncontroverted evidence. The persons entrusted with your defence had indeed themselves admitted the fact charged, for instead of contradicting or controverting it they resorted to three different modes of avoiding a direct issue, namely, 1st, to a challenge of the array, which after a discussion of two days had been found to be false and ungrounded; 2ndly, to an unavailing and irrelevant cross-examination; and lastly, to avoiding the merits of the case by resting upon a certain point of variance, which, when referred to the decision of the twelve Judges, had been without hesitation pronounced perfectly futile and untenable.

The act for which you have been found guilty has been declared by the legislature a high misdemeanour; not because it is contrary to any principles of religion, morality, or justice, but for its political character and tendency. The statute has declared that all representations by delegation are unlawful, for purpose shall afford no cloak to protect them from its operation. – Such is the precaution of the statute, that it proceeds to arrest them in their earliest steps, towards acting in pursuance of their appointment; and the very publishing of a notice of their meeting, before any possible knowledge could be had of their transactions, is pronounced a high misdemeanour. Neither *pretence* nor *no pretence*[2] forms an object for consideration; the construction and constitution of the meeting is what the legislature has pointed its attention to, and not the object or purpose.

It is not, Sir, the province of the Bench to vindicate the acts of the legislature; but it would be easy to shew that no hardship is imposed by this statute. – It restrains both Protestants and Catholics, yet by a superabundance of caution, it saves the sacred right of petition as established at the Glorious Revolution by the Bill of Rights. This all of his Majesty's subjects here enjoy, whether Protestants or Catholics, in the same spirit and purity in which it is enjoyed by the subjects in England. I shall never for my part wish to move in a larger sphere of liberty than that enlightened and brave people are satisfied with. Whether a jealous adherence to old maxims of civil freedom, or an enthusiasm in search of new additions to their rights and privileges, pervaded the whole population of that great and respectable nation, in their wildest excesses, a convention such as that which had lately agitated this country had never been known amongst them – This species of public assembly is the peculiar growth of Ireland. It is superfluous to point out how much it is in its nature calculated to produce mischief, to overawe the legislature, and to controul the deliberations of Parliament.

Such has been the Convention of 1793; such has been the Volunteer association of 1782; and such has been a memorable convention of an earlier period, which was composed precisely of the same members as the convention whose acts have lately occupied so much of the public attention – composed of peers, prelates, and commoners. An assembly of this description must by an easy and natural transition degenerate from purity of action and intention into a perfectly seditious association. I am fully aware of the high honor and public virtue of several characters who had formed members of the late committee. I am persuaded that if ever they would be betrayed into a violation of the provisions of the constitution, they would err innocently. But it is the nature of man, when he passes the boundary of the law, to forget his legitimate motives, and to launch into excesses from which his head and his heart would at first recoil. When those excesses are not controuled, they soon acquire command and dominion; all the mischievous and delusive passions rise to the top like chaff, while those of intrinsic value and merit sink to the bottom and are lost. – Under those impressions the government of this country stepped out to interfere with the proceedings of the Catholic committee. Their energy and vigilance have not been more laudable than their moderation and conciliatory exertions have been praiseworthy. When their object had been effected the Attorney General had seizd an opportunity of indulging the mild impulse of his nature; and he entered a nolo prosequi in all other actions, convinced that the loyalty and obedience of the Catholics of Ireland will bow with respect to the law.

It is fair to say, that the Roman Catholics did not wilfully violate the provisions of the act upon which able and virtuous lawyers had entertained much doubt – The transactions heretofore are therefore consigned to oblivion; but henceforward things must be otherwise. No subject, Protestant or Catholic, can any more violate the law by misadventure or from want of knowledge, therefore a transgression must necessarily be visited with rigour and severity.

Give me leave, Sir, to recommend to the consideration of the Catholics of Ireland, the sage counsel of the Solicitor General,[3] one of their best friends. I am convinced, with him, that the Catholic committee has been the most pernicious enemy catholic emancipation ever saw. It had diverted the public mind from the great and material question, and effected no good. – Emancipation cannot be legally discussed except in Parliament. It is not by trampling upon the law that its objects can be effected. It is not by intemperance that bigotry can be conciliated; it is not by violence that the legislature can be persuaded that the claims of the Catholics are just.

The Solicitor General's fascinating display of all that was great in the mind or brilliant in fancy will not be unavailing; I do not only not despair that the Catholic committee will profit by it, but I entertain the most sanguine hopes that it will be serviceable to the entire kingdom. The act shall resume its vigorous operation; it shall awake from its long slumbering, and in future remain vigilant; the Catholics will bow to it – they were heretofore only ignorant of its force. Under those impressions, and imitating the mild demeanour of the Attorney General, the court means to punish you with only a nominal penalty.

I cannot conclude, Sir, without reprobating in strong terms, some scandalous practices which you have been guilty of upon your trial, especially the transaction of the affidavit, with which you had sought to throw an unfounded imputation on a most respectable gentleman in the jury box. Having now discharged the duty that devolved on me, I shall pronounce the sentence of the Court, and that is, that you Thomas Kirwan, do pay a fine of a mark, and then be discharged.

The press reported: 'Mr. Kirwan bowed and retired with an expression of countenance which very badly acknowledged his sense of the moderation and candour of the learned Judge's speech. He was followed by a number of respectable Gentlemen, but their congratulations did not prodigiously annoy their Lordships.'

1. To be found in *A Complete Collection of State Trials 1809-13:* Cases of Edward Sheridan, M.D. and Thomas Kirwan, Merchant, for Misdemeanors; 'In the month of August last several gentlemen were arrested in Dublin (for) attending a parish meeting and acting in the appointment of representatives to represent the Roman Catholics of Ireland, for the purpose, or under the pretence, of preparing petitions to both Houses of Parliament (for the repeal of penal legislation against Catholics) contrary to 33 Geo. 3', Ibid. Wed. 6 Nov. 1811. Day's sentence appeared in full in the press, for example in the *Limerick Gazette and General Advertiser,* 11 February, 1812.

2 Counsel for the Defence claimed to interpret pretence as a secret intention on the part of the Catholic representatives.

3. Charles Kendal Bushe (1767-1843). Solicitor-General 1805-1822; Chief Justice King's Bench in succession to Downes 1822-1841. Day considered himself and Bushe as allies of the Catholics in the Irish courts.

Some Worthies on Shannonside: Spring Circuit 1812 in Munster

Friday 28th February. Start at break of day for Johnstown, whither I sent forward my equipage and servants the evening before. Mayne[1] J my associate follows, for we have arranged that I should keep ahead a stage or two through the journey, fearing that no inn on this road could accommodate at night two such great men together. Accordingly, he proposes to sleep tonight at Monasterevin while I push on 11miles more to my good snug old quarters at Backlane. I have left my poor wife in bed and indeed not in very good health. Took her Wednesday last to Dr. Archer who has prescribed for her warm milk from the cow, mixed with soda to prevent coagulation in her stomach, a warm plaster for her back, and some mixture to facilitate the expectoration of very viscid phlegm. God grant I may find my poor little woman upon my return recovered.
N.B. My viaticum £150.

Lady Denny Floyd desiring to remove Harry Hassett from her law agency wrote to him to deliver up the papers to Mr. Furlong, to wch Harry answered, that Mr. Furlong, he owned, would suit her Ladyship's occasions much more pointedly than her superannuated friend whose only fault was old age, but that he begged to assure her Ladyship that her affairs were so dark, so deep and so intricate that if her new favourite were a mile long instead of a furlong he could hardly get to the bottom of them.

Monday 2nd March. Ennis. Arrive by Limerick about four. The Judges take family dinner with Barrister Mahon, whose son is sheriff.

Tuesday 3rd Open the Commission and swear and charge the Grand Jury. Dine with our hospitable friend Mahon.

Wednesday 4th We dine with my old friend, Archdeacon Kenny.

Thursday 5th Dine with our excellent friend Finucane.

Friday 6th Dine with the Grand Jury.

Saturday 7th J. Mayne proceeds to Limerick in the morning, after closing a maiden assize. I proceed to dine and sleep at Sir E. O' Brien's.

Sunday 8th Limerick. Breakfast from Dromoland with J. Mayne in Limerick where we go with the Corporation in full robes to Church. Hear an excellent occasional sermon from Mr. Hughes, nephew of poor Cumberland. Dine this day with Lord Kiltartan where we meeet an agreeable party of English officers and their wives. I take the interchange of the militias of both islands to be the proudest as the stoutest measure of the Perceval's administration, wch by the bye is characterized for stoutness.

Monday 9th The Commissions were opened by Mayne J. last Saturday. This morning we swear in our resective grand juries, he the county, I the city.

W.11th The city business terminates so I proceed into the County and try nine records for brother Mayne. We decline the hospitable invitation of Dean Preston,[2] Mr. Dickson and Mr. George Studdert &c. A second maiden assizes.

Saturday 14th Robert Day and I proceed to Mount Trenchard accompanied by Tom Fosberry just ordained.[3]

Sunday 15th Thomas gives us prayers and we then walk to Stephen Rice's new road. A great and noble work. Henceforth the most interesting feature of the journey from Dublin to Killarney will be this piece of road along the Shannon beginning at the stupendous cliff cut down by Stephen Rice facing Foynes Island and ending at Tarbert. Henry Grady[4] and John Franks join us in the evening at dinner. I forgot to say that the worthy couple were unexpectedly summoned to Dublin and commanded us to repair nevertheless to the comforts and hospitality of my old stage, my statis benefida.

Monday 16th Beakfast as usual with the Stokeses, and spend the day and night with them. This day Mayne J leaves Limerick and dines and sleeps at Talbot House.

Monday 17th Patrick's Day, Tralee. Open the Commission. We dine with the sub-sheriff, Zeb McGillicuddy.

Wednesday 18th I dine with James Day.

Thursday 19th I dine with James Connor.

Friday 20th We dine with Barrister Rice.

Saturday 21st I dine with Counsellor William FitzGerald.

Sunday 22nd We dine with Stephen Rice.

Monday 23rd I dine with Robert Hickson.

Tuesday 24th The Assizes having closed last night, when one man was sentenced to be hanged but recommended, I proceed this morning to Killarney where I was much struck with the tasty and respectable improvement of the Church by Mr. Hyde.[5] Mayne J had left Tralee Saturday. Dine and sleep at Milstreet accompanied by Robert Day.

Wednesday 25th Breakfast as usual with Hedges at Macromp. Proceed to Cork. A beautiful road now from Killarney to Cork. Mayne J opens the commission in the city.

Thursday 26th I open the commission in the county, Dean Freeman Foreman. Foreman receives a slight paralytic stroke.[6]

Sataurday 4th April. Finish.

Sunday 5th Proceed to Dublin.

1. Edward Mayne, son of Charles Mayne of Co. Cavan. B.A. Dublin University 1777, called to the Irish bar 1781, Justice of the Court of Common Pleas 1806, of the King's Bench 1817. Died 1829. Justice (Matthias) Finucane who appears has already been noted. He resigned the Common pleas to young Mayro's appointment (Supra 53, n. 59).

2. Rev. Arthur Preston succeeded Rev. Maurice Crosbie as Dean of Limerick.

3. Rev. Thomas Rice Fosberry was 3rd son of George Fosberry of Kildimo and his wife Christina Mary, only dau of Thomas Rice of Mount Trenchard. Born 1788. (Burke's *Landed Gentry of Ireland*, 1904.

4. Henry (Harry) Deane Grady. Member for Limerick city in the Pery (independent) interest before the Union, but the grip of Prendergast Smith on the representation was restored when Grady was unseated by Charles Vereker in 1802. Had a 'low-sized and rubicund countenance, with a stentorian voice that almost blew a witness out of the chair.' (Roderick O'Flanagan, *Munster Bar*, p 155).

5. Rev. Arthur Hyde, only son of Rev. Arthur Hyde rector and vicar of St. Anne's Shandon. He became vicar of Killarney 1809 (Leslie, *Ardfert & Aghadoe*). The present church in Killarney is of a later date.

6. After his stroke Freeman laid aside official duties, and lived unil 28 March 1826. Source: Col. James Grove White, *Historical and Topographical Notes Etc. on Buttevant, Castletownroche, Doneraile, Mallow*, (Cork 1911), pp. 63-71.

Sir Edward O'Brien, 4th Bart., of Dromoland Castle (1773-1837) G. Weir.

1812: London and the Company of Judges

Canning's Catholic relief proposal will contain the compromise, or 'Veto' arrangement, and Day is present to support. But it meets again the resistance of Tory 'Ultras', including the leading English judicial figures of the Chancellor, Lord Eldon, and the Chief Justice, Lord Loughborough. Other business detains Day in London, including the arrangement of grandson Edward Denny's entry to Eton in September of that year. We will meet Edward later as a very young candidate for the county election.

Thursday 11th June. Mrs Day and I proceed for Holyhead. Viaticum £80. Friday 12th Arrive at Holyhead after a charming passage of only 11 hours, with scarcely an individual sick on board. Sir J. Purcell with his friend Mr. Callaghan and Squire Richard, alias Master Maynard Denny,[1] join Mrs. D., Robert Denny and myself in a coach, and by great exertion reach Capelcarrig (42 m.) late at night, having left Holyhead about one.

Saturday 13th Continue our romantic and beautiful journey with the same party to Shrewsbury (about 68 m.) where we arrive about nine, having left Capelcarrig at 5 a.m. From Holyhead to Capelcarrig, 42m., from Capelcarrig to Shrewsbury, 68m. From Holyhead to Shrewsbury 110.

Mrs Abingdon, actress

Sunday 14th June. The party divide, Mrs. Day and I proceeding in the Union coach for London, while the other four turn off to Worcester. Breakfast at Wolverhampton, dine at Stratford-Upon-Avon, sup at Oxford and

Monday 15th arrive at 9 a.m. in Oxford Street, having dispatched Mrs. Day. From Uxbridge across the country in a chaise to Richmond, 12 or 14 miles. Stop at Beall's Hotel, Jermyn St. Proceed on business to Palmer, Gray's Inn, who takes and introduces me to Mr. Ryder and Mr. Frere.[2] Everything promises well, as well as this harvest wch appears everywhere to promise very well. Go to the Lyceum in the evening to see Mrs. Lefanu's popular and entertaining 'Sons of Erin.'[3] Miss Duncan, an accomplished Canadian, uniting the humour of Mrs. Abingdon[4] with the grace of Miss Farren.[5]

Tuesday 16th Remove to St. James's Coffee House. Visit and see Lord Carleton, Lord Redesdale, Tom Rice, Grattan, Patterson &c. Decline all invitations but one from Lord Redesdale to meet a judicial party next Sunday at 6. Go in the evening to enjoy the unrivalled Catalani,[6] and a very good tenor, Traumanzani, in the serious opera of Clemenza di Tito. Exquisite dancing by Vestris,[7] Mad'le Angiloni, Mad'e Didelot. Suffer more by the narrow and cramped position in wch I have been seated in the gallery than by the whole journey from Dublin.

Wednesday 17th Go to the House of Commons. Sheridan is charged with duplicity between the Prince and the Talents in a conversation with Lord Yarmouth. Enters into his exculpation.[8] Proceeds with a mixture of his old ability with some symptoms of decay. After going for some time into some of the circumstances of the negotiation between Lord Moira[9] and Lords Grey and Grenville, he is taken ill just as he arrived at the commencement of his exculpation, some say dramatically, but the rest stands over till Friday. Mr.Vansittart,[10] the new Cancellor of the Exchequer, opens the budget. Oh, what a wretched performer! Oh, the arrogance and effrontery of such an insufficient, mumbling reptile presenting himself in a situation lately filled by the abilities and virtues of that able and excellent man, Perceval, and not many years since by those giants, Pitt and Fox!

Thursday 18th Go to hear Canning's promised motion on the Catholic subject,[11] wch drops for want of hours.[12] Am admitted by order of the Chancellor[13] behind the Woolsack in the Lords. Hear Liverpool, Grey, Harrowby, Holland, the Chancellor, Archbishop of Canterbury &c.

Friday 19th June. Go to the Lords to hear Lord Moira's promised explanation of the treaty between him and Lord Grey and Grenville. Something personal being expected, it attracts a full house, but on Lord Ellenborough's motion all strangers are desired to withdraw, even the Commons, who are huffed and full of retaliating.

In the Commons Sheridan concludes his exculpation, but in absence of Lord Yarmouth, who is seized with fit of gout (Quaere: Was this gout also dramatic?).

Saturday 20th Spend most of the day at Gray's Inn preparing for the Commission[14] to be sped next Wednesday, 24th.

Sunday 21st Dine with Lord Redesdale[15] and meet a judicial party, viz. Lord Ellenborough,[16] Mansfield,[17] Chief Justice, McDonald, C.B.,[18] Grose,[19] J. Bayly,[20] J. Thompson, B., Chambers, J. Wood,[21] B. Recorder Sylvester and Lord Carleton. Treated with great attention and politeness by them all. The Chief Baron whom I sit next to, a kind-hearted, well-bred gentleman. I had like to forget the Master of the Rolls, Grant, and no wonder, for he did not open his mouth but to let something into it.[22]

Monday 22nd Canning brings on his motion on the Catholic subject and sustains it with great eloquence in a speech of 1 hour 40 minutes. Tierney and Whitehead sarcastic and powerful debaters. Grattan conciliatory and dignified. Eulogized by those three and applauded by the whole house. The Treasury bench feeble and contemptible in the highest degree. The motion carried by a great majority. Vansittart a great man of business though a phlegmatic, inarticulate speaker. Lord Castlereagh the best speaker on the Treasury bench. Let them secure Canning and his friends and the present ministry need not fear the Talents.[23]

Wednesday 24th June. The Commission, wch we expected would be sped today, is adjourned to 26th by the opposite commissioners. Go in the evening to Richmond, and find my friends all in very good health.

Thursday 25th Visit old friends. Spend two hours with Delafosse inquiring about poor Ned of whom I have the happiness to receive a very flattering account from every one.

Friday 26th Return to town to breakfast. A day of merciless rain. The King's hay smokes like a dung-hill. All the hay round London in danger from the constant rain of this last week or ten days. The Commission is opened and proceeded upon. Mr. Ryder examined in chief, and to one cross interrogatory, but notice is given by plaintiffs of more cross interrogation to be filed and exhibited, and the Commission to my sore mortification is adjourned to Tuesday 30th, when I expected it to be closed this day and that I should be at liberty to return tomorrow.

Saturday 27th Dine at Hampstead with my good old friends Watts and wife.

Sunday 28th Surprise with a second visit my friends of Richmond, of whom I had taken leave on Friday. John Collis, who is lately arrived from Bengal, 2nd Mate of the Carnatic, accompanies me in each of my two visits. Mr. and Mrs. Patterson come down by surprise upon the sisterhood to dinner.

Monday 29th Collis and I dine with the Pattersons. In the evening they dress for the masquerade, he in the character of a young romp, and she in that of night. Some masks drop in and they proceed together.

Tuesday 30th The cross-examination resumed. Adjourned again till tomorrow. Dine at Dolly's.

Wednesday 1st July. The examination closed.

Thursday 2nd Maurice FitzGerald undertakes carriage of the Commission and receives it from the Commissioner Baker. We agree to start tomorrow for Worcester together in his barouche post-horses.

Charles Pratt, 1st Earl Camden, by Dance. An early protégé of Pitt the Elder. Lord Chief Justice Common Pleas, England, 1761, Lord Chancellor 1766-70. Ruled that John Wilkes (writer of a libel on the King in the North Briton) was, as a member of parliament, immune from prosecution; protected Wilkes also in a ruling against general warrants

Friday 3rd He disappoints me and we put off our journey till tomorrow.

N.B. Wednesday 1st Lord Wellesley brought on his motion in the words of Canning's on the Catholic claims. His speech an able composition and well delivered. The Chancellor and Chief justice warn against the motion, vehement and undignified. Oh how contrasted to those law lords with whom my youth was familiar: Mansfield, Camden,[24] De Grey,[25] Thurlow,[26] Loughborough[27]! Lord Holland addresses with great ability the Chancellor in a speech of one and a half hours wch reminded me much of poor Charles Fox, his uncle, whose talents and failings he seems to inherit; the question negatived at four by a majority of one i.e. by Lord Glandore's proxy who used to vote for the Catholics but has quarrelled with them for their ingratitude to him at a meeting in Kerry. But why because they behaved ill shall he vote not only against all his former votes but against a measure of such importance to the country? Remarkable that the Catholic bill of 1778 was carried by the single vote of Lord Glandore, who travelled post and arrived in Dublin but the night before, and now the Catholic resolution is lost by his single vote.

Duke of Richmond has three sisters: Lady Buckley, a single sister and Lady Bathurst. He was son to Lord George who was dying before his elder brother never succeeded to the title, and the Col. Lennox followed his uncle in the title. Lord George Lennox had been Governor of Plymouth and was a quiet, regular, good officer. He was limited in income, possessing very little beyond his salary.

Saturday 4th July. The Knight and I start at 7 a.m. and breakfast at Uxbridge. Proceed through heavy roads by Oxford and through Blenheim Park the magnificent to Chapel House, where we dine and sleep in comfort.

Sunday 5th Breakfast at the good old inn of Broadway, and work on over high hills and heavy roads to Worcester where we arrive about two. Walk to King's End House, [28] about three miles, where the family receives us with ecstacy. Poor dear Jane[29] seems far gone in a consumption; alas, the pity! Return at night and sleep at Hop-Pole, Worcester.

Monday 6th Breakfast at Kidderminster, the house facing the steam-engine la-la! Climb up into Bridgenorth, and tumble down upon the iron bridge, Coalbrookdale. Sleep at Oswestry: two very good houses; recommend the Cross Keys.

Tuesday 7th Breakfast at Craniog, and dine and sleep at Bangor ferry.

Wednesday 8th Cross the ferry and proceed without delay to Holyhead where we arrive about twelve or one, just on time before embarking...[30]

Thursday 9th July. Land at Pigeon House after a fine smooth passage of 24 hours in the Uxbridge, Jones.

1. Very probably this is Rev. Maynard Denny, 3rd son of Rev. Maynard Denny of Churchill, later a clergyman.

2. Probably Canning's friend and correspondent, John Hookham Frere.

3. *Sons of Erin, or Modern Sentiment* was written by Mrs Alicia Le Fanu, sister of Richard Brinsley Sheridan.

4. Frances Abingdon (1737-1815), played at Drury Lane and Covent Garden, as well as in Dublin where she appeared on many occasions.

5. Elizabeth Farren, Contess of Derby (1759?-1829), successor to Mrs Abingdon at Drury Lane from 1782. Married the 1Earl of Derby.

6. Italian soprano Angelica Catalani (1780-1849) sang the role of Vitellia in *La Clemenza di Tito* by Mozart in London in 1812.

7. Possibly Auguste Vestris, of a notable French dancing family of Italian origin, Giuseppa Angiolinin (Italian ballerina) and Rose Didelot, dancer.

8. While the Regent considered the formation of a Whig administration after the assassination of Perceval (restoring what Day calls the 'Ministry of All the Talents' of 1806-7), Charles Grey (Howick) refused to join unless Lord Hertford and his son Lord Yarmouth resigned. They agreed, but Sheridan withheld this information from Grey (in order to keep Grey out?).

9. Francis Rawden, 2nd Earl of Moira (1754-1826). Co. Down magnate, also eminent statesman: Governor-General of India, Commander–in-Chief of the island of Malta.

10. Nicholas Vansittart (1766-1851), first Baron Bexley. Chancellor of the Exchequer from May 1812 to

March 1823. Day would have known him in a previous role, that of Irish chief secretary in 1805

11. George Canning (1770-1827). Prime minister in the year of his death. Day had sold Canning the representation of Tralee borough in 1802. Canning refused to serve under Perceval and under Lord Liverpool after Perceval's assassination in May 1812.

12. illegible: hours?

13. John Scott, Lord Eldon, Lord Chancellor of England op. cit.

14. The nature of the Commission is not explained.

15. Redesdale, Ld Chancellor of Ireland, 1802-1806, brother-in-law of Spencer Perceval PM.

16. Edward Law, first Baron Ellenborough (1750-1818). Chief Justice 1802-1818 in succesion to Lord Kenyon. Opponent of Catholic relief. Supported a vigorous prosecution of the war.

17. Probably Sir James Mansfield (1733-1821), Chief Justice of the Court of Common Pleas, not to be confused with Wm. Ed Mansfield p. 131 & n. 136.

18. Sir Archibald MacDonald (1747-1826), Chief Baron of the Exchequer 1793-1813.

19. Sir Nash Grose (1740-1814), Justice of the court of King's Bench 1787-1813.

20. Sir John Bayley (1763-1841), Justice of the King's Bench 1808-1830, court of Exchequer 1830-1834.

21. Sir George Wood (1743-1824), Baron of the Exchequer 1807-1823.

22. Sir William Grant (1752-1832), Master of the Rolls 1801-1817.

23. Canning's motion was carried by 235 votes to 106, Castlereagh and Vansittart speaking in favour, but it was lost by one vote in the Lords where Richard Wellesley was its sponsor.

24. Charles Pratt (1714-1794), first Earl Camden. Chief Justice of the Common Pleas 1761, Lord Chancellor 1766-70.

25. Sir William De Grey (1719-81) first Baron Walsingham, Attorney-General for the prosecution of Wilkes and the publishers of the 'Junius' Letter to the King, for which Day probably remembered him and Thurlow.

26. Edward Thurlow, first Baron Thurlow (1731-1806), Solicitor-General from 1770, succeeded De Grey as attorney-general in 1771. Lord Chancellor 1778-1792.

27. Alexander Wedderburn, first Baron Loughborough (1733-1805). Formerly Chief Jusice of the Common Pleas, succeeded Thurlow as Lord Chancellor in 1793, holding office to 1801 when succeeded by Lord Eldon. The mention above could refer to Loughborough's espousal of the cause of Wilkes in 1768.

28. Kingsend House, Worcester, the residence of Sir Edward Denny and his wife Elizabeth, Judge Day's daughter. Lady Denny died in 1828, Sir Edward Denny in 1831.

29. Their daughter Jane Frances, who died in 1812, is buried with her parents in the church yard of Powick, near Kingsend House.

30. Two lines are unclear.

Midland Mansions: Home Circuit, Summer 1812

Sunday 12th July 1812. Leave town at eleven with £100 viaticum for Johnstown, where I catch my agreeable associate, Lord Norbury. Dine and sleep at the infamous inn at Ballytore.

Monday 13th His Lordship opens the commission at Carlow. I try three records. We dine at Spanish Browne's with some agreeable men and women.

Tuesday 14th. Try four records. Several dine with us.

Wednesday 15th The whole day employed in the second trial of information against Walter Kavanagh. £18.4 lodgings Athy.

Thursday 16th Breakfast at Athy riding through this beautiful ride along the Barrow. Four men capitally convicted for burglary.

Friday 17th One man capitally convicted for forged notes. The two Henrys dine with us. £20 lodgings.

Saturday 18th The Commission opened by Lord Norbury at Maryborough at 3 p.m. I remained in Athy writing letters, and I meet Lord Norbury at dinner at Stradbally-Hall, the hospitable and handsome seat of Mr. Cosby,[1] son in law of our worthy old departed brother Judge Kelly. Indulge too fully in fruit after dinner, and when I thought myself in clover for the night, I break away abruptly for Maryborough, where a violent diahorrea affects me for twenty-four hours. Dine with B. Franks at Maryborough on mutton broth.

Monday 20th Rise free from complaint save some debility and lassitude. Try a long record...[2] My agreeable advocate and myself dine tete-a-tete. Rochfort joins us in the evening. £20 for lodgings.

What an evil spirit stalks through the world, and how deep a decay have morality, religion and every public and private virtue undergone within the memory even of our children!

Tuesday 21st Lord Sydney Osborne, Cosby, Revd. Mr. Pakenham (Lord Longford's brother), Mr. Pigot and others dine with us.

Wednesday 22nd Our business being easily finished in two days, I ride to Rynn to see my old aunt FitzGerald, and the Croasdailes. All well. N.B. Rynn a good half-way house between Maryborough and Philipstown, and I promise to sleep there, please God, the next time I come this circuit. Drive to Tullamore Forest where we are most courteously and kindly received by our noble host and his poor infirm lady, Lord and Lady Charleville. A magnificent castle, and on the cursory view I could take of it, admirably contrived. Does great credit to the taste and munificence of the noble owner, or rather of her ladyship, who I understand projected the whole under the

William Murray, 1st Earl of Mansfield, (1705-1793) by Reynolds. A Scotsman (b. Perth) and friend of Alexander Pope, he was suspected of Jacobite leanings in early life. Lord Chief Justice King's Bench, England, 1756-88. The phrase 'those law lords with whom my youth was familiar', may refer to Mansfield's liberal legacy on slavery, the American colonies and Catholic relief. Day believed that Mansfield would have supported Canning's and Richard (Marquess) Wellesley's proposal of 1812 to consider remaining Catholic disabilities in the next parliamentary session.

auspices of Johnson,[3] our Irish and very ingenious architect. She is distinguished for very fine taste in the arts, possesses a masculine understanding, and, what is much better, an ardent spirit of charity and benevolence. Though labouring under a heavy and, I fear, incurable malady, wch she fancies to be rheumatism but I fear is paralytic, and wch in truth might warrant if not require confinement to the room, she devotes a great part of every fair day to the noble Lancastrian school wch she herself erected at an expence of £2000, and of the county infirmary wch under her superintendence exhibits a pattern to every county in Ireland.

Philipstown

Thursday 23rd July. Ride from Tullamore Forest to Smith to breakfast. Poor Smith now become such a driveller that it is unpleasant to dine with him. In truth, this house wch used to be pleasant is now become the least so upon this circuit.

Sunday 26th After breakfast my sociable associate and I ride to Tyrrell's Pass to prayer where we hear an excellent sermon from Mr.Usher.[4] We are met there by the High Sheriff of Westmeath, Mr. Pollard, who conveys us in his handsome barouche landau to Mullingar.

Monday 27th July. Fifteen records entered. Dine with Mr. Cooper, M.P. for county Sligo, at his excellent house, Bowden Park, late the seat and creation of poor Bob Rochfort. Mrs. Cooper, sister of Colonel Varelst, a very interesting lady.[5] Three fine boys, the eldest at Eton. Cooper possesses a singularly mechanical talent: prints and binds books admirably, makes beautiful work-boxes, tables etc., by a small windmill supplies his house to the very garrets with water etc.

Thursday 30th Ride to Killucan and stop as last summer at Counsellor Purdon's to lunch. Dine at Trim.

Friday 31st I open the Commission and proceed to business. Calendar very full and bloody. Twelve men tried for burglary, robbery and carding, of whom two are convicted, the rest though identified acquitted.

Saturday 2nd After breakfast Lord Norbury get on horseback to dine ... engagement with the Henrys of Straffan, Co. Kildare (20 miles). On our way ride through the neglected demesne of the Percival family to Battersby, who shows us pretty villa, handsome Hereford cattle, and alight at Kilcock (14 miles) and drive post 6 miles to Straffan, where we are curteously received by the kind-hearted owners, Mr. Henry and Lady Emily.[6] A clever house, fine demesne somewhat in dishabille but well wooded, and the beautiful reach of the Liffey winding through it. Excellent garden. In the house a small but choice collection of pictures: the Madonna by Carlo Dulia exquisite, so admired that Lord Hardwicke had a miniature of it by Comerford, wch hangs in his collection covered with a silk curtain. But the best article of furniture there is the sweet Lady Emily herself, whose beauty is the weakest among many recommendations. Our company were Sir E. and Lady Littlehales,[7] and Mr. Arthur Henry lately married to Eliza Gun.[8] Lady Elizabeth, altogether destitute of her sister's beauty, is not deficient in her understanding, temper or sweetness of disposition. After spending a very happy day, we returned late in the evening, and arrived after this juvenile excursion of forty miles before one in the morning safe and in good spirits at Trim.

Monday 3 August. After ruling the Crown book, a highwayman is brought into court, having been pursued this morning, immediately after committing a robbery, by the country people, indicted, tried, found guilty and sentenced to be hanged. Circuit closed.

Tuesday 4th We return to town, having had, I think, the most agreeable circuit within my judicial experience - considering the shortness of the journeys, the accommodation at each town, the good weather, the good conduct of the bar, the moderation of business, and the fine temper and juvenile spirits of Lord Norbury.

Saturday 8th August. Dine at Cabra by invitation to spend some days there.

Sunday 9th Lord Norbury, Lady Norwood[9] and I go to Finglas church, but the doors not opened. His Lordship and I get on horseback. Visit Sir C. Vernon and his dairy, pheasantry and other bijouterie. Visit Connor, the young parson[10] of Castleknock, at his neat parsonage, the poor doctor, his father, dead a few months. Ride across the road into Trench's elegant villa. Pass on to the Secretary's fine gardens, where Forsythe, his steward, shows us a meadow on wch he has already cut thirty loads of hay per acre and is on the point of cutting a second crop wch will yield about twenty loads per acre i.e. fifty loads of hay per acre in one season! Call in to Lord Westmeath[11] to whom the Duke kindly lends the Lodge during the interregnum of the departed Poole and the coming Peele.[12] Proceed to Sandy Holmes, and from him to the Rathbarnes. In short, I don't remember embracing in so short a period so many agreeable visits or so many pretty places. Lord Westmeath has just learned from the Duke that the glorious news from Salamanca is not doubted.

Monday 10th August. Visit the Domvilles at Santry. Learn to our horror that poor Mrs. Domville, who lay in last Sunday senight of a fine son and heir, continued well till Thursday evening, suddenly taken ill of an inflammation, wch in spite of Dr. Clarke etc. is become a mortification, and her dissolution is hourly expected. N.B. This amiable, interesting young woman has died[13] this evening, to the inexpressible grief of her extensive and populous neighbourhood and every admirer of benevolence and virtue.

1. Thomas Cosby of Stradbally Hall, co Laois. Governor of the county and Sheriff in 1809, he m 1802 Elizabeth, daughter of Thomas Kelly, Justice of the Court of Common Pleas 1783-1801. Justice Kelly's popularity enabled him to proceed unmolested and without escort while on circuit, even in 1798 (Grattan's Life, vol. 1, p 253).

2. illegible

3. Francis Johnston, architect.

4. Rev. Hemsworth Usher was Rector of Clonfadforan (Tyrrellspass) from 1783 to 1821 (Oliver Egan, *Tyrrellspass Past and Present*, Tyrrellspass Town Development Commission, 1986, p. 93).

5. Anne dau. of Gov. Harry Varelst of Bengal, whose seat was at Sheffield, was the wife of Edward Synge Cooper of Markrea Castle, MP Sligo 1806-1830.

6. John Joseph Henry of Straffan, co Kildare m 1801 Emily Elizabeth Fitzgerld, sister of William 2nd Duke of Leinster. (Sir Bernard Burke, *A Genealogical and Heraldic History of the Landed Gentry of Great Britain and Ireland* (2 vols, London 1894).
7. Sir Edward Littlehales, Military Under-Secretary at Dublin Castle.

8. Arthur Henry of Lodge Park, Straffan (1781-1856) m. (1 Feb 1812) Eliza, third daughter of George Gunn Cuninghame of Mount Kennedy, co Wicklow. The two Henry men were first-cousins.

9. Lady Norbury was Grace, daughter of Hector Graham. In 1797 Norbury obtained a peerage for his wife as Baroness Norwood of Knockalton in Co. Tipperary.

10. Rev. George O'Connor, Vicar of Castleknock 1809-42, succeeded his father Rev. John Connor, Vicar 1767-1809.

11. George-Frederick Nugent, 7th Earl of Westmeath (1760-1814). MP for Fore in the Irish parliament from 1780 to 1792.

12. Sir Robert Peel was appointed to succeed William Wellesley-Pole as Chief Secretary in August 1812.

13. Elizabeth Frances, daughter of Rt. Rev. Hon. Charles Dalrymple Lindsay DD, Bishop of Kildare, m (21 Oct. 1811) Sir Compton Pocklington, 1st Bt. of Templeogue and Santry. Her death in 1812 followed the birth of Compton Charles, later an officer in the army (Burke's *Irish Families*, 1976).

September in Kerry
- and Spring Circuit 1813 in the North East

Thursday 3rd September. Start for Kerry , about £100 in crumena.[1] Proceed for the first time by the lower road to Lucan, Castletown, Celbridge, Straffan etc. to Naas. An interesting line, but five miles round.

Sunday 6th Breakfast with Colonel Bagwell at his fine seat, Marlfield. Go to church with the family. Ride after prayers. Oh, what noble gardens, oh how foolish to visit them if you do not desire to despise home.

Monday 7th Sleep at Fermoy. Who in Ireland has done more noble good than Anderson? The father of our mail coaches and mail coach roads; the creator of this beautiful town!

Tuesday 8th Breakfast in Cork. Dine en famille with the Digbys.[2]

Wednesday 9th Spend the day with the Alderman.

Thursday 10th Dine and sleep with the excellent couple, Tom and Lucy Cuthbert.

Friday 11th Proceed to Macromp and spend the day and night with my friend Hedges at his fine castle.

Saturday 12th Breakfast in Milstreet and dine and sleep at Cahirnane.

Sunday 13th Go to church with the Herberts to Killarney. Return to Cahirnane where I dine and sleep.

Monday 14th September. J. McDonagh and I ride along the line of the mail coach road to the river Main where the bridge is just finished. Dine and sleep at Dicksgrove. Mrs. Meredith a very interesting lady.[3]

Tues. and Wed. 15th and 16th pass at Kiltallagh.

Thursday 17th John Collis and I cross Slemish to Tralee. Dine with James Day.

Friday 18th Visit my old friend Lord Glandore, and dine and sleep there. Has lately had a hemi plagia,[4] wch providentially he has thrown off, save a weakness and drag in his leg.

Saturday 19th Dine and sleep at Churchill. Deliver to Barry Denny Sir Edward's nomination to the living.[5]

Sunday 20th Breakfast with the Hartes. Dine with Robert Hickson. His father died

Church at Kilgobbin, Co. Kerry

about ten days ago, leaving his brother, Dick Herbert and myself trustees.

Monday 21st Preside at Infirmary meeting where we resolve to pull down that disgraceful ruin forthwith. Dine with William Rowan.

Tuesday 22nd Dine with James Day.

Wednesday 23rd Leave Tralee for Dublin. Dine and sleep at Ardfert Abbey. The poor Peer occupied in preparing his tomb stone and vault in the Abbey. Drive him in my curricle round his Park. Intellect and articulation perfect, but heavy and phlegmatic.

Gift to Lieutenant Fitzmaurice[6]	£10.0.0
Lady Glandore for poorhouse[7]	£2.5.6

Thursday 24th September. Breakfast as usual with the Stokeses, who are preparing to marry their daughter Margaret with Maurice FitzMaurice, and to remove to his house as Barrack Master in Tralee new Barracks. The day proving bad I dine and sleep there.

Friday 25th. Drive to Mount Trenchard and pass Saturday 26th with my good friends. Find there two English young gentlemen, Bridgstock and Tyler. I did not know till they told me that there lives now in England their acquaintance, Oliver Cromwell, a lineal descendant and heir in law of the Usurper. He has but one child, a daughter, Oliveria, married to Mr. Russel, who with the estate wishes to take the name of Cromwell; but government, with a miserable pussilanimity, refuse to license it. Then let him take the name without their licence. Can government hinder him, or is it not perfectly legal?

Thursday 1st October. Sadleir ascends at Drumcondra in his magnificent balloon for Holyhead: a charming day, a great and universal anxiety for him. Alas, after coming in sight of Liverpool he was driven back by a contrary current of air, and after nightfall descended at sea between the English coast and the Isle of Man, where he was picked up by a fishing boat almost exhausted and conveyed to Liverpool.

Number of my books in town, upon counting, appear to be about 2000.

23 sheep at Loughlinstown.

Friday 2nd October. One sheep sent to town.

9th One sheep and one pig.

Monday 19th Dined with Mr. Peel at the Park. Arrived from Kerry two score sheep and a heifer to calve 12th April.

Sunday 25th My poor little wife, with John Collis and Robert Denny, after being wind-bound three or four days at Holyhead, and a rough passage of 24 hours, arrive, God be praised, safe and well about three o'clock.

Saturday 7th November. Went before Master Henn[8] upon the issue referred to him by the Chancellor .

Tuesday 10th do.

Saturday 14th do. At dinner given to Butterworth[9] the law book-seller in honour of his election October 1810 for Coventry by the Corporation of Stationers. After the usual effusions of loyalty, a wag of the day at the end of the long table with a loud voice desired leave to drink 'Bonaparte'. 'Out,out, out!' was echoed from all sides of the room. 'Yes', added he, as soon as the storm subsided, 'hot-pressed and bound in Russia!'

Saturday 21st Robert Denny runs away home from a fever at Carpendale's.[10]

Monday 14th December. After endless discussions before Henn, and daily vacillations between various opinions, he at last furnishes a meagre special report castrated of many material facts, to wch both parties file sundry exceptions. Chancellor directs the case to come before him on the exceptions and merits beginning of next term (1813). Hilary Term. After various hearings and discussions the Chancellor, declaring he had received no aid whatever from the report, directs an ejectment to be tried in the Common Pleas at bar next (Easter) term by a foreign jury (viz. City Dublin), limiting, however, the inquiry to two issues: 1 whether the judgment in ejectment for nonpayment etc. be or be not a bar, while unreversed to the tenant's title? 2 did Lord Milton intend to deliver the deed 17 March 1786 conditionally and as an exception or absolutely? The first being an issue of law and the second an issue of fact.

Thursday 25th February. Sir Edward Denny arrives from Worcester. Purchase from Hardell a new chariot.

1. crumena L. a bag, a purse.

2. Rev. Arthur Herbert of Brewsterfield in Kerry, brother of Richard Townshend Herbert, married Maria Digby on 16 May 1795 (Ffolliott, *Biographical Notices*). The father, John Digby, is described (passim) as 'of this city' (Cork) and 'merchant'.

3. Alicia Orpen of Ardtully m William Meredith, Sheriff 1803.

4. A form of stroke. The press reported his death at Ardfert Abbey in 1815 of 'an apopleptic fit'.

5. Rev. Barry Denny succeeded his father Rev. Maynard Denny at Churchill. It was a living in the gift of the Denny family. He was Vicar there 1812 to 1830.

6. John Fitzmaurice of Duagh House. A relative, Day recommended him for the army of Wellington in Spain where he joined the 95th Rifle Brigade (Wellington's Rifles). See Appendix 4.

7. 'In the village of Ardfert her ladyship has established an asylum for the aged, the sick, and the poor of both sexes' (*Limerick Evening Post,* 14 November, 1812).

8. William Henn (op. cit.), Master of the Irish Court of Chancery.

9. Joseph Butterworth (1770-1826), law bookseller and philanthropist, and prominent through his work with church missionary societies. Born in Coventry, MP Coventry from 1812-1818.

10. Robert Day Denny, second son of Sir Edward Denny of Tralee Castle and Betsy Day, therefore the judge's grand-son. Pupil at Carpendale's, Armagh (Major M.L. Ferrar, *The Royal School Armagh,* printed 1933). Born in 1800, T.C.D. 1819, Worcester College, Oxford, 1821, taking B.A. 1824, M.A. 1827; ordained in 1851; perpetual curate of Shedfield, Hants. Married 1833 Sarah, daughter of Thomas Grant of Soberton, Hants. Died at Cheltenham, 12 July, 1864.

1813 Spring Circuit - North East

Sunday 8th February. Leave Dublin for Drogheda. Viaticum £135. Arrive at 6p.m. Daly J.[1] my associate arrives tomorrow.

Monday 1st March. Charge the Grand Jury, Colonel Foster foreman. Try Brannigan the priest for disturbing the celebration of Divine worship at the Mass house, and insulting and menacing Dr. O'Reilly, Roman Catholic Primate[2] etc. Acquitted by a Protestant jury most improperly.

Daly J. tries one record. Proceed in the evening to the fine seat of the late munificent Primate Robinson, now occupied by Henry Codington, who entertains us to board and bed with great hospitality.

N.B. I slept at Davis's at Drogheda. Excellent cleanly lodgings. Daly slept at another house. The Corporation pay. We left each half a guinea for the maids.

Dundalk

Tuesday 2nd Breakfast in Dundalk at Martin's excellent lodgings. Dine with Sheriff and Grand Jury.

Wednesday 3rd Try five records at Dundalk, the last the celebrated case of lord Clermont and Sharpe, the fifth jury who tried it. They don't agree and remain enclosed all night.

Thursday 4th Withdraw by consent a juror. Sign a certificate for £20. Excellent lodgings; the servants and horses within the same ... with ourselves. Ride to Castleblaney, 14 miles. There pick up A. McCartney and bring him to Monaghan. Beautiful ride through Castleblaney Park.[3]

Friday 5th March. Swear and charge Grand Jury. Daly J. arrives to breakfast. Dine with sheriff.

Saturday 6th Spend all day to a late hour in court. Decline dining with Dacre Hamilton.[4]

Sunday 7th Go to church. Hear an excellent and appropriate sermon from Robin Montgomery, brother of my poor friend Jack, on the Last Supper, it being Sacrament Sunday. Dine with a good-humoured company at Blaney Mitchell's. An account arrives of Lord Cremorne's death, wch vacates the county by his nephew Dick Dawson succeeding to the title and with it an estate of £16,000 a year.[5]

Monday 8th Conclude the assizes. Assign certificate for £18.4.0, including coach-house, servant maid, breakfast and tea.

Armagh

Tuesday 9th Ride into Armagh to breakfast - 12 miles. Poor Bob receives me with joy. Dine with the bar. Bob Franks joins us here.

Wednesday 10th I go to church, being the fast day, and hear an excellent occasional sermon from young Carpendale. Try 13 records these two days. Sign a certificate for £20 for the lodgings.

Thursday 11th Ride to the excellent little Inn of Portadown - 9 miles - to sleep.

Friday. Breakfast at Lisburn, 15 miles. Survey Coulson's unrivalled demask manufactory and purchase a few articles.[6] Daly J. arrives from Armagh and we travel together to Belfast where we dine with the High Sheriff, Mr. Bristow.[7] Sleep at the Donegal Arms.

Saturday 13th March. Arrive at Carrigfergus to breakfast overwhelmed with snow, the first we have met. Swear and charge the Grand Jury. Five of the bar dine with us, McCarthy, Foster, Hamilton and Stack.

Sunday 14th Dine with Mr. Richard Ker, Redhall, a very respectable gentleman, and pleasant day.

Tuesday 16th Finish at a late hour a very heavy Crown book. Certificate for £13 in aid of £10 allowance by the corporation for the judges' lodgings on Patrick's Day. Breakfast at Belfast. Dine and sleep at

Downpatrick.

Thursday 18th Fifteen records entered. Dine with Blackwood, High Sheriff.

Friday 19th Staples, Holmes, Scriven, Ball and Blacker dine with us.

Saturday 20th Close about one. Work for Brother Daly till seven wch enables him to finish this evening and saves him the mortification of giving Monday to this county. Certify for £19.6.9

Sunday 21st Circuit being closed, we proceed to my old friend Lord Annesley, Castlewellan. On my way I set down Hamilton, crown solicitor, at Mr. Moore's Mount Panther. Moore, the husband of my old acquaintance, Mrs Bob Shaw, very like Duke of York.

Monday 22nd March. Rise with a heavy cold and rheumatism and hoarseness occasioned by the late sittings the two last evenings at Downpatrick.

Tuesday 23rd Pick up Ar. McCarthy and convey him to town. Sleep at Man of War, an admirable house.

Wednesday 24th Breakfast at Merrion Square, having completed the Circuit precisely in three weeks exclusive of the journey from the last town. The following memorandum I bet pretty exact, measuring from Dublin to Dublin:

Home circuit 129 miles; North-West circuit 264 miles; Leinster 182 miles; Connaught 301 ; North-East 220; Munster 358.

Thursday 25th Drive to Loughlinstown where I find my wife, Mary FitzGerald and Sir Edward Denny in high bloom awaiting with kind impatience my return.

Saturday 18th April. Sir Edward remains with me between Dublin and Loughlinstown till this day when he sails at 9 p.m. on board Goddard and arrives next morning at Holyhead after a charming passage of 12 hours.

Friday 15th June. Begin to mow.

Saturday 2nd July. Move Chancellor for liberty to take defence to ejectment in name of heir of Lord Milton, wch he refuses. Daly J. hearing that a criminal conversation action was brought against Morrison the architect, said that a gentleman who had heretofore made so much by his erections might very well afford to lose somewhat by them. Lord Norbury will never forgive this.

Monday 5th July 1813. The Mail Coach makes its first entrance into Tralee from Cork amidst the acclamations of the Kerry capital.[8]

Wednesday 7th Court of Common Pleas, on motion of ... Plaintiffs fix 8th November for trial of the ejectment brought against me pursuant to the order of the Chancellor.[9]

1. St. George Daly (1757-1829). MP Galway 1797, was appointed prime serjeant as the reward for promoting the Union. Baron of the Exchequer 1801, later a justice of King's Bench.

2. Doctor Richard O'Reilly, appointed coadjutor to Archbishop of Armagh Anthony Blake in 1782; succeeded Blake in 1787; Primate to his death in 1818. Day told the trial jury, 'Since the Roman Catholic worship has been fully and without qualification tolerated by the legislature, any violent, turbulent or indecorous interruption thereof in a house of prayer is a gross misdemeanour at common law. Since Popery has ceased to be a crime and Catholic congregation to be unlawful, the law has taken them like all other lawful assemblies under its protection' (RIA, Day papers, 12w12 Newspaper cutting of his address at Drogheda, Monday 1 March 1813).

3. The seat of Lord Blayney.

4. Hamilton of Cornacassa, Co. Monaghan. The christian name Dacre occurs in successive generations.

5. Richard Dawson, MP Co. Monaghan. Family descended from a Cromwellian settler, Richard Dawson. Seat Dawson's Grove.

6. Willam Coulson and Brothers, damask manufacturers, Market Square, Lisburn.

7. George Bristow, High Sheriff, Co. Antrim, 1813.

8. *The Cork Mercantile Chronicle*, 11 December, 1811: 'Their Lordships the Post-Masters General have been pleased to direct, that a six-day Mail Coach should commence running from Cork to Killarney on the 5th Jan. next.' The well-reported opening of post bags and robbery of post bags were among the abuses which it was hoped the mail coaches and the mail coach roads would eradicate.

9. The verdict in the Court of Common Pleas went in Day's favour. He wrote to Lord Glandore of 'my complete victory over a gang of the most unprincipled plunderers that even Kerry has ever produced. After four days hard fighting in the Court of Common Pleas a most reputable jury without a moment's hesitation at 7.00 Thursday evening found a verdict for me against Messrs. Blennerhassett and co. The Chancellor vindicated my character, and the Court of Common Pleas has rescued and redeemed my property, and if the cause has cost me half my property and the sleepless anxiety of ten years I have come out of the fire more pure than when I entered it...Lord Norbury strong in my favour, Judge Fox much stronger and more powerful, Judge Mayne in a cold and neutral manner, and what is very curious and was unexpected Judge Fletcher for an hour and a half breast high with me in a style the most impressive, convincing and eloquent' (Talbot-Crosbie Mss. Day to Lord Glandore, Merrion Square, 13 November 1813).

Counsellor O'Connell, 1813, from the collection of Thomas Matthew Ray in the NLI

Sentencing the Editor of the Dublin Evening Post,[1] November 1813

The Editor of the Dublin Evening Post, John Magee, was convicted in July of 1813 for a libel on the viceroy the Duke of Richmond. Richmond was a notably anti-Catholic representative of the 'No Popery' administration which came to power in 1807. Day admired the government and Richmond for their commitment to the war and for their implementation of legislation to revitalise the Established Church in Ireland. He also benefited greatly from Richmond's patronage.

Magee's libel was contained in the sentence, that the people of Ireland 'must find themselves at a loss to discover any striking feature in his Grace's administration that makes it superior to the worst of his predecessors'. O'Connell did no favours for his client during the July trial when he turned the occasion into a political rally, delivering a four-hour tirade against the governments of Westmorland, Camden, Cornwallis, Hardwicke, and Richmond. Part of the speech depicts a powerful viceroy on a progress to the South of an imaginary country in Europe (Richmond at Tralee Castle), where he confers the distribution of patronage on one religious denomination. Another part repeats Magee's libel, in 'The Duke has interfered in elections, he has violated the liberties of the subject, he has profaned the very temple of the constitution'. The speech's principal claim to fame rests on its fierce attack on the Attorney-General, Huguenot William Saurin.

When the trial finished Magee published O'Connell's court oration in full in his Dublin Evening Post, an action which was considered an aggravation of the offence by the time Magee appeared in court again to be sentenced by Day. The Chief Secretary, Robert Peel, coordinated the response of the government and the courts, writing to the Chief Justice, Downes, 'I hope the Chief Justice will not allow the Court to be again insulted and made a vehicle for treason'. Day took his cue from this instruction.

Mr. John Magee, you have been indicted for printing and publishing in a certain newspaper, entitled '*The Dublin Evening Post*', a wicked, seditious, and scandalous Libel, of and concerning the Duke of Richmond, then Lord Lieutenant of Ireland. Upon this indictment you have been tried and found guilty by a Jury of your fellow citizens; and the Court of King's Bench, before whom you now stand for judgment, full approve of that verdict, conceiving the publication to be one of the foulest Libels which has disgraced the Irish Press, even in this prolific age of Libels. The manifest and inevitable tendency of this publication, is to hold up the King's Representative to the detestation of the people whom he was deputed to govern; stigmatising him with the blackest political crimes – with fraud and falsehood in his general intercourse – with partiality, injustice, and cruelty in the exercise of the Royal functions – with oppressing his Majesty's subjects of Ireland committed to the special protection of his Grace – and, finally, with the stale and stupid old lie of Murder. Such is the short portraits presented by this scandalous Libeller, in contempt of all honour, truth, and decency, of a Viceroy selected, it would seem, for the meridian of Ireland, for his congenial and kindred virtues. I sit not here to pronounce a panegyric upon any man;

but I may be permitted to refer to the notorious fact, that the object of this scandalous publication carried with him from hence the affection and regret of every good subject, and what perhaps is no less flattering, the slander of the bad. For what is slander, but the natural incense and tribute of malignity to virtue – the shadow which follows and would obscure, but is cast back (as if in contempt) by solid and substantial worth?

Doubtless the Liberty of the Press is sacred. Doubtless a free Press is the sacred, the hallowed birthright of every British subject. But the Press like the Subject, must be amenable to its own duties and obligations. The Press should be elevated in principle, candid and salutary in admonition, intrepid in discussion, impartial and unbiased in its judgments. Pursuing such a course, the moral censorship of the Press will preserve its wholesome and valuable influence over the public mind, and the great parent of the Reformation and of the Revolution, and of our religious and political liberties, may all preside with unimpaired authority over that unrivalled Constitution which it has engendered. But the Press like every other human blessing, may by abuse degenerate into a curse; and the sad history of our own times teaches, that the very Palladium of liberty may be transformed into an instrument even of the most tremendous tyranny that ever shook the earth. Is it necessary, in the presence of an enlightened and reflecting Bar to dwell upon the recent sickening abuses and corruptions of our Press? The licentious Inquisition which it has erected amongst us, vexes and disturbs society, agitates the credulous and unthinking body of the people, drags whom it lists a culprit for trial to the filthy tribunal of the Newspapers, and gibbets the subject by a summary sentence. No integrity, no virtue shall protect him, if, in the most scrupulous and conscientious exercise of his understanding, he presumes to differ from the unfledged purveyors of a seditious Journal, or the interested and clumsy partisans of any class or sect of our society It was lately said, in a great assembly, by an incorruptible and splendid Senator, the father of his country's freedom, that there existed in Ireland a French faction. How else is it possible to account for the extravagant prostitution of our Press, than as a calumny inflicted upon their country by this French faction of Irishmen? What more effectual course could the present wretched Ruler of France (if perchance his iron domination still continue), what more effectual course for his purpose could he prescribe to his friends in Ireland (for you know he has friends in Ireland), than to keep the people, by hireling and hostile Journals, in a state of perpetual fever and delirious discontent with their governors, to alarm those governors for their safety at home, and thus to disable Ireland from taking her share abroad in this glorious and triumphant conflict for the liberties of the world?

With respect to your defence, if defence it can be called, my Lord Chief Justice has anticipated that part of the case with such strength of observation, that little remains for me to add. The abilities and learning of Mr. Wallace have been elaborately exerted in your behalf, but his efforts sunk under the damning facts of the case. No man is more sensible than myself of the privileges of an accused defendant, or less willing to circumscribe that wide range which his interest and necessities often imperatively prescribe to his Advocate. But that point, so ably argued by your Counsel, your own conduct has made it altogether unnecessary for the Court to trench or touch upon.

You have claimed and challenged that defence in all its latitude as your own. You have declared in the words of your own publication, 'That the line of defence taken for you, and and the topics upon which Mr. O'Connell has insisted are precisely those which he was instructed to adopt.' You have not only so declared , but you have applauded and panegyrised him for his able and faithful discharge of your instructions. If then the Court are to construe words as every ordinary reader would understand them, the conclusion is inevitable; you have in terms adopted and identified yourself with that defence, and become answerable for all the matter of unexampled aggravation which it conveys.- The law is clear and settled, that the conduct of a convicted defendant, intermediate his trial and judgment, may be taken into consideration, either for mitigation or aggravation or punishment; and to this doctrine no man can object with a worse grace than yourself; for many months have not rolled over our heads since, in a Libel case, a judgment little more than nominal was pronounced upon you, in consideration of contrition expressed, and atonement offered, subsequent to your conviction. Then see the nature of that defence, and whether it does not exhibit a disgusting picture of the most inveterate hardihood in delinquency, a case of deep criminality and hopeless infatuation. Instead of any acknowledgment of error or sorrow for past offence, instead of any promise or hope held out of future amendment, of future moderation or decency in the exercise of your trade, instead of resorting to any topic which penitent or prudent convicts address to the feelings of a Jury, or the discretion of the Court, you scorn all such vulgar resources, and boldly instruct your Counsel, Mr. O'Connell, to give the reins to all his powers of vituperation and calumny; and it must be confessed that the Gentleman fulfilled his instructions to the letter. The sluices of slander were opened wide, and the mountain torrent roared and rushed along, sweeping viceroys, law officers, judges, juries, the Church, the State, every thing revered and sacred in society, down its muddy and turbulent tide, without discrimination or decorum. If the court could overlook or capitulate with conduct such as this, adieu to the administration of justice. The administration of justice would become a mockery, and nearly nominal amongst us. If any man shall, under the shelter of a bar gown, and forgetting his professional duty, turn his back upon his client, and his client's cause, to indulge his own personal or political animosity to any individual – if he then, for the mere discharge of a peremptory official duty, launch into a rancorous invective against a Gentleman, who, by his abilities and his virtues has won his way with the will and consenting congratulation of all his contemporaries, to the head of his profession, if he shall with sacrilegious hands assault the sacred heights of the Bench, the very Sanctuary of Justice, and malign one of the most enlightened, unsullied, candid, mild, and merciful magistrates that ever adorned the Judgment Seat; if he shall insult a respectable jury, that peculiar pride and main pillar of British Jurisprudence, in the discharge of a laborious, painful and vexatious duty, under the solemn obligation of an oath,[2] and the protection of the court: such a man may call himself the Advocate of his profession's privileges and of the Bar; but the Bar will disavow and disclaim this self-created Advocate, and in language not to be misunderstood, will tell him to his face,

Non tali ausilie nec defensoribus istis! [3]

Were such a course to be permitted with impunity, then may our sober, unimpassioned, dignified tribunals as well be closed at once, and turbulence and passion thenceforth become the arbiters of right and wrong.

Would to God that the punishment of this day may serve to render the Press more pure and useful, and the offender more attentive to the duty which he owes to the laws, to his country, and to himself.

The sentence of the Court is, that you, John Magee, do pay a fine of £500 to his Majesty; that you be imprisoned for the space of two years in Newgate, to be computed from the day of your conviction, and that you do find security for your future good behaviour, yourself in the sum of £1000 and two sureties in the sum of £500 each; and that you be further imprisoned until such fine be paid and such security given.

1. Reported in *Faulkner's Dublin Journal,* 11 December 1813; a lengthy, though not complete, account of the speech in defence of Magee can be found in O Faolain's biography of O'Connell, *King of the Beggars,* 1938. The more complete account is in John O'Connell (Ed.) *The Select Speeches of Daniel O'Connell, MP.*

2. Day entered the following footnote at this point in the RIA manuscript of this sentencing: 'Mr. O'C. professed himself to advocate the cause of the Bar; but upon turning round for applause, was received with a loud horse-laugh and a general murmur of indignation.'

3. Translation, Out with such unbecoming behaviour and with advocates of that ilk.

'I cannot believe that Judge Day would do this': controversy continues 1814-1815

In 1814 the government's counter-attack on the Catholic movement continued. Day sentenced Magee again in February for publishing a fresh libel on Richmond; the libel was embodied in the 'Kilkenny Resolutions' from a meeting held at the Black Abbey in Kilkenny. Day tried to conciliate O'Connell: 'Your counsel, Mr. O'Connell, to whose judicious and able management of your case I am ready to bear full testimony, did not commit his professional character to any defence of the libel. He argued that you, the printer, acted only in the way of your trade, and must be presumed, therefore, to have had no malicious motive.' Neither the author of the libel nor the chairman of the Kilkenny meeting had attempted to save Magee by taking responsibility for the libel, but Magee – 'though young in years, you are an adult in delinquency' – had to share responsibility, and he was sentenced to six months, 'to commence from the expiration of your present imprisonment', and a fine of £1000 (reported in the Limerick Gazette and General Advertiser, 22 Feb.1814).

The Catholic Board was suppressed on 3 June. By then two other developments had helped demoralise the movement: in February the Pope issued his famous Rescript accepting the government's veto formula as a solution to the Catholic question, and in April Napoleon abdicated.

Napoleon escaped from Elba in early 1815 and Day attacked the Catholics for attempting to create conditions favourable to another French invasion and for exacerbating the rural campaign: at the Spring assizes of Co. Westmeath he told the Grand Jury that the disturbances were due to a 'flame ... which in my conscience I consider as originating and vomiting forth from the Dublin Crater, at Aggregate and other meetings, by Separatists and enemies to the British name and connection'. O'Connell replied at an Aggregate meeting held in Cork in April.[1] *Much of the speech is indecipherable in the newspaper microfilm of the Cork Mercantile Chronicle, but what survives is a masterpiece of irony and invective. Its target is Day for his performance on the bench in Westmeath.*

The Aggregate Meeting of the Roman Catholics of the County and City of Cork held in the South Parish Chapel on Friday April 7 1815'[2]

I dare not believe it (a reported charge to be one of Judge Day's) was pronounced by the Judge – I conceive that the attributing it to him is a mere device of the Castle writers, in order to give circulation to some of their own nonsense. I shall, therefore, treat it as a publication and not as a charge. Though, indeed, the hirelings of the Castle have shewn what little respect may be paid to a judge's charge in their mode of treating the admirable charge of Judge Fletcher.[3] It is an example that I do not wish to imitate, and there are really several reasons to believe that this charge is not genuine. In the first place, Judge Day is a man known to possess what is called common sense – and this Charge is totally deficient of that quality, as I shall presently demonstrate. In the next place, even personal delicacy would restrain Judge Day from attacking as agitators in this way. His enmity to me, individually, I have experience and am proud of because I earned it in the honest and manly exertions of my professional duty. I was Counsel against him in his great Equity Cause, and although

I was the lowest of the Counsel, in point of talent, I was exceeded by few in zeal and activity, and I believe equalled by none in the distinct enunciation of that view of the case which struck my mind, as Counsel, to be most unfavourable to morality. I never mix my politics with my profession, because that would injure my client – but I have the pleasure to feel that whether I urge a cause against a peasant, a peer, or a judge, there is but this difference, that whilst I refrain in the case of the first from any violence of supererogation, in the case of the two latter, and especially of the last, the independence of my spirit arouses itself by the virulence of its attack. I have therefore, I hope, richly earned the enmity of the learned Judge – but that very enmity ought, and I presume would, restrain him from pouring out from the Bench any species of calumny which could be attributed by the public to so foul as source as private revenge. There is, however, a superior delicacy, which ought, and I presume would, more powerfully restrain him – the delicacy attached to his Judicial station. The Charge states that the Catholic Association is an illegal meeting, liable to punishment. Now, if the Association should be prosecuted, the prosecution is most likely to be carried on in the Court of King's Bench, of which Judge Day is a member. But Judge Day would be too delicate to prejudge the question to arise in such prosecution. He would be too delicate to pronounce as this charge does, a judgment of conviction before investigation, before argument, before trial. This thing called a Charge prejudges the Association – it even invites the Government to bring us before the King's Bench by a promise of conviction. I cannot believe that Judge Day would do this. He knows well, that nothing in human nature can be so horrible or so detestable as a prejudiced, preoccupied judge – as a judge bound to condemn, to preserve his own consistency. Judge Day knows well the disgrace of such conduct, and therefore I pronounce the attributors of this Charge to him, as an abominable calumny – he never did, he never could have uttered such a villainous farrago of false accusation and absurd contradiction as this publication styled a Charge contains.

The judicial character is too valuable to be frittered away by false imputation. Let it be recollected that one great cause of the fall of the Bourbons and of the restoration of Napoleon was the generally received opinion in France, that the Bourbon judges were partial and corrupt. The first and most popular act of Napoleon was his Proclamation or decree from Lyons, restoring the former tribunals and judges. The Bourbon judges were said to be frightful partizans of the small faction of returned emigrants; it was said they prejudged every question that came before them; that they convicted before investigation, argument or trial; and even held out lures to the government to send victims to their tribunals, rather than want causes for trial, promising beforehand to get sure convictions.

It is said that they decided every question which arose between the Crown prosecutors and the people whether of law, of fact, or even of form, in favour of the Crown, and against the people, so that the Crown was never wrong with those Judges - the people were never right. They are said to have gone so far as to have made the grammar and the dictionary yield to their decision, and to have altered the very language itself under the pretence of a legal construction. These judges are said to have been as ignorant as they were wicked. If it be true that France was, as we are told, cursed with such villainous, corrupt, and partial judges, who can wonder at the late Revolution. We are indeed told that those judges were in the constant habit of praising themselves, of boasting of the impartiality and purity of their own conduct, and that there was no allusion which was punished with such unrelenting severity as the slightest allusion to the fact that the judges were corrupt and partial. Judge Day has been, I presume, filled with astonishment when he has heard that a judge in France –a species of blatant beast, more like a fatted Calf in a wig than a human being, has procured in the short reign of Louis 18th, a period of not near so long as the Richmond administration, no less than ten or twelve valuable offices and benefices for his near relations. I have been told that in a single department of France, not so large as our county of Kerry, this Judge, whilst he was he was deciding operations between the Crown and the People, obtained for one very near relative a situation resembling that of our Surveyor-General, and worth about £500 per annum of our money, for another an office equal to our Distributorship of Stamps, worth more than £700 per annum of our money; for another connection of his a place in his Barracks, like our Barrack Mastership, and worth about £800 per annum, and two livings in the Church for other near relations, worth each of them more than £1000 a year.[4] With all this weight of obligation upon him, what a conscientious Judge between the donors of those good things and the People this Judge must have been – Judge Day must have been shocked at hearing of such profligacy, and he will therefore attribute in his next genuine Charge the restoration of Napoleon to the moral effect of such causes, rather than to the revolutionary flames of any Dublin Crater.

Alas! At this moment the calumniator of the Catholics would be better described as the ally of Napoleon. For me, I seek to aid the Government; my object is to sustain and secure the Constitution and the Throne. I offer them a powerful reinforcement, not of hundreds of whiskered Croats or of savage Pandours – not of thousands of uncombed Cossacks or beastly Calmucks – the aid I offer is of millions of the bravest, finest people in the world – the People of Ireland; men who never fled from any fight, and whose unalterable fidelity to the religion they believe, is the surest earnest of their attachment to that state which they could love. I offer, without pay or subsidy, to procure for the service of England's war two armies; the one is the army which, during her present wretched policy, England must employ in Ireland to maintain her authority. And the other is the army which Ireland's love and Ireland's gratitude will rally round her standards.

The upshot of O'Connell's speech in Cork was the trial for libel of the printer of the Cork Mercantile Chronicle, Harding Treacy, in the Court of King's Bench in May 1816. His counsel was O'Connell. Tracey was convicted and sentenced to two years in Newgate and a fine of £300.[5] *The printer testified 'that he had no concern whatever in the publication of the libel, except that of being the registered printer of the paper', also 'that his health was very much impaired, and that he was advised by physicians that protracted imprisonment would be destructive of his life', finally 'that he had a wife and five children solely dependent on his labour for subsistence'.*[6] *In language reminiscent of Day at the sentencing of Magee, the Attorney-General – still William Saurin – accused O'Connell of skulking behind 'his wretched printer' and behind the protection afforded him by the court and his profession of barrister.*[7] *The case came to haunt O'Connell. In 1824 the treatment of Harding Treacy was thrown at O'Connell by his own organisation and by Harding Treacy's wife: there was allegation and counter-allegation about whether or not Treacy had been compensated for his loss of earnings while in prison.*[8] *Mrs Treacy wrote about her husband's release: 'By the kind assistance of our friends, and the unremitting exertions of Judge Day, my husband was liberated in the month of December 1816.'*[9]

1. Day had made an unsuccessful attempt to restrain O'Connell as he prepared to fight his duel with D'Esterre on the last day of January. *The Freeman's Journal*, 2 Feb. 1815, reported that O'Connell had taken refuge in Exchequer Street. 'In a short time, however, he was assailed by the most formidable interruption which he had yet encountered - Judge Day entered in his magisterial capacity to put him under arrest. The Hon. Justice said he would be satisfied if he had the guarantee of Mr. O'Connell's honour that he would proceed no further in the business. "It is not my duty, Mr. Justice", said Mr. O'C., "to be the aggressor – I will, therefore, pledge my honour that I will not be the aggressor – further, however, I must tell you that no human consideration will induce me to go."'
2. *Cork Mercantile Chronicle* 14 April 1815; *Freeman's Journal*, 18 April 1815. Not all of this report is legible.
3. Judge William Fletcher (1750-1823) was much more inclined than Day to give weight to the concerns of the liberal press and majority opinion. He spoke strongly in favour of Grattan's Emancipation bill in parliament in 1795, when he was one of the Tralee representatives; Day is not recorded as having made a contribution. More recently, Fletcher's anti-government charge to the Wexford Grand Jury in 1814 led to the smear campaign against him referred to by O'Connell.
4. Printed in *The Tralee Chronicle*, 20 March 1860 is the following letter from Robert Day to Lord Glandore, dated 26 July 1813: My Dear Lord,
   I took leave on Tuesday last of our excellent Lord Lieutenant who proposes to be off from the government before my return from circuit. I do not know that the country has ever had a better Viceroy: open, ingenious; a decided Protestant; but candid, liberal and impartial as to the Crown patronage, in the distribution of which it might be truly said of him 'Tros Tyriusve mihi nullo discrimine habetur', a man of frank unaffected manners and social habits, possessing a clear and strong understanding. He has been six years here last April, longer than any predecessor. To me my own personal obligations prove what a loss his departure will be. He gave me for one friend a pair of colours – for a nephew a valuable living – another for a nephew-in-law; Barracks for Tralee, and the Barrackmastership for a nephew-in-law; a Chief-Constableship to another relative, and to another nephew a Supervisorship of Hearths. In short, I do not know that he ever refused me a favour; and had I the effrontery to ask I am sure he would have given me more.
   I shall now dismiss this subject with the remark that the harsh reflection which has occasioned these observations is alike devoid of justice and good taste.
   I am, sir, &c
   Robert Day
5. *Dublin Evening Post*, 21 May 1816.
6 *Limerick Gazette and General Advertiser*, 28 May 1816.
7. *Ibid.*
8. See *Freeman's Journal*, 5, 6 and 14 July 1824.
9. Newspaper cutting in the Day papers, Ms. 12w13, dated 19 July 1824; she added 'Since the question has been agitated, a statement of a mock account (of compensation and/or salary paid to her husband while in prison) has appeared in the Cork Mercantile Chronicle, intended to be a corroboration of Mr. O'Connell's assertions. It is false and untrue in every particular, and was never furnished to, nor its accuracy admitted by, my husband, as falsely asserted in that paper'.

Trial of Rowan Cashel, Gentleman, Attorney, for the wilful murder of Henry O'Connor, Esq., late of Tralee, in a duel, tried at the March Assizes of Tralee, 1816, before Mr. Justice Day.[1]

On Monday 7 August 1815 a serial duellist by the name of Rowan Cashel shot eighteen-year-old Henry Arthur O'Connor in an 'affair of honour' at Ballyseedy, near Tralee. The ball 'passed through the fleshy part of the right arm and entered his side'. It was extracted by surgeon Morgan O'Connell Busteed and the injured youth lingered a few days until he died at seven o'clock on Wednesday morning. O'Connor was the son of a former Provost of the town; this and perhaps the poignancy of his loss so young caused the town to go into mourning. A few days later Judge Day arrived in Tralee from the Connaught circuit. He was accompanied by his grandson, Edward Denny, who would stand for the county in the next general election and whose candidacy Day was already promoting. They found the town in darkness, not illuminated as was the custom for the arrival of the heir to the Denny estate and the baronetcy. Told the reason why, Day issued a warrant for the arrest of Rowan Cashel.[2] It was believed that his mishandling of the trial of Rowan Cashel in the assizes of the following spring contributed to the ending of Judge Day's career. But Day was exonerated by parliament of having misdirected the jury with the charge printed here. The manuscript account of the trial of Rowan Cashell, including Judge Day's charge, came into the possession of Kerry historian James Franklin Fuller of Glashnacree House about a hundred years ago. Fuller later found a pamphlet, printed in Cork and containing the accusations against the judge by the brothers of Henry Arthur O'Connor, in a bookshop in London. He published both in the journals of the Cork Historical Society.

The Charge.

Gentlemen – The prisoner, Rowan Cashel, stands charged with the wilful murder of Henry Arthur O'Connor, and I shall now proceed to detail to you the evidence as I have noted it down. Beginning with that of Surgeon Busteed's, he states he was on the ground, and heard two shots fired, and from his evidence he will give you to understand that the second shot might be quicker than it was. That is as much as Surgeon Busteed's evidence amounts to. Mr. Richard Quill was in the Billiard Room at a difference that happened between the deceased and the prisoner; it happened about a bet of a half a crown, for which this unfortunate young man lost his life. You should be particular in observing that the first offensive words were used by the deceased, who said, on the prisoner's denying he had lost the bet, 'You shall pay me, or (accompanied by an oath) you shall not play at this table', that is to say, gentlemen, he should be excluded from this society. To this language the prisoner made answer in terms of not a very offensive nature: 'You are', said he, 'but a boy, and I shall call upon your father', whether to complain perhaps of the conduct of deceased or not, but, however, that he would call upon his father. Deceased again demanded to be paid, insisted he won the wager, and the other denied, saying if he lost he would pay as he did everyone, to which deceased replied, 'I don't know that; you don't pay me', and 'I praise the ford as I find it'. So you see, gentlemen, from a grain of mustard seed this dispute proceeded to a serious and angry quarrel, ending in the fatal consequences which followed. The prisoner, to whom insulting language was applied, used some expression as, 'If you were not', said he 'a brat of a boy I would turn you out of the room'. This, gentlemen, is the substance of the evidence of Mr. Quill. Lieutenant Arthur Morris gives you an account of what took place next day; tells you that he (very laudably certainly) came to Mr. Cashel to make it up, met the prisoner on the Mall, and walked with him into the Green; there he explained to him the nature of what he came about, and required of Mr. Cashel to arrange the business; proposed terms to Mr. Cashel, which he would not accede to, still saying 'he was but a boy, and that he would have nothing to say to him'. I do not see, gentlemen, that this was indicative of a sanguinary nature. Mr. Morris's object was reconciliation, Mr. Cashel still persisted he was but a boy. Deceased offered no apology for the adage used, 'I praise the ford as I find it'. Mr. Morris then went away, and afterwards returned and proposed to leave the matter in dispute to Mr. Quill; the prisoner refused - very unfortunately refused – to leave it to Mr. Quill, but proceeded to lay a whip on Mr. Morris's shoulder, saying that he meant it as a horsewhipping; 'to take it as a horsewhipping'. After this, Mr. Morris tells you he was called back and a reconciliation took place, between him and Mr. Cashel; this, unfortunately, did not continue long. Mr. Morris then said he was present next day, heard the shots, but could form no opinion about them. On cross-examination, he says the deceased posted the prisoner with a view to compel him to fight. Mr. Thomas O'Connor, the brother of the deceased, gave you in testimony that all three went to the Mall for the express purpose of horsewhipping Cashel. This horsewhipping, by the code of laws of honour, is not required to be an actual horsewhipping, but ideal, and amounts to the same. He tells you he took down a posting after the occurrence of the Mall affray, and after other postings had been made – these produced the duel.

Mr. Yielding and Mr. McGillycuddy made an agreement that the parties discharge their pistols at the words 'Ready, Fire'; the witness swears that he heard the words loud enough. The prisoner, he says, knew of the arrangement but said that he would prefer that each party should take his own time. There is no doubt, it appears, of the agreement being known; but did the prisoner hear the word? They were distant about twelve or fourteen yards. (Here Mr. Thomas O'Connor said: "My Lord, I did not say so. I said I thought the seconds were about that distance from the principals, but the parties fought at the distance of eight yards at the express desire of the prisoner's brother and his second, who refused to accede to the ordinary distance.") Gentlemen, I must have misunderstood, but I do not think this observation can go to you now as evidence. The shots, he swears, were separate, one after the other; the witness on hearing his brother's shot instantly wheeled about, not wishing to witness a sight which must have been disagreeable to his feelings, but did not keep his eye on his brother, but hearing no report of the second pistol turned round again and saw his brother; this, he says, he had time to do before the second shot was fired; he says that the deceased's arm was down by his side, that he raised it, and then the prisoner fired. Deceased had but one pistol, the prisoner two. On cross-examination he states that he and his brothers went to the Mall as the most public place to make the insult to be given to the prisoner as public as possible; there was a posting made of the prisoner, the language of which was calculated to provoke; it was thus – 'Having been grossly insulted by Mr. Rowan Cashel, and having been denied the satisfaction of a gentleman, I feel myself under the necessity of posting Mr. Cashel as a coward and a bully, and therefore unfit for the society of gentlemen. Signed Henry Arthur O'Connor'. This must have gone far in producing what was then done. A more exasperating thing was never written or made use of than was posted in public places. Mr. O'Connor, the witness, allows with much candour and truth that his feelings would be much irritated by such language if it was applied to himself, and says he rebuked his servant for shouting on the occasion. He does not know how many blows his brother may have given, but the posting was before the blows. He expected from the violence that there would be a fight, but he would rather there was not. He then adds that he considered a duel as inevitable, and that there were numbers on the ground.

Gentlemen, it appears to me as if these kind of things were a pastime here. He states the posting by Mr. Cashel was before the affray on the Mall, but after the posting by deceased. Mr. James O'Connor, another brother, proved the handwriting of Mr. Cashel to the posting. He said the prisoner stepped a short step, turned his person, levelled and fired, and that the prisoner had been on terms of familiarity with their family. On cross-examination he agrees with his brother's evidence as to the aggravation given to Mr. Cashel, and that he could not help fighting; he says the prisoner posted the deceased in consequence of the prior posting by the deceased. Samuel Morris heard two shots, the first as soon after the word as it could be fired, the next a short time after. The next witness was Joseph O'Connor. He appears as an amateur. He swore, gentlemen, that one had one pistol and the other two; this, gentlemen, can be of no weight, as there was no intention of firing two shots for one. He swears he heard one shot, as he expresses it, simultaneously with the word; but he after says he meant very quickly after the word, the second shot in three or four seconds after; he described to you the position of the prisoner, that he did not observe him alter it, but that he might have squared a little, and that they levelled together. William Collis next proved much the same. Francis Twiss saw the duel; there was about a second, as much as you may reckon one, two; this was as much as Mr. Twiss's evidence amounted to. Mr. John O'Connell[3] next sworn. He does not admit that he was on the ground, but does that he heard the shots, that one was after he heard the word, the other after a lapse (a pause was his expression), such as he may take aim in; he says the day before the duel, on the Mall, he heard a buzz, he went up to the crowd and heard the deceased address Mr. Cashel, the words he did not know, on which the prisoner made a stroke at the deceased, when deceased gave the prisoner a blow, and repeated the blow severely; this was on Sunday, the day before the duel. There was a great ferment caused by the posting put up by the deceased on the Castle gate. Mr. O'Connell does not hesitate to say on his cross-examination that there was heat of blood in the prisoner, that the blows received and the double posting continued in his mind until the next day, that the three young gentlemen came up very quietly, but certainly, gentlemen, not on a very quiet purpose, to flog the prisoner. Mr. John Hurly was present; heard the shots, but did not mark the interval; it might have been enough to take aim, but not a deliberate aim. He would come to no conclusion as to the time necessary to take aim; one man may take a longer time than another, but he does not know that the prisoner took more time than was necessary to take aim in, as he considers men will differ in that respect.

Gentlemen, I will now proceed to the evidence for the defence. The witnesses were Messrs. Mason and McGillycuddy. The first, Mr. Mason, told you that he stood nearer to where the word was given than the prisoner did. He did not hear the word 'Fire'; he will not say it was not given, but he says the shot may have been fired with the word – as another witness expressed it, simultaneously with it; the prisoner fired a short time after, as 'one, two'; he observed no change of position on the part of the prisoner, and concludes by saying he thought everything was fair. On cross-examination he admits, as before, an interval between the shots, that he is a relative of the prisoner's; I do not know, gentlemen, that any such remark has been made on any of the witnesses on the part of the prosecution when the brothers of the deceased were examined; he does not say the word 'Fire' was not given, but that if it was, it was in a low voice, and that if he, who was nearer tha party giving it, could not hear it, it was no wonder Cashel, who was further away, should not; he also considers if one party fires before his time, it was reasonable the other should delay his fire. Here, gentlemen, according to Mr. Mason's idea, it would appear that Mr. Cashel delayed for the word justly, and if the other fired before his time Mr. Cashel's delay was an adherence to the agreement. Gentlemen, I observe a consistency between both sides of the evidence, except that some heard the words, others did not. Mr. McGillycuddy deposes that he heard but one word, and that then the deceased fired. He stood nearer to the deceased than to the prisoner, and he was more likely to hear the word than the prisoner; that he is conversant in matters of this nature, and that the duel was a fair one.

Here, Gentlemen, the evidence closes, and I am here to explain to you that two persons meeting, armed with deadly weapons, to fight a duel, should homicide ensue it is legal murder.[4] The questions put relative to the provocation given seemed to me an attempt on the part of the prisoner's counsel to extenuate in that way the act of the prisoner. It is impossible the treatment of the deceased to prisoner could have subsided in his mind during the night; if a falling out occurs overnight, the law says that the delay causes the heat of blood to subside; that irritability must still have remained. It is the duty, gentlemen, of the judge to state the law distinctly on duels; but as society is, unfortunately, governed by a code of its own – by the law of opinion, altogether discharging municipal law from it, there is scarcely an instance where juries will receive the law of the land, but conceive an allegiance to honour as the law to go by; but such provocation as this in a court of honour flesh and blood could not endure; it was on this the witnesses on cross examination proved the consequent heat of blood, and the contumacious language of the unfortunate deceased. The conduct of Cashel deprecated a mortal collision with the deceased, but, gentlemen, they met the next day; the treatment Cashel received must have degraded him in society; if a duel did not ensue, according to this code of laws of honour, he could not hold up his head in society after it. As a judge of the King's Bench, I must deprecate that this law should countervail the laws of the land, and that we, unfortunately, cannot oppose this despotic law, by which, if a gentlemen deny to accede to, he must be stigmatised as a coward, and which they are pleased to endure in preference to such humiliating feelings and degradation. A man would rather throw himself on a jury than walk in society an isolated being; and, gentlemen, I would be unwilling to say merely that 'one, two', was a deliberate pause to take the life of another (if in a court of honour), but by the law of the land the going out and a homicide ensuing, the law constitutes murder.

The jury retired, and in a short time returned a verdict "Not Guilty".
Mr. Justice Day then addressed the prisoner nearly to the following effect: - Mr. Cashel, you have some very respectable friends and connections in this county, and I can assure you that you will be more likely by a proper attention to the duties of your profession to render yourself a useful member of society than by aspiring to the shocking and contemptible character of a duellist. I am sure you must yourself feel more sensibly than any other man the unfortunate occurrence that has taken place, and I would recommend you as a friend in future to avoid all such places and societies as may have a tendency to produce such consequences. I trust that time will remove the affliction which has fallen on the family of the young man who has lost his life. The father has yet some very fine young men, two of whom have given evidence upon this trial, and I trust these very respectable young gentlemen will be a comfort to their family. It would be much to be wished that the unfortunate occurrence would be buried in oblivion, and that these families may be restored to the former friendly intercourse which subsisted between them. But perhaps at present this may not be possible; they have lost a very fine young man, and as I understand a young gentleman of very mild and amicable manners, so that it is possible this can only be a work of time.

Sheriff – Is Mr. Cashel to be discharged, my Lord?

Judge – Oh, yes. Mr. Cashel, you are discharged.

The O'Connor family now prepared a petition to parliament, which was brought before the House of Commons in July.[5] *Its principal allegation was that Mr Justice Day 'had grossly neglected his duty in a certain trial' and was guilty of 'a most culpable degree of partiality' in favour of Cashel. It also contained the pathetic information that one of the O'Connor brothers had, shortly after publishing 'a rather violent statement of the case', and becoming thereby 'amenable to the laws of the country', fled to the house of a relative and there died of a broken heart. There was some resistance in the House to hearing the petition while there was the possibility of a libel action on foot of the 'violent statement' printed by the O'Connors about the judge. Lord Castlereagh made a strong defence of Day's character: 'no man was more entitled to public estimation, or did more honour to the official character which he held, than the highly respectable Judge against whom the libel was pointed.' The threat of libel proceedings may have at least contributed to the exoneration of Day in the House the following 19 February, because some of its statements could be proven to be wrong.*

Points from an undated Letter Addressed to Mr. Justice Day, from a 'Brother of the Deceased', printed in full in the JCAHS, vol 10, no. 61, 1904.
I, think (for I will be candid with you) that your own good sense and delicacy ought to have suggested to you, circumstanced s you were in the county, and related to and connected as you were with the prisoner, the propriety of postponing this trial, or at least transferring it to Mr.

Justice Mayne. I am authorised, sir, to state, from a most unquestionable source, that two days before this trial you read a letter in company with the Knight of Kerry and a select party of your political friends from Lady Ventry (who had before solicited you to admit the prisoner to bail) informing you that Lord Ventry (who could poll at least two thousand freeholders) had not as yet declared whom he would support. Lord Ventry, sir, you well know to be cousin german to the prisoner's father, and I ask you, in the name of wonder, how you could reconcile it to your nice discernment and delicate sense of propriety, to have insisted on presiding at this trial, and to have refused its postponement?

Why did you not take the common precaution of obliging this man (whom you addressed in something like complimentary language) to enter into a recognizance to keep the peace in future? An homicide was committed, and one of no ordinary nature, and though, sir, he (Cashel) is your relation, and also connected with you, yet I am somewhat surprised that any learned judge of your time of life and experience should let loose on society a man who had fought no less than four duels, wounded one gentleman, and, to use the mildest term, killed another.

You very kindly observed that there were some of our family still left, and that we ought to feel perfectly content and even renew habits of intimacy with the prisoner, who had been so good as not to extirpate us altogether; we certainly, sir, feel a due sense of the obligation; but I am somewhat surprised that a degree of apprehension for your grandson, for whom you are now canvassing this county, and who is about the same age, did not induce you to take this precaution.

Sir, as I have happened to speak of canvassing, I should wish to learn from you how I am to reconcile what appears to me and several others in this county a most unaccountable absurdity in your political conduct. As I take a lively interest in everything that concerns you, I wish that you would furnish me with the means of silencing the clamours of your enemies on this topic. You have ever professed yourself a most steadfast supporter of the Government of the country; you have received numerous favours from the present administration, to whom you have declared an inviolable attachment. You are daily renewing your applications for repetitions of those favours; and under these circumstances, how is it reconcilable to common honesty that you should be at this moment exerting all the influence you can muster to exclude from the representation of this county a strenuous supporter of the present administration, and to establish in his stead a gentleman who (though of considerable talent and merit) is diametrically opposed to the party to whom you profess to adhere?

Thomas Mullins, Lord Ventry, had become a rival political presence since he acquired the Blennerhassett estate in Killorglin in the late 1790s and achieved promotion to the peerage at the Union. Day had been trying to win his support in the county elections for many years. At the time of the trial of Rowan Cashel, he was attempting to detach Ventry from Col. Crosbie of Ballyheigue (who had taken one of the county seats in the 1812 general election) and switch his support to Sir Edward Denny, his grandson. The diplomacy was underway as Day set out for Munster and the Cashel trial. He wrote to the Knight of Kerry at the time: 'Every one I have applied to have promised me or you and Edward Denny, save Lord Ventry, who very naturally and prudently hangs back, and two or three more who promise me on condition only that it shall not hurt you – you who I have told everyone was my first object...'[6] *Day failed to win Ventry's support and his grandson failed to win election; the representation remained unchanged in Maurice FitzGerald and Col. Crosbie. Two final points: Daniel O'Connell supported Denny and Maurice FitzGerald, viewing Ventry and his creature Crosbie as the new monopolists of government patronage, and representatives of an anti-Catholic ministry. Day and O'Connell were now on the same side after years of disagreement. Day's requests for favours were falling on deaf government ears while Denny was acknowledged by O'Connell to be 'the descendant of one of the most ancient families in the British dominions – his ancestors had been settled in Kerry since the reign of Queen Elizabeth'; Denny was the voice of 'Independent' opinion in Kerry and enjoyed the support of nearly all of its gentry.*[7] *Denny's failure at the poll was due to some lethargic registration of the freeholders and typically efficient registration on the part of Ventry; the old opposition to Day – Ponsonby of Crotta and Bateman of Oakpark - was prominent at the return. Judge Day returned his grandson for Tralee the day he conceded the county.*[8] *A final point: when the O'Connor petition was heard by parliament at Westminster the house was told that Day and Rowan Cashel were not related (Ed.).*[9]

1. Taken from the *Journal of the Cork Archaeological and Historical Society*, July-September 1901.
2. *Limerick General Advertiser*, 8, 10, 11 August 1815.
3. John O'Connell of Grenagh, brother of 'The Liberator'.
4. Lord Ellenborough's Act, 43 Geo. 3, C. 58, *An Act for the further prevention of malicious shooting, and attempting to discharge loaded fire-arms, stabbing, cutting, wounding, poisoning, and the malicious using of means to procure the miscarriage of women....*
5. RIA, Day papers, Ms. 12w13, news cutting of the *Dublin Evening Post*, report from the House of Commons, Friday 11 July 1817.
6. NLI, FitzGerald Papers (microfilm copy), Day to Maurice FitzGerald, 27 February, 1816.
7. *Freeman's Journal*, 9 Nov. 1818, reporting O'Connell's speech at the Mail Coach Hotel, Tralee, on the occasion of a testimonial dinner in O'Connell's honour.
8. See the *Limerick General Advertiser* 17 July 1818, the *Freeman's Journal*, 6, 9 Nov. 1818.
9. Hansard, 19 February 1818, p. 558-9.

8

Nephews and Grandchildren: Retirement at Loughlinstown, 1827. [1]

Judge Day retired in early 1819. His replacement on the King's Bench was Jebb. Mary Pott, Day's wife, died in 1823; he remarried in the following year - to the chagrin of his son-in-law, Sir Edward Denny. Nephews arrive from India. His grandchildren begin to appear as adults in these final pages. Some will become clergymen in the parishes around Tralee where the Dennys own the advowsons.

Day presses the case for a nephew to become an assistant barrister for one of the counties, the legislation for which appointments (the Magistracy Act of 1787) was strongly supported by Day when in parliament. But with Canning Prime Minister from April 1827, in alliance with the liberal wing of the Whigs (led by Lord Lansdowne, the new Home Secretary, and including Thomas Spring Rice, son of Day's first-cousin Stephen Rice of Mt Trenchard, as Under Secretary to Lansdowne), Catholic appointments are now favoured. Day's promotion of his nephew is disappointed, but these pages make clear his conversion to Emancipation, his continued admiration for Canning and the liberal Tories, and his friendship with the great new standard bearer of the Catholic cause, his south Dublin neighbour William Conyngham Plunket.

I should have begun this Journal mentioning a casualty that happen'd & threatened awful consequences in my Offices on Sunday evening, 7th January. A formidable fire broke out in my straw loft, occasioned by a piece of timber communicating with a flue of the Laundry and passing through the party wall into the Loft. 3 offices were either consumed or damaged, but the neighbouring Peasants in obedience to the summons of my labourers' Bell collected immediately & by their extraordinary ... [2]

Frid. 19th January. My friends Serjt. and Mrs. Goold,[3] who have favour'd us wth their company since Th. 14th Dec. (5 weeks) break up our pleasant party & return to Town.

M. 22 Eve of Term. We go to Town & return their visit for a fortnight – decline invitations – but meet my Law friends at the King's Inn where I dined 4 times most comfortably with Bush C.J., Burton, Vandeleur &c&c.

Go to the Play Wed 24th to see and hear the divine Miss Paton (Lady Wm Lennox) in Rosetta – oh how wretched all public places look in Dublin since the Union! Not an individual in the House above the condition of a Shopkeeper.

Feb. Sun. 4th Go to St. Stephen's where Mr. Mortimer O'Sullivan[4] edifies us for an hour with a splendid Sermon – treading fast upon Kirwan on the pick-pocket of immortal memory.

M. 5 Part with our kind friends the Goolds after an agreeable fortnight & return joyfully to Sweet Home.

W. 7th March. Robt leaves us to our regret - a very heavy fall of snow. Finished my lay oats critically before the fall.

Sun. March 11 turns out most severe day – so violent a Shower of Hail drifted into the face of the Horses & Carriage returning from Church that it was wth great difficulty the Horses could be prevented from wheeling round & upsetting us – the season unseasonably stormy.

Th. 15th the Cockburns[5] & Leesons[6] dine with us & pass an agreeable day.

Sat. 17th Poor Ned, High Sheriff[7] of Kerry, leaves us to start on Monday for Tralee – the Judges arrive there Friday evening 23rd - & just open their commission. We shall think it an age till he returns & so will he.

Thurs. 22 Drive to town to meet the Knight[8] who landed last night on his way to the Assizes. Miss him – on my return find before me the 2 Miss Hitchcocks.

M. 2 April. They stay to this morning. I have had a severe cold & affection of the lungs - Thos Hewson attends me & does me good. Renewed however my Eucharistic covenant yesterday with my Merciful God who has conducted me to this late period of life (the 81st year of my age) in the full enjoyment of fine general health and of all my senses in great perfection!

M. 9th The Bowleses & Edington come to us.

Tues. 10th The Leesons dine & sleep wth us. Edward Denny returnd to us last Monday.....[9]

May Fri. 25th Call to inquire about poor Richard Mahony – bleeds quarts from his nose – a Dropsy has succeeded – can not live it is supposed a week – we return thinking these 2 days while from house an age.

26 May Sat. Tom Goold comes as usual - very much benefited in health by these occasional rustications

Sat. 2 June the Serjt & Mrs Goold accompanying him - Sunday Hitchcock & the Leesons reinforce our party.

M. 4 We all proceed to town - the Serj. on his way to Brighton & Spa from whence it is expected he will return relieved of his nervous affection which quite deranges his habits and spirits - Mrs D. & I take Mrs Goold & return to Sweet Home.

Fr 15 Term sits - drive into Town & meet my old friends the Benchers - Joy[10] just appointed Attny. Genl., Doherty is talk'd of for Solcr Genl; but will it not be a strong measure for Canning to raise his cousin over the heads of the 3 Serjeants, all very distinguish'd men, particly Lefroy?[11] The promotion of Doherty,[12] a very deserving man, will gratify me much.

Thurs. 19th Dine with the Chancr.[13] - a very pleasant day with all my Brethren - he places me above the 3 Chiefs & all, beside himself, as an older Judge & friend - we shall lose him after this term; & never did there a more polishd or courteous Gentleman adorn that Bench - pity he is so prejudiced a Politician.

Lady Denny (Elizabeth Day) 1775-1828

June. Th. 21 Dine with us the Leesons, John Marshall, Mrs. O'Brien & her son Peter - Poor Richard Mahony was released from his suffering Monday last the 19th.[14]

Sund 1 July Dine here the Vice Provost & daurs, Geo Morris & little Theodos Hictchcock.

Mon. 2 the joyful news arrives that Mau FitzGerald was appointed[15] last Friday a Lord of the Treasury - restored - but who will pay his 25 years that he is out of pocket?

July 17 Tu. Drive to the Park to see Lord Lieutenant who appoints with me tomorrow 4 o'clock.

July 18th See Lord Wellesley who graciously promises me the first vacant barristership for Robert Day,[16] with the single exception in favour of R. Catholics, which for the more impartial distribution of patronage he probably may be influenced by on the next vacancy – but even to that exception he is not sure of yielding on the first occasion.

F. 27th July. Robert Day comes in from Town with advice of the death of Gervy Bushe[17] at Kilkenny, to the grief & dismay of his numerous friends – I write an urgent but short letter to the Lord Lieutenant inclosed in one to Col. Shaw. Blake is canvassing for Wolfe, a Roman Catholic, who so back'd I fear will succeed - Rice for Howley.[18]

August 1 My hay is haggarded and forms a noble Rick – 250 loads at least - a heavenly day! God be bless'd for all his mercies. Howlen, R. Catholic, is announced Barrister.

Wednesday, 8 August – A day ever memorable for the heaviest loss the British Empire could sustain, the death of Canning, deplored by France in particular, by Europe and the World. He laid the foundations of liberty in South America, Portugal, Greece and Ireland, and had he lived he would never have ceased till he compleed the noble superstructure. It is a day that saw me in 1774 (53 years ago) the happiest of mortals, married to the best of women and the most affectionate of wives, my beloved Mary Potts; with whom I lived in harmony and happiness for 49 years. I have selected this day for making my last will.

Sunday 19. A letter of this date from Robert Denny brings a horrifying account of his poor dear mother – spasms in her stomach – 80 or 100 leeches are applied to her side – this evacuation and a serious haemorrhage reduces her to a state of great exhaustion – the seat of her disorder seems her liver, increased (as mental suffering always does) by her anxiety produc'd by the distress and degradation to which her husband has reduced his family.

Rev. Anthony Denny, (1807-1890) Archdeacon of Ardfert (1861-85), courtesy R. Warren

Sun. 26th Edward arrives from Kerry in Dublin. I drive in to him and find him in agony from Dr. Hastings's alarming account of his poor Mother – I continue to pray God for him and to confide in his mercy that He will restore her to our supplications. Edward starts this day from Howth to Barbourne. After a week of frightful suspense another letter arrives this night from Rob! That she has rallied unexpectedly and medicals think favourably &

Th. 30th I receive the joyful tidings from Edward that she is pronounc'd out of danger and recovering. The merciful God be praised! I write to her to come to me for a while with 1 or 2 of the Guls as change of air and scene must be more beneficial to her.

September, Sun. 2. Our Conventicle or New Place of Worship is open'd at Killiney – congregation of near 200 assemble, Kelly the new Curate reads prayers & Dr. Thos. Magee preaches an excellent sermon of 55 minutes. Mrs. Hitchcock, 4 daughters & youngest son, Robert Day & son & curate Kelly & young Prendergast dine with us.

Th. 13th A very agreeable party dine with us – 18 – viz.
Mr. Lamb M.P., Mr. Birch M.P., Mrs. Birch, Lord & Miss & Lady Plunket, Sir and Lady Blosse, Bush C.J., Sol. Genl. Doherty M.P., Mr. H. Grattan M.P., Mrs H. Grattan, Mr. & Mrs. Blake, Mrs. Blashford, 2 selves.

2 October. We dine with Lord Plunkett [19] & a snug sociable party of 22.

30 October. Have a long interview with Lamb[20] about Robert Day which I trust may lead to his benefit.

November, Tuesday 6th drive to town (first day of Term) to meet as usual my brethren the Benchers.

Saturday 10th Nov. We return to our beloved Retreat tired of 5 days of City life. I have been negotiating while in town between the Abp of Dublin[21] and that wrong-headed fellow Archdn Lindsay, our Rector, about re-opening our Place of Worship at Killiney, & hope to have succeeded. Lindsay and that contemptible conceited worldling the Bp of Kildare, his father, will seek an Act of Plt enabling him to endow a Perpetual Cure with land in Dalkey & the Arbp will licence our conventicle as a Chapel of Ease & require the Arcdn to appoint a Curate or in default thereof His Grace will re-appoint the 2 Clergymen who before gratuitously did duty there. This week I trust will conclude the discussion amicably. Beati pacifici.

1. RIA, Day Papers, Ms. 12w14.
2. Some pages are missing.
3. Thomas Goold, Sergeant at Law 1823, Master of Chancery 1832, op. cit.
4. Rev. Mortimer O'Sullivan (1793-1859). B. Clonmel, s. of a RC schoolmaster; ed. Mr Carey, BA TCD 1816, MA 1826, BD and DD 1837; St Stephen's, Dublin 1824-7 (JB Leslie and WJR Wallace, *Clergy of Dublin and Glendalough, Biographical Succession Lists,* Dublin 2001, p. 945); Walter Blake Kirwan (1754-1805), formerly a professor in Louvain, conformed in 1787, Preb. Howth, St Patrick's Cathedral 1789-99, Dean of Killala 1800-05, famous preacher (Ibid 1801).
5. General, afterwards Sir George, Cockburn, of Shanganagh Castle, Co. Wicklow.
6. Elizabeth, daughter of the ill-fated and mysterious Ralph Marshall (op. cit.), who m. Robert Leeson, one of the family of the Earl of Milltown.
7. Sir Edward Denny, 4th Bart (1796-1889), High Sheriff of Kerry 1827. Succeeded his father 1831.
8. Knight of Kerry.
9. Pages are missing for most of April and all of May.
10. Henry Joy, described as 'a determined Protestant' (Brian Jenkins, *Era of Emancipation,* Kingston and Montreal, 1988, p.246), and 'a strong politician of the anti-Catholic school' (Roderick O'Flanagan, *The Lives of the Lord Chancellors and Keepers of the Great Seal of Ireland,* 2 vols., vol. 2 1870, p. 513), succeeded William Conyngham Plunket as Attorney General. Joy was Solicitor General from the time when Plunket became Attorney General.
11. Thomas Langlois Lefroy, future chief justice of the court of Queen's Bench
12. John Doherty became Solicitor General; he was pro-Catholic. What appears in the Ms. is this cryptic remark: 'The promotion of Doherty, a very deserving man, will gratify me much; but a Halbert wod be a good thing, better for himself than this Jebb, this invidious Stride.'
13. The departure after twenty years of Lord Manners, the Lord Chancellor of Ireland, was signalled when George Canning's pro-Catholic administration replaced that of Lord Liverpool in April 1827. Manners sat for the last time in the Irish Court of Chancery on 31 July. His successor was Sir Anthony Hart (O'Flanagan, *Lord Chancellors,* vol. 2, p. 367).
14. Richard Mahony, son of Margared Day, daughter of Archdeacon Edward Day of Beaufort, who m. (1796) John Mahony of Dromore Castle, near Kenmare. This John Mahony and the then Robert Day were delegates at the Volunteer convention in November 1783 in the Rotunda. Richard dunm 21 June 1827 (Burke's *Irish Family Records*).
15. FitzGerald resigned office in 1807 and, remaining true to the cause of Emancipation, remained out of office until Canning appointed him a Lord of the English Treasury.
16. Barrister Robert Day. There is a letter from Judge Day in Day papers, dated June 1822, in which Day seeks the position of assistant barrister for this nephew and namesake, described by him as 'a good Crown lawyer'. It appears that at the time of the Judge's resignation in early 1819 an offer of a baronetcy was made to him by the Chancellor on behalf of the Lord Lieutenant, Lord Talbot; Day declined the offer in order to favour the other Robert Day, 'a very meritorious Nephew of my own name, well known to the Chancellor, upon whom our capricious profession has frowned'; he counter-offered, 'that an Assistant Barrister's or a Police Magistrate's situation conferred upon him I should consider as a favour conferred upon myself' (RIA, Day papers, Ms. 12w7, Merrion Sq., 1 June 1822).
17. Gervais Parker Bushe, son of Gervais Parker Bushe, Kilfane, Co. Kilkenny, and Mary, sister of Henry Grattan. He was Assistant Barrister for Co. Kilkenny.
18. There are a number of Howleys and Howlins at this time in the law; Day appears unclear which name he means to write; the name which appears as Gervy Bushe's successor in the assistant-barristership of Kilkenny is that of Richard Farrell of 34 Nth. Gt. George's St, Dublin. (*Dublin Directory* 1828.)
19. William Conyngham Plunket, 1st Baron Plunket (1764-1854). Noted orator and pro-Catholic parliamentary activist, neighbour of Day at Old Connaught. MP Dublin University 1812; made a memorable speech in 1813 in favour of Catholic relief; tabled the Catholic relief bill of 1821 which passed the Commons. Appointed Attorney General by Marquis Wellesley as part of a policy to balance Catholic and Protestant interests. Appointed Chief Justice of the Court of Common Pleas after Canning, PM, induced Lord Norbury to resign. Lord Chancellor of Ireland 1830.
20. William Lamb (1779-1848), appointed Chief Secretary of Ireland by Canning; pro-Catholic; as Lord Melbourne became Prime Minister 1834. While in Ireland as Chief Secretary (1827-8), Lamb formed

a relationship with the wife of the clergyman peer William, 4th and last Lord Branden (referred to by Day in the final pages here); she was Elizabeth, dau. of David la Touche of Marlay, Co. Dublin, therefore, apparently, sister of the Knight of Kerry's wife. She lived apart from her husband. 'Melbourne spent almost every evening with her when in Dublin: in the following year she settled in London, where he continued to visit her.' An action for 'criminal conversation' was brought by Rev. Lord Branden in the summer of 1829, which was thrown out. (David Cecil, *Melbourne*, combined edn. of *The Young Melbourne* and *Lord M.*, London 1955, p. 168.)

21. William Magee, Archbishop of Dublin 1822-31.

‘My late Inconsolable Misfortune’:
the illness and the death of Lady Denny

1828 Tu. New Year’s Day - never has there been a more genial December. Some gales & a day or two of rain - but no snow, frost or any other severity of weather. Mrs. Talbot & family join our happy little party at dinner - a cheerful little Christmas party - our 4 girls & 4 men walk long walks every day & every night dance quadrilles. I like to see young folks innocently gay & happy.

Saturday 12 January. Robert Day arrives – brings an alarming account of his dear mother’s state of health. God avert so sad a calamity for her helpless family as her death!
Sun. 13 Jan. Simultaneous meetings throughout Ireland of the Roman Catholics after mass to petition Parliament for Emancipation – dangerous measure, showing the Body their physical strength and the facility to assemble themselves on this occasion by the mandate of the Catholic Pandemonium at the suggestion of the little fiend Sheil by the instrumentality of their Priests. They separated however peaceably.

M. 21 A mosaic Ministry formed last Friday – the Duke of Wellington Premier – but Peel probably the real minister. Happy are those like myself who a beneficent Providence has placed above the storm.

Sunday 27th Jan. 1828. Received a letter from poor Maurice FitzGerald announcing his resignation of office and going out with Lord Lansdowne, though the Duke of Wellington, the Premier, earnestly urges him to stay. Considering his straits this step must be allowed to be chivalrous and worthy of a true Knight of Kerry. Would he could remain in! but what signifies office without character? And in England ratting next to sodomy perhaps is the most disgraceful deed a politician can commit.

4 Febr. We dine with the Borroweses Mer. Sq. & return home in quite a juvenile style at 10 clock in the morning.
Mon 11. Being drawn for this day to dine at the King’s Inns I take my wife & Lucy Stokes to town resolving to spend the week at Morrison’s

May 1828. My late inconsolable misfortune[1] which took place 29th of last month having made it necessary for me to leave home where one single afflicting subject engrosses my mind I resolve on slipping the scene and crossing the water for an indefinite time. Accordingly my dear Mary and myself take leave of sweet Loughlinstown on Whitsum morning 26 May, and fearing to be intercepted by Dublin friends we drive through without bating strait to Howth and spend the night at McDoole's – pas grand chose. The better course however from Loughlinstown would be to sleep at Morrison's and from there to start early so as to reach the steam boat by 8 a.m. at which hour it proceeds, and not to stop at Howth where my mind was brooding all the night upon the impending passage and sea sickness.

June 3 Tuesday. Drive to Shrewsbury and stop (as I never fail to do while well treated) at the Talbot Inn Jobson for the night – 18 miles, a large and well regulated establishment, yet very reasonable and moderate in the charges. Much improved in that particular since my last visit in September 1825. Distance from Holyhead…108 m. This venerable old city is almost insulated by the Severn, forming a quasi horseshoe round it. My original purpose was to turn into the Worcester Road to visit the afflicted family[2] bereaved of their most inestimable armament and share in their inconsolable misfortune. But I am prohibited by…[3] So we pursue the London road and drive to the nice little inn at Haygate.
6 Friday to Wolverhampton 12 miles. Stop for the night at Birmingham Royal Hotel –Saturday 7th The Royal Hotel turns out to be a dear house – tho' surrounded by collieries they charge 3 or 4 for sitting room – but what is worse, their post is execrable backstrap. However this is better than its neighbour the Swan. Breakfast most comfortably at Meriden, a beautiful spot and passing through Coventry we proceed to Dunchurch and stop at the old Dun Cow. Those 2 houses, not quite so good as the Royal Hotel, are infinitely to be preferr'd for every thing a rational traveller can desire. This day's journey amounts to 12 and 17…29 m.
M. 9th After 2 days of refreshing relaxation for our good steeds at this modest moderate & comfortable Inn of Dunchurch we start as usual before breakfast for Daventry, commonly pronounced Daintry & stop at the Wheat Sheaf - Wilson, where we bate for breadfast. After two hours proceed on to Towcaster & refresh the horses for an hour. The county of Northampton singularly beautiful – not so wooded as Warwickshire but sufficiently so for beauty and more diversified by hills and valleys. The whole county is one grand demesne. The weather singularly genial both for travellers and farmers – alternate rain and sunshine, an agreeable breeze, no dust. The personal wealth of England increases every year. Everyone is in comfort and at ease in this happy island. Nothing here is in a state of decay. You find as you travel along every place and every person progressively improving. What a contrast with the poor island we have left. While England is progressing, why is Ireland, with such superiority of climate, soil, rivers, harbours, and let me add people, retrograding? Why, but because she has been for centuries, indeed since her connexion with England, scandalously mis-govern'd. Stop for the night at the Cock Stony Stratford, now kept by Clara, formerly by my old acquaintance the Widow Forfeit. My excellent poor friend Sir Jonathan Lovett escorted me hither in her time from Liscombe on my last visit above 40 years ago to this cheerful sociable Mansion of my friend in my way to Dublin. We sat up so late that the Mail Coach from London call'd for me & took me up at midnight half-undress'd half asleep.[4]

Tuesday 10th dispatch an express across the country with a line to Lady Lovett to say "that we are thus far arrived and propose to present ourselves to my dear friend

of Liscombe before dinner tomorrow". We pay this visit in discharge of a long engagement, & in compliance with the kind & importunate invitation of my old friend & contemporary Lady Lovett, the widow of my poor departed class-fellow Sir Jonathan.
2 o'clock. The answer arrives from her Ladyship expressing infinite gratification at the prospect of receiving us tomorrow.
W. 11th Start at 11 for Liscombe. The Cock is a very respectable, reasonable house, the most reasonable I have met with on this road, cheap, assiduous and excellent accommodation for 2 days. Arrive at Liscombe at 2 – are received with impatient cordiality by my old friend and contemporary, Lady Lovett, and her 2 daughters at their fair castellated mansion emboson'd in a noble, well-wooded park. Sir Jonathan, her late husband, was my class fellow in College, and from that hour to this death in Jany 4 1812 we lived on terms of warm & uninterrupted friendship. On opening a book of my Charges lying here upon the table I find the following passage in his handwriting in the title-page. "The Gift of the Author to his friend Sir Jon. Lovet Bart. I prize as it deserves this mark of the Author's regard; & I am proud to say that this benevolent & wise man was the chosen friend of my youth as well as the admired one of my age. Jonathan Lovett."
The good Lady expects us to spend the summer her. We compromise for a fortnight - & agree to remain till Monday 23rd.

Mon 23rd Part with our dear friends with many sincere & cordial protestations reciprocally of friendship, & a promise on our part to give Her Ladyship a longer portion of time upon our return. Stop the night at White Hart, St. Alban's – 22 miles thro Leighton, Hockliff and Dunstable, passing thro the stupendous ravine or gap cut down thro the Chalk Hill west of Dunstable, and the noble Causeway raised across the valley.
Tu. 24 June – Breakfast at the Green Man, Barnet, and arrive in Town at 1 o'clock. Drive to Holm's Hotel, no 16 Parliament St. where we take first floor for £3.3 p week or, rather, 9s a night.
Wed 25th My first steps in London mechanically take me to Westminster Hall – the Courts are altogether newly modell'd. From Westminster Hall I loung'd into St. James' Park. Buckingham House is yet too little advanced to be intelligible, at least to be a fit subject for criticism but promises to be a heavy piece of architecture, worthy of Sir John Vanburgh. This specimen as well as his fantastical Pavilion at Brighton gives one but a poor opinion of the Royal taste in building - It is to be hoped that Edward's noble Windsor Castle will not be spoil'd in H.M's & Master Wyatville's[5] hands. The Park is likely to be essentially improved – the Water particularly, in wch a very pretty island has been formed, & wch it wod seem is to be surrounded wth forest trees& flowering shrubs – The 3 Parks furnish materials for excelling far the Tuilleries if thrown together; but there seems to be as little taste here for gardening as for building.
Fr. 27th visit my friends Forrest, Harman & Watts in the City. Drive to see Mr. & Mrs Gribble, & New Ormond St., Queen's Square viz. my amiable young grand-niece Maria Marshall, who on her way to her uncle & aunt Sir J Franks Calcutta, formed on

board ship a happy match with the first Mate. His father who is Captain of an Indiaman & owner of another recd. me very kindly & conducted me up to poor Maria who is return'd in very delicate health - she gives a very unfavorable account of John Frank's health & says his is reduced to half his Irish size. Would that the poor fellow's pilgrimage was expired & that he was safe-landed at home!
I work'd my way into the Opera pit last night wth much labour & bodily exertion & suffering. But I was well rewarded by the exquisite treat of the night - the divine Pasta in Nina, & the more divine Sontag in La Cenerentola - The former acted her mad character as well as sung beyond any other female I had ever seen - but in the afterpiece succeeded Sontag who sung as well & acted also well, & if in acting inferior ran away with the House with her youth & beauty. The former is a fine Italian of a certain age with piercing black eyes & thick black hair - the latter is quite a British beauty with soft blue eyes thick brown hair & probably not exceeding 20 yrs. There is a modest unconscious simplicity in the style of the latter that with great personal pretensions make her quite fascinating.
Sat 28th Spend the morning in returning visits- to Talbot, Grattan, Godfrey, Stoughton &c.
Mon. 30th June. Mrs Day and I devote the forenoon to visiting Archdeacon Pott at Kensington, the Pattersons and poor Maria Gribble who I fear is in very critical health; & the Evening to a very agreeable dinner party at Henry Grattans, 22 Bentinck St. - The Pott family are gone to Exeter, of which Diocese he is Chancellor, and I learn at the house that Mr. Salmon, married to the Archdeacon's and my niece (Sam Pott's daughter) and who returned last winter with a shattered constitution from India, has just died. Very sorry!

July, Wednesday 2nd No subject so engrosses the public conversation now as the co. of Clare election, which commenced I believe yesterday. It is generally believed that Vesey FitzGerald will be rejected and Danl O'Connell brought in upon the general enthusiasm and the shoulders of the sans culotte 40 s freeholders;[6] FitzGerald's own tenants are among the rest. He realises that if returned he must sit and that in the United Parliament no oath can be put to him; and it is confidently said that Chas. Butler and other eminent lawyers concur in such opinion. Though I lament FitzGerald's disappointment, the happy effect of O'C's return (if those lawyers be correct, which I greatly doubt) would be quite consolatory; for it would at once and without further struggle accomplish Emancipation – and thus terminate an abominable discussion which, if continued, will gradually metamorphose the Island of Saints into a wilderness of wild beasts.

Th. 3d Maurice FitzGerald had this evening a benefit on our parliamentary stage in which he performed the principal part with great success. His object was to establish that Messrs. Pitt, Cornwallis and Castlereagh had given a Pledge to the Catholics to obtain for them Emancipation in consideration of the Union. Peel candidly admits that Pitt could never have carried that vital Measure without the Catholic aid, and that the great Minister had done every thing short of giving a Pledge – had by his splendid speeches raised their expectations, had laboured to obtain the measure for them, had laid down his political life in their cause – but had never bound himself by any Pledge. It struck me that the Knight sustained his case conclusively; and has done in that debate great good to the Catholic cause. – But the Goliath O'Connell is to do all – first come in for Clare on the shoulders of the 40/- freeholders led (misled) by their Priests in exclusion of Vezey FitzGerald who has for 20 years most uniformly and consistently supported their cause.

Sun. 13 My nephew Lieut. Col. Day,[7] just arrived from India.
M. 14th My excellent friend & kinsman Stephen Rice[8] arrives & spends the day with us all the way from Brighton.
T. 15th I omitted to notice yesterday the sudden appearance of Sir Edward Denny in my drawing room –"What! To console with you upon the recent loss of your dear sweet daughter, his wife – to console you for this unconsolable misfortune by a pathetic recital of her virtues, of her Christian patience and resignation under her long and painful sufferings, and of the impressive example exhibited by her on her death bed to her surrounding family, that faith in the atonement of Christ exemplified by steady, well-doing and intense obedience to his laws is the sure road to salvation!" No such thing! He came with his attorney to demand of me an account of £2000 which he raised upon the estate in 18- on his son's starting for Kerry,[9] and which he asserted pass'd thro' my hands without accounting for it. That is, he came to insult and pick the pocket (as he attempted once before to do in the case of the sale of his seats to Moore and Fletcher[10]) of his aged Father-in-law whose poor ill-fated daughter has fallen victim to his vicious habits and infatuated waste of property[11] so ruinous to his family and subversive of every shred of personal character.

Wed 30 Poor Jas Cuff died[12] at 2 this morning at his house in Whitehall Place of a virulent cholera morbus and vacates Tralee.
Fr 8th August. Poor Cuff's death having created vacancy for Tralee, I write to Pierce Chute, the Provost, proposing Mr. Vesey FitzGerald for our representative. I write also to Edward Denny pressing him to write to Arthur Rowan the Burgess to muster strong at the election, as Dan the Liberator, Agitator General, threatens to enact the Farce of Clare at Tralee.[13] Holmes[14] has call'd upon me from the Duke of Wellington to return his thanks.

1. *The Kerry Evening Post* of 3 May, 1828, reported that Lady Denny's death took place on 26 of April, the place Kingsend House, Worcester.
2. The residence of the widowed Sir Edward and his family, Kingsend House, near Worcester.
3. words crossed out
4. The gist of the story here is that he left his trunk at the Cock but it was sent on to meet him at the Pigeon House by another and quicker mailcoach and a second vessel after he left Holyhead.
5. James Wyatt (1746-1813), architect of improvements on the House of Lords and Windsor Castle at this time, and responsible for the Pavilion at Brighton for George IV.
6. *Parliamentary Papers*, 'Reports from Committees: Vol 7, Disturbances in Ireland', 13 May–18 June 1824, Rt Hon. Lord Viscount Palmerston in the Chair, PP. 246-266. Testimony of Mr Justice Day, 2 June 1824: 'The 40/- freeholder in Ireland votes out of a lease, and that lease is of the smallest possible quantity of property, either perhaps a cabin or a very small piece of ground for a potato garden, and out of that, on which he barely subsists, it is, that this independent constituent is

supposed to be entitled to vote; he is registered upon his positive affidavit out of this wretched holding as a freeholder worth 40/- a year; this surely is but a mockery of a freehold. He and his brethren are driven by the landlord to the hustings as a salesman driving his flock into the market.'

7. Lieut. Col. Edward Day, Bengal Infantry.
8. Stephen Edward Rice (op. cit.), of Mt. Trenchard, Co. Limerick.
9, Reference to the failure of young Edward Denny (future 4th Bart.) to win the county in the general election of 1818. He appears to have forgotten the year.
10 William Fletcher was returned to the Irish parliament for Tralee in 1795, Arthur Moore in 1797. Both were legal figures, Fletcher later a judge. Their selection is clearly attributable to the influence of Robert Day with his son-in-law Sir Edward Denny. Tralee returned two members to the Irish House of Commons, and one to Westminster after the Act of Union.
11. A line is drawn in the manuscript through the words 'ill-fated' and 'has fallen victim to his vicious habits and infatuated waste of property'. One possibility is that he repents their use.
12. James Cuff, of Deel Castle, Co. Mayo (op. cit.), MP Tralee from May 1819 to his death.
13. The 'farce of Clare' (O'Connell's victory over Vesey FitzGerald in July 1828) was not re-enacted in Tralee. Sir Edward Denny, 3rd Bart., was elected on 12 September 1828 to succeed James Cuff. He was succeeded by Robert Vernon Smith, of Savile Row, county of Middlesex, in June 1829. Smith was re-elected in August 1830. O'Connell's return for Clare was the event which forced the concession of Catholic Emancipation in 1829.
14. William Holmes (d. 1851), born in Sligo of an Offaly family; 'For thirty years "Billy Holmes" was the adroit and dexterous whip of the Tory party ... a most skilful dispenser of patronage and party manager' (DNB).

'A feast under which the very table groan'd': Twilight of life in Magunihy and Clanmaurice

Day arrives in Kerry in time for the Assizes. The Kerry Evening Post of 8 August carried the following: 'We are happy to announce the arrival this morning, in this his native town, of our highly respected and venerated countryman Judge Day, in perfect health. If a life devoted to the honourable discharge of every social duty, as a benevolent landlord, a good countryman, and a liberal and kind hearted friend can ensure public esteem and affection, we can truly say that his hearty welcome to his native county must be general and sincere.' On this return to Kerry he meets his two sons by Mary FitzGerald, John and Edward. More is known of John, but Edward appears as his fathers land agent for his property in Kerry. It appears that while in the county they provide their father's security escort.

1829 August. Sat 1st. Leave Dublin for Kerry.

The Inn at Backlane (after Monasterevin) kept very well by Power, son in law and successor to the Graves family whom I remember here and at Maryborough for 70 years back.

Tu. 4th reach Limerick about one The country is improved considerably since my last visit in 1826 - the old plantations grown luxuriantly & many new plantations added

W. 5 Meet the Liberator, exulting in his recent victory in Clare. "You have succeeded with the Multitude by agitation, clamour & vituperation, & the unexpected & incredible event justified no doubt those means wch to every man of education & sentiment appear'd most unjustifiable. But having achiev'd our object & equalized politically all our fellow-subjects, let us calm & compose the troubled waters. Let the agitation subside & with it all the mud wch it threw up to the surface, & the enlighten'd & rational classes of society resume their due station & ascendancy in the state. Let the plebians, the Ignobile Vulgus upon whose shoulders you have hitherto been borne, disperse & return to their plows their looms & their spades. Let us in a word sit down in harmony & concord & feast upon the sweet fruits of our triumph. Let us enjoy together the benefits of this great Measure & now co-operate hand & heart in promoting the prosperity of our struggling common country."

The Agitator smiling nodded assents, & we parted. Nous verons.

Drive with a wretched pair of hacks to my good friend Tom Lloyd's near Rathkeale- we spend a very agreeable time there.

Th. 6 After breakfast start with a more wretched pair of horses. Young Tom FitzGerald & his Bror seized us & conducted us down to Ballydonoghue House to a very good dinner, where we were most agreeably surprised to find Marian Harte & a large family of lads & lasses just returned after 2 years absence from Florence- all looking very well. Mrs. FitzGerald, once the fair Anne Harte, seems delicate in health and impaired a little in looks.

Proceed to Listowel, where we arrive at about ten & are very cordially & impatiently recd. by Richd FitzGerald & his good wife.

F.7th Consent, in atonement for breaking our engagement to dine with them yesterday, to spend this day with the FitzGeralds, &

Sat. 8th We start - no, not start, but with the most wretched pair of horses we creep away after breakfast for Tralee Barracks. Find our hospitable friends at the Barracks all well - they insist on our giving up Dicksgrove & remaining with them. We compromise, & form this compact: to remain here till after the Assizes, proceed then to Meredith's[1] & after a few weeks at that side & satiating myself with Magonihy to return hither early next month, give our friends here & in the neighbourhood 2 or 3 weeks, then visit a few friends to the northwd & about the first week of Oct. set of by leisurely marches for the Capital.

Sund 9th John & Edwd join us in high bloom - John as the Junior Rector[2] of the diocese preach'd the late Visitation Sermon & I hear from all quarters very creditably.

W. 12th. Seized suddenly with a serious pulmonary affection & can scarcely speak or walk. Send as usual for Purdon.[3]

Th 13th a restless night - unable to repose on either side - 20 leeches are prescribed & applied to my chest, & no sooner are they removed distended with blood than I was relievd as if by magic. This bleeding near the region affected & a good scarafuning produce the desired effect.

Sat. 15th We take an airing & visit John's Lodge - very bad!

Sund 16th Torrens J. Steph. Rice & other friends pour in to see their invalid friend.

Mon. 17th O'Grady C.B.[4] arrives & Torrens[5] opens the Assizes.

Tu 25th Part wth our excellent friends of the Barracks - proceed to Dicksgrove. Wm. Meredith receives us very cordially & we agree upon a plan of Joint-housekeeping: I to find my own hay & oats, sheep wine, groceries & numerous presents of salmon, poultry, honey &c wch pour in from my tenants upon me whenever I visit Kerry.

Th. 27th Intelligence is just arrived of the marriage of Lieut Col. Day to Mary, eldest daur of the late Patk. Trant at Ramsay, Isle of Man, on the 19th inst.

Sunday 30th accompany Meredith & family to Killeentierna church - what a precious Rector have they got in the Rt. Honble & Revd Lord Baron Brandon.[6] By address & management he has screw'd up this benefice of Castleisland on his late composition to £1900 a yr; & tho' it covers almost a barony he resisted with all his might the erection of a second church. It has been done however malgre lui; but to his present curate Mr. Ware, encumber'd with a numerous family, the poor Rector can afford but £75 a year! Why does not the Bishop[7] appoint under the Statute a sallary proportiond to the Rector's income? But the poor Bp is paralytic & of course incapable of any energy - then why does not his Vicar Genl., Mr. Forster? He is inexcusable.

Monday 31th. We pay a visit pursuant to invitation to Mrs. Arabella Day now resident at Kilcolman Abbey. Edwd FitzGerald our outrider attends us - cordially recd.

Sept Tu. 1 Drive early after breakfast to Glanagillah[8] accompanied by 3 outriders- that same Edward & John & Robt Godfrey Day, two excellent young men - great progress made in reclaiming that endless bog & mountain – a chain of Lodges & villas begins to occupy the shore of the Cara (or Dear) Lake possessing beautiful views of that bold & wild scene - viz. Drew, Williams, Peter Foley & Collis, to be followed next season by Newton, Priest Foley & Ol. Stokes. In 10 years I despair not of its rivalling Killarney; provided we can awaken the slumbering Nymph Echo of Glencar. On our return we met by appointment my good woman & my sweet God nieces Margt & Ellen Day at dinner at Michael Foley's who gave us a feast under which the very table groan'd - in the evening a choice Piper greeted us with some excellent melodies & jiggs wch drew out some merry pairs of thorough-bred dancers in succession, & after a very useful forenoon & a very agreeable afternoon we return'd to Kilcolman.

Th 3 Return to Dicksgrove to dinner - pass thro the Fair at Castlemaine, & visit Clonmelane en passant –

Th 10 after a monotonous week among Freeholders & Tenants we take a drive to Killarney to taste the charms of that enchanting Region. Drove to Flesk Castle (sometimes styled Drumhooper Castle - quaere wch. is best?), the magnificent & commanding chateau of Mr. Coultsman on the Muckruss road, to the beautiful House & demesne that Lord Headley is now constructing at Minisky on the junction of the Beaufort & Miltown roads- & oh, how the Cumberland & Scotch Lakes & their boasted beauties dwindle in comparison wth the surrounding scenery of Killarney!

Tu 22 Leave Dicksgrove for good after spendng there 4 profitable weeks - poor little Kate in the very extremity of a decline. On our progress visit Marshalls of the Mainbridge, Edwd Nash,[9] & I the Kerry Pippin who is out - John attending us as outrider, & Edwd remaining behind impounded by the good nature of Wm. Meredith - meet as usual with the most cordial reception at the Barracks.

W. 23 Edwd arrives from Dicksgrove wth advice of poor Kate's release last night for a better world. So that our departure yesterday was critically in articulo mortis & left the family at large to prepare the last tribute of affection in this life to the departed Innocent whom let us trust in the mercy of God thro his blessed Son we shall hereafter meet in bliss!

Th 24. Drive to Tralee & visit some friends - what a deplorable ruin is poor Stephen Henry Rice become![10] Two men of such unparallell'd memories this county perhaps has never produced before as Rice & my beloved friend Dick Herbert, & now alas! What an intellectual wreck do those talented individuals exhibit! It may be that the sharpness of the blade has worn out & destroy'd the sheath.

"But pray, Sir, who is this Lord Headley that I hear you celebrate so often?" Why sir, His Ldp is a singular character, no less than an English Absentee; a curiosity amongst us, tho numerous on the continent as grains of sand on the shore. Lord H. is son of the late Mr. Winn not Wynne once a Welsh Judge, not a Welsh man aftewards created an Irish Peer, who married Miss Blennerhassett & in her right became seizd of a valuable estate in the Co. of Kerry, possessing besides his own hereditary estates in Yorkshire & Hampshire on wch he resided to his death. On that event the son, succeeding to the title & inheritances English & Irish, took an early opportunity of visiting his maternal property; the romantic & bold scenery of wch so struck him that

The Franciscan Friary, Ardfert.

resolving to reclaim it at once sat down in the heart of the wildest & most lawless territory of his estates & built but a farmer's lodge. Instantly he set about the great work of improvement & reform, & whilst every other Peer of Kerry were draining the county of its currency & produce to waste & squander in foreign climes (Lord Lansdowne, Kenmare, Ventry, even the poor Lord Branden as well as the rich Lord Listowel) this Englishman was empolyd in draining the morasses & bogs of his wild estate, in clothing mountains with flourishing plantations, in usurping hundreds of acres by stupendous embankment from old Father Neptune, parceling out a rude territory of hitherto unproductive & barren lands into tillage & pasture farms. From this expenditure of mints of money a magical effect has resulted. A savage & ferocious population amongst whom the King's Writ never ran nor warrant was ever executed have been metamorphosd into an orderly, well-regulated industrious Peasantry. He has already completed the shell of an elegant mansion upon a plan & elevation by Pain on his estate of Minnisky commanding a splendid view of the Lower Lake & its various islands, particularly the Prince of all, Enisfallen.

Satr 26th We start upon a cruise to the North West in discharge of some of our numerous engagements. This day we dine and sleep with Geo and Marianne Stokes at their very pretty Lodge of Ardglass.

S. 27th Breakfast at Churchill with Henry Denny[11] who gives us a cordial reception and acquits himself considering his short standing in the pulpit very promisingly. After prayers we proceed to Barrow and spend the day and night with my worth old school fell and friend Jack Collis[12] of the advanced age of 89 and who I was happy to find in the enjoyment of general good health; only somewhat impaired in memory, as appeared from his repetition more than once of the same decies repetita story. Probably he and I are the two oldest gentlemen now in Kerry. His white headed nephew, old Ned Collis, another Banna School boy swell the number of ...[13] at table, the three making together 249 years.

M. 28th After breakfast we pay a visit to Mrs. Crosbie[14] at Ardfert and after a couple of agreeable hours proceed to Robert and Elizabeth Stokes at their comfortable farm house at Banna - are join'd at dinner by Major & Mrs. Craster, Lieuts Aclam & Vereker & Mrs. & Miss Crosbie & their friend Miss Stack - in the evening comes a female reinforcement and it was spent in music and dancing – a very gay lively party – the gentlemen however indulg'd too freely in their libations to Bacchus. It was curious and quite satisfactory to find that so polite and agreeable party could be assembled amidst the wilds and sandhills that border the Atlantic. What pleasant recollections did Banna bring with it, where my old school stood and where in 1754 at the age of 8 my good father, a Protestant gentleman, placed me under a R. C. schoolmaster where the most respectable gentry of the county sent their children, a moral conscientious old gentleman and where I formed my first acquaintance with Johnny Crosbie afterwards Earl of Glandore.

Tu. 29th Michaelmas day. After breakfast we proceed to Ardfert Abbey & eat our Michs. Goose & pass a quiet, comfortable day with Mrs. Crosbie & family consisting of William[15] & John[16] (12 & 10 yrs old) & Anne & Diana, two sweet girls. She kndly sends for my old friend of Frederick St. memory, Kitty Crosbie of Ballyheige, to meet me - I visit that fine ruin, the old Abbey,[17] & transcribe from her tomb the following epitaph upon poor dear Lady Glandore, composed by my much honour'd & dearly-beloved friend & relative, her husband: '*Johannes Crosbie Comes de Glandore Hujusce Caenobii Exstirpe Frius Fundatoris Tumulum juxta positum Sibi Restauraii Curavit Anno Salutis 1812.*' [18]

W.30th Rise early & traverse & retrace the much-loved scenes of my boyish youthful & adult life with emotions of mingled pleasure & pain. Many a happy Sunday have I spent here from the neighbouring school of Banna wth my dear schoolfellow & early & late friend Johnny Crosbie; cherish'd by his father Willm. Crosbie & still more by his excellent & virtuous mother, Lady Theodosia Crosbie, daur. of th Earl of Darnley,[19] who always distinguish'd her own & her son's favourite by the flattering appellation of "Honest Robin Day", a testimonial of wch. down even to my old age I have never ceased to be proud. The fruit of that early school connection was the most cordial & disinterested friendship of John Crosbie (afterwards Lord Baron Branden, Viscount Crosbie & Earl of Glandore) thro' life; returning me twice to Parliament for his borough, a free agent & without any consideration, in preference of any gentleman of his own name, & thus laying the foundation of my future growth & unmerited elevation.

1. One of the Judge's aunts (the *nine Geraldines*), Honoria FitzGerald, married Richard Meredith of Dicksgrove, a house where the writer spends much of his time during the visit

recorded here. Day drew up the family's marriage settlements, as he did for so many of his relatives. *The Hibernian Chronicle,* 1 Nov. 1770 reports the marriage of Richard Meredith and Lucy Saunders 2nd daughter of Arthur Saunders of Currenee (sic); Richard Meredith and Lucy Meredith, otherwise Saunders, appear in a deed of 1797 (Registry of Deeds, book 519, page 399, number 340685).

2. James B. Leslie, *Ardfert and Aghadoe,* gives the following: John Robert FitzGerald Day, son of Judge Day, born Dublin, entered Trinity College, Dublin, 2 November 1812 aged 15; ordained 1821, Rector Ballymacelligott 1828-52, thereafter of Kilbonane. Married Lucy Jane, daughter of Venerable William Thompson, Archdeacon of Cork and had issue. RIA, Day papers, ms. 12w17, Saturday 11 Jan. 1832: 'O dies faste! (suggests what follows to be an entry in *Evening Post*) This morning was married at St. Peter's Church, by the Revd. Edward FitzGerald, the Revd. J. R. FitzGerald, Rector of B. (sic, Ed.) in the co. of Kerry to Lucy Jane, 2nd daughter of the Venerable Archdeacon of Cork. After the ceremony we drive to breakfast at her grand-aunt Mrs. Hamilton's, Hatch Street.' Irish Genealogical Office Ms. 107 Copy of grant of arms to the Rev. John Robert FitzGerald and Rev. Edward FitzGerald, both of Springhill, Co. Kerry, on their assuming under royal licence in compliance with the wishes of Robert Day of Leighlinstown, Co. Dublin, the name and arms of Day. Warrant dated 11 August, 1841.
3. Rowan Purdon, physician, Tralee (Holden's *Annual London and Country Directory 1811;* Pigot and Co. Directory 1824).
4. Chief Baron Standish O'Grady (op.cit.).
5. Justice Torrens presided at the Summer assizes of 1829 on the Munster circuit.
6. Rev. William Crosbie (1771-1832), 4th and last Baron Branden, Rector of Castleisland, was the son of the Dean of Limerick (op.cit.). His wife was Elizabeth La Touche, who was involved in a 'criminal conversation' with Lord Melbourne (William Lamb).
7. John Jebb was consecrated Bishop of Limerick (Ardfert amalgamated with Limerick in 1661) in January 1823, and died in December 1833. His brother was Richard Jebb who was appointed to the vacancy created by the resignation of Judge Day on the King's Bench in early 1819. Bishop Jebb succeeded Thomas Elrington; a statue of Jebb can be seen in Limerick's Cathedral.
8. A townland in Killorglin near Cara Lake where Judge Day's farms yielded an annual bulk rent of £200 (the Name Books of John O'Donovan). His son Rev. Edward FitzGerald (both he and his brother became FitzGerald Day on their father's decease) was his resident agent in these Killorglin townlands. Records for Rev. Edward's life are scarcer than those for his brother Rev. John.
9. An Edward Nash of Ballycarty (Esq.) was High Sheriff of Kerry in 1789 (*Freeman's Journal,* 12-14 March, 1789, and elsewhere).
10. *O'Connell Correspondence,* O'Connell to William Cunningham Plunkett, Cork 29 July 1826: 'Mr Rice, the assistant barrister (a man generally and deservedly beloved by all his acquaintances and by no person more than by me) has been chairman of that county (Kerry) for near thirty years, and his mental power so weakened and has fallen into ill health that he has become a mere nuisance.' He was retired by January 1829.
11. Rev. Henry Denny, Vicar Ballinahaglish (Churchill) 1830-1877; b. 1802, third son of Sir Edward Denny and Elizabeth Day. Rugby School, Matric Worcester College, Oxford. M. Sophia McGillycuddy, d. 1877 at Blennerville manor house where his son Rev. Edward was the curate. As his funeral passed through Tralee the bell of the Catholic church was rung: Leslie, *Ardfert and Aghadoe;* tradition of the bell, A. E. Stokes.
12. John Collis, of Barrow House; High Sheriff 1798 when briefly detained on suspicion of being a United Irishman.

13. The word used here appears frandavi.
14. Jane Lloyd of Beechmount, Co. Limerick was the widow of John Talbot-Crosbie (of Mount Talbot, Co. Roscommon) who inherited the estate of his uncle Lord Glandore and changed his surname from Talbot to Talbot-Crosbie. John Talbot-Crosbie died in 1816.
15. William Crosbie, later assumed Talbot-Crosbie, b. 1817.
16. John Crosbie, inherited Mount Talbot, Co. Roscommon, and reverted to the surname Talbot.
17. The ruined Franciscan Friary - not Abbey - at Ardfert.
18. He means to note Lady Glandore's (Diana Sackville) inscription which appears on the tomb: Depositum Dilectae Conjugis Dianae Comitessae Filiae Georgii Vicecomitis Sackville Augusussimi Regis Georgii III A secretis et a Sanctioribus Consilliis Ob. 29 August 1814 AE 58.
19. Theodosia Bligh, dau. 1st Earl of Darnley.

Appendix 1.

Report of Mr Day's speech at a meeting of the county of Kerry, summoned by the Sheriff Mr. Herbert of Muckruss, to celebrate the King's recovery, reported in the *Freeman's Journal* of April 16-18 1789.

He was aware that any arguments in support of the address were superfluous in a county always foremost in ardent loyalty to the best of Kings; but he could not repress his wish to enumerate a few of the constitutional and commercial blessings restored and conceded to Ireland in the course of the present reign. The first which occurred to him was the Octennial bill; that law first brought the democratic part of the constitution into action, and gave weight and energy to the people; till then the Commons were the very reverse of what they should be, dependant upon the Crown and independent of their constituents.

Next came the relaxation of the Popery laws, that code of unprecedented tyranny, those laws of Draco, conceived in cruelty and written in blood. This abominable pile has almost dissolved before the genial spirit of a tolerant and enlightened Parliament and of a benign and gracious Monarch. But the glories which followed it is impossible to contemplate without rapture – the revolution of 1782, when the privy Councils of the two kingdoms were expunged from your legislature, when you were emancipated from the usurpation of a foreign parliament, when your judges were made independent of the Crown and your army dependent upon the people, when you acquired the habeas corpus, when the West India trade was conceded to you and the commerce of the world thrown open to your industry. All this and more were done for you under the auspices of a benevolent Prince, the common and equal father of all his people.

Appendix 2.

State Trials. Oliver Bond. 23 and 24 July, 1798. ('Mr. Justice Chamberlain being much fatigued with the late sitting and the charge to the jury, requested of Mr Justice Day to pronounce the sentence'.)

Prisoner at the bar! After a very patient, dispassionate, and impartial trial, in the course of which you have had the assistance of as able, acute, and zealous counsel as the bar of Ireland affords, you have without hesitation been found guilty by a most respectable jury of your country of a crime at which every honourable and feeling heart recoils with horror – nothing less than a foul conspiracy with a society of remorseless traitors, of whom indeed you appear to have been a prime mover, whose acknowledged purpose was to wade through the best blood of the country to the subversion of the state, and to substitute for the British constitution (the source of all our comforts, prosperity and glory) a wild and fierce republic, upon the model of France. One natural, and no doubt foreseen, consequence of this flagitious plot has already taken effect, in the disastrous carnage of many thousands of our fellow-subjects, the unhappy and deluded victims of their ferocious and abandoned instigators and leaders.

It is a melancholy subject of reflexion, that a gentleman of your condition and figure in life, who, under the existing laws and constitution, which you would have subverted, have flourished and accumulated great property – in the prime of life and vigour of health – endued by nature with rare accomplishments of mind and person, should have unfortunately, not only for yourself and your afflicted family, but for the country to which you might have been an ornament, perverted those precious gifts of Providence, and have made so unhappy and calamitous a use of them. I am sure nothing is so far from my mind as to aggravate, by any terms of reproach, the sufferings of a gentlemen, fallen by his own criminal infatuation, from a proud eminence in society into the most abject and degraded state of which human nature is susceptible. Your own good understanding will open but too plentiful sources of bitter and agonizing reflection; but I trust it will awaken you, at the same time, to a due remorse and contrition. In that anxious wish, let me entreat of you to turn your back upon that world which is now closing fast upon you, to look forward to a brighter and a better world, into which you are soon to be launched, to make the only remaining atonement to your injured country by a full and candid disclosure of that malignant plot, and thus to give the best evidence of that deep and heart-felt sorrow, which is the only fit preparation for the awful presence of that just and merciful Judge, before whom you must shortly appear.

Nothing remains for me but, as the organ of the law, to perform a duty which I do with unaffected sympathy and concern, that of pronouncing the following dreadful sentence upon you:-

That you, Oliver Bond, be taken from the place in which you stand, to the gaol from whence you came, and thence to the common place of execution, there to be hanged by the neck, but not until you are dead, for while you are yet living, your bowels are to be taken out and thrown in your face, and your head is to be cut off, and your head and limbs to be at the king's disposal; and the Lord have mercy on your soul.

(Mr. Bond afterwards received a conditional pardon, but was carried off by an attack of apoplexy, before he had an opportunity of complying with the conditions.)

Appendix 3.

AN

A D D R E S S

DELIVERED TO THE

GRAND JURY

OF THE

COUNTY OF DUBLIN,

On Tuesday the 10th of January, 1797.

BY ROBERT DAY, ESQ. M. P.

ONE OF HIS MAJESTY'S COUNSEL LEARNED IN THE LAW, AND CHAIRMAN OF THE SAID COUNTY.

First published in Dublin at the request of the Magistrates and Grand Jury.

TO WHICH ARE ADDED,

Introductory *OBSERVATIONS* recommended to the attention of the PEOPLE of *GREAT BRITAIN.*

NORTH ALLERTON,
PRINTED BY J. LANGDALE, AND
DUBLIN,
RE-PRINTED BY RICHARD EDWARD MERCIER and CO. BOOKSELLERS TO THE HON. SOCIETY OF KING'S-INNS, AND TO BE SOLD AT THEIR SHOPS IN THE NEW COURTS, AND No. 31, ANGLESEA-STREET.

1797.

Appendix 4.

Extract from a letter of Judge Day, 13 June 1813, to Major General John Fitzmaurice (of Duagh House Co. Kerry) in the brigade of Wellington's 95th Rifles, from *Biographical Sketch of Major General John Fitzmaurice, K.H.*, written for private circulation by his son, 1908, Castel di Sorci, Anghiari, Italy. (Printed by Tiber Printing Press, pp. 36-39.)

I received your letter of the 3rd April with great pleasure and many thanks. It gives a clear and interesting detail of your army, its situation and prospects, and proves that you do not look superficially at the great and awful drama acting before you, but view it, as you ought, with a soldier's eye.

You have had indeed a very long and to us unaccountable interval of relaxation and rest. At a time when such heavy drafts have been made from the French army, and so considerable an accession of numbers and strength from the Spaniards to the Allied army, why we should have rested upon our arms through the whole winter and spring and never interrupted for such length of time the slumbers and repose of the enemy, is, I say, to us at a distance from the scene, unaccountable. I trust your next will give us the comfort of some active and brilliant operations.

The illustrious Wellington will add fresh laurels to his brows before he closes the campaign. I consider him a combination of the two great rival generals of old, Hannibal and Fabius, knowing alike when to attack and when to retreat and alike victorious in both. It is however unfortunate for the poor gentleman that he has not some of us wiseacres at his elbow to advise and guide him; some of our sage politicians or feather-bed soldiers, who are very brave over the bottle or on paper, and know a thousand times better than you blockheads on the spot what course ought to be taken. For instance, had I the command of the army, I should propose instantly to cross the Tormes (shouting 'hurrah' as I passed the glorious plains of Salamanca) and the Duoro, and breakfast at Valladolid upon some eight or ten thousand of the invincibles, make a luncheon of the garrison at Burgos or mask it, and march on through Vittoria (catching fresh courage from the name), dine at Bayonne; push on after dinner before nightfall for Bordeaux, and take my evening's claret with Barton and Johnson, and the other honest fellows there, at the fountain head. But I think seriously, if the Spaniards were true to themselves, and seconded sincerely and ardently "The Great Lord", as they rightly enough call him, I am sufficiently sanguine to hope he could not only drive the 'Grande Nation' and their invincible army like sheep out of the Peninsula before him, but would before the end of the campaign erect the standard of insurrection in France. Meanwhile in the North things are going retrograde. The allies have lost a great deal of ground but they have fought with infinite gallantry and skill; retreated with all the regularity of a field day after every action, without ever losing a gun or a pair of colours; killed, it is believed, many more than they have lost, are falling back upon their resources, and drawing the enemy from his, and will, I trust, shortly turn back upon him and force him to retrace his steps across the Elbe and even the Rhine. This I do not despair would be the final issue of the campaign, though the Crown Prince and Austria took no part; but the Crown Prince surely cannot prove so steeped in duplicity, so thorough a double dealer, as not to take an active part with us in the rear of the French army, after all the money he has had from us and after throwing away the scabbard, it would seem, with Bonaparte. In that case the latter placed between two fires must retreat precipitately and with infinite disaster. But if Austria joined the cause in which she, as well as the rest of Europe, has so deep an interest; were she to interpose her army from Bohemia, Bonaparte's retreat would become impracticable and he must capitulate. The latter course of events, perhaps, it would be too much to expect, but I repeat my confident hope, at all events, of a successful issue to the campaign.

Appendix 5.
Letter of Irish Judge Robert Day to James Prior, author of *The Life of Oliver Goldsmith* (1837, 2 vols.), vol 2, p 357-361.

Loughlinstown House,
20 February 1831.
Dear Sir,
I first became acquainted with Goldsmith in 1769, the year I entered the Middle Temple, where he had chambers; it was through the introduction of my friend and namesake, Mr., afterwards Sir John Day, who subsequently became Judge-Advocate General of Bengal.

The Poet frequented much the Grecian Coffee House, then a favourite resort of the Irish and Lancashire Templars, and delighted in collecting round him his friends, whom he entertained with a candid and unostentatious hospitality. Occasionally he amused them with his flute or whistle, neither of which he played well, particularly the latter, but in losing his money, he never lost his temper. In a run of bad luck and worse play he would fling his cards upon the floor and exclaim 'Bye-fore George I ought for ever to renounce thee, fickle, faithless Fortune!'

In person he was short, about five feet five or six inches; strong, but not heavy in make; rather fair in complexion, with brown hair, such at least as could be distinguished from his wig. His features were plain, but not repulsive, certainly not so when lighted by conversation. His manners were simple, natural, and perhaps on the whole we may say not polished, at least without the refinement and good breeding which the exquisite polish of his compositions would lead us to expect. He was always cheerful and animated, often indeed boisterous in his mirth; entered with spirit into convivial society; contributed largely to its enjoyments by solidity of information and the naivete and originality of his character; talked often without premeditation and laughed loudly without restraint.

Being then a young man I felt myself much flattered by the notice of so celebrated a person. He took great delight in the conversation and society of Grattan whose brilliancy in the morning of life furnished full earnest of the unrivalled splendour which awaited his meridian; and finding us dwelling together in Essex Court near himself where he frequently visited my immortal friend his warm heart became naturally possessed towards the associate of one whom he so much admired.

Just arrived as I then was from College, full freighted with academic gleanings, our

David Garrick as Richard III by William Hogarth

author did not disdain to receive from me some opinions and hints towards his Greek and Roman histories, light superficial works not composed for fame but compiled for the more urgent purpose of recruiting his exhausted finances. So in truth was his 'Animated Nature'. His purse replenished by labours of this kind, the season of relaxation and pleasure took its turn in attending the theatres, Ralelagh, Vauxhall and other scenes of gaiety and amusement, which he continued to frequent as long as his supply held out. He was fond of exhibiting his muscular little person in the gayest apparel of the day, to which was added a bag wig and sword.

This favourite costume involved him one morning in a short but comical dialogue in the Strand with two coxcombs, one of whom pointing to Goldsmith called to his companion in allusion to the poet's sword "to look at that fly with a long pin struck through it." Goldsmith instantly cautioned the passengers aloud against "that brace of disguised pickpockets", and having determined to teach those gentlemen that he wore a sword as well for defence from insolence as for ornament, he retired from the footpath into the coachway which admitted of more space and freedom of action, and half-drawing his sword beckoned to the witty gentleman armed in like manner, to follow him; but he and his companion thinking prudence the better part of valour, declined the invitation and sneaked away amid the hootings of the spectators.

Whenever his funds were dissipated, and they fled more rapidly from being the dupe of many artful persons, male and female, who practised upon his benevolence, he returned to his literary labours, and shut himself up from society to provide fresh matter for his bookseller and fresh supplies for himself.

I was in London when the 'Deserted Village' come out. Much had been expected from the author of 'The Traveller', and public expectation and impatience were not disappointed. In fact it was received with universal admiration, as one of the most fascinating and beautiful effusions of British genius.

His beautiful little 'Hermit', which by some persons had been fathered upon Johnson, and reputed to have been given by him to his protege to help the 'Vicar of Wakefield' into popularity, was by this time restored to the owner by the public, who had discovered ere now that he excelled in the art of poetry even his eminent patron.

His broad comedy 'She Stoops to Conquer' was received with scarcely less applause, though his friends Garrick and Colman had many misgivings of its success. His friends, of whom I was one, assembled in great force in the pit to protect it; but we had no difficulty to encounter; for it was received throughout with the greatest acclamation and had afterwards a great run.

I was also among those who attended his funeral, along with my friend John Day, Hugh Kelly and a few others who were summoned together rather hastily for the purpose. It had been intended that this ceremony should be of an imposing kind, and attended by several of the great men of the time, Burke, Reynolds, Garrick, and others. This determination was altered, I imagine from the pecuniary embarrassments of the deceased Poet; the last offices were therefore performed in a private manner, without the attendance of his great friends. He was interred in the Temple burial ground. Hugh Kelly, with whom he had not been on terms of intercourse for some years, shed tears over his grave, which were no doubt sincere; he did not then know that he had been slightingly mentioned in 'Retaliation', nor would he have been so noticed then could the deceased have anticipated the growth of good feeling. Slight circumstances often separate even the most deserving persons; nor are they perhaps conscious of the worth of each other until accidental circumstancs produce the discovery. - I have the honour (in great haste) to be, dear Sir,

Your faithful and obedient servant,

Rob. Day.

1. Hugh Kelly (1739-77), miscellaneous writer and theatre critic, born at Killarney, the son of a Dublin tavern keeper (DNB).

Appendix 6.

Letter to Henry Grattan Jnr. from Judge Day. [1]

Loughlinstown House, May 28, 1838.

My Dear Grattan,

On the subject of your inquiry I cannot, after such a lapse of years, be capable to afford you any important information. Both natives of the same country, I had the honour of a familiar acquaintance with Lord Shelburne, then (1782) Prime Minister,[2] and aware that I was a zealous Volunteer and the delegate from that county (Kerry), to the National Convention, my much-lamented friend[3] selected me for the channel of communication with his lordship on the vital question which then agitated Ireland. I can never forget the distinguished courtesty and complacency with which His Lordship received the question and its bearer, and I have not a doubt that he took up the subject with the feelings of an Irishman and the anxiety of a sincere patriot.

But the success of that measure, as well as the originating of it, was mainly, if not altogether, owing to the eloquence and talents of Grattan, who from the earliest life repudiated with indignation the dependence of the Irish Parliament, and resolved to assert even by arms, if driven to them, the liberties of Ireland. On that subject you cannot possess any authority now, or at any time living, equal to mine. I had the happiness and privilege of his bosom friendship, without an hour's interruption, to the day of his sad death, from our cotemporaneous life in college, where he soon distinguished himself by a brilliant elocution, a tenacious memory, and abundance of classical acquirement. He always took great delight in frequenting the galleries, first of the Irish, and then of the English House of Commons, and the bars of the Lords. You probably possess his brilliant character of Lord Chatham, whom he adored; indeed, on referring to your works, I find it set out in extenso, to use a pedantic expression.

Henry Grattan (1746-1820) by Thomas Jones (National Gallery of Ireland)

We lived in the same chambers in the Middle Temple and took a house in Windsor Forest, commanding a beautiful landscape; he delighted in romantic scenery. Between both, we lived together three or four years, the happiest period of my life. I am angry, that in the introductory life of him you are altogether silent of those years, so variegated and full of adventure and enterprise. However, I admit that it could not be expected, or even desired, that in so brief a sketch you should have noticed much of his private history.

When we resided in Windsor Forest, he would spend whole moonlight nights rambling and losing himself in the thickest plantations. He would sometimes pause and address a tree in soliloquy, thus preparing himself early for that assembly which he was destined in later life to adorn. One morning he amused us at breakfast with an adventure of the night before in the forest. In one of those midnight rambles he stopped at a gibbet, and commenced apostrophising the chains in his usual animated strain, when he suddenly felt a tap on his shoulder, and on turning about was accosted by an unknown person – "How the devil did you get down?" To which the rambler calmly replied – "Sir, I suppose you have an interest in that question!"

These observations, I fear, will appear to you a crude effusion, but certainly not cold; they are warm from the heart. I greedily seize any occasion that crosses my path of dilating on the virtues and much honoured momory of my lost and most attached friend.

Ever faithfully yours,

Rob. Day.

1. Henry Grattan (Jnr.), *Memoirs of the Life and Times of the Rt. Hon. Henry Grattan.* 5 vols. (London 1839-1846), vol. 1, pp 117-119.
2. William Petty, second Earl of Shelburne (1737-1805), 1st Marquess of Lansdowne1784, was secretary of state for the home department when Day met him in May 1782 to negotiate on behalf of Henry Grattan and the Irish patriots. He became prime minister in July on the death of Rockingham. Shelburne was a landed magnate in the south of Kerry. His father was John Fitzmaurice, son of lord Kerry (of Lixnaw), who changed his name to Petty when he inherited his uncle's estates in south Kerry. A doubt surrounds the statement that Day was at Dungannon in 1782: he certainly represented County Kerry at the Rotunda Volunteer Congress in Dublin in late 1783, which may be the subject of this recollection.
3. Henry Grattan.

Appendix 7.

Kerry Evening Post Wednesday 10 February 1841.

Death of Judge Day

'The good old Judge', as in the language of popular affection we have been accustomed to hear him spoken of, is no more! The kind relative, the true and steadfast friend, the benefactor of the poor, and the refuge of the distressed and the afflicted, has at length given up his spirit into the hands of the Judge of all flesh. It is not for us to attempt to do adequate justice to the many virtues of a character ever regulated by genuine Christian principles, and whose heart was the chosen abode of the most exalted philanthropy. Of his character as a Judge of the land for many years, the history of his country will speak. His decisions were those of justice tempered by mercy; and many a trembling wretch was rescued from ignominious death and reserved for repentance and forgiveness. As a kind, indulgent landlord, none stood higher in the estimation of the public, or in the affection of his tenantry, who, with his highly respectable and numerous relatives and friends, will never cease to revere his memory.

The painful event which it has been our duty to record, took place on Monday last, at his seat at Loughlinstown House, near Dublin. The venerable deceased was in the 97th year of his age.[1]

He retired from the Bench, of which he was a conspicuous member, in 1819, having served his country in that capacity upwards of twenty-one years. He was a contemporary of Chief Justice Downes and Justice Bradstreet. Ere going to the bar he sat for a Fellowship, and, though unsuccessful, his answering was of a respectable order. In politics he was a Whig of the old, but not of the modern school.

His latter years were employed in compiling a history of England, and in translating the Lives of the Fathers of the Church with a view to posthumous publication. It is expected by his friends that he has left many valuable papers, which will be published. Frequently of late he had expressed his regret that he had not written a history of his own time, which would have covered the period of 97 years.

By the poor of his neighbourhood his loss will be surely felt. "Large was his bounty, and his soul sincere." During the last thirty years he was a constant resident at Loughlinstown, with only a short interval, when he made a continental trip. Besides his pension he had a large fortune in the county Kerry, and he is supposed to have died rich. He has left a widow, a sister, and numerous relatives, to whom, it is supposed, he has bequeathed his wealth. Of him it may be truly said, "he never made an enemy, never lost a friend."

1. This is incorrect: he was in his 95th year.

Bibliographical notes

The Day archive in the Royal Irish Academy presents no easy task to anybody attempting a political biography of Robert Day. In a way, the archive flatters to deceive, with all kinds of genealogical and county family information. It does however contain the Charges in their original and annotated manuscript form; and the retirement diaries are a social geography of south Dublin on the eve of the railway age. For the political career, help is at hand in the contemporary press and in the *Parliamentary Register,* the press often capturing what the official record has omitted. The other main manuscript sources are the Talbot-Crosbie Mss., in the National Library of Ireland, and the FitzGerald (Knight of Kerry) Mss., copies of which are in the Public Record Office, Northern Ireland and in the NLI. But even these are concerned, for the most part, with issues relating to Robert Day's and Lord Glandore's patronage of official positions under the government, and issues relating to defending their political leadership in Kerry; there are numerous letters also about the financial affairs of the families of Rose, FitzGerald, Crosbie, and others. The Godfrey papers (private collection) contain a number of letters from Judge Day and his brothers (not surprising in view of the intermarriage of the Days and the Godfreys).

Among the neutral sources, and to assess Day's political stature, recourse can be had to the State and Rebellion papers in the National Archives of Ireland and the NLI. Judge Day is the most frequently mentioned political and judicial figure in his region at the turn of the nineteenth century. Dublin Castle kept an eye on the regions at all times, Day appearing as a correspondent in his own right and featuring in the correspondence of others. He occasionally met the Irish viceroys face to face, more often the chief secretaries and under-secretaries. Therefore he is to be found in their private papers and they in his. He made lasting friendships with chief secretaries of the 1790s, like Sylvester Douglas (Lord Glenbervie), Chief Secretary to Lord Westmorland, and Henry Pelham, who was reappointed to that position under Lord Camden having served there in the early 1780s. After the Union, and with the weight of Tralee business on his shoulders, his power at Dublin Castle waned. By the time of Robert Peel's chief secretary-ship (from 1813), Day was - to use his own expression of some years before - 'hors de combat'.

A dearth of printed sources makes it difficult to write more than a little about Day's time at the Middle Temple, beyond the bare admission records and the record of his call to the bar in Dublin. But he has left us a number of his own accounts, including in James Prior, *The Life of Oliver Goldsmith,* 2 vols, (1837) and John Forster's *Life of Goldsmith* (2 vols. London 1854, 2nd edn.), also Henry Grattan Jnr's *Memoirs of the Life and Times of the Rt. Hon. Henry Grattan,* 5 vols. (London 1839-1846). Material on the first Marquess of Lansdowne (Lord Shelburne) is quite scarce, while the principal archive, at Bowood, remains out of reach to many; but John Norris's *Shelburne and Reform* (London 1963) has much to offer to an understanding of the political context for the early career of Day, while Shelburne commands a long index entry in many biographies and specialised studies of the time; one such study, Samuel Flagg

Beamis's *The Diplomacy of the American Revolution,* will place the achievements of Grattan squarely in the context of the ending of Britain's war with her American colonies and the final peace negotiations. Shelburne's South of Kerry was alien to Day's proper sphere of the Protestant North of Kerry, which is why the Marquis of Lansdowne's *Glenerought and the Petty-Fitzmaurices* (London 1937) warrants inclusion here; while Rev. J. Anthony Gaughan's *Listowel and Its Vicinity* introduced most of us to the Fitzmaurices lords of Kerry who inherited the Shelburne estates in the south of the county.

For Robert Day's life at the Irish bar (from 1774) information is very scarce, but see the contemporary legal environment in such as William Curran, *The Life of the Right Honourable John Philpot Curran, Late Master of the Rolls in Ireland* (2 vols. London 1822), and again Grattan's *Life* by Grattan Jnr. For the outlines of legal careers I have made extensive use of Keane, E., Phair, P.B., Sadleir, T.U., *King's Inns Admission Papers* 1607-1867(Irish Manuscripts Commission, 1982), Burtchaell and Sadleir, *Alumni Dublinensis* (Dublin 1935), and Elrington F. Ball, *The Judges of Ireland,* 2 vols. (London 1926). Roderick J. O'Flanagan contributes very readable and anecdotal accounts of the times in *The Lives of the Lord Chancellors and Keepers of the Great Seal of Ireland,* 2 vols., London 1870, *The Irish Bar,* London 1879, and *The Munster Circuit, Tales, Trials and Traditions* (London 1880). Ella B. Day's very readable *Mr Justice Day of Kerry, A Discursive Memoir,* Exeter 1938, has some original letters from Day from the time of his dealings with Shelburne.

The Volunteer era political background has received generous treatment in Irish historiography (too much to cover here); however, the Volunteer movement in Co. Galway, when Day was returned for Tuam (1783), is explained in James Kelly's 'The Politics of the Protestant Ascendancy: County Galway 1650-1832', in William Nolan and Gerard Moran (eds) *Galway History and Society,* Dublin 1991, 229-270. For a detailed account of John Fitzgibbon, the man who cast his considerable shadow over the administration of Irish justice and Irish politics when Day was climbing the promotional ladder, Ann C. Kavanaugh's *John Fitzgibbon Earl of Clare* (Dublin 1997) is recommended, as is A.P.W. Malcomson, A.P.W., *John Foster, The Politics of the Anglo-Irish Ascendancy,* (Oxford Uni. Press 1978). For his parliamentary work, in particular his work in early policing and penal reform, the Irish Statutes and the complementary *Journals of the Irish House of Commons* are the essential sources. Of secondary material I have used Stanley Palmer's *Police and Protest in England and Ireland 1780-1850* (Cambridge University Press 1988), Oliver MacDonagh's *The Inspector General: Sir Jeremiah Fitzpatrick and the Politics of Social Reform, 1783-1802* (London 1981), and to include insight into early transportation to New South Wales, Bob Reece's *The Origins of Irish Convict Transportation to New South Wales,* and such contributions as David Kelly's 'The Conditions of Debtors and Insolvents in Eighteenth-Century Dublin', in David Dickson (ed.), *The Gorgeous Mask,* (Dublin 1987).

The Rebellion papers have already been cited for their wealth of Day material, covering his efforts to clear the jails and diffuse the revolutionary tensions in the country during the descent to rebellion in 1798. The era directly after the Irish Act of Union has received scant treatment from historians, making it difficult to do our subject justice. Given that Day's context was British and Imperial as well as Irish, Linda

Colley, *Britons, Forging the Nation 1707-1837* (London 1996 edn.) rehabilitated the idea of patriotism at the centre of empire building. Allan Blackstock's *An Ascendancy Army* (Dublin 1998) is a detailed study of the Irish yeomanry and of the other initiatives to support the regular army, such as the Army of Reserve and the Additional Force Act, but it is a tangled area of new legislation and amended legislation which has yet to find a clear narrative account. The Chichester Mss. in the British Library (Pelham Mss. Mss. of Thomas Pelham, 2nd Earl of Chichester) contain some important correspondence with Day from 1807. He appears in the Hardwicke Mss. (Mss. of the 3rd Earl of Hardwicke as Lord Lieutenant, 1801-6, Add. Mss. 35708, see Hardwicke papers also in Michael MacDonagh, *The Viceroy's Post-bag,* London 1904), likewise in Mss. of Nicholas Vansittart, Chief Secretary, 1805 (Add. Mss. 31229-31230), finally in the correspondence with Robert Peel (Add. 40224 and 40251), where he struggles to win favours against the claims of his county rivals. Judicial opinions arising out of court cases, including sentencing, constitute the subject matter of some of these correspondences. In this respect there is a good deal to see among the Colchester (Charles Abbot, Chief Secretary, 1801-2) Mss. at the Public Record Office in Kew concerning the trial of Sir Henry Browne Hayes in Cork in 1801 for the abduction of a Quaker girl. Day presided at this trial, and an inadequate abstract of the relevant Colchester Mss. can be found in Report No. 4 of the *Historical Manuscript Commission,* Colchester. On other, generally minor, judicial controversies, more is to be found in the Public Record Office of Northern Ireland, which has copies of the Mss. of William Wickham, Chief Secretary to Lord Hardwicke, also those of Lord Redesdale, Lord Chancellor of Ireland from 1802-6. Redesdale succeeded John Fitzgibbon, Lord Clare, to whose promotions Day's career became linked; yet the relationship of Day and Fitzgibbon is one of the aspects of the Day story which will require more research than was permitted in the preparation of this book.

It would be a mistake to underestimate Day's commitment to the Anglican revival, which, together with the excitement surrounding the expansion of Britain's empire and the defeat of Napoleon, increased the importance which he assigned to the role and popularity of King George III. Going back a little before this, there is the neglected subject of the English Jacobite legacy of the age of Dr Samuel Johnson and the years when Robert Day was at the Middle Temple. I have learned much from the provocative work of J.C.D. Clark in *English Society 1688-1832,* Cambridge1985, and there is more in the same vein in his *Samuel Johnson, Literature, Religion and English Cultural Politics from the Restoration to Romanticism,* Cambridge 1994. F.C. Mather covers some of the same ground in *High Church Prophet. Bishop Samuel Horsley (1733-1806) and the Caroline Tradition in the later Georgian Church,* Oxford 1992, while Denis Gray, *Spencer Perceval, The Evangelical Prime Minister,* Manchester 1963, takes the subject of Anglican reaction and arguments against Catholic emancipation into the years of the Tory hegemony from about 1807. Jacqueline Hill's work on the degeneration of patriotic festivals to the ownership of the unionist sector of Irish society is covered in 'Religious Tolerance and the Relaxation of the Penal Laws: an imperial perspective, 1763-1780' (*Archivium Hibernicum 1989,* xliv. P. 98-109), while the evolution of patriots such as Robert Day into unionists is covered in her *From Patriots to Unionists.* The early assaults on the penal code has been traced in Maureen Wall, *Catholic Ireland in the Eighteenth*

Century, Collected Essays of Maureen Wall, ed. Gerard O'Brien (Dublin 1989), and in more recent work by Thomas Bartlett and others. Of theses, one by a John Patrick Day, MA, UCD 1973, *The Catholic Question in the Irish Parliament 1760-82,* goes into more detail about the first cracks in the Code from the 1760s (the name of Robert FitzGerald, Day's uncle one of those involved). For the near achievement of Catholic emancipation in the 1808-13 period Oliver MacDonagh's *The Life of Daniel O'Connell 1775-1847* (London 1991) coves the ground very systematically, while Sean O'Faolain's *King of the Beggars, a Life of Daniel O'Connell* (first published 1938) contains important sections of O'Connell's speeches, including the one in 1813 containing his famous attack on Saurin, the attorney general (a more complete version of this speech is to be found in O'Connell's *Speeches,* edited by his son). Recent historians have also looked at the wider liberal programme, or where it might be said O'Connell's humanitarian concerns converged with Day's: of these I might mention only Fergus O'Ferrall's *Catholic Emancipation. Daniel O'Connell and the Birth of Irish Democracy 1820-30* (Dublin 1985). A useful contemporary source, if somewhat biased from one a little too near the subject, is Francis Plowden's *History of Ireland from its Union with Great Britain in January 1801 to October 1810* (3 vols. London 1811). Then there is the the large and growing bibliography of Irish Catholicism's emergence from the penal age, and of the post-penal and semi-emancipated and convert environment in which Day operated. For the evangelical part in the anti-slavery agitation, prison and educational reform, and reform in diverse areas at home and in the Empire, I have drawn on Ernest Marshal Howse, *Saints in Politics, The Clapham Sect and the Growth of Freedom,* and Brian Jenkins, *Era of Emancipation, British Government of Ireland 1812-1830* (McGill-Queen's University Press, Kingston and Montreal 1988). A.T.Q. Stewart's *A Deeper Silence, the Hidden Origins of the United Irishmen,* Belfast 1993, is a great exposition of the roots of northern Irish and American radicalism in the Commonwealth Whigs and the 'Glorious' Revolution of William III.

The convert community and the residual support for the Stuart Pretender, and the legal and official community, all coexisted easily and were to a great extent interrelated in the Irish world of the late eighteenth century, which were the years of Day's rise in the law. A number of old books serve to remind us of the tenacity of Irish Jacobitism. I have used John Cornelius O'Callaghan, *History of the Irish Brigades in the Service of France,* London 1870, and Mrs. Morgan John O'Connell, *The Last Colonel of the Irish Brigade,* 2 vols. (London 1892). See also Donough O'Brien, *History of the O'Brien s from Brian Boroimhe, A.D. 1000-1945* (Cairo 1949), which gives the leaders of Clare's regiment on the continent. A recent book, Eamonn O Ciardh's *Ireland and the Jacobite Cause, 1685-1766, A Fatal Attachment* (Four Courts Press, 2002) covers a huge amount of ground on the subject.

For material to assist research in the local network of Day's extended family and political connection – often the same thing – I have drawn on Mary Agnes Hickson's *Old Kerry Records* (1st series 1872, 2nd 1874). Hickson traced the line of descent of Judge Day back to the 'Rebel' Earl of Desmond (d. 1583); the link is also made by Anne Chambers in her *Eleanor Countess of Desmond, A Heroine of Tudor Ireland,* (Dublin 1986), on page 237. For Robert's generation, and the generations immediately before and after, the press yields plentiful reports of births, marriages and deaths; a compiled list using Munster newspaper sourches is that of Rosemary Ffolliott, in her *Biographical notices principally relating to counties Cork and Kerry collected from newspapers 1756-1827 with a few references 1749-55.* Burke's Irish Family Records provides the pedigrees for many of the families in this book, and there are corroborating sources in some of the private papers, while Joseph Foster's *The Royal Lineage of Our Noble and Gentle Families, together with their Paternal Ancestry (London 1887)* carries the pedigrees back to the time before they settled in Ireland. Given the clerical and legal backgrounds, there is much to draw on in the work of Burchaell and Sadleir, who have made the very valuable Trinity College Dublin admission records available in *Alumni Dublinensis,* and these are added to by Keane., Phair, and Sadleir work, *King's Inns Admission Papers 1607-1867,* (Irish Manuscripts Commission, 1982). Day came from a very Church of Ireland family, which is why the work of historians of the Church of Ireland has proved indispensable: Canon James Blennerhassett Leslie, for clergymen in Kerry, Clogher, Armagh and elsewhere (remembering that Day's connection extended throughout the Church of Ireland), Maziere Brady D.D., *Clerical and Parochial Records of Cork, Cloyne and Ross,* 3 vols. (Dublin, 1863), and Brady again in *The McGillycuddy Papers, A Selection from the Family Archives of The McGillycuddy of the Reeks with an introductory memoir, being a contribution to the history of the county of Kerry* (London 1867).

Day's contribution to education was written about more than twenty years ago in Padraig de Brun's series of articles in the journals of the *Kerry Arch. and Hist. Society* entitled 'The Kildare Place Society in Kerry' (edns. 1981 and 1982-3), earlier again in the articles of Michael Quain in the *Journal of the Royal Society of Antiquaries of Ireland* and that of the *Cork Arch. and Hist. Society* (Michael Quane, 'Banna School Ardfert', *JSRAI* vol 84 1954 156-172; M.Quane, 'Zelva School, Valentia Island', *JCHAS* 1967; M.Quane, Michael, Midleton School, Co. Cork.', *JRSAI,* vol. 82, 1952, pp 1-27). The rise of the Catholic nation coincided, or even preceded, the revived mission of the Anglican mission; a number of journal articles have surveyed the reconstruction of the Irish Catholic church in the post-Penal environment, for example those of Rev. Kieran O'Shea, and Rev. Michael Manning in the journals of the *KAHS.*

Day's career in charge of the Denny parliamentary borough of Tralee is pieced together with difficulty. *The Civil Correspondence and Memoranda of Field Marshal Arthur Duke of Wellington,* edited by his son (Ireland: vol. 5, Ireland, March 30 1807- April 12, 1809, London 1860) offers scattered references to his return of parliamentary representatives to Westminster; there are also the Reports of the *Historical Mss. Commission,* for example the correspondence of William Elliot (the Duke of Bedford's chief secretary in 1806) with Lord Grenville in *HMC* Report, Dropmore Mss., Vol. 8, 1912. There is a disappointingly small amount in George Canning's correspondence, but see Canning with Frere, Add. Mss. 38833, and the hint or two about seeking a seat free of political obligations in the Canning papers which form part of the Harewood collection in the West Yorkshire Archives at Leeds.

Of newspapers, the *Limerick Gazette and General Advertiser* and the *Limerick Chronicle,* and *Flyn's Hibernian Chronicle* and the *Cork Mercantile Chronicle* (both Cork), often supplied the absence of extant Kerry newspapers for the period covered in this book, while such as the *Freeman's Journal* and the *Dublin Evening Post* provide more of regional politics than is generally assumed. The *Freeman's Journal* carried nearly all of Day's addresses to grand juries before they appeared in pamphlet form, and many of them never found their way into his collected addresses.

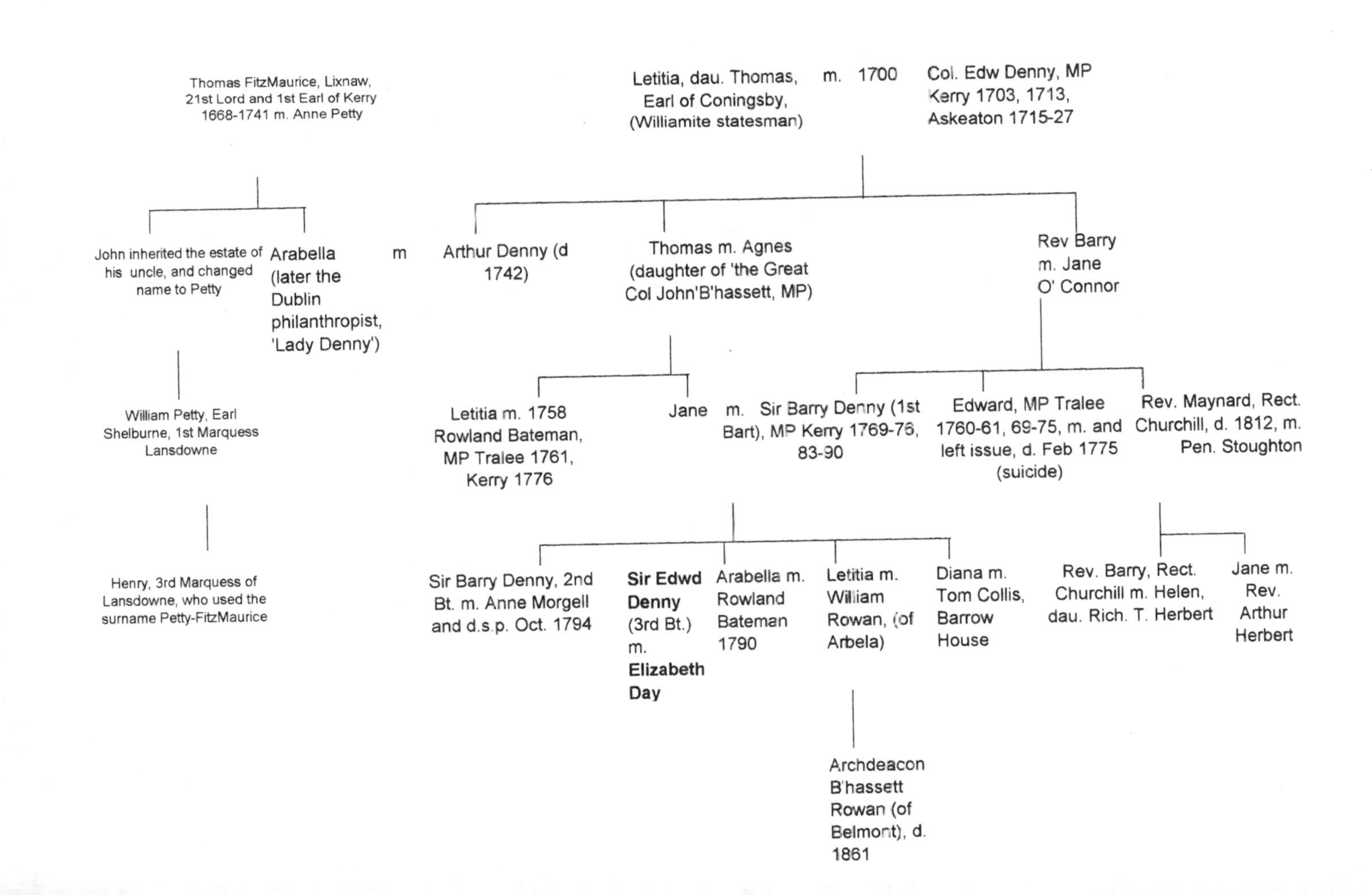
The Dennys of Tralee Castle in the Eighteenth Century
Thomas FitzMaurice, Lixnaw, 21st Lord and 1st Earl of Kerry 1668-1741 m. Anne Petty
Letitia, dau. Thomas, Earl of Coningsby, (Williamite statesman)
m. 1700
Col. Edw Denny, MP Kerry 1703, 1713, Askeaton 1715-27
John inherited the estate of his uncle, and changed name to Petty
Arabella (later the Dublin philanthropist, 'Lady Denny')
m
Arthur Denny (d 1742)
Thomas m. Agnes (daughter of 'the Great Col John'B'hassett, MP)
Rev Barry m. Jane O' Connor
William Petty, Earl Shelburne, 1st Marquess Lansdowne
Letitia m. 1758 Rowland Bateman, MP Tralee 1761, Kerry 1776
Jane
m.
Sir Barry Denny (1st Bart), MP Kerry 1769-76, 83-90
Edward, MP Tralee 1760-61, 69-75, m. and left issue, d. Feb 1775 (suicide)
Rev. Maynard, Rect. Churchill, d. 1812, m. Pen. Stoughton
Henry, 3rd Marquess of Lansdowne, who used the surname Petty-FitzMaurice
Sir Barry Denny, 2nd Bt. m. Anne Morgell and d.s.p. Oct. 1794
Sir Edwd Denny (3rd Bt.) m. Elizabeth Day
Arabella m. Rowland Bateman 1790
Letitia m. William Rowan, (of Arbela)
Diana m. Tom Collis, Barrow House
Rev. Barry, Rect. Churchill m. Helen, dau. Rich. T. Herbert
Jane m. Rev. Arthur Herbert
Archdeacon B'hassett Rowan (of Belmont), d. 1861

Judge Day's descent from O'Brien (Viscounts Clare), Butler (Earls of Ormond), FitzMaurice (Earls of Kerry), FitzGerald (Earls of Desmond) and FitzGerald (Knights of Kerry)

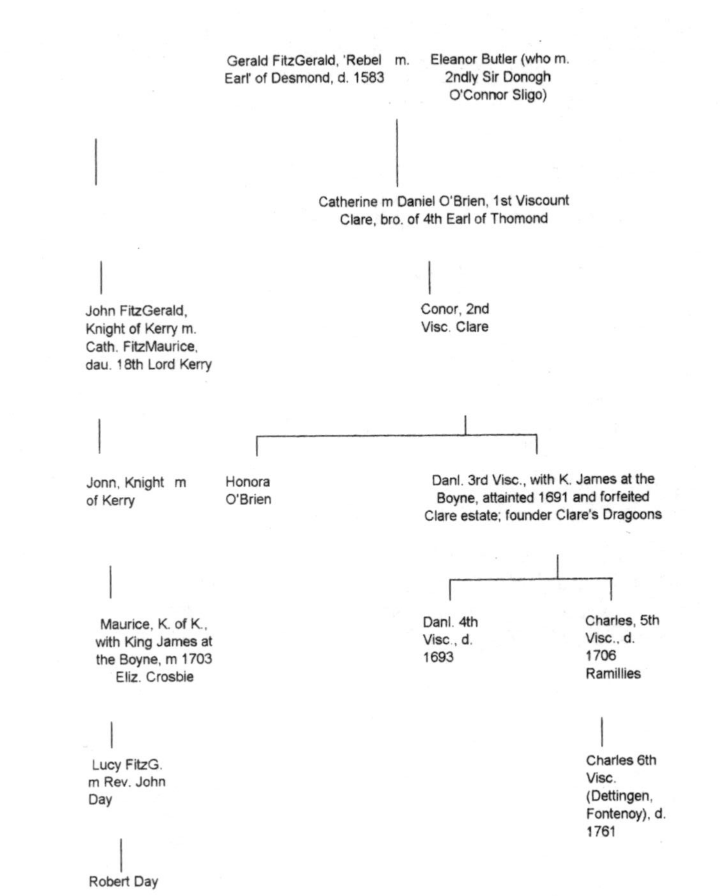

Crosbie and FitzGerald connections in Kerry and throughout Ireland

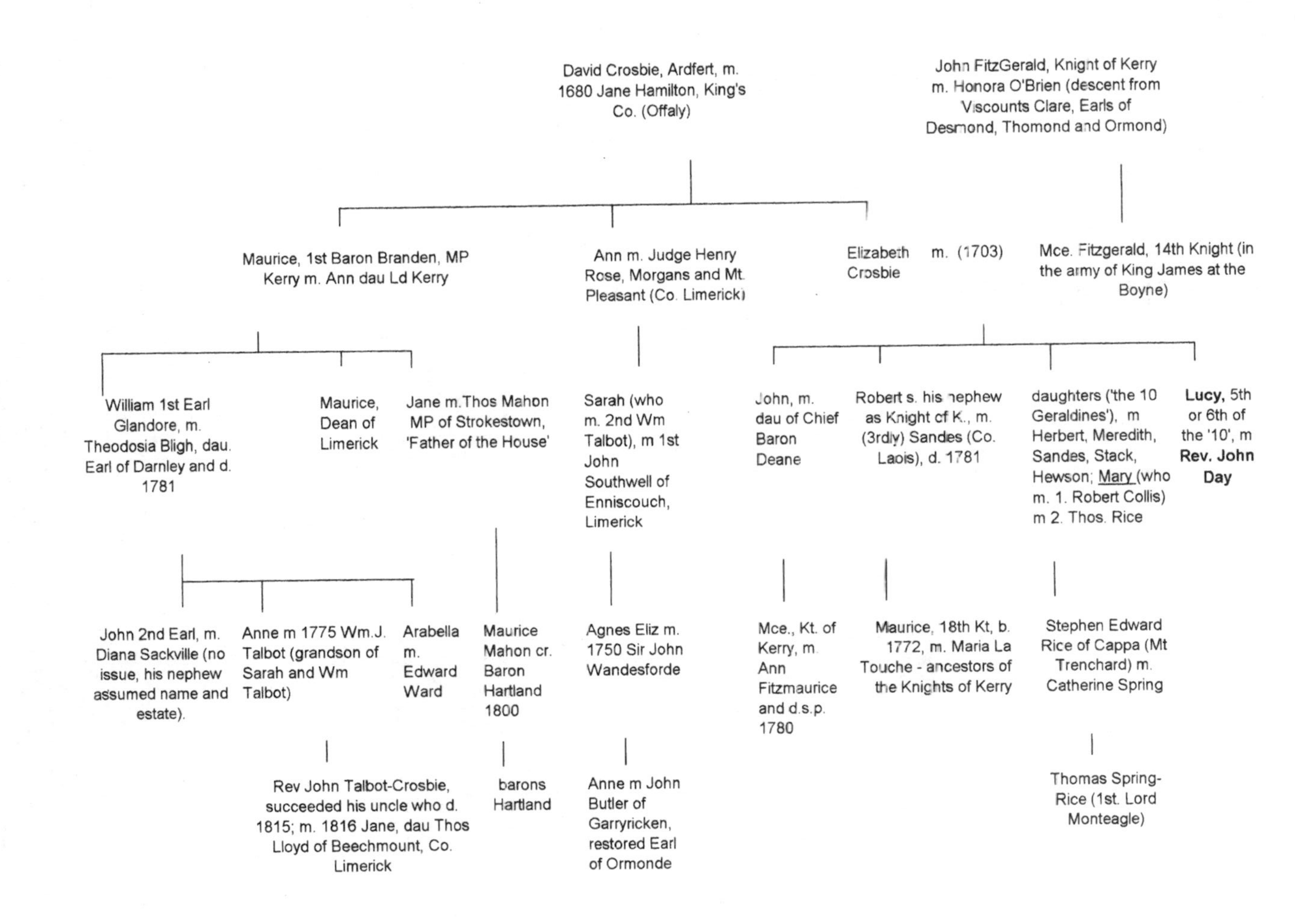

Day of Kerry

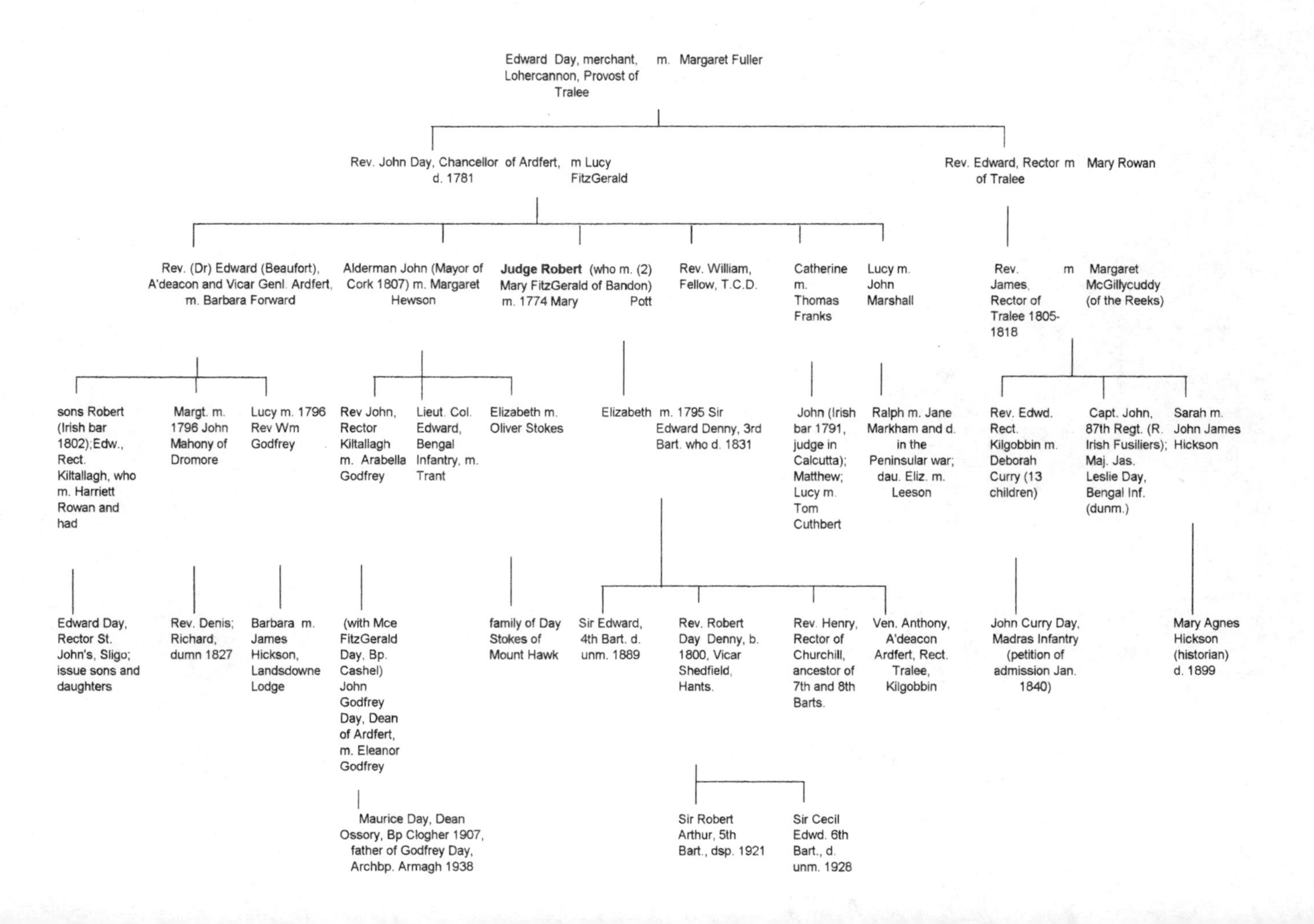

Edward Day, merchant, Lohercannon, Provost of Tralee m. Margaret Fuller
Rev. John Day, Chancellor of Ardfert, d. 1781 m Lucy FitzGerald
Rev. Edward, Rector of Tralee m Mary Rowan
Rev. (Dr) Edward (Beaufort), A'deacon and Vicar Genl. Ardfert, m. Barbara Forward
Alderman John (Mayor of Cork 1807) m. Margaret Hewson
Judge Robert (who m. (2) Mary FitzGerald of Bandon) m. 1774 Mary Pott
Rev. William, Fellow, T.C.D.
Catherine m. Thomas Franks
Lucy m. John Marshall
Rev. James, Rector of Tralee 1805-1818 m Margaret McGillycuddy (of the Reeks)
sons Robert (Irish bar 1802);Edw., Rect. Kiltallagh, who m. Harriett Rowan and had
Margt. m. 1796 John Mahony of Dromore
Lucy m. 1796 Rev Wm Godfrey
Rev John, Rector Kiltallagh m. Arabella Godfrey
Lieut. Col. Edward, Bengal Infantry, m. Trant
Elizabeth m. Oliver Stokes
Elizabeth m. 1795 Sir Edward Denny, 3rd Bart. who d. 1831
John (Irish bar 1791, judge in Calcutta); Matthew; Lucy m. Tom Cuthbert
Ralph m. Jane Markham and d. in the Peninsular war; dau. Eliz. m. Leeson
Rev. Edwd. Rect. Kilgobbin m. Deborah Curry (13 children)
Capt. John, 87th Regt. (R. Irish Fusiliers); Maj. Jas. Leslie Day, Bengal Inf. (dunm.)
Sarah m. John James Hickson
Edward Day, Rector St. John's, Sligo; issue sons and daughters
Rev. Denis; Richard, dumn 1827
Barbara m. James Hickson, Landsdowne Lodge
(with Mce FitzGerald Day, Bp. Cashel) John Godfrey Day, Dean of Ardfert, m. Eleanor Godfrey
family of Day Stokes of Mount Hawk
Sir Edward, 4th Bart. d. unm. 1889
Rev. Robert Day Denny, b. 1800, Vicar Shedfield, Hants.
Rev. Henry, Rector of Churchill, ancestor of 7th and 8th Barts.
Ven. Anthony, A'deacon Ardfert, Rect. Tralee, Kilgobbin
John Curry Day, Madras Infantry (petition of admission Jan. 1840)
Mary Agnes Hickson (historian) d. 1899
Maurice Day, Dean Ossory, Bp Clogher 1907, father of Godfrey Day, Archbp. Armagh 1938
Sir Robert Arthur, 5th Bart., dsp. 1921
Sir Cecil Edwd. 6th Bart., d. unm. 1928

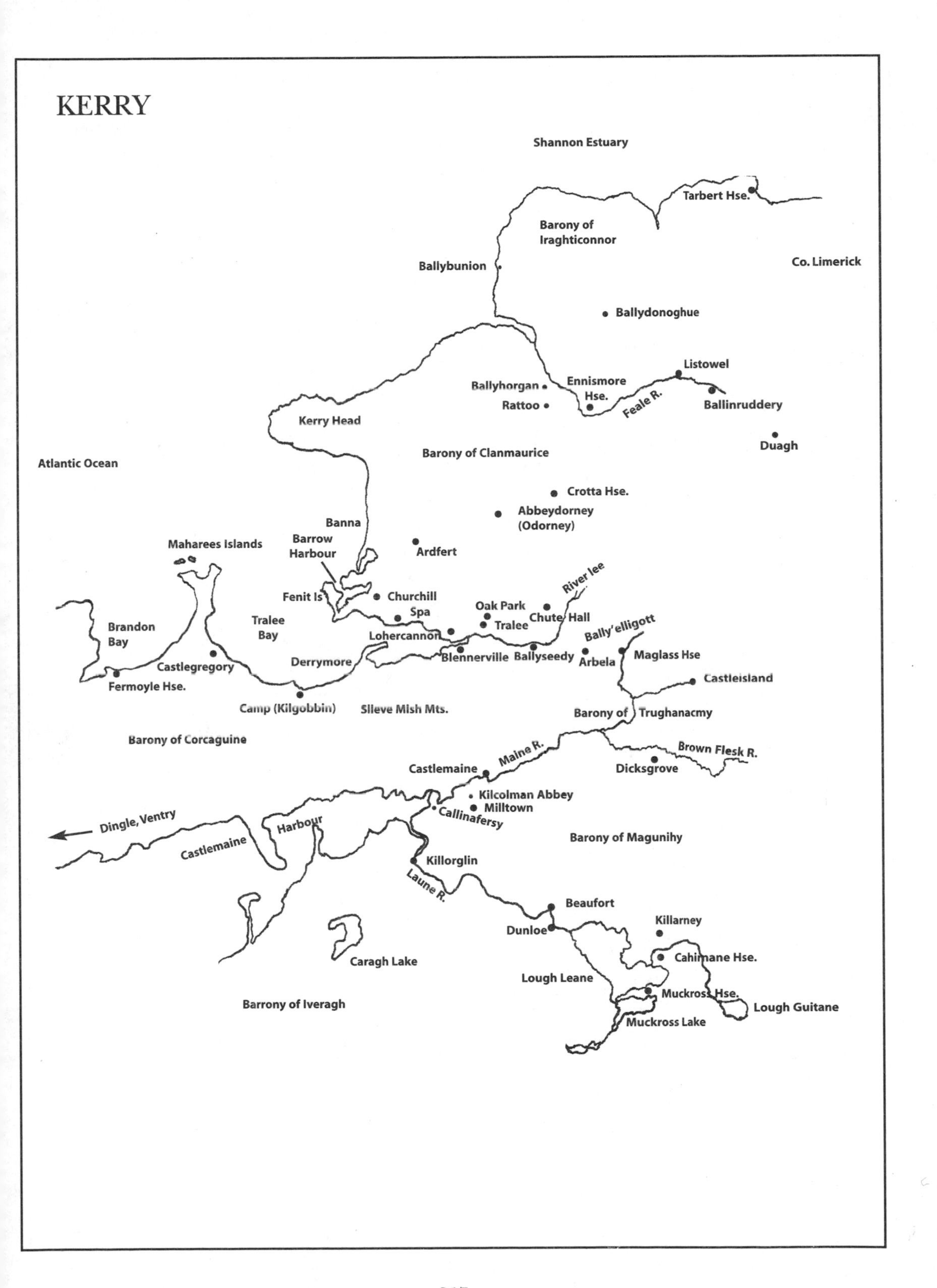
KERRY
Shannon Estuary
Tarbert Hse.
Barony of Iraghticonnor
Ballybunion
Co. Limerick
Ballydonoghue
Listowel
Ballyhorgan
Ennismore Hse.
Rattoo
Feale R.
Ballinruddery
Kerry Head
Duagh
Barony of Clanmaurice
Atlantic Ocean
Crotta Hse.
Abbeydorney (Odorney)
Banna
Barrow Harbour
Maharees Islands
Ardfert
River lee
Fenit Is
Churchill
Spa
Oak Park
Brandon Bay
Tralee Bay
Tralee
Chute Hall
Lohercannon
Bally'elligott
Castlegregory
Derrymore
Blennerville
Ballyseedy
Arbela
Maglass Hse
Fermoyle Hse.
Castleisland
Camp (Kilgobbin)
Slieve Mish Mts.
Barony of Trughanacmy
Barony of Corcaguine
Brown Flesk R.
Maine R.
Castlemaine
Dicksgrove
Kilcolman Abbey
Milltown
Dingle, Ventry
Callinafersy
Harbour
Castlemaine
Barony of Magunihy
Killorglin
Laune R.
Beaufort
Killarney
Dunloe
Cahirnane Hse.
Caragh Lake
Lough Leane
Muckross Hse.
Barrony of Iveragh
Lough Guitane
Muckross Lake

IRELAND
North Channell
Mull of Kintyre
Coleraine
Londonderry
Raphoe
Lifford
Strabane
Portpatrick
Carrickfergus
Belfast
Donaghadee
Donegal
Omagh
Donegal Bay
Moira
Portadown
Armagh
Enniskillen
Sligo
Monaghan
Ballina
Foxford
Boyle
Dundalk
Castlebar
Strokestown
Moynalty
Longford
Slane
Drogheda
Roscommon
Rathowen
Ballinrobe
Mullingar
Trim
Kilbeggan
Dublin
Galway
Shannon R.
Daingean
(Philipstown)
Tullamore
Galway Bay
Kildare
Monasterevin
Bray
Gort
Maryb'gh
N'mtkennedy
Ballitore
Roscrea
Athy
Castledermot
Rathdrum
Tulla
Ennis
Quin
Nenagh
Abbeyleix
Carlow
Arklow
Birdhill
Limerick
Gorey
Tarbert
Rathkeale
Athea
Listowel
Enniscorthy
Cahir
Clonmel
New
Ross
Wexford
Tralee
Waterford
Dingle
Mallow
Fermoy
Killorglin
Killarney
Millstreet
Macroom
Coachford
Cork
Bantry Bay